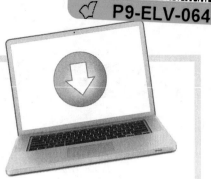

This Book Comes With Lots of
FREE Online Resources

Nolo's award-winning website has a page dedicated just to this book. Here you can:

KEEP UP TO DATE – When there are important changes to the information in this book, we'll post updates

GET DISCOUNTS ON NOLO PRODUCTS – Get discounts on hundreds of books, forms, and software

READ BLOGS – Get the latest info from Nolo authors' blogs

LISTEN TO PODCASTS – Listen to authors discuss timely issues on topics that interest you

WATCH VIDEOS – Get a quick introduction to a legal topic with our short videos

And that's not all.
Nolo.com contains thousands of articles on everyday legal and business issues, plus a plain-English law dictionary, all written by Nolo experts and available for free. You'll also find more useful **books, software, online apps, downloadable forms,** plus a **lawyer directory.**

NOLO
LAW for ALL

Get updates and more at
www.nolo.com/back-of-book/NODV.html

⚖ NOLO The Trusted Name
(but don't take our word for it)

"In Nolo you can trust."

THE NEW YORK TIMES

"Nolo is always there in a jam as the nation's premier publisher of do-it-yourself legal books."

NEWSWEEK

"Nolo publications... guide people simply through the how, when, where and why of the law."

THE WASHINGTON POST

"[Nolo's]... material is developed by experienced attorneys who have a knack for making complicated material accessible."

LIBRARY JOURNAL

"When it comes to self-help legal stuff, nobody does a better job than Nolo..."

USA TODAY

"The most prominent U.S. publisher of self-help legal aids."

TIME MAGAZINE

"Nolo is a pioneer in both consumer and business self-help books and software."

LOS ANGELES TIMES

5th Edition

Nolo's Essential Guide to Divorce

Attorney Emily Doskow

FIFTH EDITION	JUNE 2014
Editor	MARY RANDOLPH
Cover Design	JALEH DOANE
Production	COLLEEN CAIN
Proofreading	SUSAN CARLSON GREENE
Index	MEDEA MINNICH
Printing	BANG PRINTING

ISSN: 2326-5973 (print)

ISSN: 2328-0565 (online)

ISBN: 978-1-4133-2036-7 (pbk)

ISBN: 978-1-4133-2037-4 (epub ebook)

This book covers only United States law, unless it specifically states otherwise.

Please note

We believe accurate, plain-English legal information should help you solve many of your own legal problems. But this text is not a substitute for personalized advice from a knowledgeable lawyer. If you want the help of a trained professional—and we'll always point out situations in which we think that's a good idea—consult an attorney licensed to practice in your state.

Dedication

To my father, Charles Doskow, whom I admire more than I usually manage to express, and whose faith in me and pride in my work have meant so much to me.

About the Author

Emily Doskow is a practicing attorney and mediator who has been working with families in the Bay Area since 1989. She specializes in family law, including adoption, parentage issues, domestic partnership formation and dissolution, and divorce. She is a graduate of the Boalt Hall School of Law at the University of California at Berkeley and currently resides in Oakland. As an editor and author for Nolo, she has authored or coauthored numerous titles, including *The Sharing Solution: How to Save Money, Simplify Your Life & Build Community* (with Janelle Orsi), *Making It Legal: A Guide to Same-Sex Marriage, Domestic Partnerships, and Civil Unions* (with Frederick Hertz), and many others.

Acknowledgments

No one deserves more gratitude than my editor, Mary Randolph, whose collaborative spirit and unparalleled skill steadied me throughout the writing process and improved everything about this book immeasurably.

For the second edition, I'm enormously grateful to Marshal Willick for answering questions, reviewing the new Chapter 12, and generally sharing his great expertise on the topic of military divorce. Many thanks, too, to Dr. Joan B. Kelly, who generously allowed the inclusion of her wonderfully useful material on custody schedules.

Again, many thanks to Alayna Schroeder, Terry McGinley, and Drew Wheaton for their careful assistance with research, to all of my colleagues in the editorial department at Nolo for their encouragement and support, and to the production department for once again making the book look wonderful.

I am obliged to other Nolo authors for producing terrific books that cover thoroughly some of the topics I had room only to touch on: Violet Woodhouse, Mimi Lyster, Katherine Stoner, Twila Slesnick, Janice Green, and Paul Mandelstein all contributed to making this book useful and resource rich.

I am indebted to all of the divorced folks who so graciously allowed me to pry into their personal lives in the course of my research.

Huge appreciation to Andrea Palash for answering questions, reviewing drafts, and being perpetually supportive. And many thanks to family and a multitude of friends (special mention to Mady Shumofsky, Pamela Brown, Linda Gebroe, and Susanne Cohen and Jim Gaines) for their support.

Finally, I'm eternally grateful to and for my beloved partner, Luan Stauss, for her patience, practical help, encouragement, and inspiration.

Table of Contents

4   Working It Out: Divorce Mediation

5   When You Can't Agree: Contested Divorce and Trial

6 Custody Decisions and Parenting

7 Custody Disputes

8 Child Support

12 Military Divorce: Special Issues

13 Getting It in Writing: Preparing Your Marital Settlement Agreement

14 Critical Care: When Things Really Go Wrong

15 After the Divorce

16 Getting Help, Finding Information, and Looking Stuff Up

Appendix

Introduction:
Your Divorce Companion

The word divorce can conjure up images of confusion, conflict, and economic woes. And there is no question that going through a divorce is painful and difficult for just about anyone who experiences it. But although you may feel sad, you don't have to feel confused or helpless. You can educate yourself and take action. By picking up this book, you've taken the first step.

The legal part of divorce is not all that mysterious. In fact, ending the legal connections between you and your spouse is a fairly straightforward process. And it's not impossible to understand—if you have someone to explain it to you in plain English. That's the goal of this book.

You can find help here whether you're considering a divorce or are ready to go ahead, whether or not you have a lawyer, and whether you are expecting an amicable split or a long, expensive, contested process.

Throughout this book, you'll encounter one theme over and over: that it is to everyone's benefit, and especially that of your children, to make the divorce process as civil as possible. It's a simple fact that the more you are able to avoid fighting now, the easier life will be later, when you see your spouse at your son's wedding or your daughter's college graduation. There are important immediate benefits as well: You'll save thousands in legal fees, and you'll sleep better at night.

To help you work things out with your spouse and avoid a costly court battle, this book explains:

- how divorce mediation can help you reach fair agreements about the big issues: custody, property, and support
- where to find the state-specific forms and information you'll need, along with more do-it-yourself resources
- how to get help from a lawyer without losing control of the process and having it turn nasty, and
- how to prepare a settlement agreement to document what you and your spouse decide about property, custody, and support.

But if, despite your best efforts, you find yourself headed toward a trial, you'll find help here, too. The book will explain the unfamiliar legal terms you're going to be hearing and tell you:

- what a divorce trial really looks like
- how courts divide property and decide custody and support questions
- how to enforce orders for child and spousal support, and
- how lawyers and other professionals can help you when you need them, and how to find and work with good ones.

Finally, we'll help you take care of wrapping up your divorce and preparing for your new life. The book also offers guidance on some postdivorce legal issues you may run into.

This book concentrates on the legal side of divorce. But of course the emotional side of divorce can't be ignored. It's pretty unfair that just when it's toughest to think logically and form sensible long-term plans, you're called on to make decisions that will affect you and your family for a long time to come. But you can do it, and this book can help. Mindful of the emotional stresses that you're dealing with, it gives you the practical advice you need to make smart decisions.

You may feel lost and alone as you begin the process of your divorce. This book is intended to be your legal companion, providing practical and supportive advice and information along the way, and helping you through to the other side.

Get Updates, Forms, and More at this Book's Companion Page on Nolo.com

You can download any of the forms and worksheets in this book at

www.nolo.com/back-of-book/NODV.html

When there are important changes to the information in this book, we'll post updates on this same dedicated page. You'll find other useful information, such as author blogs and podcasts, as well.

Getting Oriented

Whether you're thinking about getting a divorce or have already begun the process, you undoubtedly have a lot of questions. Will you have to hire a lawyer and go to court? What will happen to your house? Who will get custody of the children? How will you make ends meet?

On top of all these practical concerns, the end of a marriage is an intensely emotional time. No matter who makes the decision, both spouses are likely to experience enormous grief over the loss of a relationship that started out full of love and hope. You probably feel disoriented and possibly somewhat lost. You need to take care of yourself, and one way to do that is by learning about the legal and practical issues you're likely to face.

This chapter gives you an overview of the divorce process and answers common questions. It also defines some important words and concepts you'll need to understand as you wade into this unfamiliar territory. Once you have this information, your divorce should be easier, smoother, less frightening, and less costly.

Taking the High Road

As you go through your divorce, time after time you'll be faced with the same kind of choice: Give a little bit or stand firm on principle. Agree to send your kids for visitation early on a day your spouse is off work or hold to the visitation schedule as if any deviation would be fatal. Go with your spouse to a parent-teacher conference or insist on scheduling separate meetings. Offer an olive branch or fire off a scathing letter.

It may not seem true now, but the best thing you can do for yourself and your family is to take the high road as often as you can. That means trying to compromise. Consider the other person's feelings. Do what's best for your kids. Think about negotiating solutions that work for everyone, not just you. Whenever possible, don't create or escalate conflict.

You don't choose the high road just because it's morally superior to pettiness and vindictiveness. Experienced divorce lawyers and family therapists will tell you that the angriest people end up hurting their own interests and dragging out the pain by their refusal to give an inch. No question, it is very difficult to make reasoned decisions when you're in emotional turmoil. You may be very angry at your spouse; you may be deeply hurt by an affair or another betrayal; you probably feel that you can't get away from the situation quickly enough. And if your spouse is abusive or otherwise impossible to work with, you may know from experience that efforts at compromise will probably be wasted. But in the vast majority of situations, a little compromise goes a long way—and if you do choose the high road, then when you look back on this time, you will feel good about the choices you made.

You'll also feel good about having done right by your kids. The other thing that experts agree on is that although divorce is difficult and stressful for kids no matter what, the real harm to kids comes from being subjected to conflict between parents. The longer that lasts, and the more severe it is, the worse it is for your children. If you truly want to shield your children from the pain of divorce, recognize that the more you take the high road with your spouse, the better job you'll do.

RESOURCE

Help in communicating with your spouse. *Difficult Conversations: How to Discuss What Matters Most*, by Douglas Stone, Bruce Patton, and Sheila Heen (Penguin), has practical advice about how to prepare for difficult talks and communicate successfully about hard topics.

Separation or Divorce?

Separation simply means that you are living apart from your spouse. A separation is not a divorce. You're still legally married until you get a judgment of divorce from a court. However, generally a separation does affect the financial responsibilities between you and your spouse before the divorce is final.

> CAUTION
>
> **Look before you leave.** In some states, moving away from your spouse can be grounds for a "fault" divorce, because if you initiated the separation and your spouse didn't want it, your spouse can say that you abandoned the marriage. While the issue of fault is much less important than it used to be, in some states, it can affect property division or support. See "Fault and No-Fault Divorce," below.

There are three kinds of separation. In most states, only one (legal separation) changes your legal status—but all three of them have the potential to affect your legal rights.

Types of Separation	
Trial Separation	Living apart to decide whether to divorce. May or may not affect property rights, depending on length of separation and activities during separation.
Permanent Separation	Living apart with the intention to divorce. Property and income acquired, and debts incurred, after separation date are the separate property of the spouse who acquires them.
Legal Separation	Legal status different from being married and different from being divorced; includes distribution of property; spouses are not free to marry again.

Trial Separation

If you and your spouse need a break from the relationship, you may choose to live apart while you decide between divorce or reconciliation. While you're separated, the same legal rules apply as when you are married, in terms of ownership of property. For example, money you earn and property you buy are likely to still be considered jointly owned by you and your spouse, depending on your state's rules about property ownership. (See "Property, Custody, and Support," below.)

Take your time deciding ...

" I wish we had spent some time apart and thought about things for a while longer. I feel like we rushed into divorce even more than we rushed into marriage—once we started talking about it, it had a life of its own. Now we really miss each other. I don't know whether we could have made it work but I would have liked to try counseling instead of just going in for the divorce."

—Divorced military spouse

If you and your spouse are hoping to reconcile, it's a good idea to write an informal agreement about some issues that will surely come up. For example, you will need to decide whether or not you will continue to share a joint bank account or credit cards and how you'll budget your spending, which of you will stay in the family home, how expenses will be shared, and the like. If you have kids, you'll need to decide how and when each of you will spend time with them. A sample separation agreement is shown below.

If you both decide there's no going back, your trial separation turns into a permanent one. That's discussed next.

Permanent Separation

When you live apart from your spouse without intending to reconcile but you are not divorced, you are considered permanently separated. In some states, living apart can change property rights between spouses— if you don't intend to get back together, then assets and debts acquired during the separation belong only to the spouse who acquires them. Once you are permanently separated, you are no longer responsible for any debts that your spouse incurs. Similarly, you're no longer entitled to any share of property or income that your spouse acquires or earns.

Because it can significantly affect how your property and money are divided, the date of permanent separation is sometimes hotly contested in a divorce. For example, if your spouse left in a huff and spent a

Sample Separation Agreement

Cynthia and Howard Bean agree that we are going to live apart beginning on February 1, 20xx. We're not ending our marriage and we aren't contemplating divorce right now.

We will continue to share ownership of and access to our joint bank and credit card accounts, and we will both continue to deposit our paychecks into the joint checking account, which we will use to pay household expenses as usual. Cynthia will continue to pay the bills from our joint account.

Howard will live with his brother. Cynthia will stay in the house with the kids. Howard will come to the house to see the kids on the following schedule: every Tuesday, Thursday, and Friday, from 5:00 to 9:00 p.m., and all day every Sunday. He may see the kids more if we both agree. Cynthia can be present during the time that Howard is at the house, or not, at her option. Other than the scheduled visitation times, Howard won't come to the house unless we agree in advance.

This agreement is valid until July 31, 20xx. After that we'll decide to reconcile or to divorce, or will make a new agreement.

_____

Signature

_____

Signature

month sleeping on a friend's couch, but you didn't discuss divorce until the month had passed, and neither of you intended to divorce before then, the date of separation is somewhat questionable. If, during that month, your spouse received a big bonus at work, who it belongs to is also arguable.

If you move out of the house and don't expect any long-term reconciliation with your spouse, there may be legal consequences if the two of you go out or spend the night together just for old times' sake. If you do briefly reconcile, you risk changing the date of separation and becoming responsible for your spouse's financial actions during a period when you thought you were responsible only for yourself.

Once you're separated and have made basic agreements about your joint assets and debts, you don't have to divorce right away. Some people stay married because of insurance—and inertia can be a factor, too.

CAUTION

You're still free to divorce even if you're formally separated. While you and your spouse agree to it, it's fine to maintain your separation without getting a divorce for as long as you want. But once one spouse wants out, it's his or her right to proceed with a divorce. Recently, a New York couple signed a separation agreement providing that the husband couldn't seek a divorce without the wife's written consent for five years from the date of the agreement. Two years later, the husband did try to file for divorce, and the wife asked the court to dismiss the case. The judge refused, saying that the law only required one year of separation and the agreement was against public policy. Your local court would probably come to the same conclusion, so don't try binding your spouse to an agreement to stay married for a certain period of time.

Legal Separation

In some (not all) states, you can get a legal separation by filing a request in family court. Being legally separated is a different legal status from being divorced or married—you're no longer married, but you're not divorced either, and you can't remarry. But the court's order granting the legal separation includes orders about property division, alimony, and child custody and support, just as a divorce would.

People choose legal separation instead of divorce because of religious beliefs, a desire to keep the family together legally for the sake of children, the need for one spouse to keep the health insurance benefits that would be lost with a divorce, or simple aversion to divorcing despite the desire to live separate lives. Some people live very happily in a state of legal separation for many years. (If you're considering a legal separation instead of divorce so that you can keep insurance benefits, check the insurance plan before making the decision. Some consider a legal separation the same as a divorce for purposes of terminating health benefits.)

Annulment

Like a divorce, an annulment ends a marriage. But unlike a divorce, when you get an annulment it's as though you were never married, at least in some ways. Although you need to divide your property just like other divorcing couples, you are legally entitled to call yourself "single" after the annulment, rather than checking the box for "divorced" wherever that comes up.

Religion is the most common reason for choosing annulment over divorce. In particular, the Roman Catholic Church doesn't sanction divorce or subsequent remarriage, but does allow someone whose first marriage was annulled to remarry in the church. But even if you get a religious annulment, in order to end your marital relationship in the eyes of the state, you must obtain a civil annulment through the courts.

Although an annulment generally takes place very soon after the wedding, a couple may seek an annulment after they have been married for many years. In that case, the court considers all of the same issues as in a divorce, divides property, and makes decisions about support and custody. Children of a marriage that has been annulled are still legally considered "legitimate" children of the marriage.

In most places, you can get a civil annulment for one of the following reasons:

Fraud or misrepresentation. One spouse lied about something that was important to the other in getting married, like the ability to have children.

No consummation of the marriage. One spouse is physically unable to have sexual intercourse, and the other spouse didn't know it when they got married.

Incest, bigamy, or underage party. Either the spouses are related by blood so that their marriage is illegal under the laws of the state where they married, or one of them is married to someone else, or one of them is under the age of consent and didn't receive a parent's approval.

Unsound mind. One or both of the spouses was impaired by alcohol or drugs at the time of the wedding or didn't have the mental capacity to understand what was happening.

Force. One of the parties was forced into getting married.

Common Law Marriage

Couples who act like they are married, hold themselves out to the world as married, and intend to be married are considered legally married. Typical indicators of a common law marriage are filing joint tax returns, referring to each other as "husband" and "wife," and using the same last name. If you live in one of the states that allows common law marriage and you meet the criteria, then you are legally married and must get a divorce to end your marriage. If this issue concerns you, see an attorney who's an expert in this area.

The states that allow common law marriage are:

Alabama	New Hampshire (for inheritance purposes only)
Colorado	Ohio (if created before 10/10/1990)
District of Columbia	Oklahoma
Georgia (if created before 1/1/1997)	Pennsylvania (if created before 1/1/2005)
Idaho (if created before 1/1/1996)	Rhode Island
Iowa	South Carolina
Kansas	Texas
Montana	Utah

Family Court

Every divorce case goes through some kind of court proceeding. Even if you and your spouse agree about how you will divide your property and handle custody, visitation, and support issues, a judge will still have to grant your divorce.

In most states, divorce cases—whether contested or not—are handled by a special court, called "family court," "domestic relations court," or "divorce court." This doesn't necessarily mean that there's a separate building (though in some places there is), but just that certain judges deal only with family-related cases, such as divorce, child custody and support, and sometimes, adoption.

Having a separate court for family cases means that the judges are knowledgeable about family law and have lots of experience with different family situations. The court clerks and assistants tend to be knowledgeable as well, which will be especially important if you are representing yourself.

Residency Requirements

Before you can use a state's court system to get divorced, you must live in the state for a certain length of time. A few states have no specified requirement; some require only six weeks; some require a one-year residency, and many more use six months as the required period.

See Chapter 3 for a list of residency requirements.

Kinds of Divorces

There's not just one way to divorce. The differences can be in the law, like fault or no-fault, or in the way you and your spouse approach it, like uncontested, contested, or default. This section describes the different kinds of divorce in general terms. All of the issues raised here are discussed in greater detail in later chapters.

No matter how you slice it, divorce is expensive and time-consuming. The most important variable is how well you and your spouse are able to put aside your anger and grief and cooperate on the big issues of money and children. The better you are at working together to make decisions for your changing family structure, the better for your bank account and for your chances of emerging from the divorce with a decent relationship with your ex.

Kinds of Divorce at a Glance		
Kind of Divorce	**How It Works**	**Hassle and Expense**
Summary	Spouses, who haven't been married long and don't have children or many assets or debts, file together	Relatively simple paperwork; lawyer usually not necessary; often only one filing fee
Default	One spouse files for divorce, the other doesn't respond	Relatively simple paperwork; lawyer may or may not be necessary
Mediated	Trained, neutral mediator helps spouses work out settlement agreement without court fight	Less expensive than a contested divorce; can help spouses communicate
Collaborative	Each spouse hires lawyer, but agrees to settle out of court using negotiation and four-way meetings	Can take longer than mediation, but cheaper, nicer, and quicker than contested case
Arbitrated	Spouses hire private judge to hear evidence and decide contested issues outside of court	Faster and slightly less expensive than trial; can be more civil than court trial and provides greater privacy; not allowed everywhere
Contested	Spouses hire lawyers and fight out issues at trial	Expensive, stressful for everyone (especially children), guaranteed to ruin chances of civil relationship in future

Summary Divorce

In many states, an expedited divorce procedure is available to couples who haven't been married for very long (usually five years or less), don't own much property, don't have children, and don't have significant joint debts. Both spouses need to agree to the divorce, and you must file court papers jointly.

A summary (sometimes called simplified) divorce involves a lot less paperwork than other types of divorce—a few forms are often all it takes. You can probably get the forms you need from the local family court. For this reason, summary divorces are easy to do yourself, without the help of a lawyer. (There's more about summary divorce in Chapter 3.)

Uncontested Divorce

The best choice, if you can make it happen, is an uncontested divorce. That's one in which you and your spouse work together to agree on the terms of your divorce and file court papers cooperatively to make the divorce happen.

There will be no formal trial, and you probably won't have to ever appear in court. Instead, you file court forms and possibly a "marital settlement agreement" that details the agreements you've made about how you want to divide your property and debts, what your custody arrangements for your children will be, and whether support payments will change hands. Your settlement, and your final divorce, will have to be approved by a judge, which shouldn't be any problem. The judge will usually approve a settlement agreement unless it's clear that the terms are completely unfair to one person or were arranged when one person was under duress.

An uncontested divorce is the least expensive kind of divorce you can get. But even it will take a bite out of your wallet. You'll have to figure out how to prepare and file the court papers, which probably involves buying books—you've already got this one, but you may want others. (Your court's website may provide free help, too—it's worth looking. Chapter 16 has a list of court websites for each state.)

You'll probably be able to handle your uncontested divorce with little or no help from a lawyer, but you may want to ask a lawyer to look over your paperwork and, perhaps, to review your settlement agreement. Many couples use a counselor or a mediator to help them come to agreement on property and custody issues. And if you or your spouse has retirement benefits through work, you might need to hire an actuary to value them or a lawyer to prepare the special court order you'll need to distribute them.

Assuming you use professionals for these tasks, you should be able to get everything done for between $2,500 and $5,000, depending on where you live and how much local lawyers and actuaries charge. (There's more about this in Chapters 3 and 4.)

If you and your spouse both stay on top of all the tasks you need to take care of, you should be able to finalize your divorce as soon as the waiting period (every state has one) is over. So depending on your state's requirements, you could be finishing your divorce within a few months, or you may have everything done and just be waiting around for the date when you can file the final papers.

TIP
A legal document preparer can help you with your divorce paperwork. In many states, legal document preparers, paralegals, or legal typists (different names for the same job) can help you prepare court forms for a divorce. They cannot give you legal advice, but they can direct you to helpful resources and then make sure the forms are properly filled out so that your court process goes smoothly. There's more about this in Chapter 16.

Default Divorce

The court will grant a divorce by "default" if you file for divorce and your spouse doesn't respond. The divorce is granted even though your spouse doesn't participate in the court proceedings at all. A default divorce might happen, for example, if your spouse has left for parts unknown and can't be found. (How to manage a default divorce is discussed in Chapter 3.)

Fault and No-Fault Divorce

In the old days, someone who wanted a divorce had to show that the other spouse was at fault for causing the marriage to break down. Even when both people were equally eager to get out of the marriage and the divorce was uncontested, they had to decide which of them would take the legal blame and decide which of the fault grounds they would use in asking the judge to grant the divorce. Adultery was the most popular choice, but abuse, abandonment, extreme cruelty (inflicting unnecessary emotional or physical suffering on the other spouse), and the physical inability to engage in sexual intercourse that wasn't disclosed before marriage also made the list.

Now, every state offers the option of no-fault divorce—and in many states, no-fault is the only option. In a no-fault divorce, instead of proving that one spouse is to blame, you merely tell the court that you and your spouse have "irreconcilable differences" or have suffered an "irremediable breakdown" of your relationship. In some states, however, in order to get a no-fault divorce you must also have lived apart for a specified period of time.

Covenant Marriage and Divorce

If you entered into a "covenant marriage" in Arizona, Arkansas, or Louisiana, you must request a divorce on fault grounds—you may not use no-fault divorce procedures. You're required to engage in marital counseling before you can file for divorce, and the waiting period before your divorce is final may be longer than that for a noncovenant marriage. You'll definitely need a lawyer's help, especially if you and your spouse disagree about getting a divorce.

Carryovers of the old fault system do remain. In some states, you have a choice of using fault or no-fault grounds for divorce. Even if you choose no-fault, some of these states' courts still use fault as a factor in dividing property and determining custody and support. This basically means that one spouse may accuse the other of misconduct and argue that it should affect support awards or the division of property.

It's unlikely you would choose to file for divorce on any of the fault grounds if your divorce is uncontested. The only reasons you might choose a fault divorce are if you don't want to wait out the separation period, or if you anticipate a major fight over property or support. However, if you do intend to argue that fault should factor into property division or support, make sure you use the right forms and check the right boxes when you file your initial court papers. You may need a lawyer's help to be sure you protect your rights.

There's a table in Chapter 5 that lists whether states are pure no-fault states, (where you can't get a fault divorce), or allow fault divorce. It also shows the length of separation required before a no-fault divorce is granted. Chapters 9 through 11 contain more information about how fault affects property and support, and Chapter 5 addresses the issue of fault in a contested divorce.

Mediated Divorce

In divorce mediation, a neutral third party, called a mediator, sits down with you and your spouse to try to help you resolve all of the issues in your divorce. The mediator doesn't make any decisions; that's up to you and your spouse. Instead, the mediator helps you organize information and communicate with each other until you can come to an agreement.

Mediation is much less expensive than going to trial, but more important is the fact that mediation is a wonderful way to preserve and even improve your relationship with your spouse. Working with a mediator to make decisions that work for everyone is a powerful, and often very positive, process.

Mediators charge anywhere from $100 to $400 or more per hour, and if you have a lot of issues to resolve, the mediation could take as many as five or six sessions. Assuming each mediation session is two hours long, you're talking between $1,600 and $3,600. And in a mediated divorce, just as in every other divorce, you may need the help of actuaries, appraisers, and other professionals to value your assets. If you have children, you might also consider working with a parenting counselor who can help you create a parenting plan.

Many couples who are mediating also use "consulting attorneys" to coach each of them through the process and prepare or review the settlement agreement at the end. All in all, you might expect to pay between $2,000 and $6,000 for your share of a mediated divorce. This is far less expensive than a contested divorce that settles before trial, and much, much cheaper than a case that goes all the way to trial. (There's a lot more about mediation in Chapter 4.)

Collaborative Divorce

Just about everyone agrees that battling lawyers escalate a divorcing couple's troubles, to no one's benefit. In response, a new process has developed, called "collaborative divorce." It involves working with lawyers, but the lawyers play a different role from the stereotypical bulldog litigator.

You and your spouse each hire lawyers who are trained to work cooperatively and who agree to try to help you settle your case. Each of you has a lawyer who is on your side, but much of the work is done in cooperation. You and your spouse agree to disclose all the information that's necessary for fair negotiations, and to meet with each other and both lawyers to discuss settlement. You all agree that if your divorce doesn't settle through the collaborative process, your original attorneys will withdraw and you'll hire different attorneys to take your case to trial. The financial disincentive for this outcome should be obvious— you'd have to pay a second lawyer to get up to speed on your case and to do the trial work.

Often other professionals are involved in the process. Most often, your team will include coaches for both you and your spouse—mental health professionals trained to work with spouses in divorce. A neutral financial analyst can help you gather the necessary documents to assess and distribute your property. All of the people assisting with your divorce stay in touch with each other and work together to help you come up with an appropriate resolution.

A collaborative process can be much faster, and much less painful, than a contested divorce. It's not for everyone, but it's a good middle ground between face-to-face mediation and all-out litigation. It offers the protection and expertise of an attorney combined with an explicit commitment to resolving things without an expensive court fight.

The downside, of course, is the potential cost if the collaborative process doesn't succeed. There's a possibility that you or your spouse might agree to something just to avoid the extra cost of going to trial. Before you agree to a collaborative process, make sure that you are prepared—both emotionally and financially—to decide how much compromise is too much.

You shouldn't choose a collaborative divorce just because you think it will be quick, easy, and inexpensive. It may be all of those things, but the commitment you make in a collaborative process is to doing what it takes to reach a solution that truly takes the needs of every person in the family into account. This can take just as long or longer than a divorce in which you hire attorneys to negotiate for you (though usually not as long as a court divorce). That means it can be expensive, as well.

If you go for a collaborative divorce, expect to pay $5,000 to $15,000 for your share. Between scheduling all the necessary meetings, gathering information, and getting lawyers to prepare paperwork, your divorce may take a year or more. Of course, if you easily reach an agreement and everyone is very efficient, you may be able to finalize things as soon as the waiting period in your state is over, and the cost may be lower.

RESOURCE

Get more information. For more information about collaborative divorce, check out *Divorce Without Court: A Guide to Mediation & Collaborative Divorce*, by Katherine E. Stoner (Nolo), *Collaborative Divorce: The Revolutionary New Way to Restructure Your Family, Resolve Legal Issues, and Move on With Your Life*, by Pauline Tesler and Peggy Thompson (HarperCollins) or *The Collaborative Way to Divorce*, by Stuart Webb and Ron Gusky (Hudson Street Press).

Arbitration

In arbitration, you and your spouse agree that you'll hire a private judge, called an arbitrator, to make the same decisions that a judge could make, and that you will honor the arbitrator's decisions as if a judge had made them. Arbitration has some of the same advantages as mediation does, including speed, efficiency, privacy, cost-effectiveness, and informality.

Arbitration has been used for many years in other kinds of lawsuits, and it's starting to gain favor among divorce lawyers as a good alternative to a court trial. The arbitrator is usually a lawyer or a retired judge, who you pay hourly. Your lawyer and your spouse's lawyer know lots of arbitrators and will probably be able to agree on someone who'd be appropriate for your case.

Just as in a trial, each side prepares arguments and evidence and presents them to the arbitrator, and then the arbitrator makes decisions. However, the presentation of evidence is usually less formal than in a courtroom. You're likely to be able to schedule a hearing with an arbitrator much more quickly than you would get a case to trial, so speed is a major advantage. It's also private, unlike a trial, which is open to the public. (Your court records will still be public if you use arbitration, though.)

Cost is another upside to arbitration; although it's still expensive, it won't cost as much as a trial. That's because it shouldn't take quite as long for your lawyer to prepare for the hearing, and the arbitration itself may be shorter because the arbitrator won't be as strict about evidence as a judge would be.

An arbitrator's decision generally is binding, which means if you don't like it, you can't ask for a do-over and go to court for a second chance. You also can't appeal the decision to a higher court, so you are stuck with whatever the arbitrator decides. Because of the inherent unpredictability of divorce cases, some people don't like that idea—though some might appreciate the certainty that arbitration offers.

> ⚠ CAUTION
>
> **Arbitration isn't available everywhere.** A few states don't allow arbitration in divorce cases. Check with your lawyer, if you have one, or with your local court clerk.

Contested Divorce

If you and your spouse argue so much over property or child custody that you can't come to an agreement, and instead take these issues to the judge to decide, you have what's called a contested divorce. The judge and court clerks will be the main players in your divorce case. (There are no juries in divorce trials, except in Texas and Georgia—and in Georgia, the jury can't decide custody or visitation, only financial issues. In a minority of other states, you can ask for a jury trial in some circumstances, but this is very unusual.) Most divorce trials are not long, drawn-out affairs like trials you may have seen on television. Many take a day or two, or even just a morning.

The trial itself may be short, but the entire process is long and hard. It will take a huge emotional toll on you, your spouse, and certainly your kids, and also cost you in dollars and cents. A contested divorce, even one that ends in a settlement rather than a trial, can cost each spouse many tens of thousands of dollars. Assuming each side's lawyer charges $250 per hour, and assuming an ordinary amount of information-gathering and pretrial court proceedings, an average divorce might run each of you $30,000—and that figure could easily go higher with a few added complexities.

Which brings us back to our initial advice: Take the high road whenever you can. The rewards aren't only monetary, but choosing compromise will definitely improve your bottom line. And less stress about money makes it easier to work out other issues, now and later. It will also expedite things—a contested divorce, especially if you are fighting over custody, can take years to resolve.

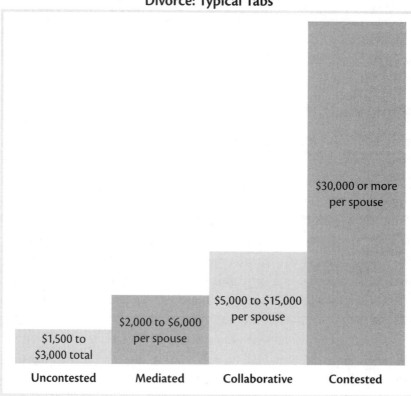

Divorce: Typical Tabs

$1,500 to $3,000 total	$2,000 to $6,000 per spouse	$5,000 to $15,000 per spouse	$30,000 or more per spouse
Uncontested	Mediated	Collaborative	Contested

Divorce for Same-Sex Couples

In 2013, the legal landscape for same-sex couples changed dramatically when the United States Supreme Court ruled that key parts of the Defense of Marriage Act were unconstitutional, and that the federal government must recognize same-sex marriages legally performed in any of the states that authorized them. At the time, there were nine states with marriage equality; as this book went to press, there were 18. Several more were in legal limbo, with their bans on same-sex marriage in the hands of the federal courts.

States With Marriage Equality for Same-Sex Couples		
California	Illinois	New Jersey
Connecticut	Maine	New Mexico
Delaware	Maryland	New York
District of Columbia	Massachusetts	Rhode Island
Hawaii	Minnesota	Washington
Iowa	New Hampshire	Vermont

States With Marriage-Equivalent Relationships for Same-Sex Couples			
California	Colorado	Nevada	Oregon

In all of these states, same-sex couples must use the same forms and procedures as opposite-sex married couples to end their legal relationship. All the same rules about custody, property, and support apply. Some other states recognize same-sex relationships from other states and allow couples to divorce there.

Now that DOMA is no longer the law of the land, divorcing same-sex couples enjoy the same federal tax advantages as their opposite-sex counterparts, including the right to transfer property at divorce without tax consequences and the ability to roll over tax-deferred retirement funds, among others. These benefits still aren't available to registered domestic partners or civil union partners in the states that offer those relationships.

Divorce for same-sex couples still carries its own complexities, and you would be well served to see an attorney with experience in this area. Issues of recognition and jurisdiction (which court can grant you a divorce) can be particularly challenging.

If you and your partner are in agreement—or can reach agreement through mediation—about how to divide your property and share time with your kids, you may be able to use one of the do-it-yourself methods described in Chapter 3, but you should consult an experienced lawyer before going forward, to make sure you're not missing anything.

RESOURCE
To learn more, see *Making It Legal: A Guide to Same-Sex Marriage, Domestic Partnerships & Civil Unions*, by Frederick Hertz with Emily Doskow (Nolo).

Property, Custody, and Support

Every divorcing couple must consider how to distribute property and debts, and whether one spouse will pay spousal support to the other. If you have kids, you'll also need to make decisions about parenting time and support. You and your spouse will either need to work out these three big issues or turn them over to a judge to decide.

Divvying Up Property

"Marital property" is the collection of assets you and your spouse have gathered during your marriage, including money, real estate, investments, pension plans, and so on. Marital debts are obligations you took on together during your married life. Both the property and the debts belong to both of you, and part of the divorce process will be to divide them up between you.

Assets or debts that either of you had before your marriage, or that you acquired after the permanent separation, are called separate property or debts. Generally, each of you will keep your separate property and be responsible for your separate debts, but in some states separate property can be divided at divorce.

If you and your spouse can agree on how to distribute your property, the court will simply approve your agreement. If you can't agree, the court will divide things for you. A few states use "community property" rules, and divide marital property equally. The rest use a system of "equitable distribution," to divide property in a way that the court thinks is fair, but that isn't always equal. Chapters 9 and 10 explain how states divide property and discuss the decisions you'll need to make about your assets and debts.

What Happens to the Children?

Divorce is stressful for everyone, but when you have children, the stakes are higher, and you are responsible for protecting these most vulnerable participants in the divorce process. There are three entire chapters about kids later in the book.

You and your spouse will need to create a parenting plan, a document that will include your decisions (or a court's) about whether you'll share custody of your children equally, or whether one parent will be the primary custodial parent. Custody means both the right to have a child live with you (physical custody) and the right to make decisions about the child's welfare and education (legal custody).

A parent who doesn't have physical custody of the kids is usually given visitation rights. If one parent has both legal and physical custody and the other has fairly limited visitation, the primary custodial parent has "sole custody." "Joint custody," which is more common, means that both parents share physical custody, legal custody, or both.

Even if you and your spouse are never going to see eye to eye about money matters, you should try very hard to come to an agreement about custody and parenting arrangements. A custody fight will harm your children more than any other kind of dispute that might come up in the divorce process. Do everything you can to avoid it.

At the beginning of your divorce process, you'll need to come up with a temporary agreement about how you will share time with your kids. You should do that as quickly as you can, to ease your children's insecurity. Whatever you decide, write it down and make sure you note that the arrangement is temporary, so that it's clear you're not agreeing to something for the long haul. It may take a while to figure out what long-term arrangement will work best.

Chapter 13 contains a sample parenting agreement; you can take parts of it and use them to prepare a temporary agreement when you first split up. See Chapters 6 and 7 for more about custody, including how courts decide custody questions and how to prepare a time-sharing plan.

Spousal and Child Support

If you and your spouse have children, chances are that one of you will pay child support to the other. When the children spend more time with one parent than the other, or if one parent earns more money, the court will award child support to make sure that the kids are always taken care of.

In some divorces, courts award spousal support, also called alimony or maintenance, to one party. A support award is especially likely after a long marriage, where one spouse's earnings are much higher than the other's, or if one spouse gave up career plans to support the other spouse or care for kids. Chapter 8 addresses child support issues, and Chapter 11 has more about spousal support. Chapter 12 addresses child and spousal support for military spouses.

Getting Help From Experts

As you can see, there are a lot of decisions to make in a divorce. You and your spouse can make these decisions yourselves, rather than having a judge make them for you—and you should make every effort to do so. At such a painful time, it's difficult to just sit down with your spouse and figure out how you are going to remake your family structure, finances, and living situations. But that doesn't mean you have to lose control of the decisions and slide into an expensive, acrimonious, and ugly divorce. You can get help. Chapter 16 has a lot more about how to go about getting the information and expert help you will need to complete your divorce. ●

First Steps After You Decide to Divorce

You've made the first hard decision—to end your marriage. Or perhaps the decision has been made for you, making the whole thing even more confusing and painful. Either way, you're probably trying to wrap your brain around the big changes coming your way very quickly. "Where will I live?" "Where will the kids live?" "What about our joint credit cards?" "Do I need a new job to support myself and the kids?" "How will I pay the bills that are due right now?"

The best way to cope is to take one step at a time. This chapter addresses some of the first—and critically important—steps to take.

> **CAUTION**
>
> **Don't make important decisions hastily.** Divorce is a traumatic experience, and your decision-making skills are probably not the best they've ever been. Although you can't put off all decisions—including some that you'll have to make with your spouse, like who will live where—try to minimize the number of long-term decisions you commit to in the first few months. If you really have to settle something, at least sleep on it, and try to find someone you trust to help you think through your options.

Breaking the News

Once one spouse decides on divorce, there's the delicate matter of discussing it out loud with the other. And once that's accomplished, there's the even more difficult issue of talking to the kids.

Your Spouse

If you're the one who's decided to end your marriage and your spouse is still in the dark, then the sooner you talk, the better. Most likely, your spouse already knows, at least deep down—most often, relationships come apart gradually over the course of time, and the outcome isn't a big surprise to anyone.

Taking the high road in dealing with your divorce can—and should—start right now. Make a plan for how you'll tell your spouse that you believe your marriage is over. If you're seeing a counselor or therapist on your own, get advice on the best way to talk to your spouse. If you and your spouse are in couples counseling, that may be a good environment to break the news. Either way, it won't be an easy conversation, so planning out what you want to say, and how, can really help. You might even want to write some notes about the words you want to use. If it's possible to break the news in a kind and compassionate way, do it—it will honor your relationship. It may also help your spouse to avoid feeling bitter about the way you did it, and though it may seem a small thing, every small kindness helps when you're splitting up. And it should go without saying that you shouldn't deliver the news via email, voicemail, or text messaging.

Don't expect that your spouse will immediately be able to discuss and make decisions about things like who will stay in the house and who will move out, or how you will spend time with your kids. It will take time to get used to the idea that you're divorcing. Solutions that may already seem obvious to you will still be shocking to someone who hasn't been considering these matters for as long as as you probably have.

Whatever you do, don't let your spouse be the last to know. If you have been considering divorce for a while and have talked to friends or family members about it, make sure you follow up with your spouse right away. Don't let your spouse hear from someone else that you're planning to leave.

RESOURCE

Difficult Conversations: How to Discuss What Matters Most, by Douglas Stone, Bruce Patton, and Sheila Heen (Penguin), has practical advice about how to prepare for difficult talks and communicate successfully about hard topics.

Other books that can help with communicating during divorce are listed in Chapter 16.

If the conversation goes all right, you might consider asking your spouse whether it would be a good time to discuss telling others in your intimate circle—your parents, siblings, close friends, and even neighbors.

These conversations can be really difficult, too, and if you can agree on how (who, when, and where) they will happen, it will probably be easier on everyone. But again, your spouse may not be ready to figure that out. If that's the case, you'll have to make your best guess about whether your spouse would want to tell others or would prefer that you take care of that chore.

Your Children

Telling children about a divorce can be one of the hardest parts of the entire process. The most important thing you can do is reassure your kids that it's not their fault and that they're not losing either of their parents. Chapter 6 has advice about dealing with your kids during divorce, including how to talk to them about the breakup—both at the start and as you all adjust to the changes.

Where Will Everyone Live?

One big decision that can't be put off for long is who will live where for the time being—that includes you, your spouse, and your children.

Who Gets to Stay in the House?

Most spouses figure out temporary living arrangements during a separation, putting off final decisions until the divorce process is further along. If you manage to do this, write up an agreement about what you've decided.

What if you can't agree? In most cases neither spouse is more entitled to stay in the family home than the other. If the house (or the lease on an apartment) is only in one spouse's name, then that spouse might be able to make the other one move out, though it would depend on factors like how long you've lived in the house together, who pays the expenses, and the like. If your spouse is the only one whose name is on the title to the house or a lease, you might be better off taking the path of least resistance and moving out now, and then arguing about ownership interests later.

Custody Considerations

In families with children, it's common for the primary caretaker to stay in the house with the kids. Often, but not always, that person is the mother.

If you expect to share physical custody, then the closer the noncustodial parent can live, the better for the kids—it will cut down on the disruption to their school and social lives. Of course, that's not always possible, especially if you live in a neighborhood of high-value single-family homes. But make as much effort as you can to keep the households near each other.

If you intend to argue that you should have sole custody, don't move out and leave your kids behind. No matter how anxious you are to get out of the house, if you go without your kids, the message you send is that you think your spouse is a good parent who can take care of the kids without help. Also, judges don't like to disturb the status quo—so wherever your kids go when you separate, that's likely where they'll stay.

If you're expecting to share custody anyway, moving out is less risky. But if you are worried that moving out might lessen your chances of getting shared custody, ask your spouse to sign an agreement that says that the move won't affect later decisions about custody and visitation.

If you and your spouse are able to cooperate, you should work together to find the best housing for the one who is moving out. If you're the one staying, why should you help? Two reasons. First, it may get your spouse out of the house more quickly; second, it benefits your kids by ensuring that both homes are appropriate for them.

If you're at a stalemate about who gets to stay in the house, you might simply agree to both stay there for a while (see "Staying Together for a While," below). You can also go to court right away and ask for a temporary order giving you the right to stay in the house for now. (Chapter 5 discusses temporary orders.) The court looks at your financial resources, the level of tension between you, the needs of your children, and whatever other information might relate to your living situation. You might argue, for example, that you need to stay in the house because it's close to your workplace but a good distance from your spouse's, or because you are the primary caretaker of the children. But the judge's decision might be that neither of you has to move out, and then you'll be back to either making it work or making a decision on your own. Try to work it out without going through this exercise if you can.

If There's Violence in Your Home

If you or your children are in physical danger from your spouse, you can do either or both of the following:

- Get out of the house quickly, taking the children with you. See a lawyer and file for custody right away, to make sure you're not accused of kidnapping.
- Go to court and get a restraining order, ordering your spouse to move out and stay away from the house and from you and the kids. Change the locks after you get the court order.

See Chapter 14 for more about domestic violence.

Staying Together for a While

Some divorcing couples keep living together even after they've agreed that the marriage is over. Often spouses agree to this for financial reasons. Other times, both spouses simply refuse to move because neither one wants to lose any ground in an anticipated custody war or because both feel they're entitled to the house, or because neither wants to give any ground at all.

Because the date of separation can become a contested issue in a divorce, staying together has some risks. If you do continue living together, make a written note of the date you believe you separated— that is, when you stopped living as spouses. If the evidence is clear that you intended to separate on a certain date, many courts do not care that you continued to live together after that point—even for some years.

If you file your divorce papers while you are still living together, you'll have to designate the date you separated. It could be, for example, the date that your spouse moved into the guest room or the date you started communicating only by email. If you can agree on what that date is, all the better. If you can't, then when you file court papers just put down the date you believe was your separation date and be prepared to argue about it later.

How can I miss you if you won't go away?

"Even though we'd agreed that I would eventually buy him out, my husband wouldn't leave the house until everything was settled and the payment was made. He said that until we were divorced it was still half his, and he delayed the divorce for as long as he could. My lawyer said I couldn't make him go, so we just lived as roommates for almost a year and a half. It was miserable, but he did still pay half the expenses and at least he was gone a lot. Still I was really happy when the buyout happened and the divorce was final. I had to get roommates in order to afford to keep the house—but they're a lot more pleasant than he was."

—**55-year-old divorced woman**

Gathering Financial Information

As soon as you can, begin to inventory what you and your spouse own and owe. This is important not only to facilitate later decisions, but also to protect against worst-case scenarios in which one spouse runs off with, or hides, property.

A financial inventory form to prompt you to remember all your assets is included in the appendix and on the book's companion page. See "Get Updates, Forms, and More" in the introduction. Include all of your property and debts, even the ones you think belong only to you or only to your spouse. In fact, it's particularly important that you list any debts that you believe are solely your spouse's responsibility. You want to make sure that your final divorce order makes clear that you're not responsible for them. Include anything that you owned before you were married and anything that you think is yours alone.

Chapter 10 explains what property is divided at divorce, and how. For now, just make your inventory. The general rule is that in community property states each spouse owns half of everything, while in other states the person who holds title owns the property. Either way, the property must be divided fairly at divorce.

Your Inventory: What to Include

Assets
- checking and savings accounts
- stocks, bonds, mutual funds, and money market accounts
- certificates of deposit
- real estate (house, condo, or any other property you own, such as a vacation house)
- retirement plans, including pensions, 401(k)s, IRAs, SEP IRAs, profit-sharing, and any other deferred compensation plans
- stock options and restricted stock unit (RSU) grants
- accrued vacation time
- medical savings accounts
- cars and other vehicles, including boats or other recreational vehicles
- valuable personal property, such as works of art, jewelry, or collections
- household furniture and furnishings
- life insurance policies with cash value
- season tickets to sporting or cultural events
- airline miles and other rewards points
- tax refunds you expect.

Debts
- mortgage
- home equity line of credit
- credit cards
- vehicle loans
- promissory notes
- student loans
- any other obligation.

> **TIP**
>
> **Ready for your close-up?** In addition to creating a written record, it's not a bad idea to use a video camera to document your major assets, like your house and automobiles. This will show their condition at the time you separated and also be proof of how you were living before the divorce, which can sometimes be a factor in support negotiations.

In addition to making a list, make copies of important financial documents, including:

- deeds
- recent mortgage statements
- insurance policies
- retirement plan documents
- business interests
- tax returns for the past five years
- wills and trusts, and
- bank, brokerage, and retirement account statements.

If you have bank safe deposit boxes, check their contents as soon as you can. Take a friend along, or ask a bank employee to witness you opening the safety deposit box and making a videotape of the contents, then make a written inventory and have your witness sign it. Don't take anything from it unless you're sure the property belongs only to you. Even in that situation, rent a second box and simply move the contents over for safekeeping under your control. You'll have to identify the property and have the court confirm that it's your separate property as part of the divorce.

Something else you should take care of right away is getting information about your spouse's retirement plans. You need to let the employer know that you are separated and planning to divorce, and find out from the human resources department the address of the plan administrator or trustee of the retirement plan. Write the employer a letter (and send a copy to the plan administrator) asking for the following:

- a "summary plan description" for all deferred compensation plans that your spouse participates in

- copies of benefit statements reflecting your spouse's benefits for the past five years
- information about company stock or stock options that your spouse holds, including vesting or exercise dates, and
- names and addresses of plan administrators, if you don't already have them.

If you can, get your spouse's signature on the letter, consenting to the release of the information. You are entitled to receive all of this information and if the employer doesn't cooperate, you can get the documents through methods discussed in Chapters 5 and 9.

If Your Spouse Has All the Financial Information

You are entitled to know what you and your spouse own and owe. But what if you don't even know what accounts there are or where they're kept, much less what's in them?

If your spouse isn't cooperative, you may need to file for divorce right away so that you can force your spouse to disclose relevant financial information.

In the meantime, a good first step is to get copies of your tax returns. If you don't know where they are at home, you can get them from the IRS by submitting a simple form (Form 4506). You can get the form by contacting the IRS at 800-829-1040 or www.irs.gov. There's more about getting financial information out of a recalcitrant spouse in Chapter 9.

Are Those New Golf Clubs, Honey?

If you think your spouse has always been completely forthcoming about money matters, think again. A recent survey found that nearly one-third of adults in committed relationships admit to having been dishonest with their partners about spending habits and even about overdue bills.

Managing Your Family's Money

Divorce usually means establishing two households on the same income that used to support only one, and that takes some creative financial planning. Take it one step at a time. Not every decision has to be made right now. All you need to do now is figure out how you will separate your assets so that each of you has enough money to keep everyone fed and housed until the divorce is final, months from now. Then you need to make sure the agreements about your temporary financial arrangements are clear. With the passage of time, what works financially—and what doesn't—will become clearer, making it easier to work out your final settlement.

Make a Budget

The first thing to do is make a budget. Why? Because it's essential that you know what you are bringing in and what you are spending. You will probably need the information when you file for divorce in any event—most states require that you file a statement of your assets, debts, income, and expenses at the outset of your case. If you have a lawyer, your lawyer will want the information even if it's not required by the court.

For another thing, it's very common to underestimate what you spend and, more important, what you will need to keep both households afloat. So, even though it can be tedious and requires an attention to detail that may be hard to muster right now, do your best to create a meaningful budget and stick with it.

It's easiest if you can work together with your spouse on this project. If that seems feasible, make a few copies of the budget forms in the appendix and on the book's companion page. See "Get Updates, Forms, and More" in the introduction. That way, you and your spouse can each fill them out and then share information. When you're done, you should have a comprehensive picture of your financial status and needs during the separation and divorce.

If you can't work with your spouse on this, then just do your best to estimate your spouse's income and expenses. This will help you figure out what support you need and what your spouse might be able to pay—or vice versa.

If you've never made a budget before, start by keeping track of your daily, weekly, and monthly expenses, from predictable ones, such as your phone bill, to the unexpected need for a new transmission. Include every bit you spend, whether it's for parking meters or cappuccinos. Then total those expenses and include them in the monthly budget in the appropriate category. For expenses that you pay regularly but less often, like yearly homeowners' insurance, semiyearly property taxes, or even haircuts every six weeks, either divide the amount to come up with a monthly figure or keep a separate list of major annual and irregular expenses, and use it to help you plan.

 FORMS

In the appendix and on this book's companion page, you'll find forms that you can use to start working on a budget, along with legal updates on the topics covered in the book, and more. See "Get Updates, Forms, and More" in the introduction.

- **The Monthly Income form** will give you a sense of what's coming in and also help you gather the information you'll need when you start to do support calculations later. If you have information about both you and your spouse, include it all; otherwise, do your own and estimate your spouse's.

- **The Daily Expenses form** will help you keep track of where your money is going. Be sure you write down everything you spend money on in the first column, and then use each daily column to track expenses for that item. (If your item is rent, then it will appear in only one of the daily categories, but if it's Starbucks, you may learn a little something about how often you indulge in certain treats.) If it's easier, you can create a daily expense form on which you list the types of expenses you typically have, and copy that so that you don't have to write the items in each time.

- **The Monthly Budget form** gives you a place to put your projected monthly expenses and then see how closely you stick to them over time.

If a regular salary is your only source of income, it should be pretty simple to fill out the Monthly Income form. But if, like many people, you're self-employed or work on commission, you'll need to average your income over some months to come up with an accurate picture. And it's important to include investment and other income, such as rents, on the Monthly Income form.

> CAUTION
> **Don't overuse your credit cards.** While it's always important to keep an eye on how you use credit, it's especially so now. Circumstances can conspire to make credit card spending seem attractive or even necessary: You probably have less money than usual, you may be setting up a new household, and you're emotionally stressed. Even so, don't fall into the "I give up, let's just pull out the plastic" trap. If you don't control your credit card balances, you may emerge from the chaos of your divorce only to find yourself in the quicksand of uncontrolled debt.

Start Keeping Your Income Separate

If you don't have a separate bank account already, run right out and open one, and start depositing your paycheck into it. Even if you are the sole support of your family and you and your spouse have agreed to keep a joint account for paying family expenses, make sure the money you earn goes first into your own account before being transferred to the joint account. As soon as you have permanently separated, your income becomes your own, separate property.

This doesn't mean you won't pay over some of it, possibly even most of it, to your spouse as support, but that's a different issue. Having your own account makes clear that you and your spouse have separated and that your income is your own. (The importance of this varies depending on whether you live in one of the nine "community property" states, listed in Chapter 9, where everything you earn during the marriage is considered to be jointly owned, or another state, where your earnings have been your own all along.)

If you pay for family necessities like food, clothing, housing, or health care out of money that is only yours, your spouse might be required to reimburse you later—generally when your final settlement agreement is being completed. Except for that, for the most part, debts that either of you agrees to after the date of separation are considered your personal responsibility. (See "Close Joint Credit Accounts," below.)

Dealing With Joint Assets

How you deal with your jointly owned property depends on whether the divorce papers have been filed yet—and also on how much you trust your spouse.

Before Papers Are Filed

Before either you or your spouse files divorce papers, you may use jointly owned assets as you see fit. You and your spouse do, however, share a legal responsibility not to do anything that would harm your jointly owned interests. (And, of course, you can't do anything that would harm your spouse's separate property.) You must manage jointly owned property for the benefit of both of you.

You have this responsibility (called a fiduciary duty, in legal terms) even if your spouse isn't living up to it. But what if you're afraid that your spouse will clean out the joint accounts? Theoretically, before divorce papers are filed there's nothing keeping you from taking half of the money out of your joint bank accounts—as long as you do it in a way that doesn't cause harm. But as a practical matter, it's not the greatest idea. First, if your divorce is acrimonious, your spouse's lawyer will have a field day questioning you about taking the property in anticipation of the divorce. Second, if your divorce isn't acrimonious yet, it probably will be after you clean out half of all the accounts. Better to talk to your spouse and make some agreements about disbursing cash for necessary expenses during your separation.

If you do take money out of joint accounts before you file and without your spouse's knowledge, keep extremely careful records of how much you withdrew (and how you use it), and put the money in a separate account in your name. Don't take more than half, and make sure that you don't touch any assets that might possibly be considered your spouse's separate property.

You also have the right to withdraw money from or borrow against your own retirement accounts, as long as you don't take more than 50% of the total value of the asset. (But there are reasons not to make such a withdrawal, discussed in Chapter 10.)

After Papers Are Filed

When you file for divorce, the court automatically issues an order that restricts both you and your spouse from taking or transferring any of your jointly owned property. You must leave your joint savings, checking, and investment accounts and everything else as they are unless you and your spouse agree to use them. It's best to agree on how you'll use joint money, and stick to those agreements. It's perfectly fine, if you've always used a joint checking account to pay household expenses, to keep doing that. It's also fine to divide the money and each keep whatever percentages you agree on.

If you and your spouse agree that one of you can take some of the jointly owned property, make sure you write down the agreement. And whether you take your share on your own say-so before filing, or according to agreements you made with your spouse at any point, you'll need to account for all of it later when you and your spouse formally divide up your property. If the court later decides you took more than your share, you'll have to pay it back somehow—either by trading some other asset for it or by paying cash.

Just because the law and the court papers say you can't transfer money after court papers are filed doesn't mean people don't try. If you think your spouse might try to transfer co-owned property after you've filed, immediately notify your bank and brokerage house that you are in the process of a divorce and that they should not allow withdrawals or transfers without the written consent of both spouses. Send a letter advising the financial institution that it must honor the court orders that are an automatic part of your divorce. Enclose a copy of the form that contains the restraining orders, and something that shows your case number and the date you filed for divorce.

You might want to do the same with the plan administrator for your spouse's retirement plan, and don't forget about any equity line of credit you have. And if you or your spouse uses the Internet to make investment transactions, immediately send an email to the trading firm advising them that a divorce action has been filed and that no further transactions should be made on the account without both spouses' authorization.

Protecting Your Financial Privacy

Your financial information is now your own—make sure it stays that way. If you and your spouse are still living together, it's prudent for you to get a post office box where you can receive personal and business mail. And if you have a shared family computer, don't use it for divorce-related email correspondence or document preparation. Even after you delete something, a skilled computer user can retrieve it.

Decide How to File Your Tax Returns

Depending on when in the year you separate, you may have to deal with the issue of tax filing quite early in your divorce process. You can file jointly for any tax year in which your divorce was pending, but not for the tax year in which it became final. You are considered to have been divorced for the entire year in which your divorce becomes final. So if you separate in July, and get a final decree of divorce the next May, you can file jointly for the separation year but not for the following year.

If you have a preference for filing one way or the other, you can also time your divorce (consistent with the court's timing, of course) so that you make the divorce effective before or after the tax year ends.

In many situations, joint tax filing for married couples is advantageous— for one thing, you can take the child care credit only if you're filing a joint return. But it's not always the best option, so be sure you have your tax professional calculate the tax liability in a variety of ways to see what will work best. In certain circumstances a separated spouse can file using "Head of Household" status, and you may want to explore this option if you have your kids more than 50% of the time. Sometimes, one spouse will balk at the idea of filing jointly, either on general principle or because of fear of being liable for the taxes or penalties related to that return. You can't force your spouse to file jointly, but you can always ask.

Divorcing spouses in community property states should consult a tax professional before making filing decisions. These states treat income earned from separate property (for example, dividend income from stocks that one spouse owns separately) differently than other states, and this affects what you report on your income tax returns. Community property laws can also affect dependent exemptions.

If you do file jointly, you are 100% responsible for any taxes due. (So is your spouse.) And if you file jointly and are entitled to a refund, you must figure out how to divide it just as you do all of your other shared assets.

The "Innocent Spouse" Rule

The IRS allows for the fact that sometimes one partner in a marriage prepares joint tax returns that the other spouse signs without knowing what's actually in them. The Innocent Spouse Rule says that a spouse who unknowingly signs a fraudulent tax return can be excused from liability for penalties based on that return.

It's difficult to prove that you were an innocent spouse, but if you've been victimized by your spouse's overreaching on a tax return, give it a try. IRS Publication 971, available at www.irs.gov, has the information you'll need to get started learning about these rules. *Divorce & Money*, by Violet Woodhouse with Matthew J. Perry (Nolo), also has extensive information about innocent spouse rules. If you think you have a problem after reviewing these materials, talk to a tax expert. (To avoid problems, have your own accountant review joint tax returns before you sign them.)

RESOURCE

The IRS can actually help. For details on the ins and outs of taxes and divorce, check out the comprehensive IRS publication *Divorced or Separated Individuals*. It's IRS Publication 504, available at www.irs.gov or by calling 800-829-3676.

Protect Your Valuable Separate Property

If you're worried that your spouse might take, or even damage, any particularly valuable items of your separate property, protect them. If you have larger items, like art or furniture, that belong solely to you, you might want to rent a storage unit and move them there. Smaller items, like jewelry or important and valuable papers, can go in a safe deposit box or be left with a trusted friend. Be sure to do this before divorce papers are filed. And be sure to document everything you do by having a witness or videotaping the property in your home and then in the storage unit.

Close Joint Credit Accounts

Even in the crisis time after you first separate, the bills have to be paid. Make sure that you decide who will pay which ones, especially ones that might trigger late fees or hurt your credit rating if you miss a payment. Both of you are responsible for all of the debts that you incurred together before you separated—and if you live in a community property state, possibly for some debts incurred by either of you after separation as well.

Whether or not you trust your spouse to continue to be responsible with your joint credit, get in there and close the accounts, using the process described below. If you don't, your good credit could be at risk from your spouse's actions.

If your spouse runs up debts on a joint credit card account after you separate and doesn't pay, the creditors won't pay any attention to your date of separation—they'll come after you because you are the other owner of the account. And although you might eventually get your spouse to reimburse you for whatever you have to pay, you'll go through a lot of hassle getting there, not to mention the potential for damage to your credit rating. (There's more about dealing with debts in Chapter 10.)

CAUTION

Before you close joint accounts, make sure you'll be able to establish credit in your own name. If you don't have a separate credit card account, be sure to open one before closing joint accounts. If you can't get credit in your own name and you think you'll need to use the credit cards you have, then it's probably better not to close the account—although you'll bear the risk that your spouse will be irresponsible with credit, you'll also be sure that you have the resources you need. (See "Get Your Own Credit Card," below.)

To close a joint credit account, write to the credit card issuer with your instructions. (There's sure to be a customer service address on your statement, or you can call the 800 number on your statement and find out where to send correspondence—but definitely close or at least confirm the closing of an account in writing.) Make sure they put a "hard close" on the account, which means that neither you nor your spouse will be able to reopen it later. A sample letter to a credit card company is shown below.

If your credit cards have balances, acknowledge that in the letter and ask to close the account for new charges, leaving it open for billing purposes until you have paid them off. Also, acknowledge that they may not be willing to close the account just on your say-so—they may want both owners to confirm before actually closing the account—but insist that your relationship with the account is terminated. If you don't hear back from the credit card company, check your credit record to see that your instructions were followed.

RESOURCE

Taking control of your financial situation. *Divorce & Money: How to Make the Best Financial Decisions During Divorce*, by Violet Woodhouse and Matthew J. Perry (Nolo), has more about debt and credit issues in divorce, as well as general financial advice.

Solve Your Money Troubles: Debt, Credit & Bankruptcy, by Margaret Reiter and Robin Leonard, and *Credit Repair*, by Robin Leonard (both from Nolo), offer very useful general credit and debt advice.

Other resources are listed in Chapter 16.

Sample Letter Closing Credit Account

May 12, 20xx

To: University Credit Union
Re: Account Number 4612305

My spouse, James Brown, and I are in the process of getting a divorce. Our court case is in Milton County, Illinois, Case Number F333555. I am requesting an immediate "hard close" of this account so that neither party may incur new charges. If the account has an outstanding balance, you may keep the account open for billing purposes only. Please advise me immediately of any outstanding charges on the account.

If my authorization alone isn't enough to close the account completely, please terminate my relationship with this credit card account immediately. I have destroyed my card attached to this account. Any charges made to the account after the date of this letter will be the responsibility of James Brown alone. James Brown does not have my permission to reestablish the card at any time using my name or credit.

Please notify the three national credit bureaus that this account has been "closed by consumer" and send me written confirmation that you have done so.

Thank you for your assistance.

Sincerely,

Sarah Brown
Sarah Brown

Get Your Own Credit Card

If all you have is joint credit, get yourself a credit card in your own name immediately. Your ability to get new credit cards, rent an apartment, take out a mortgage, and more all depend on the information that's stored in your credit report. It's a good idea to get a copy as soon as you separate, so that you'll know what kind of credit you have on your own. If you and your spouse own everything jointly, your credit will be tied to your spouse's. If you've had some joint and some separate accounts, you'll have an easier time getting credit on your own because you'll have your own individual records.

Each major national credit bureau—TransUnion, Experian, and Equifax—must, under federal law, give you one free copy of your credit report each year. The federal Fair Credit Reporting Act requires this.

How to Get Your Free Credit Report

You can order a copy of your report by phone, online, or mail.

> 877-322-8228
>
> www.annualcreditreport.com
>
> Annual Credit Report Service
> P.O. Box 105283
> Atlanta, GA 30348-5283

You must provide your name, address, Social Security number, and date of birth when you order. You also may be required to provide information that only you would know, such as the amount of your monthly mortgage payment.

If you want additional copies of your credit report within a year, or you need to correct information in your credit report, you'll probably need to contact a credit bureau directly.

How to Reach Credit Bureaus		
Equifax	**Experian**	**TransUnion**
P.O. Box 740241	P.O. Box 2002	P.O. Box 105281
Atlanta, GA 30374	Allen, TX 75013	Atlanta, GA 30348-5281
800-685-1111	888-397-3742	800-888-4213
www.equifax.com	www.experian.com	www.transunion.com

Make Temporary Agreements About Support

You and your spouse also need to think about temporary child and spousal support. The decisions you make now need not be set in stone. Your main goal is just to make things work so that you can manage your day-to-day life and prepare for the decisions to be made later when you finalize your divorce.

If you're the person receiving support, don't sell yourself short in terms of what you need. And in your agreement (discussed below), spell out how well the temporary support actually meets your financial needs, in case you need to argue later that you accepted less than you actually needed on a temporary basis.

If you've been supporting the family, you'll do everyone a favor if you voluntarily keep supporting them while the divorce is pending. If your spouse has to go to court to get you to pay, you may well end up paying the lawyers' fees for both sides, in addition to being ordered to pay support. If you're not sure how much you should be paying, or if you think what your spouse is asking for isn't fair, use one of the support calculators listed in Chapter 8 to get a general idea of what your local court might order, and agree to pay that amount.

Whatever you and your spouse agree to about your finances at this early stage, write it down. And make sure you state that the arrangements you're making are temporary and subject to change. This is especially important when it comes to child and spousal support, for two reasons. First, judges often look at what's being paid on a temporary basis and decide that it's appropriate for permanent support because it's been working so far.

The second reason for putting your support agreement in writing is that you want the payments to be treated appropriately for tax purposes. Child support is neither taxable to the recipient nor deductible to the payor—in other words, it's tax-neutral. But to get this tax treatment, you must identify the payments as child support. Spousal support payments, on the other hand, are taxable income to the recipient and deductible for the payor—as long as they are made under a written agreement.

A sample agreement for temporary support is below.

Get Temporary Court-Ordered Support If You Need It

If you and your spouse separate and you don't have a job or another source of income, you might soon find yourself in dire financial straits. If your spouse has been supporting your family (either entirely, or by paying more than you do into the family coffers), you're entitled to continued support. If your spouse isn't paying support voluntarily, you can ask a court to order your spouse to make support payments during the divorce proceeding. It's called temporary or "pendente lite" (during the pending action) support. The court can issue a permanent support order later.

If you want to get the papers filed right away or you think you're in for a battle, you may want a lawyer's help to get this request done quickly and get some money coming in. You'll have to rustle up some cash to pay the lawyer, but it's possible the court will order your spouse to pay part of your lawyer's fees right away. Chapter 16 can help you find and work with a lawyer; Chapter 3 has information about doing it yourself.

Sample Temporary Support Agreement

We separated on August 1, 20xx. It is our intention to settle our divorce through mediation, and our first mediation session is scheduled for September 15, 20xx.

In the meantime, we agree that Carey will pay Susan on the first of August and the first of every month after that until this agreement is terminated, $1,000 per month as child support for Chris and Barry Jameson, and $300 per month as spousal support. Susan will pay all household expenses other than the mortgage and homeowners' insurance. Carey will pay the mortgage and insurance on the house at 275 Aurora Lane, as well as the property taxes when they come due, and Susan will continue to live there with the boys. Carey has his own apartment and will pay all his own living expenses.

This agreement is temporary, and is in effect until February 28, 20xx, unless one of the following occurs sooner: (1) We make a different agreement, written and signed by both of us, or (2) a court orders a different amount of support or says that Susan is required to share in the mortgage payments.

Neither of us gives up our right to ask a court for a different financial arrangement at a later time, and neither of us intends by this agreement to indicate that we think these should be our permanent arrangements.

Carey Jameson
Signature

Susan Jameson
Signature

August 1, 20xx
Date

August 1, 20xx
Date

Getting a Job

If you've been a stay-at-home parent or homemaker, it's likely that divorce will require you to reenter the workforce—a daunting thought when it's been a while. Your first step is to assess your skills and experience and polish up your resume. Career counselors generally advise that you prepare a resume that doesn't use a traditional chronological format, so that the gap in time won't be so prominent. Instead, use a "functional resume" organized around your job skills and training. Prospective employers are not allowed legally to ask you about your marital status or whether you have kids. Still, employers are going to want to know what you've been doing, and there's certainly no shame in having stayed home to care for your children. You might want to address that issue in your cover letter instead of your resume.

Next, consider contacts you have who might be useful to you in finding work—either something to tide you over until you get settled, or a job that you might want to stay in for a while. If your job skills are simply out of date, look into getting some retraining. Community colleges, adult schools, and private training programs all offer programs that may help.

Sources of help when you're reentering the workforce:

- state employment development departments
- private career counselors
- job websites
- placement services from a college or professional school you attended, and
- college programs for "reentry" students.

Some websites that might be helpful include www.careerplanner.com, www.careerbuilder.com, and www.jobhuntersbible.com, which is related to the classic career counseling book *What Color Is Your Parachute?*, by Richard Bolles (Ten Speed Press).

Getting Legal and Other Professional Help Early

At some point during your divorce, you're very likely to need some professional help. Even if you intend to handle the paperwork yourself and are sure the divorce won't be contested, it's often a good idea to talk to a lawyer somewhere along the way to make sure that you aren't giving up any important legal rights unknowingly. You may also need help from other experts, like actuaries, accountants, or real estate appraisers.

Don't delay getting advice—the sooner you learn the ins and outs of your situation, the better off you'll be. And even if you and your spouse agree about what you want to do, don't take any major actions, like selling real estate or other assets or transferring large amounts of money, without talking to someone first about the legal and financial consequences. For example, it might seem like a good idea for your spouse to pay you a lump sum for a couple of years of support in advance because you need cash immediately for major expenses and know you'll have income later. But support payments can have tax consequences for both the person who pays and the recipient, and you'll need advice about structuring the payment. (There's more about this topic in Chapters 8 and 11.)

Chapter 16 has an extensive list of the different types of professionals you might talk to in the course of your divorce.

Taking Care of Yourself

Divorce is one of the most stressful life events that anyone goes through. Only the loss of a loved one and moving are even in its class, difficultywise—and divorce generally involves both of those as well. Even when you are the one initiating the divorce, the enormous changes that result are bound to throw you off and leave you feeling, at the very least, a bit lost—and at worst, genuinely confused and depressed. There's no question that you will need time to grieve the loss of your family as you have known it. Make sure you pay attention to your emotional state and get the support you need to get through the divorce and the adjustment period that will follow.

Don't be reluctant to seek help from a counselor or therapist. Low-cost counseling can be found through county mental health programs, schools that train social workers and psychologists, and community health care centers. If you are part of a religious community, you're likely to find short-term counseling there. And don't hesitate to get help for your kids if you think they need to talk to someone outside of the family.

Even if you don't think therapy is for you, you might be surprised at the many therapy options available these days. Take the time to learn about what might work for you. If you don't want to go to individual counseling, try a divorce support group. If traditional "talk therapy" doesn't sound like your cup of tea, consider more body-based therapies like massage. You might even consider learning to meditate. Give something a try—you can always switch therapists or programs or stop when you feel it's time.

Whatever you do, avoid sitting at home moping, burning old photos, and plotting revenge. Just taking a walk and enjoying fresh air, sunshine, or fall colors can help you feel more grounded. If you have hobbies, try to stay engaged with them. If you've lost touch with old friends, now is a great time to reconnect. It's not uncommon to lose some friends in a divorce—either because they pick sides, or simply because some of the people you're used to being with as a couple aren't as comfortable with you as a single person, or vice versa. So, renew old relationships and find new ones—it will help you to stay busy and avoid dwelling on negative things. Finally, to state the obvious: Eat right and get plenty of sleep and exercise. You will get through this. ●

When You Can Agree: Uncontested Divorce

Although we hear about people whose knock-down, drag-out divorce cases last for years and tear their families apart, most people manage to part ways with much less conflict. That doesn't mean that their divorces are free from emotional turmoil or disagreement—only that they figure out a way to move through all of that and complete the legal part of their divorces with some level of cooperation. In other words, they take the high road.

This chapter goes into the nuts and bolts of the uncontested divorce— a divorce in which you and your spouse figure out how to handle the big issues (property, support, and custody) yourselves, instead of fighting it out in front of a judge. It will help you figure out what you'll actually need to do from the beginning of your uncontested divorce to the end.

Even if you're convinced that your divorce will be full of acrimony and conflict, please read about uncontested divorce. It's important to see that a divorce doesn't have to be that way, and you can also learn some useful techniques to minimize conflict. If you can manage to keep the process relatively civil, it will have huge long-term benefits for you, for your ex-spouse, and especially for your children.

Kinds of Uncontested Divorce	
Kind of divorce	**What It Is; How It Works**
Summary divorce	A streamlined procedure, this is for couples who haven't been married long and don't have children or much property.
Default divorce	One spouse files for divorce, and the other doesn't respond.
Mediated divorce	A couple gets the help of a trained neutral mediator to reach agreements about financial matters and child custody.
Collaborative divorce	The divorcing spouses hire lawyers and everyone pledges to resolve property, support, and custody issues out of court; spouses negotiate directly.
Lawyer-negotiated divorce	The divorcing spouses hire lawyers with the intention of resolving issues out of court, with the lawyers negotiating on behalf of the spouses.

Basics of the Uncontested Divorce

You can file for an uncontested divorce if you and your spouse:

- both want to get divorced
- agree on how you will divide your property and debts, and
- agree on how you will share custody of your kids.

An uncontested divorce doesn't mean you'll agree on everything right from the start. It just means you'll decide the issues in your divorce yourselves, possibly with the help of a mediator or lawyer, but without needing to ask a judge to decide. Getting your divorce will mostly involve paperwork. Depending on where you live, you may not need to go to court at all; you may be able to do everything by mail.

The three steps in getting an uncontested divorce are:

1. File the initial papers to get the proceedings in motion, and deliver copies to ("serve") your spouse. Depending on your state's rules, you may also have to exchange financial documents.

2. Negotiate with your spouse and decide how to divide up property and how to handle support, custody, and visitation.

3. Complete and file the final papers (including your marital settlement agreement, which sets out all your property, support, and custody decisions) to make your divorce official and get a court's approval of the agreements you've made.

The steps almost always go in that order, although sometimes people agree about property, debts, and child custody before they even start the paperwork.

You might want to have a lawyer look over your marital settlement agreement before you finalize your divorce, if you've done the rest of the divorce process on your own.

Summary Dissolution for Short-Term Marriages

If you've been married no more than a few years and don't have a lot of entanglements, you can use a streamlined procedure for getting divorced. Typical requirements for a summary (simplified) divorce, which you and your spouse must file jointly, include:

- You have been married for a relatively short time, usually less than five years (though a few states allow summary divorce when you've been married as long as eight or ten years).
- You both agree to give up any right to spousal support.
- There are no children of the marriage (if either you or your spouse has children from another marriage, you can still do a summary divorce).
- You don't own a house, either together or separately, and neither of you has a lease on any property that's for a term longer than a year from the time you're filing.
- You don't have significant assets, either jointly or separately owned (generally this means in the $25,000 to $30,000 range).
- You don't have significant debt (in most states, that means more than about $5,000 to $15,000).

Some states may have different requirements—for example, a minimum length of time you must be separated before you file for summary divorce. Usually, a summary divorce involves filing only one or two fill-in-the-blanks forms that you can get from the court, paying a filing fee, waiting a certain period of time—how long depends on your state, but varies from one month to a year—and then asking the court to make an order granting the divorce. You're rarely required to make a court appearance, and you can probably prepare the paperwork yourself, without a lawyer.

Not all states offer a summary divorce option. If you're interested, your first step is to figure out whether your state allows it, and if it does, whether you meet the requirements. Chapter 16 lists ways to get information about divorce laws and how to do research on your own. If you find you are a candidate for a summary dissolution, talk to your spouse about it—and if the two of you agree, see the section below called "Preparing and Filing Legal Papers."

Summary Divorce, Step by Step
1. Agree on how you'll divide your property and debts.
2. File divorce forms with the local family court.
3. Wait a few months (exact time depends on state law).
4. Request final divorce decree from the court.

Default Divorce

A default divorce is another form of uncontested divorce. It's uncontested because one spouse never even files court papers—everything gets done based on the filing spouse's paperwork. If you file for divorce and your spouse doesn't respond—that is, doesn't file any papers with the court—you can get a default divorce.

You might also use default divorce procedures if you and your spouse agree to do it that way and your state allows it. And you'd have to get a default divorce if you haven't been able to find out where your spouse is, even after making a genuine effort.

If You Serve Your Spouse and There's No Response

If you prepare the paperwork to start your divorce, file it with the court, and deliver it to your spouse (all of which is explained below), and your spouse fails to respond or file any paperwork within the required time period, you can try to get a default divorce. (This is called "taking the default" of your spouse.) However, it's a good idea to get in touch with your spouse to find out whether the deadline has simply been forgotten. Although, technically, you can seek a default divorce as soon as the time limit passes without a response, your spouse could also come back and try to get the default invalidated later by saying that the delivery wasn't proper or there was a good excuse for missing the deadline.

It's better to give your spouse every chance to respond—even write a reminder letter, keeping a copy to show the court if you do ask for a default. If your spouse never does respond, get the default paperwork and complete the divorce yourself.

By Agreement

In some states, you can agree with your spouse that you'll have the divorce entered by default. In that case, one of you will file for divorce, and the other will simply not file any responsive papers. The person who filed would then go ahead and ask the court to sign the final judgment of divorce, the document that ends your marriage. (See "Preparing and Filing Legal Papers" and "How the Other Spouse Can Respond," below, for more about how this would work.)

The main reason for agreeing on a default divorce over an uncontested divorce where both spouses appear is if one spouse is agreeable to getting divorced and to dividing property fairly, but doesn't want to be involved in the court process or do any paperwork. In that case, the filing spouse can take care of the details and the other can just sit back and let it happen. You may also save on filing fees—the defaulting spouse doesn't have to pay the fee for filing responsive papers. (The only exception to this is if your divorce is by default but you have a settlement agreement signed by both of you—then the nonfiling spouse may be required to pay a fee.)

If Your Spouse Is Missing

Sometimes, married couples drift apart without ever getting a divorce—especially if they marry young and then grow into different lives, or if the marriage was one of convenience. Neither person really cares that they don't know exactly where the other is—until someone starts thinking about marrying again and realizes that there's some paperwork that needs taking care of.

If you don't know where your spouse is, your first task is to look. You're required to make a sincere effort to locate a missing spouse before asking the court to grant a default divorce. That means doing at least the following things:

- Find the last known address of your spouse. You will have to tell the court how, when, and from whom you obtained it.
- Check that address. If the people living there have no information about where you can find your spouse, ask the neighbors on the right and left. You can do this either by letter, in person, or by sending an investigator.
- If the last known address is a mental or penal institution, ask the person in charge of the institution for current address information, and then contact that address.
- Ask every relative, friend, former employer, and other person you know who might be likely to know where your spouse is. You'll have to submit a written summary of your efforts to the court, listing their names and relationship to your spouse, and the dates and results of your inquiries.
- If the court requires it (check with your county clerk or social worker), contact the military services to see whether your spouse is in the military. The military became much more closemouthed about the location of service personnel after the 2001 terrorist attacks, and each branch has its own procedures, so you'll need to be persistent if you are required to check on this. Chapter 12, on military divorce, lists resources.
- If your spouse owned a house, phone the tax assessor's office in the county of your spouse's last known address. Ask for current information.
- Put your spouse's name into an Internet search engine such as Google. There are also Internet services that you can use to locate people for a small fee; this is a good thing to do if you can afford it, because it will show the court that you really tried.
- Follow up any other lead you can think of, including contacts with unions, trade associations, or licensing agencies that may have information.

Keep very clear records of all the information you collect. You'll use it to show the court that you can't serve your spouse with divorce papers and that you are entitled to a default divorce. There's more about that in "Serving Papers," below.

> ### Default Divorce, Step by Step
>
> 1. File divorce forms with the local family court.
> 2. Try to find your spouse.
> 3. Get the court's permission to go ahead with the divorce without notifying your spouse (see "Serving Papers," below).
> 4. Submit final divorce paperwork to get a final judgment of divorce.

There's a good chance you'll be able to take care of the paperwork for a default divorce yourself if you're so inclined.

Preparing and Filing Legal Papers

Most of the work in an uncontested divorce is paperwork. Once you and your spouse agree on the big issues of property, custody, and support, all you need to do is get it all into the forms your court requires. That process can be worky, but should be fairly straightforward.

How do you learn how to prepare the legal papers you'll need and submit them to family court? This section explains some general rules that hold true pretty much everywhere. But every court has its own rules, too, so you'll need to get hold of whatever instructions and forms your court provides in pamphlets, handbooks, or online. Chapter 16 explains how to find those resources.

Will You Need Help?

Years ago, if you wanted a divorce, you just about had to hire a lawyer—but times have changed in a big way. It's now estimated that in more than 70% of divorce proceedings, at least one party is self-represented. But whether or not you hire a lawyer, you won't be entirely on your own.

Courts have responded to the flood of people representing themselves by becoming increasingly accessible to people without lawyers. In some places, courts operate self-help centers for family law matters. At these centers, clerks will help you find the right forms, fill them out, and file them. The clerks can't give legal advice, but they can help you navigate the court's procedural rules.

Many states and counties also have their own websites with extensive information for people representing themselves in court matters, including divorces. Some states make all forms and instructions available online; others provide much less. (See Chapter 16 to find out what your state offers.) There are also lots of do-it-yourself materials on the market. Be sure to check out anything written specifically for your local court or area.

If you and your spouse both choose self-representation, you will probably save yourselves lots of time, money, and heartache. Of course there are reasons to hire a lawyer, too. If you're not sure whether you need an attorney, see Chapter 16. That chapter lists websites for each state and has extensive information about what's available and how to decide what kind of help you need.

How to Start the Divorce Proceeding

You begin a divorce by filing a document, usually called a "petition" or "complaint" for divorce or dissolution. It asks the court to grant a divorce. In general, it's a fairly simple form to fill out.

Petitions differ enormously from court to court—to give you an idea of how different they can be, they vary in length from one page up to more than 40. Some states have different forms for marriages with children and without, for contested and uncontested divorces, and for fault and no-fault divorces. Most petitions require at a minimum that you state:

- the date and place of your marriage
- the date of your separation
- whether you have children and, if so, their names, ages, and birth dates, and
- your basis for seeking a divorce (this will usually be something along the lines of "irreconcilable differences").

Some petitions also let you state what you are seeking in the divorce: for example, a division of property, a decision about child custody and support, or restoration of your former name. You may also have the option to check a box indicating that you're basing the divorce petition on "fault" grounds like adultery or abandonment. If you're doing an uncontested divorce, you won't check any of those boxes—instead, you'll choose "irreconcilable differences" or the like.

A sample petition—not the simplest, not the most complicated—is shown below.

If You Want Your Former Name Back

If you took your spouse's last name when you married and you now want to go back to using the name you had before your marriage, make sure you take care of it during the divorce. Otherwise, you'll have to pay additional court filing fees and go through a separate procedure to change your name. In most places, the petition form will ask you whether you want a name change as part of the divorce—if it doesn't, then the final order is likely to have a place where you can ask for that. Or you can include a provision in your marital settlement agreement if you write one.

You aren't required to take your prior name back. You might want to keep your married name because it's the same as your children's. Some people think they're likely to remarry and don't want too many name changes over the course of time. And some feel it's important to get rid of their married name as part of moving on. It's entirely up to you—your spouse has no say in the matter.

Which Spouse Files for Divorce?

If you're expecting to get a default divorce, go ahead and file the papers yourself. If you and your spouse have agreed on an uncontested divorce, you'll need to decide who files. Usually it doesn't matter much, so don't get into an argument about it. (The main issue is convenience—if your spouse has moved to a different county and you think you're going to be the one doing most of the work of the divorce, file in the county where you live.)

Residency Requirements

Before you can file for divorce in the state where you live, you must have lived there for a certain period of time. A few states don't require a specific period of residence, but most have a residency requirement ranging from six weeks to one year. (If you or your spouse is in the military, residency requirements don't apply, and most of the time, you may file in the state where the military spouse is stationed—see Chapter 12 for more about that.) The requirements for each state are listed below.

Alabama	6 months
Alaska	Must be a resident at the time of filing
Arizona	90 days
Arkansas	60 days
California	6 months*
Colorado	91 days
Connecticut	No requirement for filing**
Delaware	6 months*
DC	6 months*
Florida	6 months
Georgia	6 months
Hawaii	6 months*
Idaho	6 weeks
Illinois	90 days*
Indiana	6 months
Iowa	1 year
Kansas	60 days
Kentucky	180 days
Louisiana	6 months
Maine	6 months
Maryland	1 year
Massachusetts	1 year (none if cause of divorce occurred in state)
Michigan	180 days
Minnesota	180 days*
Mississippi	6 months
Missouri	90 days

Residency Requirements (cont'd)	
Montana	90 days
Nebraska	1 year
Nevada	6 weeks
New Hampshire	1 year
New Jersey	1 year
New Mexico	6 months
New York	1 year
North Carolina	6 months
North Dakota	6 months
Ohio	6 months
Oklahoma	6 months
Oregon	6 months
Pennsylvania	6 months
Rhode Island	1 year
South Carolina	3 months (unless only one spouse is resident, then 1 year)
South Dakota	Must be a resident or service member stationed there at the time of filing
Tennessee	6 months
Texas	6 months
Utah	3 months
Vermont	6 months*
Virginia	6 months
Washington	At least one spouse must be resident or servicemember stationed there at the time of filing
West Virginia	1 year if marriage was out of state (none if marriage was in W. Virginia)
Wisconsin	6 months
Wyoming	60 days

* Same-sex couples need not meet residency requirements, if they married in state and their current state of residence will not allow them to divorce. (A Vermont same-sex couple may avoid residency requirements only if there are no minor children of the marriage.)

**Must establish residency for 12 months before final judgment can be entered, unless one party lived in Connecticut at marriage and returned with intention to stay, or the cause for dissolution arose after either party moved to Connecticut.

The filing fees for the petitioner (the spouse who files first) and the respondent (the other spouse) are about the same, but if you want to you can add up both fees and split the total cost. (See "Filing Fees," below.)

Your New Best Friend: The Clerk of the Court

Court clerks are the people who work in what is basically the court system's front office. They are the public face of the court, and they handle almost every piece of paperwork that comes into or leaves the court. The clerks are not lawyers and are not allowed to give legal advice. At the same time, it's their job to help people who have questions about what papers they need, how to fill those papers out, and what they need to do next.

Here are a few things to remember when dealing with the court clerks:

- **Be friendly, patient, and courteous.** The wheels of justice do not always turn swiftly or smoothly, and you may have to wait in a long line just to ask what seems to you like a simple question. The nicer you are to the clerk, the more likely it is that you'll get your question answered and get the help you need.
- **Submit papers that are neat, complete, and on time.** Double-check everything you do—or better still, have a friend check it—to make sure the clerk won't have to give it back to you. (There's more about how to prepare legal papers below.)
- **If the clerk says that your question requires legal advice, ask whether there's any part of it that the clerk can answer.** For example, if you want to know how to get an order for temporary child support, the clerk should tell you where to get the forms you will need to file, where you should file them, and how to schedule hearings. You'll have to figure out how to fill out the forms yourself, though.

Sample Petition for Divorce

FL-100

ATTORNEY OR PARTY WITHOUT ATTORNEY *(Name, State Bar number, and address)*:	FOR COURT USE ONLY
Susan L. Johnson 444 Elm Street Oakland, Ca 94619 TELEPHONE NO.: 510-555-1234 FAX NO. *(Optional)*: E-MAIL ADDRESS *(Optional)*: sjohnson@yahoo.com ATTORNEY FOR *(Name)*: In Pro Per	

SUPERIOR COURT OF CALIFORNIA, COUNTY OF Alameda
STREET ADDRESS: 1225 Fallon Street
MAILING ADDRESS:
CITY AND ZIP CODE: Oakland, CA 94612
BRANCH NAME:

MARRIAGE OF
PETITIONER: Susan L. Johnson

RESPONDENT: Richard P. Johnson

PETITION FOR	CASE NUMBER:
☑ **Dissolution of Marriage** ☐ **Legal Separation** ☐ **Nullity of Marriage** ☐ **AMENDED**	

1. RESIDENCE (Dissolution only) ☑ Petitioner ☐ Respondent has been a resident of this state for at least six months and of this county for at least three months immediately preceding the filing of this *Petition for Dissolution of Marriage.*

2. STATISTICAL FACTS
   a. Date of marriage: June 5, 1997
   b. Date of separation: April 4, 2012
   c. Time from date of marriage to date of separation *(specify)*:
      Years: 14   Months: 9

3. DECLARATION REGARDING MINOR CHILDREN *(include children of this relationship born prior to or during the marriage or adopted during the marriage)*:
   a. ☐ There are no minor children.
   b. ☑ The minor children are:

Child's name	Birthdate	Age	Sex
Chantal Johnson	May 15, 1999	13	F
Daniel Johnson	October 12, 2001	10	M

   ☐ Continued on Attachment 3b.
   c. If there are minor children of the Petitioner and Respondent, a completed *Declaration Under Uniform Child Custody Jurisdiction and Enforcement Act (UCCJEA)* (form FL-105) must be attached.
   d. ☐ A completed voluntary declaration of paternity regarding minor children born to the Petitioner and Respondent prior to the marriage is attached.

4. SEPARATE PROPERTY
   Petitioner requests that the assets and debts listed ☐ in *Property Declaration* (form FL-160) ☐ in Attachment 4
   ☑ below be confirmed as separate property.

Item	Confirm to
Antique dining room set	Petitioner
Stamp collection	Respondent

NOTICE: You may redact (black out) social security numbers from any written material filed with the court in this case other than a form used to collect child or spousal support.

Page 1 of 2

Form Adopted for Mandatory Use Judicial Council of California FL-100 [Rev. January 1, 2005]	**PETITION—MARRIAGE** **(Family Law)**	Family Code, §§ 2330, 3409; www.courtinfo.ca.gov

American LegalNet, Inc.
www.USCourtForms.com

Sample Petition for Divorce (cont'd)

MARRIAGE OF *(last name, first name of parties):* Susan L. Johnson Richard P. Johnson	CASE NUMBER:

5. DECLARATION REGARDING COMMUNITY AND QUASI-COMMUNITY ASSETS AND DEBTS AS CURRENTLY KNOWN

    a. ☐ There are no such assets or debts subject to disposition by the court in this proceeding.

    b. ☑ All such assets and debts are listed ☑ in *Property Declaration* (form FL-160) ☐ in Attachment 5b.

          ☐ below *(specify):*

6. **Petitioner requests**

    a. ☑ dissolution of the marriage based on   d. ☐ nullity of voidable marriage based on

        (1) ☑ irreconcilable differences. (Fam. Code, § 2310(a).)   (1) ☐ petitioner's age at time of marriage.

        (2) ☐ incurable insanity. (Fam. Code, § 2310(b).)   (Fam. Code, § 2210(a).)

    b. ☐ legal separation of the parties based on   (2) ☐ prior existing marriage.

        (1) ☐ irreconcilable differences. (Fam. Code, § 2310(a).)   (Fam. Code, § 2210(b).)

        (2) ☐ incurable insanity. (Fam. Code, § 2310(b).)   (3) ☐ unsound mind. (Fam. Code, § 2210(c).)

    c. ☐ nullity of void marriage based on   (4) ☐ fraud. (Fam. Code, § 2210(d).)

        (1) ☐ incestuous marriage. (Fam. Code, § 2200.)   (5) ☐ force. (Fam. Code, § 2210(e).)

        (2) ☐ bigamous marriage. (Fam. Code, § 2201.)   (6) ☐ physical incapacity. (Fam. Code, § 2210(f).)

7. **Petitioner requests** that the court grant the above relief and make injunctive (including restraining) and other orders as follows:

	Petitioner	Respondent	Joint	Other
a. Legal custody of children to	☐	☐	☑	☐
b. Physical custody of children to	☑	☐	☐	☐
c. Child visitation be granted to		☑		

        As requested in form: ☐ FL-311 ☐ FL-312 ☐ FL-341(C) ☐ FL-341(D) ☐ FL-341(E) ☑ Attachment 7c

    d. ☐ Determination of parentage of any children born to the Petitioner and Respondent prior to the marriage.

| e. Attorney fees and costs payable by .... | ☐ | ☑ | | |
| f. Spousal support payable to (earnings assignment will be issued) .... | ☑ | ☐ | | |

    g. ☑ Terminate the court's jurisdiction (ability) to award spousal support to Respondent.

    h. ☑ Property rights be determined.

    i. ☐ Petitioner's former name be restored to *(specify):*

    j. ☐ Other *(specify):*

          ☐ Continued on Attachment 7j.

8. **Child support**—If there are minor children born to or adopted by the Petitioner and Respondent before or during this marriage, the court will make orders for the support of the children upon request and submission of financial forms by the requesting party. An earnings assignment may be issued without further notice. Any party required to pay support must pay interest on overdue amounts at the "legal" rate, which is currently 10 percent.

9. **I HAVE READ THE RESTRAINING ORDERS ON THE BACK OF THE SUMMONS, AND I UNDERSTAND THAT THEY APPLY TO ME WHEN THIS PETITION IS FILED.**

I declare under penalty of perjury under the laws of the State of California that the foregoing is true and correct.

Date: June 20, 2012

Susan L. Johnson

    (TYPE OR PRINT NAME)   ▶   (SIGNATURE OF PETITIONER)

Date:

    (TYPE OR PRINT NAME)   ▶   (SIGNATURE OF ATTORNEY FOR PETITIONER)

NOTICE: Dissolution or legal separation may automatically cancel the rights of a spouse under the other spouse's will, trust, retirement plan, power of attorney, pay on death bank account, survivorship rights to any property owned in joint tenancy, and any other similar thing. It does not automatically cancel the rights of a spouse as beneficiary of the other spouse's life insurance policy. You should review these matters, as well as any credit cards, other credit accounts, insurance polices, retirement plans, and credit reports to determine whether they should be changed or whether you should take any other actions. However, some changes may require the agreement of your spouse or a court order (see Family Code sections 231–235).

FL-100 [Rev. January 1, 2005]   **PETITION—MARRIAGE**   Page 2 of 2
                            (Family Law)

Where to File

You'll file your divorce papers with a court clerk at a county courthouse. Big counties have more than one courthouse, and some counties have special family law departments. Check your local court's website, if there is one, or call the court to find out where you should file. For advice on how to find your local county courthouse, see Chapter 16.

Finding Forms

Most states have fill-in-the-blanks forms for divorce cases. Usually, you can get these forms at your local courthouse or from the court's website or a state website. (Chapter 16 lists court websites by state.)

You should do whatever's easiest and most convenient for you, but all things being equal, consider going to the courthouse to pick up your forms—it gives you a chance to begin establishing a relationship with the court clerks. Many court clerks will give you a divorce packet that includes all of the forms you need to get your divorce started (and in some cases, finished).

On the other hand, especially if you live in a large county where you're not likely to get a lot of attention from the clerks, the convenience of the Internet may outweigh the opportunity for the personal touch. Be aware, though, that some court websites don't have all the forms you need.

How to Fill Out Court Papers

We all fill out lots of forms in the course of our daily lives, and interacting with the court system means filling out even more than usual—and in a particular, nitpicky sort of way. Follow instructions slavishly—don't cut corners or skip steps—and you'll be fine.

Most fill-in-the-blanks court forms require that at or near the top of the first page you list your name, telephone number, and current address. Just below that, usually on the left, there will be a box for you to list your name and the name of your spouse. Use your full legal names, including middle names or initials. Even if you are planning on taking back the name you had before your marriage, don't use it on these papers unless you've already changed it back legally. You can have your name changed as part of the divorce.

Court Forms You'll Probably Need

- The **petition** or **complaint** that starts the divorce proceeding.
- A **summons** that you will need to serve along with the petition. The summons is a form that tells your spouse that you are suing for divorce and orders both of you not to dispose of marital assets or make changes on insurance or other documents, not to take your children out of state without the other's permission, and not to do anything else to disturb the status quo.
- A **cover sheet** that you must submit in some places along with your forms, usually asking for information such as what county you live in, how many children you have, and how long you have been married.
- **Financial information sheets** that you must give either to the court or to your spouse early on. (See Chapter 9, which discusses financial disclosure issues.)
- **Responsive forms** that your spouse will use to file a response to your petition. (You may have to deliver blank copies to your spouse along with the papers you've filled out.)
- **Proof of service** form that shows the date that your spouse received the divorce paperwork.

TIP

Even though all of these documents are set up with two "opposing" parties, that doesn't mean you can't have an uncontested divorce. You and your spouse can decide together what your forms will say. You can't file a joint petition unless you qualify for a summary dissolution, described above. But your spouse's response can ask for all of the same things that you want— an end to the marriage and a court order reflecting your agreements about property, custody, and support.

Occasionally, you'll need to prepare a document from scratch. See "Preparing Court Documents From Scratch," below.

You can fill in the forms on your computer, with a typewriter, or by hand. Whichever method you use, it's a good idea to practice filling out a copy of the forms before you make final copies to give to the court.

On computer. When you download forms from the Internet, they usually will be formatted so that you can type the information into them and then print them out. Unfortunately though, you probably won't be able to save electronic copies once you are finished filling them out—so if you discover a mistake after you've printed the document, you may have to go back and start again.

Typing. You can print out blank copies and use a typewriter to fill them in. (Yes, typewriters do still exist, often at public libraries.)

By hand. If you don't have a computer or typewriter, it is acceptable in most places to handwrite the information. However, make sure that you use a black pen and that you print very, very neatly. If your handwriting is not good, ask a friend to do it for you. It's important that the court personnel be able to read what you have written.

Sign all forms in blue ink. Signing in blue will help you (and the court clerks) distinguish the original from the copies.

One last word about forms: If, after you file a document, you discover that you made a serious mistake or omission in the wording, you can fix it. You'll need to get another copy of the same form, type "Amended" in front of the existing title, fill it out properly, and then file the amended form. (Usually, you won't have to pay a filing fee for the amended form.)

Preparing Court Documents From Scratch

If there's no fill-in form for what you need and you have to prepare your own documents, get ready to nitpick. Most courts require that documents be typed on 8½" × 11" numbered legal paper. The two sample pages below show what this paper looks like. Numbered legal paper is available at most office supply stores and comes as an option with some word processing software. Some courts accept plain paper; you can call the court clerk and ask, or check your court's local rules.

Sample Caption

1	MARTIN KORNBLUM
	In Pro Per
2	1111 Gray Street
	Anytown, Illinois 12345
3	510-555-1212 Telephone
	510-555-1213 Fax
4	
5	
6	
7	
8	CIRCUIT COURT OF THE STATE OF ILLINOIS, COOK COUNTY
9	
10	In re the Marriage of) Case No. F 22222
	)
11	Petitioner: MARTIN KORNBLUM)
	)
12	and) (title of document)
	)
13	Respondent: SHIRLEY KORNBLUM)
	)
14	_____)
15	
16	
17	
18	
19	
20	
21	
22	
23	
24	
25	
26	
27	
28	

Many courts have rules relating to earthshaking matters such as whether plain paper is acceptable, whether your document must have a footer, whether you must double-space your documents, and what size font is big enough. The local rules might be available on your court website, or you can ask the clerk for a copy. Some states, like California, have abolished local rules in favor of statewide procedures. The court clerk should be able to direct you to those, too.

Whenever you make a form of your own, it needs to show what case it belongs to. There are two ways you can do that. If you're creating an entire document, it should have a full "caption," like the one shown in the example above, stating your name, the court you're in, the names of the people involved, and the title of the document. If you're preparing an attachment that will go with another form, then at the top it just needs to give the basic information that will allow it to be identified—for example, "Marriage of John and Sarah Brown, Case Number FA-0345, Attachment to Property Declaration of John Brown." The sample attachment below shows what this would look like.

It's okay to use white touch-up correction fluid or tape to correct typing errors. Keep your text lined up with the line numbers on the left-hand side of the legal paper. Many courts also require that each document have a footer—a line at the bottom of the page that states the name of

Sample Attachment

1	In re the Marriage of Kornblum Case No. F2222
2	Attachment to Motion for Child Support, Item F.1.
3	
	[Begin text here, numbering each item to correspond with the numbering that identifies it in
4	*the document to which you are attaching the additional page(s).]*
5	
6	
7	
8	

the document. Check the local rules on this, too. If you're not sure, go ahead and put it in—it won't hurt.

Make sure your papers are hole-punched at the top with a two-hole punch (you can find those at copy shops, or the clerk will lend you one when you file the papers).

Filing the Papers

Filing court documents means handing them across a counter to the court clerk or sending them in by mail to be filed. When you begin your divorce action, and possibly if you file a request (usually called a motion) later, you'll also hand the clerk a check for the filing fee. (See "Filing Fees," below.)

When you file a document, give the clerk the original and three photocopies. In most cases, the clerk will keep the original for the court file. The clerk may keep one or more of the copies, too, depending on court policy. The clerk will stamp the front page of the other copies and hand them back to you. The stamp will prove when you filed the original document. These copies are called "file endorsed," "file stamped," or "conformed."

When you file your initial complaint or petition for divorce, the clerk will assign a case number and place the number on the first page. You will put the case number on all other documents that you file in your case, and refer to it in all your communications with the clerk's office.

You can mail documents you want to file to the clerk, but it's the second best way to get them filed. Aside from the obvious danger of delay or loss, you'll lose the chance to start establishing a personal relationship with the clerk's office staff, with whom you may be dealing later. (If you do mail the copies to be filed, keep an extra copy at home in case the others are lost in the mail.)

Filing Fees

Filing fees vary enormously from state to state, but you can be sure that you'll have to pay at least $100, and possibly as much as $400, to start your divorce. Your spouse—or you, if your spouse was the filing party—will then have to pay a similar fee to file a response.

If you make any interim requests from the court, such as for custody, support, or a determination of who stays in the family home at the outset, there will probably be a filing fee if a court hearing is necessary. These fees are much less than the initial filing fee, though—more in the range of $20 to $50. You can find out the fees by calling the court clerk or, in many places, by looking at the court website. See Chapter 16 for a list of court websites by state.

Serving Papers

After you have filed your initial papers with the court, the next step is to "serve" the papers on your spouse. Serving papers simply means having them delivered in a legally approved way, according to your state's law. The most important thing to know is that you cannot serve the papers yourself. You have to have someone else do it, and sign a document stating that they did so, usually called a "proof" or "declaration" of service.

You can have your spouse served personally or by mail. If your spouse is missing and you're asking for a default divorce, you'll have to ask the court to either allow you to serve your spouse by publication or release you from the obligation to serve your spouse. See "Service When Your Spouse Is Missing," below. Whichever way you get your spouse served, given that you're trying for a cooperative divorce process, it's courteous to let your spouse know the paperwork is coming.

Personal Service

Serving someone personally means hand-delivering the documents to that person. You can either hire someone to do this—a process server or, in most places, the local sheriff—or ask a friend to do it. (You can't do it yourself, because you are a party.) If you want to hire someone, check with the court clerk about having the sheriff's office serve the papers, as that is often the least expensive route. Or look in the phone book under "process servers" or "private investigators" to find someone who is experienced with serving papers.

Your local court clerk should be able to give you more information about getting your spouse served with the papers. And make sure you double-check what needs to be served. In many places, you're required to serve blank copies of responsive documents along with the petition and summons, so that your spouse has the necessary papers to prepare a response.

Service by Mail

In most states, you can serve divorce papers by mail and include a form that your spouse signs to acknowledge that the papers were received. Usually the acknowledgment form is available along with the rest of the divorce forms you get from the court or online. Have someone else drop the papers in the mailbox and sign the form—remember, you're not allowed to do the serving.

Service When Your Spouse Is Missing

If you can't find your spouse after trying all the suggestions listed in "If Your Spouse Is Missing," above, you will have to ask the court to either:
- allow you to serve your spouse by publication, or
- dispense with the service requirement.

Which you ask for depends on your spouse's last known address and how long it's been since you last saw your spouse. If the last place you know your spouse lived is in the same county where you live or a nearby area, or if it's not been that long since the last time your spouse was known to be in the area, the court will probably require that you publish notice of the divorce in a local paper. Only certain papers are authorized to publish legal notices, so you need to find one that is. You'll probably be required to publish notice of the divorce petition once a week for about four weeks.

If your spouse has been missing for a long time and the last known address is either quite far away or very old, the court may allow you to simply proceed with the divorce without publishing notice. This is called a "waiver" of the notice requirement.

Your local court forms may include forms for asking the court about publishing or waiving service. If they don't, you'll have to prepare your own. You'll need a document asking for what you want, and a declaration stating all the things you did to try to find your spouse. If the local court doesn't have forms that you can use, you can probably find sample forms in your county law library. Chapter 16 explains how to find forms that way. "Preparing Court Documents From Scratch," above, explains how to create the documents you need.

Proof of Service

After your spouse is served with the divorce papers, you need to let the court know that service has been accomplished. You do this by filing a form called "proof of service" with the court clerk, after having the process server sign it and enter the information about where, when, and how your spouse was served.

How the Other Spouse Can Respond

After one spouse files for divorce, the other can either file responsive documents with the court or choose to let the case proceed by default. (See "Default Divorce," above, for an explanation of that process.)

The first responsive paper is often called, unsurprisingly, a "response" or "answer." Usually, a response form looks much like the petition, and the responding party—usually called the "respondent" or "defendant"— is required to set out many of the same facts that are contained in the petition. This is to make sure that you agree about such things as how long you've been married, when you separated, and where you and your children live. The response also lets the other party register disagreement with any requests that were made in the petition—for example, the requests relating to division of property. If you've worked that all out, though, there shouldn't be any surprises in the response.

The court may require other documents to be filed with the response— for example, a cover sheet or financial disclosure form. The court clerk can help with finding the right forms and your court's rules.

Negotiating a Settlement and Preparing a Marital Settlement Agreement

As part of your uncontested divorce, you and your spouse will probably want to prepare a marital settlement agreement, sometimes referred to as an MSA. The MSA will set out your agreements about how you'll split your property and debts, describe whether and how much spousal support (alimony) will change hands, and detail your arrangements for child support, parenting time, and visitation. In some places, the court forms will be detailed enough that you can use them instead of preparing a separate MSA, and you will probably be able to make the assessment yourself. If you can use the forms, do—the court will prefer it. And if you have no kids and you've already divided up your property, you may not need an MSA either.

How to Work Toward an Agreement

Negotiating the terms of an MSA isn't always easy—as you're no doubt aware, the fact that you're trying for an uncontested divorce doesn't mean that you and your spouse agree on everything. You're going to have to sit down and figure out what the issues are and then engage in some give and take until you resolve them. You can do this in a few different ways.

Face-to-face negotiation. You and your spouse could sit down together over the kitchen table and, with the help of this book and other materials, identify the issues that need resolving—and then resolve them. This is, obviously, the least expensive way of reaching agreement. However, for some people, it's also the most difficult, because it means making decisions about very emotional issues with the person from whom you are trying to separate emotionally, without any buffer between you. Chapter 4, on mediation, has information about communication and negotiation that will be helpful if you decide to try one-on-one discussions with your spouse.

Negotiation with the help of a family member or friend. If you think that you and your spouse are likely to be able to agree on most issues, but you might benefit from that buffer of having another person present, you could ask a mutual friend or a family member to sit in with you. This person could be the recorder, writing down agreements as you come to them, and could help you stay on track with your agenda. It's a pretty hard job for the average person, and you'll need to make sure that whoever you ask is someone with whom you and your spouse feel equally comfortable, and who will feel comfortable in the role. Whatever you do, don't pick someone who's likely to insert a lot of their own opinions into the process.

Mediation. Mediation is a process in which a trained, neutral third party, the mediator, sits down with you and your spouse and helps you reach agreement about the issues involved in your divorce. Mediation gives you the best possible chance of an outcome that both you and your spouse can live with. It also supports the possibility of an ongoing, cooperative relationship with your spouse—something that will have a positive lifelong effect on your children. There's much more about mediation in Chapter 4.

The Big Issues

How do you know what you need to discuss and decide? Here are the big ones, each of which is covered in later chapters:

- **Children.** Develop a parenting plan that deals with custody, visitation, and child support and answers other questions involving your kids. (Chapters 6 through 8)
- **Assets and debts.** Divide your property and debts, including your family home, cars, personal items, financial accounts, and amounts you owe. (Chapters 9 and 10)
- **Alimony.** Decide whether either of you will pay spousal support (alimony) and if so, how much. (Chapter 11)

Once you have completed your negotiations, you'll be ready to draft your marital settlement agreement. Chapter 13 lists the issues you need to address and guides you through the process of preparing an MSA.

Finalizing Your Uncontested Divorce

If you've filed for divorce, submitted all the required forms and information to the court, finished your negotiations with your spouse, and prepared a marital settlement agreement, congratulations! You are almost there.

You may not even have to go to court to get your final divorce order. You will, however, have to fill out some paperwork and submit it to the court. Either you or your spouse can prepare and submit the final paperwork.

You'll usually be required to submit a signed statement (declaration) that tells the court:

- when you filed your divorce petition
- when your spouse was served (or when you got permission to publish or skip service)
- that your spouse hasn't responded, if that's the case, and
- what you are asking the court to do (such as grant the divorce, restore your former name, and approve your settlement agreement).

Along with the declaration, you may have to provide proof that you made whatever financial disclosures are required in your state. Usually, you can do this by signing and filing a form saying that you gave your spouse all the information that's required.

If you have signed a marital settlement agreement, you'll either need to submit the entire agreement or check a box on one of the final divorce forms that says you've prepared one and that you've resolved all the issues in your divorce. Make sure that the order says that the marital settlement agreement is "incorporated" into the judgment—then the terms of the settlement agreement will have the force of a judge's order.

Finally, you'll submit an order for the judge to sign, granting the divorce and declaring that you are no longer married. This form will often be called an order, a judgment, or a decree of divorce. For the rest of this book, we'll refer to it as the final order. Every divorce case must have a signed order that ends the marriage.

Often, you'll be asked to submit one more form along with the final order—it might be called "Notice of Entry of Judgment" or "Notice of Entry of Order." On this form, you'll put your name and address and your spouse's name and address, and, in some places, you'll be required to attach stamped envelopes with the addresses on them as well. This will allow the clerk to send you and your spouse a notice when the judge signs your final order.

If you're doing a default divorce, you'll submit these papers yourself. Otherwise, either you or your spouse can prepare and submit the final paperwork.

Ask the court clerk whether a court hearing is required before the judge will grant your divorce. If there is a hearing, most likely you and your spouse will simply have to appear and confirm for the judge that you both understand and agree to the divorce and the terms of the marital settlement agreement. (See "Going to Court," in Chapter 5, for advice about courtroom etiquette.)

Just as nearly every state has a residency requirement before you can file for divorce, most also have a waiting period before your divorce can be made final. The waiting period usually runs from the date that the responding party was served with or acknowledged receiving the court papers. Sometimes, however, it begins on the day the paperwork is filed to begin the divorce. (In legal jargon, that's the date the court "acquired jurisdiction" over that person.) Make sure you find out whether your state has a waiting period and what it is. Even after you have filed your settlement agreement and final documents, you are not officially divorced until the waiting period has passed and the judge has signed the final divorce order. If you don't find the waiting period in any of the forms or instructions you're using for your uncontested divorce, ask the court clerk or use any of the resources listed in Chapter 16 to find it.

Most of the time, the process of negotiating your settlement and preparing your papers will take you as long as the waiting period, so you won't have to worry about it. But if you complete your paperwork quickly, you can still submit it to the court. When you prepare the final order of divorce, you'll have to list a date that your marital status ends. If you're past the waiting period, you can leave the date blank for the court to fill in. But if you're not, calculate the date that the waiting period ends, and enter that date. The judge may sign the order in advance, but the order will state that you're not divorced until that date.

You'll need to figure out how you'll get the final, signed divorce order back. One way is to leave a postage-paid envelope with the clerk along with your final papers when you submit them, with enough postage for return of copies of all the documents you've submitted. The court won't necessarily mail you a copy of the judgment if you don't leave the envelope for them. You could also pick up the judgment when the clerk sends you a notice saying it's ready.

Always make sure your divorce is complete ...

One attorney tells a story about a client who came in seeking help with an adoption. "The client had been married many years before, and the social worker investigating the adoption asked to see her divorce judgment. She couldn't find it. After some research with the court, we discovered that she and her husband had never submitted a final divorce order for the judge's signature in their uncontested divorce. Her husband had remarried and had three children with his new wife, and the client had moved on as well, but all the time they were still legally married to each other! We were able to get the judge to enter the divorce judgment retroactively, so that the husband's second marriage was not bigamous. But it was a big hassle. My client thought it was funny, but the husband's second wife wasn't at all amused.

TIP

If you want your divorce finalized before the end of a calendar year, submit your request early enough. Courts usually receive a rush of paperwork toward the end of the year as people try to get their divorces finalized before the tax year ends. (Your filing status for tax purposes will still be "married" if you aren't divorced by December 31 of the tax year.) If it's important to you to be divorced before the end of the calendar year, make sure you get your paperwork in early—at least eight weeks before the end of the year—so that the judge has time to review it and sign the order before December 31.

Papers You'll Need to Finalize a Default or Uncontested Divorce

- Declaration (statement under penalty of perjury)
- Marital settlement agreement
- Financial disclosures (if required)
- Notice of entry of judgment
- Judgment (for the judge to sign), and
- Other forms required by your local court.

Working It Out: Divorce Mediation

Perhaps you are one of the fortunate divorcing people who can negotiate directly with your spouse with a minimum of acrimony, come to an agreement about dividing property and parenting your children, and prepare and file your court papers for an uncontested divorce, all without outside help. If so, *mazel tov*! You can skip this chapter (and the next one, too).

But if you're like most people and would appreciate a little help in the negotiations, divorce mediation may be a boon to you at this difficult time. And if you have kids, you may end up in mediation whether you want to or not. Many courts now require parents to attend mediation sessions if they can't agree about custody or visitation.

Unless the court orders it, mediation is a voluntary process, and you will use it only if you and your spouse both agree to it. You can go to mediation at any point in your divorce, even if you've already hired lawyers. Divorce mediation has an extremely high success rate—the vast majority of cases that go to mediation get settled there.

Why Divorce Mediation Works

Divorce mediation is a process in which a neutral third person, called a mediator, sits down for a series of meetings with a divorcing couple to help them reach an agreement on all of the issues in their divorce. Most couples arrive at agreements they can live with—which means they don't have to fight about any of these issues in court. Mediation offers many advantages over court battles.

You stay in control. You don't turn your divorce over to lawyers, who then start to run the show. Instead, decisions stay where they belong: in your hands. After all, you know best the condition of your finances, the needs of your children, and your plans for the future.

Conflict is dampened, not fueled. When lawyers do the talking, conflict tends to escalate. But in mediation, you communicate directly with your spouse instead of through third parties. The mediator is trained to help you communicate effectively and keep you focused on the present and future, not on what happened in the past. You each have the opportunity to share your concerns, beliefs, and desires and have them listened to (and maybe even understood) by the other person in a neutral setting, so resentment and misunderstandings can be eased.

You can still get legal information and advice. Mediators can provide legal information that helps you make informed decisions, though they won't give legal advice to either of you (that's because they are neutral and don't represent either of you). You and your spouse can both hire lawyers if you wish, to get legal advice and be sure your rights are protected. You can also hire a mediation coach—a lawyer or a nonlawyer with expertise in communication and negotiation, who will give you advice and support through the mediation process.

You'll save a ton of money. Even if you and your spouse both hire consulting lawyers and use other professionals to help you negotiate your divorce, the cost of mediation is much less than that of a contested divorce. (See "What Does Mediation Cost?" below.)

You can do what works best for your family. In mediation, you don't have to go by what the law would say about dividing your property or dealing with your kids—you can be creative about solutions and do what works best for you. For example, a court might order that you get half of your spouse's pension, which you wouldn't receive until your spouse reached retirement age. But if you'd actually much rather keep the house and let your spouse keep the pension, in mediation you can do it that way.

The process is much less stressful than court. Mediation is informal and unintimidating. You keep control over when and how often you meet and how much help you get from advisers. Mediation is private; nothing that happens in the mediation session goes into the public records except the ultimate outcome. And you avoid the drama and public spectacle of a divorce trial. Your contact with the divorce court is limited to submitting paperwork—you probably will never have to appear before a judge. (Learn more about trials in Chapter 5, and you'll probably be even more inclined to give mediation a try.)

You'll have fewer disputes later. Because you remain in control of the decisions, you and your spouse are much more likely to be satisfied with the result and to comply with all the terms of your negotiated agreement. That means everyone—including your children—is happier in the long run.

What have you got to lose? Deciding to try mediation doesn't mean that you're stuck with it if it doesn't work for you. You can stop at any point and go on with a contested divorce. From a financial perspective, you have very little to lose by trying mediation. Even if it doesn't work, the information sharing and negotiation you do will make your contested divorce process more efficient. (See "If Mediation Doesn't Work," below.)

"Alternative" Dispute Resolution

You may hear mediation referred to as a method of "alternative dispute resolution." Arbitration, which we discussed in Chapter 1, is another so-called alternative procedure. This is something of a misnomer—the term "alternative" refers to alternatives to trial, but given that trials are actually the least common way for a case to resolve, mediation and arbitration really should be known as the standard ways to settle a divorce case, with trial as the alternative.

What Does Mediation Cost?

Mediation is generally much less costly than a contested divorce case. It's certainly more efficient, and when professionals are being paid by the hour that makes all the difference.

Here's an outline of a scenario showing how mediation is more efficient and less costly than litigation. Mediator and lawyer fees vary a great deal by geographic area, but taking an average hourly rate of $250 and assuming your mediation takes 12 hours, you and your spouse together will pay the mediator $3,000. Let's say you each also pay consulting attorneys for nine hours spent coaching you, reviewing the settlement agreement, and filing papers for your uncontested divorce. That's another $4,500. You may also hire an actuary to value a pension plan ($500) and a CPA to review your settlement for tax consequences ($400). You have one meeting with a child psychologist to discuss how best to help your child cope with the divorce ($200). That's a total of $8,600.

Now let's say that instead, you and your spouse each hire lawyers of your own to negotiate for you. You each have initial consultations ($500 each) and give the lawyers financial documents to review. Your lawyer spends time putting those documents in the required form to send to the other side (which is what your spouse has become), and reviewing the documents from your spouse (many of these may be the same documents). The lawyers talk to each other, too. That's probably another $3,000 total.

Over the next few months, there's some wrangling about the visitation schedule and support payments, and your lawyers make a trip to court to argue those issues in front of the judge (at least $2,000 from each of you). You hire competing appraisers to value your home ($1,000), you each hire a CPA to look at the tax issues in your divorce ($800), and you have several visits with a custody mediator to work on your visitation schedule ($550). Your lawyers coordinate all of this and review the reports of these other professionals, then argue with each other about what the reports mean—and you are kept up to date on these negotiations, which also involves the lawyer's time. Another $1,500 each.

After all of this, your lawyers may encourage you to try mediation with the lawyers present—a great idea, but another $1,500 from each of you to pay the mediator and your own lawyer for a half-day session, plus the $500 you'll each pay your lawyer to prepare for the mediation.

At this point you've spent more than $8,000 yourself—almost twice what you would have spent to have your divorce completed in an average mediation process. And you haven't even paid for the lawyers to prepare and haggle over a settlement agreement if you settle in mediation (another $1,000 at least). If the mediation isn't successful, you're looking at another 50 to 75 hours of your own lawyer's time preparing for and presenting your case to a judge.

You can do the math on that, and it isn't pretty: You and your spouse could end up paying tens of thousands of dollars each for your divorce trial. Can you think of other ways you might want to use that much money?

Typical Costs: Mediation vs. Pretrial Costs Using a Lawyer			
Mediation (one spouse's share)		**Contested Divorce** (one spouse's share of pretrial costs)	
9 hours consulting attorney	$2,250	Initial consultation with lawyer	$500
		Lawyer reviews documents, talks to your spouse's lawyer	$1,500
		Court hearing	$2,000
		Lawyer reviews reports, negotiates with your spouse's lawyer	$1,500
12 hours mediation	$1,500	Mediation prep and time in mediation	$2,000
Actuary	$250	Appraisal	$500
Accountant	$200	Accountant	$400
Custody evaluator	$100	Custody evaluator	$275
TOTAL	**$4,300**	**TOTAL**	**$8,675**

Is Mediation Right for You?

Mediation is a good option for almost everyone, but there are a few exceptions. For one thing, if you think you have a chance in the court system of getting everything you want, and it's important to you to not to compromise, mediation is unlikely to satisfy you. Other circumstances that are likely to preclude mediation are:

- **Violence.** If you're intimidated by your spouse, who uses bullying or emotional abuse to try to control and manipulate you, you may not want to mediate. A lawyer might help you to protect your rights more effectively. See "If You've Been the Victim of Domestic Violence," below.

- **Drug or alcohol abuse.** The reasons for this should be obvious. Someone who has an addiction problem should be in some kind of recovery program before you consider mediating.

Some people think that mediation won't work unless divorcing spouses get along well. But you don't have to like or even completely trust your spouse in order to mediate successfully—you only need to be confident that your spouse will show up and make a real effort to settle. If you're not sure, give your spouse the benefit of the doubt and try it. But if you are somewhat mistrustful, make sure you have a consulting attorney— a lawyer of your own who can advise you about your best interests throughout the mediation process. (See "Choosing and Working With a Lawyer," below.) And if one of you blames the other for the divorce and is still very angry, you may need a cooling-off period before you start mediation.

Your chances of success in mediation are enhanced if:

- **Neither you nor your spouse is interested in reconciliation.** If either of you still wants to try staying married, you'd be better off going to marriage counseling first. Mediation isn't about making the marriage work—it's about making the divorce work.
- **You both consider it a priority to maintain good relations with each other.** You might feel this way for the sake of your children, or because you want to honor the relationship you had and the history you share.
- **You both disclose everything about your finances.** Most mediators will ask you to disclose financial information to your spouse voluntarily, as part of the mediation. If one person is withholding information—and particularly if you suspect that your spouse might be hiding assets (see Chapters 5 and 9 for more about this), you can still consider mediating. But you'll want to have your own attorney who can help you make sure you are getting all the information to which you're entitled.

If You've Been the Victim of Domestic Violence

Many mediators and battered women's advocates feel that mediation can't work when there's a major power imbalance between the parties, as is true where one party is a batterer and the other a victim. But others believe that the mediation process itself can be empowering for people who are leaving abusive relationships, and can provide an opportunity for them to stand up for themselves in a way they weren't always able to during their marriages.

If your relationship has involved physical violence and you want to try mediation, consider using a court-sponsored mediation program rather than a private mediator. (There's more about these programs in "Court-Connected Mediation," below.) It will cost less, and the mediators in court programs are generally experienced in dealing with domestic violence issues and will ensure that you and your spouse have separate sessions with the mediator, rather than meeting together. If you do use a private mediator, ask that mediator to meet with you separately.

Suggesting Mediation to Your Spouse

What should you do if you are interested in mediation but you think your spouse won't be, or might reject the idea just because it comes from you? How you raise the issue may make all the difference, so plan your approach carefully.

If you and your spouse have lawyers, start with them. Virtually all family law attorneys are familiar with mediation. Assuming your lawyer is solidly promediation, ask your lawyer to propose it to the other lawyer. That way your spouse's own lawyer will be the one bringing it up to your spouse.

If you're working directly with your spouse to get the divorce process going, then you'll have to figure out the best time to raise the subject. You surely know by now that both of you are on an emotional rollercoaster, and that some days are much, much better than others. Not only do you need to assess your spouse's mood and feelings before going ahead with the discussion, but also your own. Are you able to calmly give your reasons for wanting to mediate, and discuss any reluctance that your spouse might have? Or are you likely to fly off the handle if your spouse questions the process or your motivation for proposing it?

If a calm discussion seems unlikely, try writing a letter to your spouse. Explain in simple terms what mediation is and why you want to try it, and give an estimate of the costs and time involved. Then give your spouse some time to think about the idea. You might suggest that your spouse take a look at one of the books about mediation listed at the end of this chapter.

Follow up with a phone call when you think that both you and your spouse might be ready to talk. Be prepared to answer questions and concerns your spouse might have.

Being Prepared for Your Spouse's Concerns	
Common concerns	**Possible responses**
"The mediator will be biased in your favor because you are ... [*fill in the blank*]".	"You can say what criteria we use for choosing the mediator" or "You can choose the mediator".
"I'm already paying for a lawyer. I don't want to pay for a mediator, too."	"Mediation is usually less expensive than having lawyers negotiate a settlement. Avoiding conflict saves money."
"We've already done couples therapy."	"Mediation is about resolving issues and moving forward, not rehashing the emotional conflicts of the past. It's not therapy."
"It's too painful to sit in a room together and talk."	"How painful would it be—for us and for our kids—to sit in a courtroom together and battle it out through our lawyers?"

If your spouse is worried about possible bias, you can also explain that mediators are trained to be neutral and not favor one party over the other. On the issue of cost, mediation has the potential to be faster than having lawyers negotiate for you because a skilled mediator can help you cut to the chase, identify the issues, and work together to resolve them. Even if you hire a consulting attorney, the process still may go more quickly and, thus, be less expensive. (See "What Does Mediation Cost?" above.) And whether or not it is faster or cheaper, you always have the advantage of being in control of your own process, rather than turning it over to the lawyers and courts.

Lots of people worry that mediation is too much like couples therapy. While it's true that one focus of mediation usually is communication, the mediator won't be trying to help you reconcile or solve all of your relationship problems. Mediation is focused on getting results. It's designed to help you keep your eyes on the prize: resolving the issues you need to resolve and getting your divorce finalized. It may have the fringe benefit of improving your communication with your spouse, but it's not therapy. Also, some mediators are more touchy-feely than others, and you can choose one you're both comfortable with. (See "Choosing a Mediator," below, for more about mediation styles.)

If your spouse feels strongly that spending hours in mediation sessions will be too emotionally difficult, it's possible that mediation won't work for the two of you. Some people are willing to cooperate but want to avoid direct contact by using the lawyer as a buffer. You could start by taking the path of least resistance and working with your lawyers for a while. The cost, not to mention the realities of having someone else control your divorce process, may change your spouse's mind.

Choosing a Mediator

For most divorcing couples, it's not difficult to agree on a mediator, but for some, it's a struggle. It helps to reach some basic agreements with your spouse before you start searching. There are lots of different kinds of mediators, and knowing what qualities you are looking for will make your search much easier. It's important that you both be comfortable with the mediator, so take whatever time is needed to find the right person.

Types of Mediation

There are a few different places to turn to find mediators. If you have kids and are asking the court to resolve a dispute over custody or visitation, most courts will require that you mediate your disagreements about your kids. In that situation, you can hire a private mediator or use a mediator connected with the family court.

Court-Connected Mediation

Many family courts offer low-cost (or even free) mediation to divorcing couples. These programs usually cover only issues related to your children, so if you want to mediate property issues as well, you'll probably want to hire a private mediator to mediate your entire divorce. You could use two mediators—one for custody and visitation issues, and one for property and financial issues—but it would mean a lot of meetings and could get confusing. Even if you're planning on hiring a private mediator, you may be required to attend a minimum number of sessions of court-sponsored mediation.

Court mediators are skilled and experienced. But there often is a limit on the number of sessions to which you are entitled, and you don't have much control over scheduling.

Private Mediation

Most couples who can afford it hire a private mediator because of the greater flexibility and choice it allows. You select and pay your own mediator and can control scheduling, number of sessions, what can be covered, and so on.

Private mediators charge from about $150 to $500 an hour, depending on their background, experience, and location. How long your mediation takes will depend on how complicated the issues are and how well you and your spouse negotiate and compromise. With a very motivated couple and straightforward issues, just one or two sessions might be enough. If the dynamics are difficult or there are lots of complex financial or custody issues, the number of sessions could move up toward double digits.

Community Mediation

In many places, nonprofit community mediation agencies provide low-cost mediation to divorcing couples. Community mediators are nearly always volunteers. They are trained to work in panels of two or three mediators, and to deal with many different kinds of issues. Some of the mediators may be lawyers or therapists who mediate professionally and also donate their time; the rest are from all different walks of life.

Some community mediation services don't do family cases, deferring to mediators with family law or counseling expertise. And you probably wouldn't want to go to a community mediation service if you have retirement plans to divide or need to determine what level of support is fair. But if you and your spouse agree on most things but simply can't work out one thorny issue about parenting time or who gets to keep the good china, you might try community mediation for that single issue. The biggest advantage of community mediation is its very low cost.

If you use a community mediation service, you'll still need a lawyer or document preparation service to prepare your divorce papers, including your marital settlement agreement.

Therapist and Lawyer Mediators

Many divorce mediators are lawyers or therapists. Whether you prefer one over the other depends on your needs and your inclinations.

Lawyers. The major advantage of a lawyer-mediator is that you can get legal information about your divorce. A lawyer can also prepare the court forms and a settlement agreement if you and your spouse come to an agreement.

No mediator can, however, give you or your spouse legal advice. Because mediators don't represent either spouse, but work with both of you together, they can't tell either of you how to protect your own interests. They can only give legal information—for example, telling you how much child support the judge is likely to order if you don't come to an agreement yourselves. For advice about what's in your best interest, you'll need to hire a consulting attorney.

Therapists. If you've been in couples counseling, a therapist-mediator may be something of a redundancy. But if you and your spouse haven't had any counseling in the process of your divorce, and you're comfortable getting legal information and advice elsewhere, a therapist-mediator might work for you—especially if you feel that there's a lot of misunderstanding and blame between you. The therapist has skills to keep a lid on that sort of thing and to support more productive communication. Therapists also tend to charge somewhat less than lawyers for mediation services.

Both. Another good option is to work with two mediators together, one lawyer and one therapist. The combination of skills that they bring to the table can really streamline the process and help you make decisions. The therapist-mediator can help you work with barriers to communication, while the lawyer-mediator keeps track of the issues that need to be decided, provides legal guidance, and keeps the process moving toward a resolution. Be prepared to pay—you'll have two professionals involved, and it won't be cheap.

Nonlawyer/Nontherapist Mediators. Some mediators offering services to divorcing couples aren't lawyers or therapists, but laypersons trained in the basics of family law and skilled in the process of mediation. If your case isn't legally or emotionally complicated, and what you really need is help communicating and making decisions, a lay mediator can probably help you at a much lower cost than a professional. A search for mediators in the yellow pages or online will turn up mediators of all kinds, including nonlawyer, nontherapist mediators.

The best of both worlds ...

" My husband and I chose to go to mediation with a married couple who worked together as mediators—the husband was a lawyer and the wife a therapist. The lawyer took the lead in the mediation. He gave us legal information and helped us negotiate. He also wrote up our agreement, and did the court paperwork. The therapist stepped in when things got intense and we had trouble communicating or were super emotional. I thought they were great, and my husband liked them, too. I think that the two kinds of skills they had made things go faster than they might have otherwise. It was expensive in terms of the hourly cost, but not more than going to court! To me the cost was totally worthwhile."

—Divorced mom

Making a Short List

As is true with most services, the best way to find a divorce mediator is by getting a personal recommendation from someone whose judgment you trust. You can ask lawyers, financial advisers, therapists, or spiritual advisers you know for referrals.

If you can't find direct, personal referrals, here are some other ideas:

- Check the Internet: www.mediate.com has links to mediator referrals, as do many other divorce websites and lawyer directories, including Nolo's directory at www.nolo.com (click "Find a Lawyer").
- Contact national mediation or family law organizations, including the Association for Conflict Resolution (www.acrnet.org), the Association of Family and Conciliation Courts (www.afccnet.org), and the American Arbitration Association (www.adr.org).
- Call your local community mediation center and ask for a recommendation.
- Call your local bar association or a local organization of therapists or financial professionals.

- Call your local legal aid office.
- Check the phone directory or search online for "mediation," "divorce mediation," or "dispute resolution."

Make sure that you get referrals for divorce or family law mediators, not general or business mediators. When you've collected a few names, you'll need to interview some.

Interviewing Mediators

If you and your spouse can cooperate, you can work together to screen potential mediators. You can either split the list and each contact some of the mediators, or you can both contact each of them and compare notes. There's no set number of mediators you should talk to—start with a couple each, and stop when you've found the right one.

Some mediators have websites, and that's a good way to begin gathering information. (But don't hold it against the ones who don't. Websites are expensive to create and maintain, and many mediators work as solo businesspeople, rather than in big firms with big budgets.) There's no substitute for direct contact, though. Because the mediator's personality and manner will be so important to the process, you need to feel comfortable. If the mediator is overbearing or curt on the phone, you have gathered valuable information. On the other hand, if you feel immediately comfortable talking with the mediator about your questions and expectations, you can move that person to the top of your short list.

Some mediators are concerned that talking with either spouse separately before the mediation might make the other spouse question the mediator's impartiality. Instead, they may ask an assistant to answer your questions. In this case, you might try a three-way conference call with both you and your spouse on the phone, or separate calls with you and with your spouse.

If the mediator doesn't feel comfortable with either of these options, you'll have to decide whether you're willing to go to a meeting without having spoken directly beforehand. This may depend on what other prospects you have and how you felt about the mediator's manner in setting these limits. Don't reject someone out of hand because of a policy about premediation contact—instead, use it as a factor in your decision-making process.

Here are some issues to explore during your screening process.

- **Scope of the mediation.** Some mediators work only on property issues and ask you to see a separate custody mediator or parenting counselor to deal with parenting issues. If the mediator has such a policy, and you have custody issues, who will help you work on them?

- **Fees.** Will there be charges in addition to the hourly fee for mediation time and time spent drafting documents? (You may be charged for such things as copying, postage, and long distance telephone calls.) Does the mediator have any kind of sliding scale based on your income? Can you pay with a credit card or work out a payment plan?

- **How long it will take.** Obviously, the mediator can't tell you exactly how long your mediation will take. But you might be able to get a range of how many sessions are needed in a typical divorce mediation.

- **Scheduling.** What are the mediator's scheduling and cancellation policies? Is it easy to get an appointment within a week or two, or will you have to struggle to find time to get together?

- **Training.** What is the mediator's professional background and training? In most states, mediators aren't regulated by any government agency, other than the state bar (if they're lawyers), so be sure to find out how many hours of mediation training the mediator has had (in both general mediation and divorce mediation—the minimum should be 40 hours in each). Also ask what mediation organizations the mediator belongs to— membership can demonstrate commitment to the profession and to keeping up with trends and new information.

- **Experience.** How many divorce cases has the mediator worked on? In general, what is the rate of settlement?

- **References.** For reasons of confidentiality, the mediator shouldn't give you names of clients, but possibly could refer you to colleagues who can serve as references.
- **How you'll begin.** What will happen at the first mediation session? The answer you get to this question can give you a sense of the mediator's personal style and approach to the mediation.
- **Style.** Some style differences are based on the mediator's personality, but there are also different schools of thought about mediation. A "facilitative" mediator will focus on communication between you and your spouse, and will help you understand each other's goals and interests so that you can reach an agreement. A mediator who is more "directive" will tend to control the process a little more tightly. A directive mediator is more likely to give an opinion about how to resolve your differences and to direct the discussion.
- **Working with other professionals.** Will the mediator recommend (or require) that you hire other professionals, such as consulting attorneys, accountants, actuaries, or tax advisers? This is not uncommon, especially if you and your spouse have retirement plans, which are often difficult to value (that is what an actuary would do). Some mediators require that you have an attorney review whatever agreement you come up with. None of this should deter you from hiring a particular mediator, but it's important to know ahead of time.
- **What you'll end up with.** Will the mediator prepare your marital settlement agreement or your uncontested divorce paperwork? If not, will you get a referral to someone who will?

Make sure you take notes as you speak to different mediators—and include not only the answers to the questions listed above, but your general impressions of the mediator. After you and your spouse have interviewed all of the mediators on your list, you should be able to narrow it down to a few that you both think you could work with. Then you and your spouse will need to agree on whether to meet with more than one mediator in person. This can be expensive, so if you can choose one mediator who both of you like, you'll save time and money.

In any case, look at the first meeting as an experiment. If you've done your screening and interviewing, you're likely to feel good about your choice once you get there. But if you don't, you can always try a different mediator.

Choosing and Working With a Lawyer

It's a really good idea to have a lawyer help you through the mediation process. Lawyers in this role are often called "consulting attorneys." You can hire a consulting attorney to work with you throughout the process (usually the best option) or just to review the settlement agreement before it's finalized. Some mediators require that you have a consulting attorney review the agreement before they'll allow you to sign it, but even if your mediator doesn't require that, you should consider it a crucial step in wrapping up the mediation.

Your consulting attorney may attend mediation with you if the mediator requests it—unlikely, but possible if things are really at a stalemate—or if you want the support and expertise. Usually, though, they stay in the background. Assuming the consulting attorney isn't involved in the mediation, you'll check in between mediation sessions to talk about the negotiations and get advice about legal questions and the proposals that you are considering. The lawyer will help you negotiate, do what you can to get the most out of the mediation process, and make the best decisions you can. In essence, a lawyer coaches you through the mediation.

Choose a consulting attorney early if you can, before your mediation process is underway. Your best bet is to meet with someone before you go to your first mediation session, so that you can get advice about your rights and figure out your priorities before you go in.

Your consulting attorney needs to have a positive attitude about mediation. You need a lawyer who's willing to act in your best interest and be your advocate by explaining your rights to you. But your lawyer must also help you decide where to compromise and what kind of negotiated settlement will work best for you and your family.

Many lawyer-mediators also work as consulting attorneys, so you can use the same resources listed in "Choosing a Mediator," above, to help you find one. Or you can use the steps outlined in Chapter 16. If some of your prospective consulting attorneys aren't also mediators, be sure to ask for their opinions about mediation's chances for success and how many of their divorce cases settle through mediation. The answers you hear may be very illuminating. For example, if a lawyer you interview assures you that mediation can work only in a few types of cases, or that people come out of mediation with less than if they had gone to court and fought, you should probably think twice about using this person as a consulting attorney. A lawyer who is determined to fight for everything you might be legally entitled to, and who doesn't want to compromise, is not a good consulting lawyer.

In most cases, the consulting attorney shouldn't ask for a large retainer (as do some lawyers who represent people through the whole divorce process). It's reasonable to pay for a few hours of work up front, but after that it should be a pay-as-you-go proposition.

Where the Law Comes In

In mediation, you and your spouse are free to work things out however you want to. You don't have to do exactly what a judge would do. You may have very good reasons for doing something different. For example, perhaps you are willing to give up a percentage of support to which you would otherwise be entitled in exchange for your spouse's willingness to stay on the loan for your house, which you can't afford to live in otherwise.

But it's often helpful to know what decision a judge is likely to make in a given situation, and your mediator or consulting lawyer can give you informed predictions about that. Likewise, most states have guidelines for things like child support, and you may want to know how those calculations would come out in your situation.

The Mediation Process

There are as many ways of mediating as there are mediators—because it's such a personal process, the mediator's personality is an important factor. But all mediations tend to take a similar path in terms of procedure. Here's the nutshell version:

1. The mediator, or an assistant, will usually speak briefly with each of you before the first meeting.
2. At the initial session the mediator will explain the process, and each of you will have a chance to speak about your perspective and your goals. Then you'll begin discussing specifics.
3. You'll have as many subsequent meetings as you need to work through all the disputed issues. Divorce mediation works best in multiple sessions of a few hours each, giving you time to gather information and consult with your lawyer in between.
4. Once you've reached an agreement, either the mediator or a consulting attorney will prepare a written settlement agreement, and then you'll be able to finalize your divorce.

There's more about each of these steps below.

The Intake Interview

You've already interviewed the mediator—now, before your first session, the mediator will interview you to get background information and a sense of the most challenging issues. The mediator will probably talk to you and your spouse separately by phone before the first mediation session. However, some mediators don't do an intake interview before the initial meeting, preferring to hear from both parties while everyone is together.

The First Session

At the first mediation session, you'll all meet in the mediator's office or conference room. Most likely the room will contain a table, comfortable chairs, and something to write on that everyone can see—a chalkboard, a white board, or an easel with big sheets of paper. You'll be seated in a way that allows each of you to see and communicate with each other.

Is Your Lawyer Invited?

When you start the mediation, you may already have a consulting attorney. Generally, family law mediation sessions involve just the divorcing spouses and the mediator, and lawyers don't attend. This keeps costs down and ensures that you and your spouse do the talking and make the decisions. Even if you're a little bit nervous about it, try the first mediation session without your attorney—unless your spouse insists on bringing an attorney, in which case you should probably do the same. If you find that you can't state your position clearly or stand up for yourself alone, then consider bringing your lawyer to later sessions. You can also discuss the issue of your lawyer's presence with the mediator, who may have opinions or suggestions, especially after meeting with you.

The Mediator's Opening Remarks

Most mediators begin by telling you something about what you can expect. This will probably include the fact that the mediator is a neutral party and won't be providing legal advice, and how the process will go—for example, whether you'll all work together the entire time or will sometimes meet separately with the mediator. The mediator will make sure that you understand the nature of the process and will find out whether anyone has time limitations or other needs for the session.

The mediator may also take care of some housekeeping business, if that hasn't happened already—for example, asking you to sign an agreement that says that you'll keep what's said in the mediation confidential, and that you understand that the mediator can't disclose any of what goes on there if, later, there's a court proceeding. At the same time, the mediator will be trying to make you feel comfortable and establish rapport with both you and your spouse.

Telling It Like It Is

After the mediator has gone over the basics, you and your spouse will each get a chance to make a short statement about your situation and what you hope to gain from mediation. Some mediators will ask you to answer a few specific questions. Others will just let you say whatever you want to about your marriage, your divorce, what's brought you to mediation, and what you would like to get out of it. The mediator will usually ask each of you not to interrupt the other (a good policy even if you're not reminded of it by the mediator). After each of you has a chance to speak, the mediator may ask some questions to clarify or get more information about what you've said, and make sure you've been understood.

What Do You Need to Work On?

Next, the mediator will begin assessing where you already agree and where you need some work to reach an agreement. Here's where the white board or easel and pad will start to be useful. For example, if you have worked out a custody arrangement, the mediator can put "parenting schedule" on the list of items that you don't need to discuss. You can move on to something else, like a buyout price for the house or the amount of spousal support to be paid.

Tips for Your Opening Remarks

Before the mediation, consider what you might want to say when you first have a chance to speak. It's your opportunity to set a positive tone for the mediation. You can do that in a number of ways.

- Refrain from spending lots of time talking about why your marriage is ending. Unless you think the problems in your marriage will affect how the mediation goes, leave the past in the past. State your intention to focus on the present and the future.
- Use positive terms to state your expectations from the mediation. For example, "I'm hoping we can resolve everything quickly and cooperatively," is better than "I want her to stop being so unreasonable."
- Say what's most important to you, and state your willingness to compromise on things that are less important. For example, "Getting the issue of the house buyout resolved is critical to me. I think lots of other things might fall into place if we can get that resolved, and I'm open to whatever scenarios might work best for all of us."
- Offer your commitment to doing what's best for your kids and for the family as a whole. Stay focused on those goals.

Making a Plan and Moving Forward

Once you have a sense of what needs to be accomplished, you, your spouse, and the mediator will plan how you are going to accomplish it.

You may or may not get down to actually negotiating during the first session. You may need to get more information before you can even discuss the topics that are on the table. For example, if neither you nor your spouse knows exactly how much you still owe on your house loan, and you don't know the fair market value of the house, then you can't have an intelligent negotiation about a buyout. The mediator will help you figure out what information you need before you can go forward, and will assign each of you tasks to complete before the next time you meet. It's important to keep the momentum going by not letting too much time pass between sessions—a couple of weeks at the most—but you also need to be sure you have enough time to accomplish whatever you've promised to do.

> **TIP**
> **Strike while the iron is hot.** Try to schedule the next session before you leave a meeting with the mediator. Doing it later by phone or email usually means a longer delay.

Negotiating an Agreement

Later mediation sessions begin with a brief assessment of what's been accomplished so far and then a bit of planning for that day's work. Which issues do you want to tackle? Did each of you bring all the information that's needed to work on resolving them? Do some issues depend on others, so that you need to do things in a particular order? The mediator may ask you to deal with simpler issues first. Resolving them builds trust and encourages compromise when it comes to the more difficult issues. Settling a divorce, like almost any other dispute, has an aspect of horse-trading about it. If you let your spouse take the expensive stereo system that she spent so much time assembling, she may be more likely to agree that you can have the computer you have been sharing.

You'll then negotiate issues one by one in the order that you decided on. It's not always neat and tidy, and you may need to cycle back into the information-gathering stage. If you don't seem to be making progress, the mediator may ask everyone to stop, remind themselves about why they're there, and renew their commitment to settling the issues without a court fight.

During the negotiation, the mediator will help you and your spouse to express your opinions, positions, and what's important to you, and will help you to listen to each other effectively. The mediator will encourage you to brainstorm about possible solutions and come up with a wide range of options so that you can be creative about settlement possibilities.

Try to be open to compromise, and really listen and try to understand your spouse's point of view. Understanding doesn't mean you have to agree with it, but it's difficult to have an effective negotiation if you don't know what your spouse wants or why. You are also more likely to get more of what you want if your spouse really understands what it is and why you want it. Invest the time in that mutual understanding, and you'll be on your way to a successful negotiation.

Reality Testing

When you have reached agreement on everything, or seem to be coming close, the mediator will help you make sure that it will actually work by doing what is often called "reality testing." Using all of the information gathered about your family throughout the course of the mediation, the mediator will ask detailed questions about how the proposed settlement might work in real life. This may force you to go back to the brainstorming or negotiating stages, but it will be well worth your time—you will end up with an agreement that will last.

Your consulting attorneys should also do some reality testing, and you may make some revisions to the agreement after they get through with it. Be patient with this part of the process—it's another piece that's critical to making sure you have an agreement that will stand the test of time.

It seemed like a good idea at the time …

" My wife Rachel and I were determined to share custody of our children exactly 50-50 when we divorced. We went into mediation with that agreement and announced it to the mediator, saying it was agreed and we should just use the mediation to talk about our property and spousal support.

"We worked everything else out with the mediator's help, and then the mediator made us talk about the parenting plan some more so that he could include it in the settlement agreement. He asked us what our kids do in terms of activities, where each of us lives, what our schedules are like, and where the kids go for their soccer, music lessons, and gymnastics practice. Once we started talking we could see that an exactly equal time-share wouldn't work well for our kids, so we had to go back and start over on the time-sharing.

"The mediator helped us come up with a schedule that should work for us all. Rachel's a schoolteacher so she has time in the afternoon to ferry the kids around—so we agreed the kids would be with her more of the time. That meant the child support calculation changed and I have to pay more, which of course I'm not happy about, but I'm more unhappy at losing time with the kids. And neither of us likes the idea that Rachel has to continue to do more of the chauffeuring. But the mediator was great. He let us both talk about what we didn't like about it and let us take our time accepting that this is the best thing for our kids, at least for now. In the end, we both feel comfortable with the solution we came up with."

—Divorced dad

How to Make Your Mediation a Success

There are a number of things that you can do to help keep the mediation process moving forward and get the most out of it.

Don't hold back any information. Disclose all the financial information that's in your possession at the very beginning of the process, if you haven't given it to your spouse already. This will make the mediation go more quickly and be more effective. If you have a real need for confidentiality, such as for sensitive business information, ask your mediator about the possibility of preparing a special protective order, a binding legal document that a judge will sign, stating that neither you nor your spouse will disclose the information outside of the mediation session.

Do what you say you will. Don't procrastinate or make excuses that delay the process. For example, if you agree to get estimates of how much it will cost to do some critical repairs to prepare the house for sale, don't wait until the last minute to make those appointments. If the estimates aren't ready for the scheduled mediation session, you, your spouse, and the mediator will all waste time.

Show up. Don't cancel a mediation session unless it's truly an emergency. Momentum is an important ingredient in the mediation mix.

Take your communication cues from the mediator. The mediator is, no doubt, an effective communicator; take the opportunity to improve your own communication skills. Use neutral language and a calm tone as much as you can.

Compromise wherever you can. When it feels like you can't compromise, try to make clear to your spouse and the mediator what it is that's important to you about the issue. It's easier to find ways to resolve challenging situations when the reasons for the position you are taking are on the table.

RESOURCE

Divorce Without Court: A Guide to Mediation & Collaborative Divorce, by Katherine E. Stoner (Nolo), is a detailed explanation of both divorce mediation and collaborative divorce (discussed in Chapter 1 of this book).

A Guide to Divorce Mediation, by Gary Friedman (Workman Press), explains divorce mediation and provides case studies from actual mediation cases.

After the Mediation, the Paperwork

If you and your spouse negotiate a complete settlement of your divorce, you'll then need to complete the divorce paperwork. That paperwork includes

- a marital settlement agreement incorporating the decisions you made in mediation, and
- all of the court forms that are required to finalize your divorce legally.

If you each have your own attorneys, they can complete the paperwork. If you don't have lawyers, the mediator can prepare the paperwork— most mediators are happy to do this for you. Or you and your spouse can do it yourselves, using the instructions and resources in Chapters 3 and 16 and whatever additional information you need for your own state. However, it's a good idea to hire a lawyer to review your settlement agreement, just to make sure it complies with all of your state's requirements. Chapter 13 has a sample marital settlement agreement.

If Mediation Doesn't Work

Mediation works for most couples. But sometimes you can do everything in your power to make mediation successful and still not resolve all of the issues in your divorce. In that case, you have some options.

Have your lawyers try to settle the divorce. You probably resolved at least some of your issues during mediation. Use those agreements as a starting point to have your lawyer negotiate with your spouse's lawyer. It may be that after a bit of time has passed, you'll feel differently about the proposals that were made during mediation. It's also possible that the lawyers will use their negotiating skills to come up with a proposal that's acceptable to both you and your spouse.

Try collaborative divorce. This is a particular way of working with lawyers, where everyone pledges to try to settle the case and the lawyers won't represent you if you do ultimately insist on a trial. See Chapter 1 for more about collaborative divorce.

Hire an arbitrator or a private judge. You can hire an arbitrator, who is a private attorney or a former judge, or a private judge, who is always a retired judge, to decide the issues you couldn't resolve. This option is quicker and less expensive than court. See Chapter 1 for more about arbitration.

Go to court. Whatever you can't decide, a judge will. Of course, this should be your last resort. A contested trial, even one that deals with only a few of the issues, will be time-consuming, damaging to your relationship with your spouse, and shockingly expensive. (If this is the way you may have to go, turn to Chapter 5 for more about contested divorce.) ●

When You Can't Agree: Contested Divorce and Trial

A contested divorce is one in which you and your spouse can't agree on the big issues—and most likely, the small ones, either—so you hire lawyers to fight it out for you. You may end up settling, after your lawyers have spent lots of time and lots of your money arguing with each other on your behalf. Or you may end up in front of a judge, going through a divorce trial that ends with the judge making decisions about your family and your future.

Even if you are totally convinced that you and your spouse are going to have a perfectly civil divorce, it's a good idea to know what happens when spouses take their personal and financial grievances to court. If nothing else, it will serve as a cautionary tale. Someday, things may look bleak and you'll think you just can't compromise any more, or your ex may be acting like such a jerk that you can't remember why you ever got married in the first place. On that day, knowing what a contested divorce looks like might be the best thing in the world for you. It will help you to take a deep breath (or a break) and return to negotiations with a renewed sense of purpose: to avoid spending the money, wasting the time, and losing the mental and emotional energy that will be sapped out of you in a contested divorce proceeding. Oh, and did we mention the harm to your children and the lifelong bitterness that a court fight can create?

Given the time, expense, and overall awfulness of a divorce trial, why would anyone choose one? Well, maybe neither you nor your spouse is willing to compromise on issues that you both feel strongly about. For example, if each of you is utterly convinced that conceding custody of your kids to the other would be terrible for the kids, you're going to have to let a judge decide. Likewise, if your spouse is the primary income earner in your family, but refuses to pay what you consider a reasonable amount of support or insists on dividing property in a way you think is completely unfair, you may have to try to convince a judge to see your side. If you think that your spouse is hiding assets or lying about their worth, you might need a judge to review the evidence and decide who's telling the truth. And of course, if you can't get your spouse to negotiate with you at all—in other words, it's their way or the highway—you'll have to get a court to step in.

Before you decide to go to trial, though, take a good hard look in the mirror and ask yourself whether it's really necessary. Are you truly concerned about the kids, or just mad at your spouse for leaving you in the first place? This is no time for being vindictive. Punishing your spouse will punish your entire family, now and for a long time to come.

This chapter describes the process of a contested divorce, from the first meeting with an attorney to deciding whether or not to appeal after the trial. It assumes that you are going to have a lawyer, because you'll need one.

Representing Yourself in a Contested Divorce (Not)

In a contested divorce, the stakes are high, and there's a lot of animosity and not much spirit of compromise. In other words, it's the type of situation for which lawyers were invented. Can you represent yourself? Well, if your spouse doesn't have a lawyer and the two of you want to slug it out in the courtroom without the benefit of legal counsel, go for it. At least you'll be on equal footing. There are certain advantages, besides the cost saving, to representing yourself—for example, you maintain control over how your case is handled, which can reduce your anxiety. With the increase in unbundled legal services (having a lawyer help you with only part of your case) and self-help centers, it's becoming easier to get help and support for some parts of your case without hiring a lawyer to take care of everything.

However, in many contested cases, especially in locations where self-representation isn't very common, you're probably better off hiring a lawyer. Courtroom procedures can be complex, and the law is not always as accessible as you would like. If you're going all the way to trial, you probably feel that there's a lot at stake—so make sure you have as much help as you need.

If you are considering representing yourself in a contested divorce, look for do-it-yourself materials from your local court (check the list of websites in Chapter 16). Chapter 3 has basic information about filing papers and dealing with courts in uncontested divorces; you'll have to find more help if you're going it alone in a contested case. For example, check out *Represent Yourself in Court*, by Paul Bergman and Sara Berman (Nolo).

> **One divorced dad who represented himself in a custody trial said ...**
> "I think a person who can think rationally and has the emotional wherewithal can do self-representation, especially with some help from a coach. It's like house painting—90% is preparation. I didn't end up using my legal coach much after she first helped me with the petition to modify custody. I relied a lot on books like *Represent Yourself in Court*, and on Bender's legal forms in the law library. The hardest thing is to keep your equanimity, not get too up or down about the things that happen. It can be really hard on a partner, too, so you have to make sure it doesn't take over your life."

TIP

Consider arbitration as an option. You may want to consider arbitration instead of court. Ask your lawyer about it after you read up on the basics in Chapter 1.

Finding the Right Lawyer

If it is your spouse, not you, who is making an expensive and nasty divorce trial necessary, keep in mind that you don't have to get nasty yourself. You still can, and should, take the high road. This begins with your choice of a lawyer. Try to find a lawyer who will do everything possible to resolve the case before it gets to a trial and will respect your desire to spare your family a bitter fight.

Don't think that just because your spouse hired an aggressive lawyer, you have to do the same. There's more than one way to represent a client, and the best lawyers are versatile. They begin by doing everything possible to settle, and if that's not possible, they work as aggressively as is required to protect their clients' interests.

Dos and Don'ts When You're Shopping for a Lawyer

Don't:

- Go around asking your friends for the most cutthroat, litigation-happy, no-holds-barred divorce attorney they've ever heard of.
- Hire a lawyer who badmouths your spouse even before their first meeting.
- Choose a lawyer who tells you that you can get whatever you want out of your spouse if you just fight hard enough.
- Rely on a lawyer's statements that your spouse will have to pay all of your attorney's fees, so it doesn't matter if you litigate like crazy. You might get your fees back, but then again, you might not.

Do:

- Look for a lawyer who will represent your interests whether that means fighting it out in court or making sure you get into mediation.
- Ask your divorced friends and family whether they liked their attorneys, and find out why.
- Meet with more than one lawyer to get a sense of what personal style works for you.
- Find a lawyer who will treat both you and your spouse with respect and who considers the welfare of your kids the top priority.

Where to Look for a Lawyer

There are a lot of places to go looking for a lawyer. The best one, though, always is a recommendation from someone who knows the lawyer and the lawyer's work in cases like yours. If you've ever used a lawyer for any other type of case or services, ask that lawyer for a referral to a divorce lawyer or for help checking out the reputation of lawyers whose names you get from others. If you have a marriage counselor or an individual therapist, ask for referrals. Ask family members, friends, and acquaintances. If the same name pops up more than once, pay attention—but don't choose your lawyer just on that basis.

If you can't find a personal referral, try professional associations of family law attorneys. The American Academy of Matrimonial Lawyers (AAML) is a national organization with admission standards that require members to be experienced and skilled practitioners. It shouldn't be a deal-breaker if the lawyer isn't a member, but membership is a good indication that the lawyer is reputable and competent. The AAML has an online directory (www.aaml.org) that lists members.

Your state may have an association of divorce lawyers, and your local bar association surely does. They very often have referral services. The downside to these services is that the lawyers who place themselves on the referral panels sometimes do so because they are inexperienced or are having difficulty getting clients. But this is not always the case, and at the very least you can be assured that the bar association will have made sure that the lawyers are licensed to practice law and have professional liability (malpractice) insurance.

Other options for finding lawyers include the divorce websites listed in Chapter 16. These sites often have lawyer directories and may also have chat rooms where you can ask for recommendations. There's also a lawyer directory at www.nolo.com, which provides quite detailed profiles of listed lawyers.

No matter how you search for lawyers, check with your state's regulating agency (usually the state bar) to make sure they haven't been disciplined and to confirm their education and experience. It's also a good idea to search online for information about any lawyer you're considering hiring.

Interviewing Lawyers

Nothing substitutes for a personal interview. Think about what you want to know from your lawyer and how you want your lawyer to treat you, and then make appointments with a few prospects. A lawyer who is going to earn a lot of money on your divorce case should be willing to spend some time with you while you check out whether you two are a good fit.

Conflicts of interest may keep you from your lawyer of choice. Don't be surprised if an attorney you contact declines to consult with you.

You may or may not learn why, but in most cases it will be because your spouse has already consulted that lawyer. The lawyer shouldn't tell you that your spouse has been there, because that would violate confidentiality rules—most likely you'll just be told that the lawyer's not available. The same would be true if your spouse contacted a lawyer you had already spoken to, and to whom you gave confidential information about your marriage or divorce.

Some lawyers offer brief initial consultations free of charge so that you and the lawyer both have a chance to decide whether or not to work together. Others charge for the consultation, especially if they are giving you strategic advice about your case. Here's a list of suggested questions to add to the ones you already have, to help you figure out what kind of lawyer you're talking to. You may be able to get answers to some of the basic questions about education and length of time in practice by checking out your lawyer's website or the website of the state bar association.

Don't ignore your gut feelings about the lawyers you interview. If you think a lawyer isn't a good fit, you're probably right.

Questions to Ask a Potential Lawyer

- How long have you been in practice?
- How long have you been doing family law?
- How many family law cases have you completed?
- Do you do any other kinds of cases? What kinds?
- Who else in your office would be working on my case? Under what circumstances would someone other than you work on my case? What will the charges be?
- Can I expect to have my phone calls and messages returned within 24 hours by you or someone on your staff?
- How many divorce cases have you brought to trial?
- How often do your divorce cases go to mediation?
- Do you encourage people to mediate their disputes?

Questions to Ask a Potential Lawyer (cont'd)

- Are you a certified specialist in family law? (Check your state bar's website first to find out whether your state grants certification.)

- Have you published any articles about family law?

- Are you familiar with the judges and the courts in the county where my divorce will be filed?

- Do you believe that kids should ever testify in a divorce trial? (If this is something you want to protect your kids from, asking this up front is a good idea—you don't want to argue about it on the eve of trial.)

- Are there attorneys in the community with whom you have particularly good or particularly bad relationships? (This can give you a sense of the lawyer's experience, and also of whether they themselves are difficult to work with. If they tell you that there are six other lawyers who are simply impossible, you might want to think about the common denominator.)

- Do you know my spouse's lawyer? Have you worked on cases with the lawyer before? Would you say you have a good relationship?

- What do you think your reputation is among other family law lawyers?

- What do you think is the likely outcome of the custody dispute (or dispute over the home buyout or whatever) that my spouse and I are having?

- What is your opinion about arbitration? Are you experienced in taking divorce cases to arbitration?

- Are you able to estimate how much I'm going to pay in attorneys' fees? What about expenses of the case?

- Will we have a close working relationship, where you accept my input on strategic decisions like when to file a motion or how much support to ask for?

- Have you ever been disciplined by the state bar? What were the circumstances?

- Have I forgotten to ask anything? What else can you tell me about yourself or your practice?

Paying the Lawyer

If you are going the contested route, get out your checkbook.

The Retainer

Virtually all divorce lawyers ask you to pay a "retainer" or deposit when you hire them. The retainer is your first payment toward the fees that you will owe as the case goes along.

The amount of the retainer depends on the lawyer's hourly rate, common practice in your area, and whether the lawyer thinks you might be able to collect some fees from your spouse during the divorce. Because you are anticipating litigation, the lawyer will expect to put in a significant number of hours—and pretty much every divorce lawyer charges by the hour. Many lawyers ask for $10,000 to $15,000 up front. If the lawyer charges $250 per hour, $10,000 will last only 40 hours, a relatively short time given the legal work the lawyer will do. And $250 is an average. If you live in a metropolitan area and your lawyer is a specialist, you could pay twice that.

The retainer goes into the lawyer's trust account, and the lawyer withdraws it as the fees are earned. In other words, lawyers pay themselves with money from their trust accounts. You should get a bill every month itemizing the time that the lawyer has spent, listing any expenses that have been incurred on your case, and giving an accounting of how much the lawyer paid to the law office and how much of your retainer is left in the trust account. When the money gets low, the lawyer will probably ask you for more. Many lawyers now accept credit card payments.

Lawyers are subject to very strict ethical rules that control how they must deal with trust accounts, which contain money that isn't theirs. You are always entitled to know how much of your money is available to pay fees.

The Fee Agreement

The lawyer should give you a fee agreement before you write your first check for the retainer. It should spell out the terms of your relationship and cover, among other things, the following issues:

Hourly rate. The contract should state the lawyer's hourly fee and the rates of anyone else who might work on your case. You may, for example, be asked to pay for the time of a paralegal who works for the lawyer. The hourly rate for a paralegal or less-experienced lawyer in the firm should be significantly lower than that of the lawyer in charge. Some lawyers charge a higher hourly rate for time actually spent in the courtroom during trial.

Billing practices. Check how often the lawyer will bill you, how quickly you'll be expected to pay, and what level of detail you'll get on your bill about the work that's being done on your case. Ask to see a sample bill to see whether the details look adequate to you.

Expenses. In addition to the hourly charges, you may be charged for expenses such as copying, postage, or fax filing fees. Make sure those charges are spelled out in the agreement and that the agreement limits what you are required to pay for them. You might want to ask for a clause that says the lawyer will check with you before incurring expenses that exceed a certain amount, like $250.

Services of experts. The agreement may require you to pay the fees of other professionals hired to work on your case: an actuary, a custody evaluator, or a real estate appraiser, for example. Often, lawyers include a clause that says they can hire experts without your approval, and then bill you. You might want to ask for a limiting clause, stating that experts who will charge more than a certain amount must be cleared with you first.

Refund for unearned fee. Don't sign a fee agreement that says that your retainer is nonrefundable. If there is money in the trust account when your case is over, you should get it back. In fact, a nonrefundable retainer is likely to violate ethics rules in most states, so you might think twice about the lawyer, too.

Sample Attorney-Client Agreement

Attorney-Client Agreement

This agreement is made between Margaret Camaro, Attorney, and Steven Thorpe, Client. Attorney and Client agree that Attorney will provide legal services to Client according to the following terms.

1. **Engagement.** Client hereby employs and retains Attorney to represent the Client in connection with dissolution of marriage to Eleanor Hall-Thorpe.

   No other legal matters are covered by this Agreement. Specifically, the services to be rendered by Attorney do not include preparation of a Qualified Domestic Relations Order dividing retirement or other benefits. If such an order is needed, Attorney will refer Client to another attorney who specializes in preparation of QDROs. This agreement also does not cover appellate work, for which a new fee agreement will be required.

   Attorney will begin working on Client's case when Client has returned a signed copy of this Agreement to Attorney, along with the retainer described in Paragraph 7, below.

2. **Attorney's Obligations.** Attorney agrees to provide competent legal services in the promotion of Client's interests and the protection of Client's rights, to make every reasonable effort on Client's behalf, and to work toward achieving a favorable outcome. Attorney will keep Client informed of progress and respond promptly to inquiries. Attorney makes no promises or guarantees about the ultimate outcome or resolution of the case, but will offer informed opinions and advice about possible outcomes and legal conclusions.

3. **Client's Obligations.** Client agrees to provide all relevant information and documents that Attorney requests and will be forthcoming and truthful with Attorney at all times. Client will pay fees and reimburse costs expended in accordance with this agreement. Client will keep Attorney informed of Client's current contact information at all times.

4. **Information.** Client authorizes Attorney to gather whatever information is needed to effectively provide the services described above and to negotiate in Client's behalf pursuant to Client's instructions.

5. **Costs.** All expenses, including filing fees, service of process, depositions, appraisals, witness fees, court reporter fees, transcripts, telephone, postage, photocopying, messenger service, travel, and similar expenses, as well as all legal costs and fees charged by investigators, accountants, custody evaluators,

Sample Attorney-Client Agreement (continued)

and other experts consulted for their professional advice necessary to prepare and present Client's claims are to be advanced by and paid for by Client. No professionals will be consulted without Client's prior consent.

6. **Termination of Attorney-Client Relationship.** Attorney may withdraw at any time upon giving Client reasonable notice, if such withdrawal would not prejudice Client's case. Client may discharge Attorney at any time upon written notice to Attorney.

7. **Attorneys' Fees.** In consideration for services rendered and to be rendered by the Attorney on behalf of Client, Client agrees to pay any and all costs incurred, and an hourly rate for services of Attorney and Attorney's staff as listed below:

Attorney and other partners	$300/hr
Associates	$225/hr
Paralegals	$75/hr
Law clerks	$100/hr

Attorney will bill Client in increments of tenths of an hour and will submit billing to Client at least once per month. Bills are due when presented.

Client will pay an initial deposit of $10,000, which will be held in Attorney's trust account. Hourly charges will be charged against the deposit, and Client authorizes Attorney to transfer funds from the trust account to Attorney's business account as charges are incurred and billed. When the deposit is reduced to $2,500 or less, Attorney may request further deposits of no more than $5,000, which Client agrees to remit within ten days of request.

At the conclusion of the case, any unused balance will be refunded to Client.

If Client fails to pay fees or to replenish the trust account as described, Attorney may file a motion to withdraw from the case.

8. **Retention of File.** When Client's case is completed, Attorney will retain Client's file for at least five years. If Client does not retrieve the file after that, Attorney may destroy it without further notice to Client.

_____   _____
Date   Steven Thorpe, Client

_____   _____
Date   Margaret Camaro, Attorney at Law

Ending the agreement. The fee agreement should say that you can terminate the lawyer's services whenever you want to, and that the lawyer can also end the lawyer-client relationship, but not in a way that would affect you negatively. Sometimes the language used for this is that the lawyer can't withdraw at a time that would "prejudice" your interests.

It's guaranteed that these won't be the only provisions in the agreement. The sample agreement above has fairly typical provisions. Make sure you read over the contract your lawyer gives you very carefully, ask the lawyer about anything you don't understand, and have a trusted friend review it as well to catch anything that you didn't see.

What You Can Expect to Pay

The total cost of a divorce trial depends mainly on the length of the trial and your lawyer's hourly rate. Lawyer hours are, by far, the major expense in a trial.

From the lawyer's mouth ...

" In my most recent trials, one was basically three long hearings and the total cost was about $15,000, which is unusual—it's a rare case that costs less than $25,000. The last moveaway case I did cost my client $50,000, and the most expensive trial I ever did was a case with a lot of money at stake—my client paid me $120,000 by the time all was said and done."

—Divorce attorney

Here's an estimate of the costs of a two-day trial with the most basic expert testimony. Let's assume the lawyer charges $250 per hour— probably a fairly conservative estimate. Expert witnesses sometimes charge less for their out-of-court work but more for court testimony, so we'll use an average for each of the experts.

The Price of Fighting It Out			
Lawyer fees	**Cost**		
Initial meeting and information gathering	10 hours @ 250/hr	= $	2,500
Discovery	50 hours @ 250/hr	=	12,500
Trial preparation	100 hours @ 250/hr	=	25,000
Pretrial motions	30 hours @ 250/hr	=	7,500
Court time	15 hours @ 250/hr	=	3,750
Expert fees			
Custody expert	40 hours @ 250/hr	=	10,000
Actuary	15 hours @ 200/hr	=	3,000
Vocational expert	20 hours @ 200/hr	=	4,000
Court reporter fees		=	2,500
Total		$	70,750

This estimate doesn't take into account costs like copying or investigative fees. It also doesn't include any of your time spent in preparation and in trial, which will cause you to miss work (and stress you out more than you can probably imagine).

Some trials may be less expensive, but as you can see, even a one-day trial at a low hourly rate and with no expert witnesses involved will cost you tens of thousands of dollars. A more complex one will easily take you into the six-figure realm. And there's a chance you might end up paying your spouse's attorneys' fees as well as your own if you lose and the judge thinks you have the ability to pay. (See "Attorneys' Fees," in "After the Trial," below.)

Is Fault a Factor?

Some states still allow you to allege fault as the grounds for your divorce if you want to. There's a difference between alleging fault as the reason you're getting divorced, and alleging fault as a reason for the judge to divide property or award support in favor of one spouse. Unless you do want the judge to consider fault in dividing property and awarding support, or unless you don't want to wait out a long separation period required by your state before you can qualify for no-fault divorce, there's no reason to allege fault when you file your divorce papers. And even if you want the judge to consider your spouse's wrongdoing when deciding the issues, you don't have to allege fault as the reason for the divorce if you don't want to. Take your lawyer's advice on this, as it may depend on local practices.

Some states are purely no-fault states, meaning fault is entirely irrelevant to all aspects of the divorce. And some are mixed—you can't use fault as a basis for getting divorced, but judges can consider it in setting support or dividing property. In those states, however, the judge gets to decide how much weight to give the element of fault, and most don't use it much. Domestic violence is an exception to this—even in states where fault is otherwise irrelevant, judges may consider abuse as a factor.

Two charts, below, explain fault rules for every state. The first chart, "Grounds for Divorce," shows each state's rules about what you need to prove in order to file for divorce. The second, "Effect of Fault on Property Division and Support," summarizes each state's rules about when fault is relevant. If the entry says "maybe," it means that the state law is wishy-washy, listing fault as one among a number of factors, or simply saying that judges have discretion in what factors they consider. In most of those states, you can assume that although you'll be allowed to allege it, proving fault won't do much for you.

State	Fault	No-fault (other than separation)	Separation	Length of separation
Grounds for Divorce				
Alabama	✓	✓	✓	2 years
Alaska	✓	✓		
Arizona		✓		
Arkansas	✓		✓	18 months
California		✓		
Colorado		✓		
Connecticut	✓	✓	✓	18 months
Delaware	✓	✓	✓	6 months
District of Columbia			✓	6 months if both parties agree; otherwise 1 year
Florida		✓		
Georgia	✓	✓		
Hawaii		✓	✓	2 years
Idaho	✓	✓	✓	5 years
Illinois	✓	✓	✓	6 months if both parties agree, otherwise 2 years
Indiana	✓	✓		
Iowa		✓		
Kansas	✓	✓		
Kentucky		✓		
Louisiana	✓		✓	180 days
Maine	✓	✓		
Maryland	✓		✓	12 months
Massachusetts	✓	✓		
Michigan		✓		
Minnesota		✓		
Mississippi	✓	✓		
Missouri	✓	✓	✓	12 months if both parties agree; otherwise 2 years
Montana		✓	✓	180 days

Grounds for Divorce (continued)

State	Fault	No-fault (other than separation)	Separation	Length of separation
Nebraska		✓		
Nevada	✓[1]	✓	✓	1 year
New Hampshire	✓	✓		
New Jersey	✓	✓	✓	18 months (6 months if marriage is irretrievably broken
New Mexico	✓	✓		
New York	✓	✓	✓	1 year (must have a written separation agreement)
North Carolina	✓		✓	1 year
North Dakota	✓	✓		
Ohio	✓	✓[2]	✓	1 year
Oklahoma	✓	✓		
Oregon		✓		
Pennsylvania	✓	✓	✓	2 years
Rhode Island	✓	✓	✓	3 years
South Carolina	✓		✓	1 year
South Dakota	✓	✓		
Tennessee	✓	✓	✓	2 years
Texas	✓	✓	✓	3 years
Utah	✓	✓	✓	3 years
Vermont	✓		✓	6 months
Virginia	✓		✓	1 year[3]
Washington		✓		
West Virginia	✓	✓	✓	1 year
Wisconsin		✓	✓	12 months
Wyoming	✓[1]	✓		

[1] Divorce may be granted on the basis of "incurable insanity"; otherwise, divorce is no-fault.

[2] No-fault divorce will be denied if one party contests ground of incompatibility.

[3] May be reduced to six months if there are no minor children.

Effect of Fault on Property Division and Support

State	Fault Divorce?	Can fault reduce share of marital property?	Can fault reduce or prevent spousal support award?
Alabama	Yes	Yes	Yes
Alaska	Yes	No	No
Arizona	No	No	No
Arkansas	Yes	Yes	Yes
California	No	No	No [1]
Colorado	No	No	No
Connecticut	Yes	Yes	Yes
Delaware	Yes	No	No
Dist. of Col.	No	Yes	Yes
Florida	No	Yes	Yes
Georgia	Yes	Yes	Yes
Hawaii	No	No	No
Idaho	Yes	No	Yes
Illinois	Yes	No	No
Indiana	Yes	No	Yes
Iowa	No	No	No
Kansas	Yes	Maybe	Maybe
Kentucky	No	No	Yes
Louisiana	Yes	No	Yes
Maine	Yes	No [2]	No [2]
Maryland	Yes	Yes	Yes
Massachusetts	Yes	Yes	Yes
Michigan	No	Yes	Yes
Minnesota	No	No	No
Mississippi	Yes	Yes	Yes
Missouri	Yes	Yes	Yes
Montana	No	No	No

Effect of Fault on Property Division and Support (continued)

State	Fault Divorce?	Does fault reduce share of marital property?	Does fault reduce or prevent spousal support award?
Nebraska	No	No [2]	No [2]
Nevada	No	Yes	No
New Hampshire	Yes	Yes	Yes
New Jersey	Yes	No	Yes
New Mexico	Yes	No	No
New York	Yes	Yes	Yes
North Carolina	Yes	No	Yes
North Dakota	Yes	Yes	Yes
Ohio	Yes	Yes	Yes
Oklahoma	Yes	Yes	Yes (limited)
Oregon	No	No	No
Pennsylvania	Yes	No	Yes
Rhode Island	Yes	Yes	Yes
South Carolina	Yes	Yes	Yes
South Dakota	Yes	Yes	Yes
Tennessee	Yes	No	Yes
Texas	Yes	Yes	Yes
Utah	Yes	Yes	Yes
Vermont	Yes	Yes	No
Virginia	Yes	Yes	Yes
Washington	No	No	No
West Virginia	Yes	Yes	Yes
Wisconsin	No	No	No
Wyoming	No	Yes	Yes

[1] Court may consider convictions for domestic violence.

[2] Economic misconduct may be considered, whether or not it is related to fault in ending the marriage.

Getting Started

Once you've hired your lawyer, what's next? Depending on your situation, the lawyer may advise asking for an immediate court hearing to get temporary orders about support or visitation. There's more about that below. Either way, there will be a flurry of activity and a lot of work for you to do.

Getting Your Financial Information Together

To work effectively on your behalf, your lawyer needs all of the relevant financial data from your marriage—and you'll have to provide it. You may have already started the process of figuring out your income, assets, and obligations by filling out the worksheets in Chapter 2.

Your lawyer may also give you forms to fill out. You can transfer any information you've already put in your worksheets over to the lawyer's forms or onto the disclosure forms provided by the court, if your local court uses them. It may be tedious, but it can't be avoided, so don't procrastinate.

> **TIP**
>
> **Cooperate with your lawyer.** One of the best things that you can do for yourself is to be responsive when your lawyer asks you for information or asks you to do something. Every time your lawyer has to call and remind you to do something, send something, or call someone, the meter is running. Better to spend your time than your money.

Temporary Orders

From the moment you start your divorce, every time you have an opportunity to compromise that won't be damaging to you in the long run, do it! An early opportunity will come when you and your spouse try to negotiate temporary custody and support agreements that will be in place while the case is pending. If there's any chance you and your spouse can work out a temporary agreement about spousal or child support and sort out your parenting schedule, try to make that happen.

If you and your spouse can't figure it out and if your lawyer can't negotiate an agreement with your spouse's lawyer, then you'll end up going to court for a hearing. These short pretrial hearings are sometimes called "law and motion" or "short cause" hearings, and they are for the sole purpose of establishing temporary orders.

To have a law and motion hearing, your lawyer will have to schedule it, prepare the necessary court papers, respond to your spouse's papers, and appear in court to argue on your behalf. You can imagine how much that will cost.

Sometimes, however, the expense of getting temporary orders is necessary. The wheels of justice do not turn quickly, and it could be a year or more before your case goes to trial, especially if you live in a large urban area. If you're in dire need of financial support in the short run, you may well need a hearing. But if your lawyer says there's going to be a hearing right away, ask some questions. Find out what the judge is likely to order (how much child support, for example), consider what you might agree to right now, and ask your lawyer to try to work something out with your spouse's lawyer without going to court.

Whatever you agree to doesn't have to be what you want in the long run, but you can save yourself a lot of money if you compromise in the short run. Don't, however, agree to a parenting schedule that's drastically different from the permanent schedule you hope to get. Judges tend to like to stay with the status quo where children are involved, so make sure that whatever custody schedule you agree to is pretty close to what you'll want in the future.

CAUTION

Make sure it's clear that the agreements you're making are temporary. Make sure that whatever you agree to is put in writing, clearly stating that the agreement is temporary. You don't want to compromise your future position when you decide to take the high road and compromise now. This is particularly true in regard to your parenting schedule.

As your case proceeds, you may have a number of motion hearings, or you may have none. Motion hearings are less predictable than many elements of your case, because the judge has very little time to review your paperwork and make a decision about your request, which is only one of many on the court calendar. The judge spends a morning or an afternoon conducting lots of short hearings and making decisions about limited, specific issues.

If you can stay out of motion court, great. But if you can't, make sure you work with your lawyer to keep your requests clear, specific, and as limited as possible.

These hearings may resolve some of the issues that are in dispute, and they may also give you a clue as to what kind of permanent orders the judge will eventually issue. Some of the disputes that might come up include:

- who gets to stay in the family home
- how much alimony or child support will be paid
- whether either spouse may use or sell assets owned by both
- where the kids will stay and what the parenting schedule will be, and
- whether one spouse will be permitted to move away with the children.

Getting temporary orders in place can be a big relief if you've been worrying about money and your spouse has been unwilling to pay enough support. And if your kids' custody changeover times have turned into opportunities to argue about money or custody, having a temporary order can ease the tension.

Going to Court

You will usually need to accompany your lawyer to any hearings that are held in your case. If you've never been in court before, don't worry. Courtroom rules are pretty straightforward.

Especially in short hearings, and sometimes even at trial, your testimony will usually be given to the court in the form of a signed statement called a declaration or affidavit. You won't need to speak. But everything you do will make some kind of impression on the judge, and the judge is the only one deciding your case. The same judge might later preside over your trial, so your demeanor in the courtroom matters, whether you have a speaking part or not. Probably the most important thing to do is always present yourself as respectful, reasonable, and mature.

If you have a longer hearing or a trial, dressing and behaving appropriately are especially important because you will be spending quite a few hours, and possibly even a few days, in the judge's presence. Here are some tips for making your going-to-court experience a bit easier.

Dress appropriately. Dress in a way that shows respect for the judge and the other people in court. Don't wear shorts, T-shirts, or other extremely casual clothes, and don't show a lot of skin. If you typically wear jeans to work and you don't want to dress differently for court, just make sure that your jeans are clean and neat and that you're wearing a nice shirt, sweater, or sports jacket with them. When in doubt, go with the more conservative option—it will never work against you.

Be respectful. Don't disrupt court procedures, even if you think your spouse's lawyer is telling massive untruths about you. Don't snort or roll your eyes at the testimony of your spouse or the experts. (But do take clear notes for your lawyer about how to respond to testimony that's untrue or distorted.) Don't speak directly to the judge or the other lawyer unless they are speaking directly to you. (In that case, answer respectfully, and address the judge as "Your Honor.") Write your lawyer a note or whisper discreetly. Turn off your cell phone and pager all the time that you're in court.

Be on time. Get to court early so that you're not stressed out about having time to find parking, get through the metal detector, and find your courtroom. Give yourself enough time on your parking meter to wait as long as necessary for your case to be heard. (Especially with law and motion, lots of cases are scheduled for the same time and then taken one by one, so you may have to wait a while.)

Be prepared. Bring a pen and paper, so that you can take notes about what your spouse's lawyer says.

Gathering Information for Trial: Disclosures, Discovery, and Digging Up Dirt

The term "discovery" refers to the process by which each side asks the other for information before a trial. The discovery process is designed to promote fairness at trial by making sure the playing field is level and that neither side is surprised by information the other side withheld. Financial disclosures also promote settlement—the more information you have, the better able you are to be creative (and realistic) about settlement options and to figure out your bottom line.

Mandatory Disclosures

In many states, family courts require that you disclose a long list of financial information to your spouse. You are then required to sign and submit to the court a form saying that you have complied with the local rules for disclosures. You'll probably be required to provide:

- recent pay stubs and other income-related information
- tax information—your returns, if you've filed separately from your spouse, but also any information in your possession related to accounts that you own or control, such as the annual report of interest earned on stocks
- recent statements from brokerage accounts
- recent bank statements
- current information about your retirement plans
- current information about any insurance you own, such as life or long-term care insurance
- documentation of obligations, such as student loans, car loans, equity lines of credit, and mortgage statements
- recent credit card statements, and
- information about financial opportunities that have come up since your separation, arising out of assets that you and your spouse own jointly (for example, you own stock that increases greatly in value during your separation, and your broker advises that it's an optimal time to sell).

Again, as soon as your lawyer asks you for this material, gather it up as quickly as you can. There's no benefit in waiting or in withholding information. You may not have all of the information at hand or at home, which means you'll need to get some of it from various financial institutions. If you do this work rather than having the lawyer or paralegal do it, you'll save yourself some money. You should be able to make phone calls or send letters or emails asking for current balances, account histories, or whatever else you might need. You have the right to information for any account that has your name on it. However, for information about accounts that have only your spouse's name on them, your lawyer may need to make formal requests using forms called "subpoenas," which have the force of law behind them, in order to figure out whether you own some share of those assets.

Requesting Information

If you don't get enough information from your spouse through the basic disclosures required by the court, or if your local court doesn't impose such requirements, you can make formal requests for information.

Interrogatories. Interrogatories are written questions that you send to your spouse, who then has a specified time (usually 30 days) to respond with answers or object to the questions. You can ask about anything related to the division of assets and debts, such as asking your spouse to list all existing interests in bank and brokerage accounts, or to list the names of all limited partners in a business your spouse is involved in.

Requests for Production. You have the right to ask your spouse for written financial records—tax returns, bank statements, brokerage statements, retirement account statements, and anything else that will provide information that you need to engage in an informed negotiation. But you should know that in some states, all documents that either of you turns over will become part of the public court record of your divorce case. If your spouse owns a business, the business might have a strong interest in keeping some of the information confidential. If there's no reason for you to want the material publicized, and for most people there isn't, you might offer to agree to a protective order that would keep the information out of the court record or from being passed on to other people not connected with your divorce. (That's called catching flies with honey instead of with vinegar.)

Requests for Admissions. These are written yes-or-no questions, where you ask your spouse to admit or deny certain facts. They are not used often in divorce cases, but can be useful. For example, you might ask your spouse to admit that as of the date of separation, the value of a certain asset was *x* amount. Once your spouse admits facts, you can use the response to challenge any contradictory testimony that comes up at trial.

Depositions. You can ask your spouse to appear and answer questions under oath about anything related to the divorce. You can also ask other people who have information about your marital finances to appear for questioning. Depositions take place in a lawyer's office (usually the lawyer who has requested the deposition), not in court, but the person being questioned is under oath, and everything said is taken down by a court reporter just as in a courtroom.

Subpoenas. You can get information and documents from people—and institutions—who aren't directly involved in your divorce, like banks and credit card companies, using subpoenas.

Your lawyer will definitely want to take your spouse's deposition if you suspect that your spouse is hiding assets, or if your spouse took care of all the financial matters during your marriage and you don't know much about what's going on. You might also want to take your spouse's deposition if there are issues about whether certain property belongs to one of you separately or to both of you. For example, if your spouse claims you made a gift of an expensive piece of art work, and you are arguing that it's a jointly owned asset, you could use a deposition to ask your spouse to lay out all the facts that support the theory that the work was a gift and, thus, separately owned by your spouse.

Probably you and your spouse will both be called for depositions. But the most important depositions will be those of anyone you've hired—or anyone who's been appointed by the court—to evaluate your kids and make a recommendation about what custody arrangement would be in their best interests. Chapter 7 addresses contested custody cases.

Is Your Spouse Hiding Assets?

Unfortunately, it's not uncommon for people in a divorce to try to hide assets. They may fail to disclose bank accounts, claim that an asset is less valuable than it really is, or make deceptive payments to a straw person to hide the money's location. Some of the most common ways that spouses hide assets from each other are:

- fudging the books of a business to make it look less valuable than it is, or to show more accounts payable or payroll obligations than the business actually has
- underreporting income on tax returns and financial statements
- failing to identify or disclose retirement accounts
- making secret agreements with employers to defer bonuses or pay increases until after the divorce is final; or, for someone who owns a business, delaying profitable deals or contracts
- "repaying" fake debts to friends or relatives, thus appearing to reduce assets, and
- putting friends or family on the payroll at work when they are not actually working (this has the dual benefit of increasing the business's expenses and allowing the asset-hiding spouse to retrieve the money later from the cooperative coconspirator).

If you think your spouse might be hiding assets, it's probably well worth your while to hire a forensic accountant—a person who's trained to uncover financial shenanigans like this. Talk to your lawyer about it. There's more about forensic accountants in Chapters 9 and 16.

And don't try any funny business yourself. You don't want to end up like the man who transferred a parcel of land to his brother to keep it out of the marital estate, and then couldn't get it back from the brother even after filing suit.

Witness Lists

One of the things your lawyer will find out before trial is who your spouse's witnesses are going to be. Your lawyer may then ask you for whatever information you have about these people, including negative things that will help your lawyer try to discredit them. Some of these witnesses may be people you considered your friends at one time, so the idea of letting your lawyer attack them because you once saw them lose control and smack their kid may be pretty distasteful to you.

You are in the driver's seat on this. You'll have to listen to your conscience and your lawyer's advice—and if they conflict, you'll have to make some difficult decisions.

Evidence of Fault and Other Wrongdoing

If you live in one of the few states where proof of one spouse's adultery or other bad behavior works to the other's advantage in a dispute over property or support, your trial might include such evidence. (There's a list of these states in "Is Fault a Factor?" above.) And if you're in a contested custody case and you have strong suspicions about your spouse's parenting (for example, that your spouse leaves the kids with a caregiver most of the time, or neglects or abuses them), you need to gather evidence to document your concerns and support the position you're going to take in court.

Under no circumstances should you ever use your children to get information about your spouse. If you must look for evidence, talk to your lawyer about hiring a reputable private investigator who is licensed, bonded, insured, and experienced. Be clear with the investigator about what kind of information you want and how many hours you are willing to authorize. Don't be a do-it-yourself investigator—there are laws, which vary from state to state, about recording phone conversations or photographing people without their consent, and you don't want to run afoul of the law this way.

Settle, Settle, Settle!

As you prepare for trial, you will have a number of opportunities to settle. You might think that if you haven't settled yet, it's not going to happen now. Nothing could be further from the truth. Over 90% of court cases settle before trial begins. The closer it gets to trial, the more motivated you and your spouse should be to avoid spending the money and time that a trial demands and exposing yourself to the uncertainty it brings.

Even if you and your spouse can't stop fighting about property or support, put everything you have into avoiding a custody trial. There is nothing more damaging to your children's chances of recovering emotionally from the divorce. There's extensive information in Chapter 7 about custody evaluations and your kids' relationship with the court system if you are in a custody fight.

Chances to settle may present themselves in a couple of different ways.

Negotiating Along the Way: Written Settlement Offers

As you move toward your trial date, your spouse's lawyer may write to your lawyer with a settlement proposal. (Of course, you can also ask your lawyer to propose settlement terms as well.) If you've tried to negotiate before, the new proposal will probably take into account the sticking points in the earlier conversations, and either come at them differently or concede a point or two.

Always look over a settlement proposal carefully to see what is new, whether your spouse's priorities have shifted, and whether there's additional information that changes your perspective. Discuss every offer with your attorney, even if it seems certain you won't take it. Talking may generate new ideas for a counterproposal.

Your lawyer cannot accept or reject a settlement offer without your say-so. Make sure your lawyer knows that you want to be made aware of every settlement proposal that comes in, even if it looks like you won't take it. You are the boss, and if you decide that the new terms that your spouse is proposing are finally good enough for you, you have the right to settle the case even if your lawyer thinks you can get more at trial. Of course, you'll want to consider your lawyer's advice carefully, but in the end, it's always your call.

Last-Minute Negotiations: Settlement Conference

You'll probably have a mandatory settlement conference very shortly before your trial is set to begin. (The date is usually set at the pretrial conference discussed below.) The court will assign a mediator or settlement conference judge to try to help you settle. It usually won't be the same judge who is going to hear your trial, but another judge from the same court, or a mediator—probably a local lawyer experienced in family law, approved by the court. At the settlement conference, you and your spouse and both lawyers meet with the mediator or judge to discuss the current status of the case, what offers and counteroffers have been proposed, and where the settlement discussions have stalled out. The mediator or judge will help you try to bridge the gap and see whether the case can be resolved. This is a point at which many cases settle.

Even if your court-sponsored settlement conference comes and goes without a settlement, your lawyers can continue negotiating. There may be phone calls, more letters, and in some cases, another meeting with the judge or a mediator on the very day the trial is scheduled to begin.

Evaluating Settlement Offers

How do you evaluate a settlement offer? After all, you've already invested many thousands of dollars and immeasurable time and energy into getting ready for the trial. You'll have to look at the interplay between these key issues:

- How much better is this offer than previous ones?
- How close is the offer to what you want—and how many of the things that are most important to you are satisfied by it?
- How certain are you of your legal positions—in other words, how likely do you think it is that you will win everything you want? (Trials, as any lawyer will tell you, are unpredictable.) And how much better off would you be if you did win?
- How much will it cost you to go to trial?
- How relieved will you be to stop preparing for trial and get back to the rest of your life? (Imagine waking up the next morning with the settlement arranged and the divorce nearly finalized.)

Consider these questions and discuss them with your lawyer. And don't give short shrift to the last question—your emotional health and happiness are as important as anything else.

The Pretrial Conference

The last hearing before your trial will probably be a pretrial conference, at which the lawyers and parties (you and your spouse) appear and discuss with the judge all of the issues involved in planning the trial. (See below for more about what those issues are.)

Not all judges require a pretrial conference, but they are fairly common. Some judges like to have the pretrial conference well in advance of the trial, and some do it much closer to the actual date. The judge will almost always be the same judge who will hear your trial, so this is your opportunity to define the issues and state your positions.

At the pretrial conference the lawyers and the judge, with input from you and your spouse, choose a date for your trial. The lawyers estimate how long the trial will take, and the judge sets aside the time needed. Of course, the judge has heard the discussion of the issues, and may also have an opinion about how long the trial should take. As you might expect, the judge's opinion will be the one that prevails. The lawyers also submit lists of the witnesses they expect to call at trial.

The judge will tell the lawyers how they should prepare and present evidence—right down to details about whether exhibits should be labeled with numbers or letters—and what kind of written trial brief they should submit in advance of the trial. A trial brief explains what the legal issues are from each party's perspective before the trial. As the trial proceeds, the judge can use the trial brief to place the evidence in context.

The judge will want to hear a bit about the issues that are going to be disputed at the trial. Usually these fall into the major categories of child custody and visitation, property division, and support issues, but not every trial deals with all three. For example, sometimes you and your spouse may work out your parenting issues, but not your property division, or vice versa.

There's much more about each of the "big three" divorce issues in the chapters that follow.

Anatomy of a Divorce Trial

Very, very few court cases—divorces included—go all the way to trial. Even the most hotly contested cases generally settle without trial, sometimes only hours or days before.

As the trial date grows closer, preparation will heat up. Your lawyer will spend many hours preparing a trial brief, an opening statement, and evidence to present to the judge. And you will probably be required to spend many hours with your lawyer and other law firm staff, preparing your testimony and going over documents to make sure that your lawyer completely understands the financial and personal issues.

Most trials follow a similar pattern, one you've probably seen on television many times. But there's no jury; in almost every state, a divorce trial is held in front of one judge. (Texas and Georgia are the only states that allow jury trials in divorce cases if you request it.) That means that in most places, all of the decisions in your case will be made by one person: the judge.

A lot happens during a trial. But even with all the back and forth that's described below, a trial can be as short as one day. It also can be much longer. It depends on whether you were able to resolve any of your issues before going to trial or whether the judge has to decide every single thing, and on how complicated your legal and financial issues are. The more complicated they are, the more witnesses and evidence you'll need to present, and that means more trial time. Also, even a trial that doesn't take that many total hours can take a long time in terms of weeks or months. The courts are so busy, especially with the effects of recent budget cuts, that judges sometimes break up trials into one or two-hour pieces and schedule them over a period of time. This means not only that it will take longer to get things resolved, but also that you'll pay more, because your lawyer will bill you for more preparation and travel time.

TIP

Be prepared. If you're going to trial and you haven't been to the courthouse for any hearings, visit before your trial starts. You can even watch another divorce trial if you want to get a sense of how things go.

Opening Statements

Let's assume you are the petitioner—that is, the person who filed for divorce. Your lawyer will begin the trial by telling the judge what you are asking for, and how the evidence will show that you are entitled to it. Next, your spouse's lawyer will have a chance to do the same thing. The lawyers aren't supposed to argue in their opening statements, only to tell the judge what the evidence will show and what they want the judge to decide. In divorce trials, the opening statements tend to be brief— there's no jury to talk to, and the judge has heard most of your factual contentions before.

Petitioner's Case: Evidence and Testimony

You (the person seeking the divorce) will have the first chance to prove your case. Your lawyer will present evidence, both by submitting documents and by having witnesses testify. You will undoubtedly be one of the witnesses (see "Testifying in Court," below). There will probably be others, including financial advisers, actuaries, a forensic accountant if you used one, and any custody evaluators who evaluated you, your spouse, and your kids. You may also have hired expert witnesses to testify about things like the value of your home or business or the best interests of your children. And you may ask friends and family members to testify about things they've observed that are in dispute—for example, who has been the children's primary caretaker or the date that your spouse moved out of the house.

Listening Etiquette

Most of the time that you're in court for your trial—except when you're actually testifying—you will be sitting next to your lawyer and listening. It's important not to react to anything that your spouse or a witness is saying. If what's being said is wrong or untrue, write a note and give it to your lawyer. Don't whisper to your lawyer, and don't address the witness, the judge, your spouse, or your spouse's lawyer unless you have the judge's permission. Keeping your cool can only help your cause, and losing it can really hurt you.

The testimony that the people on your side give under your lawyer's questioning is called "direct" testimony. After the direct testimony, the other lawyer will get a chance to cross-examine each person. Your lawyer then gets to question each person again in what's called "redirect" examination. This can go on as long as the judge will let it, except that each time the lawyers can only ask follow-up questions on topics that have been covered before. They can't go over the same ground or bring in something new, so the process gets shorter with each round.

It's a recent trend for judges to ask for direct testimony in writing—in other words, your lawyer writes up all the things you would say in court in the form of a sworn declaration, and submits it to the judge and the other side. At trial, your spouse's lawyer can ask you questions about the declaration, as though you had testified out loud to what's in it. (Your spouse will submit testimony, too, and your lawyer can ask questions about it.) Some people don't think this is fair, because it doesn't give you your day in court in the same way that in-person testimony does, and some lawyers have challenged the practice. There are no legal rulings one way or the other yet, so if your judge wants testimony in writing, that's the way you'll have to go.

Testifying in Court

If you testify at your trial, your own lawyer will ask you questions, and then your spouse's lawyer may cross-examine you. The goal of the cross-examination is to show that some or all of what you have said is not true or complete. Be prepared to be challenged on every aspect of your testimony. Your lawyer will prepare you for the cross-examination before you go into court, probably by playing the role of the other lawyer and asking you the questions the other lawyer is likely to ask you. But expect the unexpected—there's no way that you or your lawyer can anticipate every question the lawyer might ask you.

It can be nerve-wracking to be on the stand answering questions. The most important thing is for you to stay calm. Take your time in answering the questions; think about the answers before you speak. Always tell the truth, even if it doesn't make you look good. If you don't understand a question, say so. The lawyer will repeat or rephrase it until you know what you are answering. Keep your answers as brief as you can while still being truthful and complete. And never be sarcastic or rude, no matter how awful your spouse's attorney is to you. Don't exaggerate or be overly dramatic in your testimony, though it's okay to show your feelings when you are testifying, within reason.

If you get nervous, try looking at a friendly face in the courtroom—in fact, if you know you'll be nervous, bring a friend to sit in the front row. Pour yourself a drink of water, which will almost always be handy when you are testifying. If you are shaking, put your hands in your lap and take a deep breath to try to calm down. And if you feel faint or sick, ask the judge for a short break to pull yourself together.

Respondent's Case: Evidence and Testimony

After your lawyer has questioned all your witnesses and submitted all your paper evidence, the other side gets its chance to do the same thing. They will probably have expert witnesses of their own, and your spouse will likely testify just as you did. The direct and cross-examination process will happen just as it did when your lawyer presented your case.

Petitioner's Rebuttal

Next, you will have a chance to respond by putting on witnesses who can contradict (rebut) what your spouse's witnesses said. Your witnesses can't repeat what they said earlier, but can respond only to what the other side's witnesses said.

Respondent's Surrebuttal

Sometimes, a judge gives the respondent the opportunity for what's called "surrebuttal," which is where the respondent's witnesses respond to what your witnesses said on rebuttal. Again, they can't bring up anything new or repeat themselves—they must limit their testimony to contradicting what was said in the rebuttal case.

Testimony From a Child's Lawyer or Custody Evaluator

In contested custody cases, it's very common for a judge to appoint a lawyer to represent the children or a custody evaluator to review your family situation. The lawyer might be called a "guardian ad litem," and the job of this lawyer—or custody evaluator—is to pay attention only to the interests of the children, ignoring financial matters. The guardian ad litem or custody evaluator will have the opportunity to offer testimony—usually after both sides have already presented their testimony. That's because the guardian ad litem's testimony doesn't belong to either spouse—the guardian is appointed by the court. There's more about custody evaluations in Chapter 7.

Closing Arguments

After all the testimony has been heard and all the evidence has been presented, the lawyers get a chance to sum up their cases to the judge. This time, they can argue all they want. Sometimes, the judge asks for closing arguments in writing—this is more likely if there are sticky legal issues that the judge wants time to consider, or if the trial has gone on for a long time.

The Judge's Ruling

You almost certainly will not find out who wins and who loses as soon as the trial is over (unless you live in Texas or Georgia and a jury heard your trial). Usually the judge will not rule from the bench immediately at the end of the trial, although you may have a sense of what's coming from comments the judge made during the trial. Instead, the judge takes the case "under submission" and takes some time to consider the evidence and review the legal arguments. The judge then prepares a written ruling.

After the Trial

If you have gone all the way through a trial and received a ruling, or came close to trial and then settled, you will probably be feeling about as wrung out as you ever remember—though you're probably relieved that the trial itself is over. But you are not quite done yet.

Attorneys' Fees

When a trial ends, there's always a winner and a loser. In most places, the winner has the right to ask the court to have the loser pay back attorneys' fees that the winner expended on the trial. The judge usually has the power to say yes or no to this request, and will base the decision on the winner's resources, the loser's ability to pay, and the relative merit of each side's position. For example, if the judge thinks you were completely unreasonable in your child support demands and thus wasted the court's time arguing about it—and the opposing lawyer's time preparing for the argument—you might have to pay your spouse's attorneys' fees.

The very real possibility that you'll be forced to pay your spouse's attorneys' fees should be another disincentive for going all the way through a trial.

The End Result, in Writing

After the trial or arbitration, or after you finally settle, the decisions that were made must be reduced to a document that's called a "judgment." The judgment is the court's way of officially saying what the outcome of your case was and making a record of what each spouse is required to do in the future.

The process starts with the judge, who submits a written ruling to both of the lawyers. Then the lawyer for the winning party prepares another document—an "order" or "decree" that sets out the rulings and orders that the judge made, as well as any other matters that you and your spouse agreed to outside of the trial. This document tells you what your rights and responsibilities are once the divorce is final. The other lawyer reviews it, and there may be some haggling, but eventually a final version is approved by the judge. It has the force of law. In other words, if you or your spouse ever violate its terms, the other person can ask the court to make the violator do what the judgment says.

The final divorce order that the judge issues is the document that declares that you are legally divorced.

Appeals

Even when it's all over, it may not be all over. If either you or your spouse believes that the judge in your trial made a serious mistake in applying the law, you have the right to appeal the judgment to a higher court. These are called courts of appeal or appellate courts. Because appeals are expensive and take a long time to resolve, they are quite uncommon. In many cases, there's simply no legal error on which to base an appeal. And sometimes, even though there was a mistake, it didn't affect the outcome of the trial, which is also required for a successful appeal.

If you do appeal, then while you wait for your case to slowly move through the appellate system you will have to comply with existing court orders about your kids, because custody and visitation can't be kept in limbo. But if the appeals court eventually finds that your trial judge was wrong, it can reverse all of the trial judge's orders—or you can be ordered to go through a whole new trial.

How do you decide whether to appeal? Your lawyer's advice will be critically important, because appeals are based on legal issues, your lawyer's specialty. However, apart from the validity of your claims, there's the issue of money. Many trial lawyers don't do appellate work, so you may be referred to an appellate specialist. Either way, your lawyer will put in anywhere from 100 to 200 hours or more preparing your appeal, at an hourly rate between $175 and $500. You'll also have to pay for a copy of the trial transcript, which can be pretty expensive (up to $500 or $600 per trial day) depending on how long your trial was.

In the end, it's a weighing process—how unfair do you think the decision was, how likely does your lawyer think it is that you would prevail, and how willing are you to invest the necessary resources in the appeal? If the balance on all those questions tips strongly toward going ahead, then do it. But if you're wavering on any of them, think long and hard before making a commitment. At the same time, watch the clock— you have only a limited amount of time, usually 30 to 45 days, to file a notice of appeal after your judgment becomes final.

Picking Up the Pieces

Chapter 15 is all about what to do after the divorce is final. It lists lots of practical things like transferring title to property and naming new beneficiaries on your insurance policies. And yes, you'll need to do all those things. But if you have kids, your next step is to try to move from the highly conflicted relationship you have been in for many months, and possibly years, into a relationship with your former spouse that lets you parent your children together in the most positive possible way.

Depending on whether you are the winner or the loser in the trial— and one of the major downsides of a trial is that there can be only one winner—you may be more or less inclined to try to bury the hatchet for the sake of your kids. But even if you didn't get everything you wanted in the trial, this is the time to shake it off, grow up, and start putting your kids first. The decisions have been made, and even if you think they are wrong, you have a responsibility to comply with whatever orders the court made. Make it easier on everyone by doing that with the best attitude and spirit of cooperation you can muster. ●

Custody Decisions and Parenting

There's no way around it: Divorce is hard on kids. For most parents, dealing with their children—breaking the news, trying to help them through the many transitions, figuring out custody and support arrangements, and worrying about their well-being—is the most challenging part of the divorce.

When it comes to figuring out how you're going to take care of your children during and after your divorce, you have two choices: Work it out with your spouse, or have the court decide for you based on the judge's interpretation of what's best for your kids.

No matter what you and your kids' other parent disagree about, you should be able to agree that it's good for your kids if you can minimize the conflict they witness and protect them from contact with the courts and from lots of uncertainty about the future. (And custody cases are notoriously unpredictable.)

So, the high road appears before you again. Take it, and do everything you can to reach an agreement with your spouse about parenting. It doesn't matter what kind of jerk your spouse is or how angry you are—as long as there's no verbal or physical abuse going on in your ex's house, you still need to support the other parent's relationship with the kids. (See Chapter 14 if you're concerned about abuse.) And try to do it graciously and with a positive, cooperative attitude. Accept the inescapable truth that hurting your kids' other parent hurts your kids. Sit down and negotiate a parenting plan that will work for everyone. It's guaranteed to pay off in the long run.

This chapter addresses the high road: agreeing with your spouse about custody and visitation. Chapter 7 deals with contested custody and other difficult parenting issues. Chapter 8 explains support.

TIP

It isn't just Dear Abby who says so. Research has shown that basic parenting skills like effective listening, consistent routines for kids, clear discipline that both parents participate in, and especially, minimal exposure to parental conflict can significantly help children's mental health after a divorce.

Physical and Legal Custody

The first thing you need to know about custody is that there are two kinds: physical and legal.

Having *legal custody* of your children means that you have the right to make decisions about their welfare—things like where they go to school, what religious education they receive, whether they need academic tutoring or psychological counseling, and when they go to the doctor.

Courts prefer that after a divorce, both parents continue to participate in making these decisions just as they did when they were married—in other words, both parents share legal custody. This is called joint legal custody. But a judge may give one parent sole legal custody if:

- There is so much hostility that parents simply can't communicate at all, even about important decisions affecting their children.
- One parent lives a great distance away.
- One parent is abusive or neglectful.
- One parent simply isn't involved in the child's day-to-day life and doesn't spend time with the child.

Finally, a few judges order joint legal custody, but then designate one parent as the tiebreaker in the event the parents can't agree.

Physical custody refers to where the children live on a regular basis. Courts generally prefer that parents have joint physical custody so that children have regular contact with both parents. Joint physical custody doesn't always mean an exact 50-50 time split. But if one parent has the kids most of the time, that parent is usually granted sole physical custody; the other parent gets the right to regular parenting time, also called visitation.

TIP

Check your state's default visitation schedule. Some states have standard time-sharing plans that courts use unless spouses agree to a different plan. You can use these as a starting point for your discussions of time-sharing and other issues. You can generally find standard orders on the court-related websites listed in Chapter 16.

Courts make decisions about legal and physical custody separately. For example, it's not unusual for parents to have joint legal custody, but for one parent to have sole physical custody and the other to have regular visitation. Legal custody, remember, just refers to making decisions about your child's life, and you can make those jointly, no matter where your child lives.

How custody is characterized now can affect you later. For example, in California and some other states, a parent with physical custody has a presumed right to move away with the kids; to keep the kids nearby, the noncustodial parent must go to court and show that the move would be harmful to the kids. So if your spouse's attorney tries to tell you that it doesn't matter whether you let the other parent have sole physical custody even though you spend significant time with the kids, don't buy it. Check with a lawyer about whether the decision could come back to haunt you later.

The High Road: Agreeing With Your Spouse on a Parenting Plan

Many spouses disagree to some extent about how they will share time with their children. But you don't have to be on good terms or in complete agreement about everything in order to negotiate an effective parenting plan. You just need to be willing to put your children's needs first.

If It's Tuesday, This Must Be Mom's House: Typical Custody Arrangements

Divorced parents share custody in a wide variety of ways. Especially as many fathers are more actively involved in parenting than were the dads of previous generations, parents are coming up with new and different time-sharing agreements.

What will it really be like to continue parenting with your ex when you don't live together anymore? You can no longer use the fly-by-the-seat-of-your-pants method that might have worked when you all lived together, to determine who took care of what on any given day. Instead, you'll need an agreed-upon plan about sharing time with your kids, and about what your responsibilities are now.

> ## Giving Your Kids a Say
>
> Your kids may have strong opinions about where they want to live and how much they want to visit the noncustodial parent. Very young children obviously won't have much say about custody and visitation, but older kids have their own activities, commitments, and attachments, which they deserve to have considered. Generally, they'll want to be where their friends are and will resent a schedule that interferes with their activities. If you and your spouse don't end up living near each other, you'll have to figure out how flexible you'll be when teens don't like the plan you've come up with.
>
> If you talk to your kids about custody or visitation, make sure you don't pressure them. Just listen to what they have to say and tell them you'll take their views into account. Never tell them that you'll be sad or lonely if they want to spend time with your ex or live in the other parent's home instead of yours.

Sole Custody and Visitation

A very common arrangement is for one parent to stay in the family home with the kids. The children spend most of their time there and see the other parent at regularly set times. In legal terms, one is the custodial parent and the other the noncustodial parent who has visitation rights. Other terms frequently used are "residential" and "nonresidential."

One fairly standard plan is the "Wednesday night dinner and every other weekend" arrangement. In other words, one parent has sole physical custody, and the other parent has visitation rights for one dinner a week and every other weekend.

Joint Custody

Some parents share physical custody 50-50 or something fairly close. But to make this work it's crucial for the parents to live near each other; otherwise kids can't move easily back and forth or continue with their regular activities. Also, carefully consider the frequency of changeovers as you develop your parenting plan. Having changeovers too frequently every week can cause stress for both children and parents, especially in the early days after you separate.

If your kids seem to be experiencing wear and tear from the transitions, or if you're really having a hard time being in the same place as your spouse, try not to make a plan that calls for changeovers every day or two days. Instead, opt for a weekly visitation schedule, or schedule the changeovers to occur after school, so that one parent drops the kids off and the other picks them up. That way you won't have to be in the same place at the same time, and the kids won't have to worry about that either.

On the other hand, if you get along okay and the changeovers aren't too stressful, it can be good for kids to feel that they really have two homes. (See tips on making this work in "If You Share Physical Custody," below.)

One schedule that is particularly popular these days is the so-called 2-2-3 plan. The child is with Parent 1 on Monday and Tuesday, Parent 2 on Wednesday and Thursday, and alternates Friday and weekends. This gives each parent a five-day/four-night stretch every other week and means that both parents are with the child on both weekdays and weekends. Option 6 in the "Sample Parenting Plans" section, below, encompasses a 2-2-3 plan.

Bird-Nesting

An uncommon but very child-centered custody arrangement is called bird-nesting. The kids stay in the family home and the parents take turns living there with them, usually on an equal basis. This can be hard on the parents, and also on the pocketbook—unless the parents are willing to alternate time in just one living space away from the family home, each parent needs a separate place to live when they're not with the kids. And parents say it's important to have ground rules about leaving the house tidy for the other parent, and not bringing dates to the shared house. But some parents would rather inconvenience themselves than cause the kids the stress of the back-and-forth lifestyle.

> **Transitions are hard on the kids ...**
>
> "I really wish we could have afforded to do a bird-nesting thing," says one divorced mom years later. "Even though my husband and I lived only about eight blocks apart, my daughter packed up every last thing she owned every time she changed houses—clothes, guitar, books, everything. She was really stressed out by all the back and forth. We thought about leaving the kids in the house and switching in and out ourselves but it was just too expensive, and also I didn't want to be around the place where things had gone so wrong in my marriage. So we managed, but I regret the anxiety it caused the kids."
>
> **—Divorced mom of two**

Sample Parenting Plans

When you're just beginning to figure out what life's going to look like once you separate, it can be hard to imagine what kind of time-sharing arrangement would be best for your family. There are lots of ways to work on this. You can:

- sit down together with your spouse and discuss what you each think your kids need
- ask a mediator, therapist, or child custody evaluator to help you make decisions
- use one of the websites or other resources described below
- use some combination of the above.

It can also be helpful to see some examples of what other families have done. Here are some sample parenting plans developed by Joan B. Kelly, Ph.D., a noted expert in the field of child custody. Each option shows the time-share, the number of nights per 28-day period that the child spends with the nonresidential (noncustodial) parent, and some of the factors that affect whether the particular arrangement being described is a good one for your family.

Option 1: Four Overnights

Every other weekend: Friday afternoon to Sunday evening

Factors to consider:
- 12 days separation from nonresidential parent is too long for many children
- Nonresidential parent's relationship with child is diminished; minimal involvement in school, homework, special projects
- Little time off for residential parent
- Can benefit children when nonresidential parent is very angry or rigid
- Can add a midweek evening visit to reduce separation time, but that creates more transitions and can be rushed or too hectic.

Option 2: Six Overnights

Every other extended weekend: Friday afternoon to Monday morning

Factors to consider:
- Nonresidential parent connects with school experience
- Dropoff and pickup at school or day care means reduced opportunity for conflict at transition
- Three-night period means fewer transitions for child
- Won't work if nonresidential parent lives too far away to drop off child at school or day care.

Option 3: Eight Overnights

Every other weekend and weekly midweek overnight: Friday afternoon to Sunday evening and every Wednesday afternoon to Thursday morning

Factors to consider:
- No separation from either parent greater than six days
- Nonresidential parent engaged with school and homework
- Residential parent gets an evening off during the week
- No transition on Wednesday evening after visitation.

Option 4: Ten Overnights

Every other extended weekend (Friday afternoon to Monday morning) and every Wednesday afternoon to Thursday morning

> Factors to consider:
> - Same as in Option 3, plus nonresidential parent more engaged in school and homework
> - No separation from either parent greater than seven days.

Option 5: Twelve Overnights

Parent A: Sunday to Thursday; Parent B: Thursday to Sunday

> Factors to consider:
> - Only one transition per week
> - Parent A has mostly school time; Parent B mostly weekend time, so there's an imbalance in activities they're each involved in.

Option 6: Fourteen Overnights

Split time between parents and alternate schedule each week as follows:
Parent A/Week One: Sunday evening to Wednesday morning
Parent B/Week One: Wednesday afternoon to Sunday evening
Parent A/Week Two: Saturday evening to Wednesday morning
Parent B/Week Two: Wednesday morning to Saturday evening

> Factors to Consider:
> - Both parents have weekday and weekend time
> - Only one face-to-face transition per week
> - No separation from either parent longer than four days
> - Completely equal time-share.

Option 7: Fourteen Overnights

Split midweeks and every other weekend:
Parent A: Monday evening to Wednesday evening each week, and every other weekend
Parent B: Wednesday evening to Friday morning each week, and every other weekend

Factors to consider:
- All transitions occur at school or day care
- No separation from either parent greater than five days
- Completely equal time-share
- Both parents have weekday and weekend time
- Can be a challenging schedule for children with physical or learning disabilities or difficult temperaments

These are merely some examples of possible schedules. You and your spouse can use them to discuss what is appropriate for your kids—and not all of these plans will be appropriate for all children (for example, some kids do better with transitions than others, and kids with learning disabilities or other school-related issues might not do well with transitions in the middle of the week).

For additional examples, as well as tools that can help you sketch out your own possible parenting plans, check out these websites:
- www.afccnet.org: the website of the Association of Family and Conciliation Courts has lots of resources for parents. Click the link for "Resource Center" and then "Resources for Parents."
- http://courts.alaska.gov/forms/dr-475.pdf. This link takes you to the Alaska state court Model Parenting Agreement.
- If you're interested in research on child development and divorce, Dr. Kelly also has some academic articles that you can review. "Children's Living Arrangements Following Separation and Divorce: Insights from Empirical and Clinical Research" was published in *Family Process* journal, Volume 46, pages 35–52, in 2007, and "Developing Beneficial Parenting Plan Models for Children Following Separation and Divorce" was in *Journal of American Academy of Matrimonial Lawyers*, Volume 19, in 2005.

Splitting Up the Kids

Although it's not common, some parents do opt to separate their kids, each taking primary custody of one or more children. Separating siblings during a stressful time like a divorce isn't generally a great idea, but there may be situations where it makes sense—for example, if there's an enormous age gap between the kids and they don't have much of a relationship, if one kid has drug or behavioral problems that you think you could deal with better in isolation from siblings, or if one child is simply having problems with one parent and both could use a break.

If you're considering a split custody arrangement, it's probably a good idea to talk to a custody evaluator or parenting specialist who has experience dealing with children of divorce, and have that person evaluate your family's situation and give an opinion on how the kids will handle it. A custody evaluator is a therapist with special training in helping children of divorce by assessing the family situation and offering suggestions (or, in a contested situation, recommendations to the court) about the best parenting arrangement. See "Your Kids and the Court Process" in Chapter 7, to learn where to locate a custody evaluator.

How to Negotiate a Parenting Agreement

Divorced parents need a parenting plan—a document that addresses various aspects of your kids' lives and sets out your agreements about how you'll deal with them.

There are different ways to come up with this kind of parenting agreement.

Face-to-face discussions. Logistically, the easiest way to make these decisions is to sit down with your spouse, make a list of the issues, and discuss them all as rational adults who both have your kids' best interests as your first priority. Your emotions, of course, may complicate this pretty scene considerably. Some parents are able to set aside feelings about their separation long enough to work out a parenting agreement, but for others, a little bit of help can go a long way.

Help from a friend or family member. You can ask for that help from a friend or family member, if you think there's someone on whom you both can agree and who has the temperament to help the two of you work toward an agreement. Make sure it's someone you both trust to stick with the process, to be neutral about what you decide, and to keep your confidences. It's a rare friend who has the ability to act as an amateur mediator—but there are other ways your friends can help you, such as being a sounding board to vet ideas and proposals and give you an honest reality check.

Help from a mediator or custody evaluator. Mediation is a great way to work out your parenting plan. A mediator is trained to work with difficult issues and reach practical solutions that will work for both of you. (There's a lot more about mediation in Chapter 4.) If you're having trouble agreeing on a parenting plan, you might want to consider hiring a mediator to help you with just this issue, even if you and your spouse are able to work out all of the other questions that need to be decided in your divorce.

Identifying the Issues

You may be surprised at the level of detail in a parenting agreement. There's a lot more to deal with than just the amount of time the kids will spend with each parent—probably including some issues that you haven't thought about yet. But the more you can anticipate possibilities and deal with them in advance, the less conflict you will have in the heat of the moment. Here's a list of issues you'll need to cover in your parenting agreement. There may be others, too—the specifics will, naturally, depend on your family situation.

Basic time-sharing
- Where the kids will stay
- How the kids will get from one place to another
- Who, besides you and your spouse, is allowed to pick the kids up and transport them

Contact outside of visitation
- Schedule for the kids to be in touch with the parent they're not staying with, and how they'll be in touch (phone, text, videochat)
- Agreement about using email for contact
- Whether the kids are old enough for cell phones, or whether the residential parent will be responsible for making the contact happen

Family birthdays

- Where the kids will spend their birthdays
- Who is responsible for the birthday party, and whether it's okay to have two parties
- Whether you'll make special arrangements for your birthday or your spouse's, as well as the kids' birthdays

Holidays

- Alternating holidays each year or splitting the day between parents every year to share equally
- Definition of a holiday (when the kids don't have school for Presidents' Day, for example, is the person who's responsible for them on Mondays still on duty, or is that Monday treated differently?)
- Special holidays for one parent, like Mother's or Father's Day
- Sharing time during long school vacations, like spring and winter breaks

Religion

- If each household has a different religion, whether there's a middle ground, or whether the kids will practice the religion of each household when they're there (this may not be an issue if you've agreed on your kids' religious training so far, but if you and your spouse don't see eye to eye on religion, it may take some serious negotiation)

School

- Where the kids will go to school (if you want them to go to private school and your spouse is willing but can't afford it, will you put your money where your mouth is?)
- College planning
- Staying united on making sure your kids stay motivated and succeed in school

Activities

- How you'll decide on activities, especially if you disagree about the relative importance of such things as sports and music lessons
- Whether there's some limit on how many activities the kids can be involved in

Going out

- Agreeing on whether your kids are old enough to be going out with groups of friends or dating, and what the ground rules are (while writing it in the agreement may not be necessary, make sure you discuss it and see whether you can agree on what's appropriate)

Privileges and discipline

- Whether TV and computer time is to be limited in both homes
- Nutrition and junk food consumption
- What they're allowed to see at the movies
- Whether teens can go out with their older friends who are already driving
- Appropriate consequences for breaking rules or failing to do chores (remember, kids engage in divide-and-conquer strategies whenever possible, so try to come to some agreement if you can)

Medical care and insurance

- Who the kids see for medical and dental appointments
- Whether you're required to notify the other parent every time you get medical attention for the kids, even if it's routine
- How quickly you must notify the other parent in an emergency
- Whose policy will cover the kids, and who will pay for it if it's not included as a job benefit
- How uninsured expenses will be divided
- What you'll do if the kids need mental health care.

RESOURCE

For a comprehensive list of issues and step-by-step instructions for making a comprehensive parenting plan, see *Building a Parenting Agreement That Works*, by Mimi Lyster Zemmelman (Nolo). For more about custody generally, see *Nolo's Essential Guide to Child Custody and Support* by Emily Doskow (Nolo). Also, websites listed in Chapter 16 provide or direct you to sample parenting plans. A couple of excellent ones are Arizona's "Planning for Parenting Time," available online at http://supreme.state.az.us/nav2/parentingplansworkgroup/documents/PPWguidelines.pdf, and Alaska's "Model Parenting Agreement" at http://courts.alaska.gov/forms/dr-475.pdf.

> **Remember who's affected by your divorce ...**
>
> "We are both older, and we agreed on the divorce so neither of us was being dumped and we aren't wallowing in our hurt and desires. We both know that the really vulnerable person in this equation is our son. We have really striven to make sure that we don't lose sight of that. And I do think that most divorcing people do lose sight of who's the weakest."
>
> **—Divorced mom of eight-year-old**

Helping Your Kids Cope With Divorce

Although there is a lively debate in psychological circles about just exactly how much long-term impact divorce has on children, there is little question that it creates enormous changes in their lives, especially during the separation process. From your perspective, you have a single focus: protecting your kids as much as possible.

There's also no disagreement about the fact that parents are the most important people in a child's life, or that a highly conflicted divorce is much, much harder on kids than one that minimizes their exposure to parental conflict. In case you haven't yet gotten the message, here it is again: Do not bring your kids into your conflicts with your spouse. Don't fight with your spouse in front of the kids or say negative things about your spouse to the kids or within their hearing. You may privately think that your spouse has turned into a toxic waste product, but your kids shouldn't have to take sides. No matter how angry you are, leave your children out of it.

> **"I wish I wasn't there."**
>
> A nine-year-old child of divorced parents is clear that witnessing his parents' fights is the worst part of having divorced parents. "When they fight about me, I wish I wasn't even there anymore. I wish they would just learn to work it out and I wouldn't have to listen anymore."

Telling Your Kids About the Divorce

The challenges of parenting during divorce begin when it's time to tell your children that you and your spouse are divorcing. Start by making a plan, and don't wait—kids have strong antennae, and you'll be doing them a favor by telling them what's going on. Try to have the conversation at a time when it's normal for you to be with your kids— don't interrupt or cancel their usual activities.

It's best for you and your spouse to talk to the kids together—this can reassure them that you both love them and will always be their parents, even though you won't be living together anymore. And it's best to do it before making any major changes, like having one parent move out. It's important to reassure them that the divorce isn't their fault, and that your decision has nothing to do with them or their behavior. While you shouldn't overshare, if you can give them a reason for the divorce, all the better—even if it's just that "We aren't happy living together anymore." An amazing number of kids place blame on themselves, perceiving the facts in topsy-turvy ways you'd never imagine. Having a sense that there was a reason other than their behavior can help. Make sure they also understand you thought about it for a long time before making a decision.

If something like infidelity or substance abuse is a factor in your divorce and your kids are asking why the breakup is happening, you may need to offer an answer that is true, but vague: "Some of the reasons are private, but the main reason is that we are fighting so much that we are not happy living together anymore." The adult concerns that are probably driving your decision to divorce are not actually what your children are concerned about. They are much more worried about where they will sleep at night and who will tuck them in—or if they're older, whether they'll have to switch schools.

TIP

Make a plan. Before sitting down to talk with your kids, decide on what you are going to say and how. If you and your spouse will be together, get on the same page before sitting down with your children—and don't argue with each other while you're talking with them! The last thing you want is to disagree in front of the kids about what is going to happen in terms of custody and living situations. If you and your spouse are going to be talking to the kids separately, make a plan of your own so that you don't stumble or feel confused—and you and your spouse should still try to get together about what the kids are going to be told so that you don't contradict each other.

If your kids are close in age, you can talk to them at the same time, but if they are further apart and in very different developmental stages, you might need to have more than one conversation. If that's the case, at least make sure the conversations happen close together in time, so the kids have the same information at the same time.

When you do talk, try to stay as calm as you can—this will help them understand that even though it's hard and painful, you are making a decision you can live with. (And it's upsetting for kids, especially young ones, to see their parents cry or be very obviously agitated or out of control.)

Different kids, of course, will react differently. Some will cry, while others will go quiet. Watch for signs of upset, and make yourself available to talk to them as they absorb the news and start to adjust. Let them know that they can say anything to you and that it's okay for them to express their anger, disappointment, and sadness.

Most kids want to know practical things: who will pick them up at school, where will the dog live, when is the move happening, what should they tell their friends. Be prepared with the answers to these questions; it will be reassuring to your children.

TIP

It's a good idea to let the people who'll be around your kids know about the divorce—their teachers, caregivers, and even their friends' parents. That way, if they notice behavioral changes signaling that your child is having trouble coping, they'll understand why and will know they should alert you to what's going on.

Reassure the kids that they will still see the parent who's moving out or who will be the noncustodial parent. As soon as that parent has a new place, make sure the kids get to see it, and make sure they have a current phone number and email address right away. If you're the parent moving out, stay in close touch with your kids by phone and email right after the separation—and if you're the custodial parent, support and encourage this contact no matter how hard it might feel.

Keep repeating to your kids the important messages that:

- The divorce is not their fault.
- They will always have both parents, and they have your permission and encouragement to continue to love their other parent.
- Their lives will return to being more predictable and routine after the initial transition is weathered.
- You will tell them the truth about what's going on and listen to their feelings.
- You will always love them and so will their other parent.

RESOURCES

"Split: A Film for Kids of Divorce (and their Parents)" features children's perspectives on divorce. No adults or experts show up in this powerful video. Find it at www.splitfilm.org.

Speaking of Divorce: How to Talk With Your Kids and Help Them Cope, by Roberta Beyer and Kent Winchester (Free Spirit Publishing), has lots of concrete suggestions for how to have all the different conversations you'll need to have with your children as the divorce progresses.

Mom's House, Dad's House: Making Two Homes for Your Child, Revised Edition, by Isolina Ricci, Ph.D. (Simon and Schuster). This book is a perennial bestseller for a reason: its straightforward approach to coping with separating your households and the impact on your kids.

Helping Your Kids Cope with Divorce the Sandcastles Way, by M. Gary Neuman, L.M.H.C., with Patricia Romanowski (Random House). The "sandcastles" method of working with children of divorce has been praised by professionals and parents.

The Good Divorce: Keeping Your Family Together When Your Marriage Comes Apart, by Constance Ahrons, Ph.D. (HarperCollins). While a "good divorce" might seem like an oxymoron, this book is based on the premise that even after divorce, you are still a family—just one with a different structure. It's focused on working through the transition in the most positive way possible.

Being a Great Divorced Father: Real-Life Advice From a Dad Who's Been There, by Paul Mandelstein (Nolo), helps fathers deal with the unique parenting challenges of divorce.

Kids and Emotions

Just as you are riding an emotional roller-coaster, your children are dealing with feelings they may never have experienced before. You have an opportunity to affect their future in a positive way by how you deal with their feelings during this vulnerable and difficult time.

No matter how old your kids are, talking with them and making yourself available to listen to what they have to say is probably the single most important thing you can do. Don't force them, but do ask them regularly how they are doing and then make time and space to listen. If you have more than one child, make sure you spend time alone with each one in a way that encourages them to talk to you. Don't judge anything they say—listen carefully and with curiosity, and respond gently and without anger, no matter how difficult it is to hear what they are saying. Keep your body language neutral and open (that means don't cross your arms or legs), and make eye contact.

Most kids go through a hard time when their parents first separate, especially if they have to move. If you do move, it's important to give your kids as much input as possible into making the new house a home, so that they can feel that they belong there.

Children will act out differently depending on their ages and their unique personalities. While some acting-out behavior is to be expected—and of course, some of these behaviors come with the territory at certain ages—you should also expect to see improvement over time. But when you see a combination of behaviors or things are looking really extreme or are disrupting your family life, it's probably time to intervene.

Settling in ...

A divorced mom reports that "the therapist told us that children can deal with divorce, but what they can't deal with is disappearance [of their parents and their life as they know it]. She said that the more our son could be empowered, the better, and that we should let him make as many decisions as possible about his room in the new place. When we first told him [about the divorce], he cried, but then we immediately took him over to see the other house and then he started running back to our house to bring stuff over." And just as you will adjust to the new living situation, so will they. Children are quite resilient, and the less conflicted your divorce is, the better they will do. No matter what, though, you're bound to see some reactions from your kids.

For younger kids, you might seek outside help if you see extremes in the following areas:

- regression in learned skills, either physical or cognitive
- regression in toilet training
- change in sleeping habits, night terrors, or desire to sleep with you
- change in eating habits
- physical complaints or frequent illness, or
- tantrums, resistance to discipline, or difficult interactions with peers.

With school-age and teenage kids, pay attention to:

- rebellion against discipline, chores, or family interactions
- secrecy
- problems with schoolwork or peer relationships at school
- change in eating habits
- change in sleeping habits, or
- physical complaints of headaches, stomachaches, or other ailments.

If you are concerned, your first step should be to check in with your spouse and find out whether the same behavior is going on when your child is with the other parent. Your spouse might have some interesting observations. Armed with complete information, you can next try contacting your child's teacher or school counselor. They may have some insight if they are familiar with your child—or just have general knowledge about helping kids through divorce—and they might be able to give you a referral to a child psychologist if you think you want advice or counseling for your child.

Kids and New Relationships

If you are already involved in a new relationship when you are still dealing with the nitty-gritty of your divorce, you are coping with some complicated issues. Kids often have a hard time with parents having a new love interest after a divorce, and you'll need to learn to juggle the responsibilities of being a single parent with the pleasures and perils of a new relationship. Don't rush into anything, and be especially careful about bringing a new partner into your home to meet your kids until you're sure the relationship is serious. (There's more about new relationships and blended families in Chapter 15.)

> **TIP**
>
> **Don't ask your new partner to pick up the kids.** If you are in a new relationship, try to keep your new partner away from changeover times for a while. A spouse who encounters your new love every time the kids are dropped off or picked up (or who finds out that the new partner is picking up the kids from school) is bound to feel anxious at the very least. There's more about dealing sensitively with new relationships in later chapters, but for now, the signs on the high road point to restraint in this area.

> **RESOURCE**
>
> **Give your kids something to think about.** There are lots of books for kids about divorce. Check your local library or bookstore for age-appropriate books. A few good ones for each age group:
>
> *Two Homes*, by Claire Masurel (Candlewick Press), is a picture book for very young children about going back and forth between Mom and Dad's houses.

Also for the very young set, *Standing on My Own Two Feet*, by Tamara Schmitz (Price Stern Sloan).

At Daddy's On Saturdays, by Linda Walvoord Girard (Albert Whitman & Co.), is for young grade school children and has text and pictures about a young girl learning to adjust to seeing her father on weekends.

Dinosaurs Divorce: A Guide for Changing Families, by Laurene Krasny Brown and Marc Brown (Little, Brown & Co.), is an extremely popular book for good reason—it uses humorous drawings and simple, but straightforward, text to deal with the really difficult issues of divorce, including having two homes, birthdays and holidays, stepparents you don't like, and what to do when your parents badmouth each other.

How I Survived My Parents' Big Scary Divorce, by Audrey Lavin (BookSurge), is another title for the four-to-eight-year-old set, about a feisty young girl coming to terms with her parents' divorce.

Kids' Divorce Workbook: A Practical Guide that Helps Kids Understand Divorce Happens to the Nicest Kids, by Michael S. Prokop (Alegra House), offers space for kids to write and draw about their feelings, alongside the words and drawings of other children dealing with divorce. An excellent resource for kids who might be more comfortable with writing or drawing.

Help Hope & Happiness, by Libby Rees (Script Publishing), is written by a ten-year-old and contains her advice for kids on coping with divorce; the book is only available from its UK publisher at www.shop.scriptpublishing.co.uk or www.amazon.co.uk.

What in the World Do You Do When Your Parents Divorce? A Survival Guide for Kids, by Roberta Beyer and Kent Winchester (Free Spirit Publishing), is aimed at kids seven to 12 years old, and explains divorce, new living situations, and dealing with difficult feelings in ways that should resonate with the preteen set.

The Divorce Helpbook for Teens, by Cynthia MacGregor (Impact Publishers), is a thorough, plain-language book that does not condescend as it offers guidance on navigating the challenges of divorce.

Making Shared Parenting Work

The challenges of shared parenting may be the greatest ones you face as part of your divorce, because they involve the people you most want to protect from suffering, and because the challenges don't end when the divorce is final. You will continue to have a relationship with the kids' other parent for many years to come, probably for the rest of your life. In fact, that is a result devoutly to be hoped for, because it would mean that you and your spouse were able to cooperate enough to share in your kids' lives even as they become adults. But that's the hoped-for future. In the here and now, you need to work out shared parenting, and you need to do it with the focus on what is best for your kids.

Staying close ...

A mom whose ex rented a place a block away so that their son could easily walk back and forth says that the proximity is sometimes difficult for the adults, but seems to work for their son. "I think the hardest thing for him is not being with me, but he and his dad have a deeper relationship than they've ever had, and it's really wonderful to see. He spends two weeknights, and Saturday day and overnight with his dad and the rest with me. If he really wants to come to my house, he can. We're not inflexible, and he spends enough time with his dad that if there's a night he wants to spend with me, Greg doesn't feel threatened. What he's going to end up having is two happier households."

If You Share Physical Custody

Shared physical custody, where the kids spend significant amounts of time with both parents, can be a great choice for kids. It means that they get to have two really involved parents and to feel a sense of "home" wherever they are, rather than feeling that they have one home and one place they go to visit their other parent. A real 50-50 custody arrangement requires a high degree of cooperation between parents, so don't do it unless you are willing to be in contact with your ex regularly as time goes by. And think about some of these tips:

Make both houses home. Kids should have all the stuff they need in both places: toys, school supplies, clothes, and the right breakfast cereal. And having some consistency in rules between the two homes is more important when the kids are spending significant time in both places.

Consider getting some outside help. There are classes for divorcing parents in most communities, or you may be able to find a therapist experienced in dealing with shared custody situations. Even if you're optimistic about your ability to manage a shared physical custody arrangement, it can't hurt to get some tips from people who have been through it or helped other families.

Stay in touch. It's important that you keep in touch with your spouse about what's going on with your kids. You can let the school know that you both should receive progress reports and information about events, but there's lots of other information that you'll want to share. Some parents use a notebook that goes back and forth with the kids, in which they make notes about things like a developing cold, a new aversion to orange juice, or an upcoming sleepover that you've agreed to.

Email is a common way for divorced parents to communicate, and there are also interactive websites where you can set up message boards and calendars for communicating about day-to-day scheduling and parenting issues. The cost is reasonable. For example, check out www.ourfamilywizard.com, www.jointparents.com, www.sharekids.com, or www.parentingtime.net; all offer programs that allow you to keep an expense log and to negotiate schedule changes like trading days, for between $100 and $200 per year. There are also some free apps, like cofamilies.com, which offers a simple scheduling tool with no other bells or whistles.

Be mindful of the learning curve. In many relationships, one parent is the primary caretaker for the children. That parent knows where the information about the kids' doctor and dentist is kept, who drives the carpool on what days, and when picture day at school is happening. If you haven't been that parent, get ready for a crash course in management as you start to take care of the kids on your own. You may be surprised to find just how much your spouse has been doing to keep the kids functioning in their busy lives—and a bit overwhelmed at your new responsibilities.

> **RESOURCE**
>
> **Family planning.** Free Spirit Publishing offers quite a few resources for families going through divorce, including a kit titled *Juggling Act: Handling Divorce Without Dropping the Ball: A Survival Kit for Kids and Parents*, by Roberta Beyer and Kent Winchester. The kit includes both of Beyer and Winchester's books (*Speaking of Divorce* and *What in the World Do You Do When Your Parents Divorce?*), along with a calendar and communication system for parents. The calendar comes with stickers that make it user-friendly for kids and helps them to get involved in dealing with the schedule in a positive way. And parents find the communication tools helpful.
>
> Another communication tool for parents sharing custody is the *Co-Parenting Journal*, by Joseph A. Ekman and Bruce Bess, distributed through the About the Kids Foundation at www.aboutthekids.org.

(Extended) Family Matters

You may be painfully aware that you and your spouse aren't the only family members concerned about their ongoing relationship with your kids after the divorce. Grandparents, aunts, uncles, and others often have a lot invested in how your custody and visitation arrangements get set up, as well as in where you live. And just as you will continue to have your spouse in your life at least until your children are adults, you're likely to also keep your in-laws.

Your spouse's family

If you're the parent with primary residential custody, or if there's a 50-50 split, you have another excellent opportunity for taking the high road in your divorce. Reassure the grandparents on your spouse's side that you intend to support their relationship with your kids in whatever ways are appropriate. If they don't have much of a relationship to start with, you don't have to go out and cultivate one. But if they live nearby and are involved in your kids' everyday lives, let them know that doesn't have to change. The same goes for aunts, uncles, and cousins your children are close to.

On the other hand, if your relationship with your spouse's relatives deteriorated with the divorce or was never good, you may want to let your spouse deal with keeping the kids in contact with that side of the family.

Try not to get into a legal fight about this if you can at all avoid it. The law in this area is not simple, and states differ on how they handle nonparent visitation. In general, nonparents don't have a lot of legal right to ask for visitation with your kids if you don't want to allow it. However, some states use a "best interests of the child" standard in reviewing these visitation cases and some have specific laws covering grandparent visitation, so if you really don't want your child's grandparents to have any visitation, you may need to show why the contact would be bad for the kids. And unless you have hard evidence that the grandparents or other relatives are abusive or otherwise dangerous to your kids, you don't have any control over who the kids see when they're with the other parent.

All in the family ...

"We all had good relationships before the divorce, and we've tried to keep that going for our daughter's sake," says one divorced father. "My wife's family was angry at me for a while after we separated, but she always supported my relationship with our daughter and I just kept showing up at big family events until they remembered that they like me. I can tell that Lily is thrilled when we're all together and that makes it worthwhile."

Stepparents

Perhaps your spouse has children from a previous marriage whom you've been parenting during your marriage but haven't adopted. Courts are split on whether you should get visitation with these kids, who aren't legally related to you. But most states have laws that say at least that you can go to court and ask for visitation, and some states look to the best interests of the child, rather than the rights of the parents, in making decisions on stepparent visitation. The length of your marriage and the degree to which you acted as a parent will be the major factors in the court's decision. The judge may also consider the level of conflict in your relationship with your spouse and with the child's other legal parent.

Major life events

Especially if your kids are young now, you'll be dealing for many years with big events like school graduations, bar and bat mitzvahs, big birthday parties, important sports events, and even your children's weddings and the births of their own children. And it won't just be your kids' events—there are also the other relatives who have milestones, too. Most likely, your child wants to have all the important people around for these events. Voila! Here's another opportunity for you to take the high road.

If you're the one organizing the big events, make sure that everyone in your spouse's family to whom your child feels close gets an invitation from you, not just from your spouse. Make it clear that they are welcome, and be gracious when they show up. The same goes for your spouse's new love interest (assuming that enough time has passed to make it not completely gauche of your spouse to bring a date). You may have to take some deep breaths, but keep your focus on your children's welfare and you'll be fine—and your kids will be better than fine. They'll have a sense of belonging to a family and of being valued and important, as well as the opportunity to see you modeling maturity and kindness.

If One Parent Has Primary Physical Custody

Both custodial and noncustodial parents face lots of challenges—different ones—as they adjust to new household structures. If you are the custodial parent, you have your kids with you the majority of the time. This may feel like a victory to you, but don't waste time gloating about it. As the parent with greater access, you have an important responsibility to support your children's relationship with the other parent, no matter what your own feelings are about your spouse.

If you're the noncustodial parent, be careful you don't fall into the trap of trying to overcompensate for not being there all the time. Make sure your time with the kids is quality time, but don't spend it all at the amusement park or the mall. Your challenge is to establish a second home where your kids feel comfortable, safe, and loved.

What about noncustodial parents who live so far away that they can't visit weekly, or maybe even monthly? Regular phone calls are a must—and if you're the custodial parent, you need to be sure not to interfere with your spouse's relationship with the kids, no matter how inconvenient it may be sometimes. Modern technology is good news for faraway parents. Email, instant messaging, Skype, FaceTime, and webcams can be good ways to stay in close contact on a daily basis.

Couples are beginning to agree to—and courts are starting to order—"virtual" visitation. As you would expect, virtual visitation means the use of webcams for kids and parents to (literally) see each other. You can schedule regular visitation times just as you would in-person visits. It makes a big difference to a child to actually see a distant parent's face, as opposed to just talking on the phone—especially when kids are younger and often don't enjoy phone contact.

The website www.distanceparent.org provides information and resources for distance parenting. Virtual Visitation at www.internetvisitation.org is a clearinghouse with news, information, and resources for parents trying to bridge distance between themselves and their kids. You can use www.google.com or www.skype.com for video connections.

10 Rules for the Custodial Parent

1. Make sure your children understand that even though time is not shared equally, you and your spouse are still equal parents.

2. Never bad-mouth your spouse to your kids. Ever. And that includes complaining that you don't get enough financial support to afford things that the kids want. Don't complain to your kids about being lonely or depressed because of the divorce.

3. Never ask your kids to take messages of any kind to the other parent or to tell you about the other parent's comings and goings.

4. Never ask your kids to take sides, express loyalty to you over the other parent, or say which parent they want to spend more time with.

5. Let your kids contact their other parent anytime they want to, and give them privacy.

6. Always have an upbeat, positive attitude when you send your kids to their visits with the other parent.

7. Never condition visitation on receiving support payments from the other parent. (The other parent has a legal right to the visits, separate from the obligation to pay support.)

8. If your kids want to spend more time with the other parent than what's scheduled, consider their requests with an open mind and be as flexible as you can. If they're reluctant to go for visits, try to find out what's bugging them, but also make sure they understand it's not up for discussion.

9. Cut the other parent some slack about exact compliance with the parenting schedule. If your ex is chronically late, that's one thing. But if there's one occasion when the movie went longer than expected and they showed up at your door 20 minutes after the kids were supposed to be back, don't make a fuss.

10. Keep the lines of communication with the other parent open, and share information about what's going on with your kids during the time they're with you.

10 Rules for the Noncustodial Parent

1. Make sure your children understand that even though time is not shared equally, you don't love them any less, and you are still an equal parent.

2. Never bad-mouth the other parent to your kids. Ever. And that includes complaining that you can't afford things that the kids want because you have to pay so much support to the other parent. Don't complain to your kids about being lonely or depressed because of the divorce.

3. Never ask your kids to take messages of any kind to the other parent or to tell you anything about the other parent's comings and goings.

4. Never ask your kids to take sides, express loyalty to you over the other parent, or say which parent they want to spend more time with.

5. If your kids want to contact their other parent when they're with you, let them. Give them privacy.

6. Make the most of your time with your kids, but don't fall into the "party parent" role. Do normal activities with them, like grocery shopping and homework.

7. Never condition support payments on compliance with the visitation schedule. (Your spouse has a right to support that's separate from the visitation orders.)

8. If your kids want to spend more time with you than what's scheduled, be as flexible as you can. If they don't want to come for visitation, try to find out what's bugging them, and don't assume that the other parent is poisoning them against you.

9. Be as prompt as you can with picking up and returning the kids, and cut the other parent some slack if once in a while the kids aren't completely ready or something isn't exactly right.

10. Keep the lines of communication with the other parent open, and be consistent about checking in about what the kids are doing when they're not with you. Attend school and sports functions whenever you can, even if they're during times that aren't "your" times.

Trying to Get Along With Your Ex

If your divorce is very contentious and you and your spouse can't agree on anything, you're going to have to figure out how to coparent with the least damage to your kids. After all, no matter how difficult you find their other parent, the kids are still entitled to have meaningful relationships with both of their parents. Here are some ideas that might help:

- Ask neutral friends—or a court-sponsored transfer system—to help you with changeovers. Minimize your contact as much as you can.
- Get into mediation as soon as you can—preferably even before you separate—and develop a temporary parenting agreement that you can live with, relieving you from having to negotiate for a while. Hire a mediator who has experience with custody issues and who is comfortable working with lots of conflict.
- Use email to communicate, and say only the minimum that's needed to deal with the issue at hand. Websites like www. ourfamilywizard.com, www.parentingtime.net, www.jointparents. com, or www.sharekids.com can help by providing a structure for communicating by email.
- Try not to make changes in the parenting plan after it's in place. Life is unpredictable, and sometimes you may need to ask your spouse to be flexible, but make sure it's really crucial before rocking the boat, even in ways you think should be no big deal.

When It Comes to Divorce, Grownups Are Kids, Too

Not all children of divorce are young—sometimes, they are adults themselves. Adult children of divorce have some special challenges, the primary one being a general assumption that having parents divorce shouldn't affect them much, as they are grown and out of the house. But divorce can be devastating to adult children, too—especially if parents forget that it's still important to set some boundaries and leave the kids out of the worst of the conflicts.

Here are a few ideas for divorcing parents of adult children:

- Don't force your adult kids to listen to the gory details of your divorce. It's no more appropriate now to give them too much information than it was when they were young.
- Don't ask them to take sides or testify against the other parent in a court proceeding.
- Don't abandon them out of guilt or a sense that they no longer need their parents.
- Do take the time to tell them about the divorce in a kind and caring way.
- Do understand that they may feel abandoned, just as a younger child would.

You can do it. Parenting during and after divorce provides a wealth of opportunities for you to learn your way along the high road. The best way to take advantage of those opportunities is to keep your unwavering focus on your children's welfare. If you do, you'll be sure to find your way.

RESOURCE

Divorce is different for older adults, too. If you have adult children, chances are you fall into the category sometimes called "graying divorce." If you're interested in learning about some of the issues unique to your demographic, see *Divorce After 50: Your Guide to the Unique Legal & Financial Challenges*, by Janice Green (Nolo). ●

Custody Disputes

What if you think your spouse's ideas about custody are all wrong for the kids, and the two of you just can't agree about time-sharing? What if you are convinced that the kids would be much better off staying with you the majority of the time, with your spouse having only weekend visitation, but your spouse insists on 50-50 custody? What if your spouse doesn't comply with the visitation schedule you've established, or drinks or does drugs in front of the kids? This chapter addresses all these difficult custody problems and explains what a custody trial will mean for your kids.

The Low Road: Fighting It Out in Court

When it comes to custody disputes, the high road can become a bit rocky—but once again, take a deep breath and think about what's best for your kids. It's almost always better for kids to spend time with both of their parents, and in most circumstances, that's what a court is going to order. How much time and effort (not to mention money) are you willing to put into trying to limit your spouse's contact with the kids, knowing that you're likely to be unsuccessful? Go to mediation and try to work something out—and be sure you are truly making every compromise you can that puts the kids first.

Also, make sure your desires are consistent with reality. Do you work 70 hours a week? If you do get more time with the kids, who will be taking care of them when you're at work? Are you really available to parent, or are you just trying to get the other parent's goat by contesting custody? Remember that your kids' well-being is at stake here, and take a good hard look in the mirror. If you're resisting shared custody, ask yourself whether the things that you think make your spouse a weak parent are really all that serious. Are you really concerned about your kids, or are you just trying to control things?

How Courts Handle Custody Disputes

If you're fighting with your spouse about custody or visitation, prepare to be deeply involved with the court system. In fact, your first stop should be a mediator's office to see whether you can avoid a full-blown custody trial. Even if you run right out to your lawyer and ask for a court hearing, the court will send you to mandatory mediation with a court mediator before you can have your day in court. Go to mediation as the court requires—or meet with a private custody mediator chosen by your lawyer.

Courts in some states have special programs to handle what appears to be an increasing number of high-conflict custody cases—and if you go to court repeatedly over issues involving your children, you could end up involved in such a program. In these programs, you might be assigned to one judge who follows the case from start to finish. (Otherwise, it's more likely you'd appear in front of a number of different judges over multiple court dates.) In addition to having one judge oversee the case, you could be required to meet with a social worker for counseling before you can schedule your divorce trial. Some judges also appoint "parenting coordinators" who meet with battling parents regularly to monitor how things are going in terms of day-to-day compliance with the court orders. This keeps the judges from having to micromanage divorces such as when a parent comes back to court complaining that the other parent didn't pick the kids up from school on time and should be punished with a change in the visitation schedule.

Even in moderately conflicted cases, judges often order parents to attend child-rearing classes and require them to draw up parenting plans. In Texas, for example, each divorcing couple is required to set up and follow a parenting plan—the court even appoints a parenting coordinator to assist the divorcing parents in figuring out the plan, which must include a process to resolve future conflicts.

How to Argue for Custody

When you file your first court papers asking for the divorce (or respond to your spouse's papers), you state in general terms what you want in terms of custody. For example, you state whether you agree to share joint legal custody or are seeking sole custody with visitation to your spouse. In most states, you're also required to file a statement describing where and with whom your children have lived for the past five years, to comply with a law called the Uniform Child Custody Jurisdiction Enforcement Act (UCCJEA). See "Interstate Custody Fights," below.

Interstate Custody Fights

If parents live in different states, which court decides custody issues? The answer comes from a law called the UCCJEA, which most states have adopted. It's designed to do two things: prevent parental kidnapping, and give information about where children in a divorce are living, so that the court knows whether the children are under the court's authority (jurisdiction). If your spouse moves during the course of your divorce and tries to file custody papers in another state, you'll need a lawyer. The law about which state gets to decide custody issues is complex and the decision is important, because once a state has jurisdiction over a child custody dispute, it's hard to move the case to another state.

If you want to learn more about these rules, a good place to start is a publication by the Department of Justice, which you can find at www.ncjrs .gov/pdffiles1/ojjdp/189181.pdf.

If you want the court to issue a temporary custody order while your divorce is pending, you'll probably move quickly on to a motion hearing (described in detail in Chapters 3 and 5). Either you or your spouse will file a motion stating what you want, and the other will respond, arguing for something different. You may also submit declarations—written statements by you and possibly from witnesses, giving the judge facts that you think support your position. You'll then go to court for a hearing, where the judge will make a temporary order. That order will be binding until you either agree to change it or have a full trial, after which the judge will make a permanent order.

Factors a Judge May Consider in a Custody Dispute

Nearly all states use a "best interest of the child" standard in disputed custody cases. This is a rather amorphous standard, and one that lends itself to judges' subjective beliefs about what's best for children. Most states' laws include a list of factors for judges to consider, and there are some that are nearly universal. There's a big debate right now in child development circles—at least as those circles interact with custody rules—about attachment in very young children, and the wisdom of scheduling overnight visitation in cases where the divorce occurs early in a child's life. If you are in that debate, you will find expert opinions on either side, and you'll probably want to consult an attorney about the views of local judges.

The Evolution of Custody Rules

These days, most judges believe that it's good for children to have ongoing and regular contact with both of their parents. But it hasn't always been that way. Back in the 1800s, fathers almost always got custody, because of their role as head of the family. In the early 20th century, the preference shifted to mothers, especially in cases involving very young children (the "tender years" doctrine). That rule prevailed for many years, but as more women entered the workforce and family structures and roles shifted, some judges began to focus on the children's best interests without a preference for either parent. Still, in practice, many courts favor mothers in custody cases. In the last couple of decades, fathers have begun arguing for greater rights to custody, and another shift may be in store.

Age of the children. Although the "tender years" doctrine is officially out of fashion, some judges still believe that younger children should live with their mothers, especially if the mother has been the primary caregiver. (Certainly, a nursing baby will do so.)

Each parent's living situation. There's a bit of a chicken-and-egg dilemma surrounding the issue of where parents live and how that affects custody. Sometimes, the parent who stays in the family home is granted custody of the children because it allows the children stability and continuity in their daily lives. Sometimes, the parent with custody is awarded the family home, for the same reason. If you are crashing in your best friend's guest room while you get back on your feet after the divorce, don't expect to get primary custody of your kids. If you truly want to spend a significant amount of time with your children, make sure your living situation reflects that.

The proximity of your home to your spouse's may also factor in to the judge's decision. The closer you are, the more likely the judge will order a time-sharing plan that gives both parents significant time with the kids. The location of their school and their social and sports activities may also matter.

Each parent's willingness to support the other's relationship with the children. The judge will look at your record of cooperating—or not— with your spouse about your parenting schedule. The judge might also want to know things like whether you bad-mouth your spouse in front of the kids or interfere with visitation in any way. The more cooperative parent is going to have an edge in a custody dispute—and a parent who's obviously trying to alienate a child from the other parent will learn the hard way that courts don't look kindly on that type of interference. In other words, taking the high road can serve your self-interest here.

The judge will also look at how you and your spouse communicate and cooperate in making decisions about your children. A judge is much more likely to grant joint legal custody where you are able to make decisions effectively.

Each parent's relationship with the children before the divorce. It sometimes happens that a parent who hasn't been much involved with the kids' lives suddenly develops a strong desire to spend more time with the children once the marriage has ended. In many cases, this desire is sincere, and a judge will respect it, especially if the parent has been dedicated to parenting during the separation period. But the judge will definitely take some time to evaluate a parent's change of heart and ensure that the custody request isn't being made primarily to win out over the other parent.

Children's preferences. If children are old enough—usually, older than 12 or so—a judge may talk to them to find out their preferences about custody and visitation. Some states require courts to consider kids' views, but others disapprove of bringing the kids into it at all. The judge also may learn about the children's preferences from a custody evaluator. (See "Your Kids and the Court Process: Custody Evaluations," below.)

Religion and Custody

In some states, whether or not a parent provides religious training to children can be factored into custody and visitation decisions. For example, in some states, courts have concluded that learning two religions is not harmful to children, while others have reached the opposite decision and ordered one parent to stop teaching religion to the child. Courts have also made orders that a parent take the children to church during visitation times (because they're used to going to church on other Sundays) and that religious practices that are outside of the mainstream (like Jehovah's Witnesses) are not inherently harmful to children and can't be limited by court order. In other words, the courts are all over the map, and the rules depend on where you live.

If you have sole legal custody of your kids, you can pretty much make whatever decisions you want about their religious education (though in most cases, you can't control what they do when they're with the other parent, and an Oregon court recently ruled that even a parent with sole custody couldn't have his 12-year-old son circumcised over the other parent's objections). But if you share legal custody with your spouse, you can't make unilateral decisions about things like sending your kids to religious school. If you and your spouse disagree, you'll have to work it out, take it to mediation, or ask a judge to decide.

Continuity and stability. When it comes to children, judges are big on the status quo, because most of them believe that piling more change on top of the traumatic transition of divorce generally isn't good for kids. So if you're arguing that things are working fine, you've got a leg up on a spouse who's arguing for a major change in the custody or visitation schedule that's already in place.

Sexual orientation and gender identity. If one parent comes out as lesbian or gay, or begins a gender transition, after separation, what impact does it have on custody and visitation decisions? The answer depends in large part on where you live. If you are in a relatively open-minded state with a significant LGBT population, like California or New York, sexual orientation shouldn't be a factor in custody or visitation decisions. In fact, in some states, the law forbids using sexual orientation alone to deny custody or limit visitation. That doesn't mean you won't come up against a homophobic judge, even in those states. And in some states, courts are allowed to, and do, consider sexual orientation as a major factor in custody and visitation decisions. It's quite common in those states for judges to rule that a parent's same-sex partner can't be around when children are visiting, or that the parent can't expose the kids to a "gay lifestyle." And in the worst-case scenario, parents can be denied all contact with their children on the basis of their sexual orientation.

The same can be true for transgender parents, who may face even more prejudice than same-sex parents, as well as a lack of knowledge in many courts about the transgender experience.

If you're in a same-sex marriage in one of the marriage equality states or in a domestic partnership or civil union in a state where the legal relationship is the equivalent of marriage, and you and your partner are both legal parents of your kids, your sexual orientation will have no impact on the court's consideration of custody and visitation matters. The same standards that apply to all divorcing couples will apply to you.

RESOURCE

If you think you've suffered illegal discrimination in family court because of your sexual orientation, there are organizations that can help you. Contact the National Center for Lesbian Rights at www.nclrights.org or the Lambda Legal Defense and Education Fund at www.lambdalegal.org for information. If you're a transgender parent, contact the Transgender Law Center at www.tlc.org.

Abuse or neglect. Obviously, if there's clear evidence that either parent has abused or neglected the children, a judge will limit that parent's contact with the children. There's more on dealing with abuse in Chapter 14.

The Absent Parent

While it's fairly common for parents to fight for more time with their kids, it sometimes also happens that one parent simply disappears when the couple splits up. Can you track down a spouse who's done a vanishing act and insist on visits with the kids? Not really. The courts have systems for enforcing support, but not visitation. (A judge in Tennessee tried imposing a monetary penalty each time a father failed to exercise his visitation rights, but the court of appeal voided the order.) If your spouse doesn't want to see the kids, there's not much you can do except keep in touch and keep sending the message that visits are possible.

Your Kids and the Court Process: Custody Evaluations

In general, your children won't be too much involved in the court process. You'll go to hearings that involve child custody and support without the kids even knowing that you're doing it—if their schedule is changed, they'll just find that out later. But don't fool yourself that you can be involved in a custody fight and still protect your children from paying the price.

If you ultimately aren't able to work out a custody agreement with your spouse, the court will probably order a custody evaluation. The evaluation itself is a document that an evaluator prepares for the judge to review, giving the evaluator's opinion about the best custody and visitation arrangement for your family.

A custody evaluation is done if:

- the judge orders it, or
- you and your spouse agree to it.

A custody evaluator is a mental health professional, usually a psychologist, with special training and experience in reviewing family situations and making recommendations to judges about what custody arrangements and parenting plan or schedule would be in the best interests of the children involved. Sometimes the court appoints a "guardian ad litem"—a lawyer who represents the children's interests—instead of a custody evaluator, but the process is very much the same either way.

The evaluator's recommendation is not binding on the court, but as a rule, a judge gives it a lot of weight—it's the only neutral information the judge has about your family situation and dynamics.

Choosing the evaluator

The judge might assign a custody evaluator to your case. Or the court might give you a choice of two or three people and let you either choose among them or reject one of the choices. You and your spouse may be able to agree on an evaluator recommended by one of your lawyers. If you do, the judge will probably go along with your choice.

If you're choosing an evaluator yourselves, or if you're choosing from among options given to you by the judge, ask your lawyer to get some information so you're comfortable with the choice—even if your lawyer has recommended the evaluator. (Don't question the evaluator directly, as you don't want to do anything that might negatively affect the evaluator's impression of you.) You want to know about the evaluator's experience generally, and if your family has special issues (for example, a relocation question or a child with special needs), about whether the evaluator has dealt with similar issues before. It's also appropriate to ask whether the evaluator has a history of recommending in favor of either fathers or mothers.

It's unlikely, but if none of the options offered by the court are acceptable to you after you do your research, you can ask the court to give you more options. But don't assume your request will be granted. If you and your spouse agree to an evaluation but you can't agree on the evaluator, you can hire competing evaluators. After you've read what the custody evaluation involves, however, you may be less inclined to do that.

Cost. How much the evaluation costs will depend on whether it's court ordered or voluntary. If the court orders the evaluation and you use the county's evaluator, you'll pay a much lower hourly rate than if you hire a private evaluator. A county custody evaluation will probably cost between $1,000 and $2,500, and you could pay $10,000 or more for a private evaluation.

The evaluation process. To some extent, how the evaluation process is structured will depend on the specific evaluator. But almost all evaluators:

- interview both you and your spouse up to three times (interviews will be planned, not unannounced visits)
- interview each child once or twice
- spend time with each child with each parent, to observe your interactions (at the evaluator's office, your home, or both)
- gather information from teachers or caregivers, doctors, therapists, and other witnesses, and
- look over your court file.

Many evaluators use psychological testing as well—for both children and parents. Some do the testing themselves and some (including a guardian ad litem who's a lawyer, not a mental health professional) send you to another professional for testing.

If anything happens in the evaluation that concerns you—for example, the evaluator appears to have a strong bias in favor of your spouse or asks questions you think are inappropriate—talk to your lawyer immediately, before the report is submitted. Concerns raised after the report is completed will be discounted if the recommendation goes against you.

What you should do if you're being evaluated

Your meetings with the evaluator present a difficult situation. You want to be yourself, yet you probably can't avoid going out of your way to present yourself favorably. That's entirely natural, and it's also natural for you to be anxious when you meet with the evaluator. Some important dos and don'ts are listed below.

Dos and Don'ts of Custody Evaluations

Do:

- Acknowledge both your strengths and your weaknesses as a parent.
- Be truthful in answering questions about your history and current situation. Answer the question that's asked, rather than using it as a jumping-off point to state your case.
- Acknowledge the benefits to your children of having positive relationships with both of their parents.
- Express your willingness to consider different custody and visitation arrangements, but clearly explain (once, not over and over again) why you prefer one over another.
- Keep your focus on your children's well-being and what's best for them.
- Follow up promptly and thoroughly if you're asked to provide paperwork or information—for example, verification of employment or medical information about your children.

Don't:

- Say negative things about your spouse; if you're asked about your spouse's strengths and weaknesses as a parent, be as evenhanded as you can, and don't dwell on either.
- Ask the evaluator to provide therapy or advise you on how to deal with your spouse or your children.
- Coach your kids about what to say or do.
- Be late or miss appointments with the evaluator.
- Disobey custody orders that are in place while the evaluation is pending.

CAUTION

Don't try to manipulate the evaluator. There's a lot of material out there about custody evaluations, especially on the Internet. A lot of it comes from an extremely adversarial perspective, promising to show you how to manipulate the process to get the evaluator to do what you want. But if you're in need of a custody evaluation, you and your spouse are already in a highly polarized situation—and you will best serve your children by recognizing that the help of an experienced professional might be just what you and your spouse need. That means you need to cooperate with the evaluator, rather than trying to get something out of the evaluation. Look at the evaluator as the person who may actually be able to help you and your spouse come to a better understanding of your children's needs and your family's best course of action.

Talking to your kids about the evaluation

There's little doubt that your children will be frightened and confused by the evaluation process, and will wonder whether the decision will hinge on what they say. You can't avoid the difficult truth that the reason for the evaluation is that you and your spouse have different opinions about how the kids should be cared for. But you can explain to them that the evaluator is trying to learn about the family, in order to help you and your spouse learn to parent together in a way that works.

Never coach your children about what to say, and especially don't tell them to speak negatively about their other parent. Reassure them that all they need to do is to tell the truth.

The report

The evaluator's report will be given to you, your spouse, and the court at the same time. Depending on the parameters given at the outset, the evaluation might make recommendations about:

- custody, visitation, and time-sharing
- whether therapy is appropriate for the family together or for any individuals or subsets of the family
- how you and your spouse should deal with conflicts in the future, and
- how to deal with specific issues like substance abuse.

The report might recommend a reevaluation for a specific time in the future, especially if your children are very young.

After you get the recommendation, sit down with your lawyer and discuss it. If it's at all acceptable to you, you're probably better off agreeing to the recommended course of action and giving up your day in court, where you might end up getting less. Of course, if your spouse doesn't agree as well, you'll have to go to court anyway. But take the opportunity to try to get things resolved without an ugly courtroom fight—and maybe even to learn something about parenting during and after your divorce.

If the Custodial Spouse Interferes With Visitation

For many parents, having to deal with an ex-spouse about visitation is really hard, especially right after the separation before anyone has settled into a new routine. Some parents try to minimize contact between their children and the other parent, hoping the difficulties will go away if they're avoided.

Nothing could be further from the truth. If you're hoping that quietly sabotaging contact between your spouse and your kids—by making the kids unavailable for phone calls, inventing excuses why visitation just can't happen some days, or giving your kids subtle messages that they should resist visitation or shouldn't be close to the other parent—will have a good result, think again.

First of all, it's not good for your kids, who need both of their parents' support during this big transition. Second, it will only make things more difficult for you and your spouse in the long run. Third, it may backfire against you in court. If your spouse reports your behavior to the judge, you could lose your custody rights or some of your visitation time, or have to deal with the judge appointing someone to oversee visitation and make sure the court orders are being carried out.

If your spouse is interfering with visitation, first try direct communication. Ask your spouse whether the visitation schedule is working out and if it isn't, what the problem is. Don't accuse or threaten. There may be an explanation that you haven't thought of, so be open-minded. However, it's also important to remind your spouse that there's a court order in place and that you expect compliance. If you continue to have problems, suggest mediation—and try to find a mediator who's trained in dealing with custody matters. A little intervention can go a long way in a situation that hasn't escalated too far.

But what about a spouse who simply refuses to comply with court-ordered visitation? There's not much you can do except go back to court and ask the judge to intervene. If necessary, the judge will send law enforcement officers to pick up your kids and bring them to you for visitation. And you may even be able to get the judge to order a change in custody. It's definitely in your best interest to have a lawyer help you with this kind of custody fight. A parent who refuses to honor visitation rights is a parent who's probably beyond a talking cure.

If One Parent Wants to Move Away

One of the most contentious issues that divorcing couples deal with is one parent's desire to move away. A move across town, or even to a different city within driving range, may not be a big deal, but when one parent wants to move across the country, sparks may fly.

It's most common for moveaway issues to come up when some time has passed after the divorce—as you start to make a new life for yourself and consider your options, moving might seem like a good plan. (Chapter 15 deals with postdivorce moveaway fights.) But the prospect of a move could also arise during the process of negotiating your divorce.

If you're the one who wants to move with your children, you probably have lots of good reasons. Maybe you have a great job opportunity, or your new partner does. Perhaps you want to live closer to your parents so that they can help you with child care and getting back on your feet after the divorce. Could be you've never liked where you live, and you moved there only because your spouse wanted to.

You may be surprised that your spouse doesn't immediately see the logic of your plan when you present it. But very few parents, especially those who spend significant amounts of time with their kids, are happy about the idea of a major move that takes the kids out of the area.

You need to consider your kids' welfare, too. If your intention is to share joint custody with your spouse, it's really hard on the kids to move a great distance away. Even though there are creative ways to stay in touch, they are not a substitute for frequent contact. Especially in the early days after the divorce, try not to stress your kids this way if you don't absolutely have to.

What if you really need to move and your spouse objects? First and foremost, do not take the kids and leave town without your spouse's agreement. The old saying "It's easier to ask forgiveness than permission" absolutely does not apply here, and you may be accused of violating your visitation plan at best, and of kidnapping at worst. Your first step should be to the mediator's office to try to work things out—which for you means getting your spouse to agree to the move.

Before the meeting, think about how you can go the extra mile to make the move more palatable to your ex. Are you willing to pay a greater share of travel costs? Are you willing to give up the kids on holidays, or for longer periods of time during vacations—maybe even for the whole summer? There are a lot of logistical issues to consider. Remember that you are disrupting everyone else's routine, and be prepared to compromise.

If mediation doesn't work, you may have to ask a judge to decide whether or not the move can happen. This is a roll of the dice. Most judges do not favor a move that will take children away from an involved parent, school activities, and friends. At the same time, they are sympathetic to arguments of economic necessity. In some places, the court decides what would be in the "best interests" of the children, but in others, the court will allow a custodial parent to move unless it would harm the children—a much lower standard than considering only what the children's best interests would be. Most states put the burden of showing the move is in the children's best interest on the parent who wants to move. In California, a noncustodial parent can't even get a hearing on the best interests of the child without showing that it's likely the move would be detrimental to the child.

You might end up with permission to move—but without your children. Instead of letting the kids move, the judge might change custody to the parent who's staying in town. If you're in a fight, the parent staying where the kids are growing up will have a significant advantage. And if the judge thinks that you're moving for the purpose of keeping the kids away from your spouse, watch out. You're likely to get an earful as well as have your request denied.

 SEE AN EXPERT

Don't represent yourself in a moveaway case. The legal rules involved in cases about moving are complicated and change with some frequency. If you and your spouse can't agree about a proposed move, find an experienced custody lawyer to help you protect your rights.

Drug and Alcohol Abuse

Substance abuse, whether it's a cause or an effect of divorce, can become a major issue in decisions about child custody and visitation.

If You Have or Had a Substance Abuse Problem

If you abused drugs or alcohol in the past but are clean now, your spouse will likely try to use your history against you if you're fighting over custody or visitation. So get your ducks in a row right away. Get signed statements from anyone who knows about your recovery, to the effect that while you had a problem in the past, you are dealing with it in a mature and focused way and have been successful in your recovery efforts. If you have persuasive evidence that you are successfully staying away from drugs and alcohol, a judge probably won't treat you any differently than any other parent.

If your recovery is very recent, however, be prepared for the possibility that a judge might place some restrictions on your relationship with your kids. You're unlikely to get primary custody, for one thing. And you may have limited or even supervised visitation until you can prove that you are staying clean. Unless the restrictions are really Draconian, don't fight it. Just keep your nose clean and rely on your lawyer's advice about when it's the right time to return to court and ask for increased visitation or an end to supervision.

If you have a current substance abuse problem, that's a very different story. Your visitation with your kids will definitely be limited, will most probably be supervised, and may be discontinued if you (or your friends or relatives) are found to be abusing drugs or alcohol when the kids are around. Drug abuse isn't limited to illegal substances, either. If you're abusing antianxiety or pain medications, you may well be a danger to your children. Recognize the signs, come out of your denial, and get some help.

RESOURCE

Get the help you need. The United States Department of Health & Human Services Substance Abuse and Mental Health Services Administration website at www.samhsa.gov has information about recognizing alcohol or drug abuse, understanding what it may be costing you, and getting help, including a treatment facility locator.

www.soberrecovery.com casts a wide net in collecting recovery resources online—you can get information about treatment resources and treatment facilities by geographic location, demographics, or type of substance.

The Drug & Alcohol Resource Center provides online and telephone information at no cost. The site is maintained by a private recovery treatment provider, but there's also a lot of free information about substance abuse, detox, recovery options, and treatment centers all over the country. Information is available at www.addict-help.com or by phone at 800-390-4056.

If Your Spouse Has or Had a Problem

If you're dealing with a currently alcoholic or substance-abusing spouse, get ready to walk a fine line. You are, of course, responsible for protecting your safety and that of your children, and you need to fight for a custody and visitation arrangement that will do that. At the same time, your spouse is still your kids' other parent, and has a right to see them within parameters that protect their safety. So unless your spouse's alcohol or substance abuse poses a significant danger to your children, you probably won't be able to avoid some kind of contact between your spouse and the kids.

However, you can take steps to limit that contact, and you can ask the court to order that all visits be supervised. Some courts have affiliated agencies that provide visitation supervision, and the judge may order you to make use of these services, which are generally provided at low or no cost. There are private agencies that provide supervision for court-ordered visitation as well. You can also ask the court to order that the visits be supervised by a friend or family member, but that has disadvantages. Trained workers at an agency will be sure to stick to the boundaries of the court order, and probably won't hesitate to refuse or end a visitation session if it appears that your spouse is using drugs or alcohol or is behaving inappropriately. A friend or relative might have a harder time knowing where to draw the line.

If your spouse has had substance abuse problems in the past but is making a sincere effort at recovery, it behooves you to make a sincere effort to support that effort. Again, without compromising your children's safety, try to facilitate visitation, and be open to changes in the visitation schedule as your spouse gets further along in the recovery process. If the substance abuse was a major factor in your marriage and your divorce, it may be very difficult to give your spouse credit for working at recovery—especially if there have been broken promises or failed efforts in the past. Still, try to offer the benefit of the doubt to the greatest extent possible, as long as you have clear evidence that there's been no backsliding. ●

Child Support

Allparents must support their children financially, whether or not the parents are married. Both you and your spouse are responsible for giving your kids all the necessities of life until they become legal adults. This chapter explains what that means and helps you figure out whether one of you will pay child support to the other and, if so, how much. You'll also learn how long support lasts, what the tax implications are, and more. This chapter covers only child support. Spousal support (alimony) is covered in Chapter 11.

Who Pays Support?

Which parent makes support payments to the other depends a lot on where the kids spend their time. If one parent is the custodial parent, then the other parent almost always is required to pay child support. The reasoning is that both parents are responsible for supporting the kids, and if the kids live with one parent most of the time, chances are that custodial parent will need some help paying for the housing, food, clothing, and everything else the kids need.

However, it's not completely unheard of for a parent with primary custody to pay child support to the other parent. If the custodial parent's income is significantly higher than the other's parent's, the noncustodial parent may receive support based on the amount of time spent with the children.

If you and your spouse share custody 50-50 and there's a big income disparity between you, the higher-earning spouse usually pays child support to the lower-earning spouse even though you're each caring for the children half the time.

> CAUTION
>
> **If you're the parent receiving support, make sure you use it for the kids.** Given that most custodial parents are women and that statistically, women often suffer major financial downturns after a divorce, it's unlikely that you're using your support to get pedicures or buy yourself a little something. But just in case you were considering it, remember that child support is for your kids' living

expenses, not for anything that doesn't benefit them directly. That doesn't mean you have to spend it all on Keds and Cheerios—a family vacation and even a new television are legitimate expenses—but just that you should be mindful where the money is going, so you don't end up in court explaining your finances to the judge because your spouse complained.

Temporary Support While the Divorce Is Pending

It may take a year or more before your divorce is final, and you might not know the permanent child support figure until then. In the meantime, there are bills to pay and mouths to feed. You need some kind of temporary arrangement about child support.

Just like everything else in your divorce, this is a decision that's best made between you and your spouse, without court intervention. You know best the size of your collective financial pie and how it could be sliced to best serve everyone. So try to agree on a temporary amount of child support, and then write up a quick agreement that says what the support amount is, when it is to begin, when in each month it will be paid, and that you agree the amount is temporary. To help you figure out the amount, see "Estimating Child Support in Your Family," below. Before you even do that, you can buy yourselves some time by simply looking at your expenses and ballparking the amount that needs to change hands right away.

If you're not able to reach an agreement yourselves, you can take the issue either to mediation or to court. Sometimes, if you're the custodial parent and things aren't moving quickly enough, going to court for a temporary order (sometimes called "pendente lite," meaning it applies while the divorce case is pending) is your best option. Chapter 5 discusses these temporary court orders.

Working It Out Yourselves

If you and your spouse can decide on an amount of support that seems fair to you, you can be done with the whole issue. Child support is a very good issue to resolve yourselves, without the intervention of a court. Lawyers will tell you that typically, spouses are more likely to stick to the terms of a negotiated agreement than a court order. You'll also save money doing it yourself. But probably the most important aspect is the symbolic value of working together for your kids' welfare. It's great practice for the years of cooperative coparenting that you have ahead of you, too. After you read about all the issues that go into deciding support, have a frank discussion about how much money there is, what the kids' needs are, and what will work for everyone.

Starting With the Guidelines

To get a general idea of what a court would order as support, use your state's child support guidelines. See "How Courts Decide Support Amounts," below. If you and your spouse agree to an amount of support that's different from the guidelines, a court will usually accept the agreement. You are free, within limits, to make whatever decisions you want—you could even decide that one of you is going to stay home with the kids until they reach a certain age and, to facilitate that, the other parent is going to pay more support than the guidelines would otherwise require. Your agreement should briefly state the reasons that the support amount agreed on is way outside of the guidelines, and say that you both believe that the amount is fair and is in your kids' interests.

Child support guidelines are designed to provide children with the basic support needed to feed, clothe, and care for them. It will account for things like one parent's paying for the children's health insurance. Baseline child support doesn't take into account things like tutoring, sleepaway summer camp, music lessons, or snowboarding trips. If you and your spouse are trying to calculate support yourselves, don't leave out those extra expenses. Remember your child is going to keep growing, and you need to anticipate events and expenses like sports uniforms and equipment, a bar or bat mitzvah, braces, SAT and college prep expenses, driving lessons (maybe even a vehicle), a graduation gift, and college tuition. Address those issues either by stating what you'll do about them, or stating that you'll discuss them at a specified time and try to agree what to do then. Include a provision that if you can't agree, you'll go to mediation.

Factoring in Changing Circumstances

You can make agreements in advance about temporary reductions or increases in support tied to certain events. Here are a few examples.

When the kids are away. You might agree to a provision that if the kids go off to summer camp or live away from their regular residence for more than a month, child support is reduced for that month (depending, of course, on who's paying for camp). It doesn't make sense to have a reduction for less than a month, because the expenses that the custodial parent pays won't be that different if the kids are only gone for a week or two. The custodial parent still has the regular expenses of running the household, which is for the kids' benefit.

College. A child who goes off to college may be living in a dorm. You could agree that support payments will be made to the school rather than to the other parent during the months that the child is at school, and will revert to the custodial parent during the summer or other periods that the child is at home.

Financial conditions. You can agree to an automatic increase in support to keep pace with inflation, or agree that if the paying spouse's income goes down by a certain percentage, support will be reduced by that same percentage.

How Courts Decide Support Amounts

Given that judges decide most child support awards by looking at guidelines that you can look at yourselves, there's not much point in wasting your time and money arguing in court about it. But before you begin estimating child support and negotiating with your spouse, it helps to know what a court would do and how judges make their decisions.

Basic Support Guidelines

Every state has a formula for calculating child support. The formulas themselves can be quite complicated, but it's pretty easy to find the amount by using software or websites for your state. Some helpful resources are listed in "Estimating Child Support in Your Family," below.

The biggest factor in calculating child support is how much the parents earn. Some states consider both parents' income, but others consider only the income of the noncustodial parent. In most states, the percentage of time that each parent spends with the children is another important factor.

Most states consider at least some of these other factors in calculating child support:

- child support or alimony either parent receives from a previous marriage
- whether either parent is paying child support or alimony from a previous marriage
- whether either parent is responsible for children from a previous (or subsequent) marriage
- which parent is paying for health insurance, and the cost
- which parent is paying day care costs, and the cost
- whether either parent is required to pay union dues or has other amounts deducted from paychecks
- ages of the children
- whether either parent receives irregular income such as bonuses or incentive pay, or expects severance pay or other lump sum payments, and
- whether either parent lives with a new partner or spouse who contributes to household expenses.

Some states use very individual factors—for example, New York looks at local taxes and also alimony that one parent is paying in the current marriage, not just previous marriages (this is unusual; most courts believe that child support is more important than alimony and calculate child support first, and then evaluate what's left in setting alimony). And states define "income" differently—some use gross income, some use net, and some include gifts, bonuses, and overtime while others do not. If a parent has significant investment income, it may be counted as income for purposes of calculating child support.

Setting Support Higher or Lower Than the Guidelines

If you think that the guidelines shouldn't apply for some reason but your spouse doesn't agree with you, you'll have to tell it to the judge. Judges are allowed to deviate from the guidelines if there are good reasons, but you'll have to be pretty persuasive.

For example, if you're the paying parent, you might argue that because you are paying for your kids' private school and all of their uninsured medical expenses, the support payment should be less than the guideline amount. (But even if you're providing some extras, the base amount of support has to be enough for the necessities.) Or if you have custody of a disabled child who requires extra care and has unusual medical expenses, you might think the support paid to you should be higher than the guideline amount.

In any case, be prepared to show the judge documentation of your position. A budget showing all of your expenses relating to the kids will impress the judge with your attention to their needs and the seriousness of your position.

Here are some circumstances that might cause a judge to set support above or below the guideline amount:

- **The noncustodial parent can afford more.** If the paying parent earns a great deal of money, has other significant assets, or receives in-kind compensation like employer-provided housing or a vehicle, the judge may order a payment that's more than the guideline amount.
- **The guideline amount is more than what's needed.** If the noncustodial parent makes so much money that the guideline support amount would be much more than is needed to pay for the children's regular expenses, the judge might reduce the amount somewhat. But both parents will always be required to contribute to supporting the kids.
- **The paying parent can't pay.** If the noncustodial parent earns very little money, has other expenses that make it impossible to meet

the guideline amount, or has recently lost a job, the court may order a lower support amount. The judge is also likely to order the parents to return to court at a set time so that the judge can review their current circumstances.

- **A child has special needs or interests.** A child with unusual medical, psychological, or educational needs may require a higher amount of support. Also, if your child is an avid musician or involved in sports or other activities, you can ask the judge to order the paying parent to pay an additional amount so that the child can continue a favorite activity.

- **The paying parent is shirking.** A parent's earnings sometimes don't reflect true earning potential—for example, say a parent is trained as a lawyer but works as a bookstore clerk. In that case, especially if the judge believes the parent is purposefully avoiding paying support by taking a low-paying job, a court might calculate support based on what the parent could be earning (that's called imputing income). Even when the parent isn't deliberately shirking, some courts will impute income if a change in income represents a disregard of parenting responsibilities, as a North Carolina judge did when the father quit his engineering job to start a church and "follow Jesus Christ," reducing his income by 70%.

Estimating Child Support in Your Family

There are a lot of resources that can help you estimate what you might expect to pay in child support. The Internet is your best friend for this, so if you aren't connected at home, find a café or public library where you can get online and do some research. There are three ways you can get a general idea of how much support is likely to be ordered in your case:

- Ask your lawyer, who undoubtedly has software that will calculate support for your state. This will give you the most accurate idea of what support is likely to be.
- Use an online calculator (or downloadable worksheets) specifically designed for your state by either the court system, the child

support enforcement agency for your state, or a commercial website. This will give you a decent estimate of support. The best websites for finding a child support calculator for each state are listed below.

- If your state doesn't have any resources to help you, use the online calculators at www.alllaw.com. (Click "Family Law" under "Topics," then use the calculator link and find your state.) This will give you a ballpark figure, but is not as reliable as either of the other methods. (Many other websites that say they offer child support calculators actually redirect you to alllaw.com.)

When you use an online calculator, remember that the result won't be the exact amount of support that a judge might order. For one thing, you may not know your spouse's exact income or deductions, or how much the kids' health insurance costs. For another, the calculators are all different from one another, and the free one that you are using will give a somewhat different result from the official one that the judge would use in court. And as discussed above, the guidelines are not necessarily the be-all and end-all of what a judge would order. If you take the matter to court, you will have the opportunity to try to persuade the judge that even though the guideline says that support should be a certain amount, other factors should be considered and the amount should be more or less.

The list below shows you where to find your state's official child support calculator, if there is one, or worksheets, guidelines, or regulations. However, the tools on those sites, especially some of the worksheets or regulations, may not be as easy to use as the simple calculators available on www.alllaw.com. You'll have to determine what works best for you.

If there's nothing listed, that means the state doesn't provide a calculator and that a lawyer, the free calculators at www.alllaw.com, or a commercial calculator that you pay for are your options for estimating support.

At the website listed, sometimes you'll have to use your common sense and click through to the page that has the information you want. In every case where you need to do that, it's very clear what links you need.

State Child Support Calculators	
State	**Support Information/Calculators**
Alabama	www.alacourt.gov/childsupportobligations.aspx
Alaska	https://webapp.state.ak.us/cssd
Arizona	www.azcourts.gov/familylaw/childsupportcalculator.aspx
Arkansas	http://courts.arkansas.gov/subsection/support-charts-affidavit
California	www.childsup.ca.gov (click link to "calculate child support")
Colorado	www.courts.state.co.us/Forms/SubCategory.cfm?Category=Divorce
Connecticut	www.jud.state.ct.us/Publications/ChildSupport/2005CSguidelines.pdf
Delaware	http://courts.delaware.gov/SupportCalculator
Dist. of Col.	http://csgc.oag.dc.gov/application/main/intro.aspx
Florida	dor.myflorida.com/dor/childsupport/
Georgia	www.georgiacourts.org/csc/
Hawaii	www.hawaii.gov/jud/childpp.htm
Idaho	No official calculator; guidelines at www.isc.idaho.gov/files/ICSG-July_1_2012.pdf
Illinois	www.childsupportillinois.com/general/calculating.html
Indiana	www.in.gov/judiciary/2625.htm
Iowa	www.iowasupportmaster.com/childsupport
Kansas	www.kscourts.org/rules-procedures-forms/child-support-guidelines/2012-guidelines.asp (Microsoft *Word* worksheet and schedules are included in guidelines, which are complex)
Kentucky	http://chfs.ky.gov/dis/cse.htm
Louisiana	www.dss.state.la.us (select Parenting, then Child Support)
Maine	www.ptla.org/calculating-your-child-support
Maryland	www.dhr.state.md.us/CSOCGuide/App/disclaimer.do
Massachusetts	www.dor.state.ma.us/apps/worksheets/cse/guidelines-short.asp
Michigan	http://courts.mi.gov/Administration/SCAO/Resources/Documents/Publications/Manuals/focb/2013MCSF.pdf
Minnesota	http://childsupportcalculator.dhs.state.mn.us
Mississippi	www.mdhs.state.ms.us/csemdhs.html#receive (very basic child support table)
Missouri	http://teamlex.com/Areas/form14.htm

State Child Support Calculators (continued)

State	Support Information/Calculators
Montana	www.dphhs.mt.gov/csed/packet/guidelines.shtml
Nebraska	http://supremecourt.ne.gov/forms/supreme-court-child-support-forms.shtml
Nevada	No official calculator. Statutory guidelines at www.dshs.wa.gov/pdf/esa/dcs/nvchildsupportcalculation.pdf
New Hampshire	www.dhhs.nh.gov/DCSS/calculator.htm
New Jersey	www.judiciary.state.nj.us/csguide/index.htm (Appendixes IXB and IXC)
New Mexico	https://elink.hsd.state.nm.us/eCSE/pubCalculator.aspx
New York	https://newyorkchildsupport.com/child_support_standards.html
North Carolina	http://info.dhhs.state.nc.us/olm/manuals/dss/cse/man/CSEcJ-02.htm#P175_16711
North Dakota	www.ndcourts.gov/chldspt/
Ohio	No official calculator
Oklahoma	www.okdhs.org/onlineservices/cscalc
Oregon	http://oregonchildsupport.gov/calculator/pages/index.aspx
Pennsylvania	www.humanservices.state.pa.us/csws/
Rhode Island	www.cse.ri.gov/services/establishment_childsup.php (no calculator, just general guidelines)
South Carolina	www.state.sc.us/dss/csed/calculator.htm
South Dakota	www.dss.sd.gov/childsupport/services/obligationcalculator.asp
Tennessee	www.state.tn.us/humanserv/is/isdownloads.html
Texas	No official calculator; legal aid agency site provides info at www.lanwt.org/txaccess/change_childsupport.asp
Utah	http://orscsc.dhs.utah.gov
Vermont	www.dcf.vermont.gov/ocs/parents/guidelines_calculator
Virginia	www.dss.state.va.us/family/dcse/links.cgi (select Guideline for Determination of Child Support)
Washington	www.courts.wa.gov/forms/documents/CSWorksheet.pdf
West Virginia	www.legis.state.wv.us/WVCODE/code.cfm?chap=48&art+13#13 (scroll down for worksheets)
Wisconsin	http://dcf.wisconsin.gov/bcs/order/guidelines_tools.htm
Wyoming	www.courts.state.wy.us/Pro Se Divorce Forms/DWCP/DWCPentire.pdf (DWCP 12 is a computation form)

How Support Is Paid Each Month

Once you've agreed on an amount—or the court has decided on one for you—your next step is to figure out how it will be paid. You have a few options:

- You can agree that the paying spouse will send checks directly to the recipient, on a schedule you set up together.
- You can agree that the paying spouse will transmit the money in another way, like through an electronic funds deposit or even a PayPal account.
- The recipient can get an income withholding order (IWO) (also known as a wage assignment), making the paying spouse's employer responsible for deducting the support amount from the paycheck and sending it.
- The recipient can register the child support order with your state's child support enforcement agency, and the paying spouse (or the spouse's employer) can pay the support to the agency, which in turn pays the recipient spouse.

Each of these options is discussed in detail below.

CAUTION

Lump sum child support is unusual. It might seem easier to pay child support in advance in a lump sum. A few states allow this, but most don't, so don't do it before talking to a lawyer about your state's rules.

Direct Payment

If you're entirely certain that the paying spouse will never miss a payment and you want to keep things really simple, you can agree on the amount and date of the payments and just go from there. Your final order and your marital settlement agreement will set out the terms of the support payments, so if you're supposed to get support and don't, you can always go in and enforce the terms (with an income withholding order, for example) later. But getting the order will take longer than if you put the enforcement mechanisms to work right away, as the methods described below do.

If you do decide on direct payment, include a provision in your settlement agreement saying that the paying spouse's wages can be garnished if there's no payment for a certain number of months. States automatically include income withholding orders in child support orders, but it's up to you whether you want to ask the employer to exercise the order. (There's more about withholding orders below.) If the paying spouse is self-employed, you might want to consider having the paying spouse post a bond or deposit a few months' worth of support into a separate account, with an agreement that the recipient spouse can withdraw money from the account only if support isn't paid for a certain number of months.

Income Withholding Orders

All child support orders automatically include a provision allowing automatic deductions from the paying spouse's paycheck. There are limits on how much can be taken from each paycheck, but at the very least, it will be a start on getting support. This works only if the paying spouse has an employer—you can't garnish the self-employed. You don't have to use an IWO; it's up to you. But having an automatic deduction is a good way for both spouses to make sure support arrives on time each month.

Once you have a court order stating the amount and terms of payment, the recipient spouse is responsible for getting the IWO in place. Garnishing wages isn't all that complicated, and probably won't require a lawyer's help. You'll have to send the court order and some fairly simple paperwork to your spouse's employer. (You may also have to register with your county or state child support enforcement agency—in some states the agency will be involved in the payment process in all cases.) After you do, the employer becomes responsible for taking the money out of your spouse's check to pay the support. The employer also is required to notify you if your spouse changes jobs within the company or leaves the job.

State child support enforcement office websites are listed below. Many of the websites include information about how to garnish wages in a divorce.

If you're the paying spouse, the automatic deduction of an IWO may seem intrusive, and some people might find it slightly embarrassing. But withholding orders are so common now that the stigma is pretty much gone—because they're automatic, there's no implication that you are a deadbeat. An IWO does make things easy for you. You don't have to mail a check to your former spouse each month, and you never have to worry about being late or where the money is going to come from. It might feel like your paycheck is miniscule after the deductions, but at least all the money that's left is yours to do with as you see fit—you've already met your most important obligation, supporting your kids.

Using Your State Child Support Enforcement Agency

Federal law requires that every state have an agency dedicated to child support enforcement. If you need help getting your spouse to pay child support, your state agency or in some places, a county agency doing the same work, can do the following for you:

- help you get an income withholding order served on your spouse's employer
- receive payments from your spouse and distribute them to you
- keep track of the payment history in your case
- follow up if payments aren't made on time (the agency can enforce support through wage garnishments, taking money directly out of your spouse's bank accounts, intercepting tax refunds, invalidating your spouse's passport, suspending your spouse's driver's license and professional licenses, and going to court for a contempt order that means your spouse is subject to criminal prosecution)
- ensure that health insurance for your children is in place and continuing under the support order by helping you prepare the appropriate order
- monitor your spouse's efforts to get work if nonpayment is because of loss of a job, and
- work with you and your spouse to come up with a plan to pay overdue support (arrearages), if payments haven't been made for a while.

You may have to pay a small administrative fee or a tiny percentage of your support payment to the agency for these services. To find out how to get an account with your local agency, go to the website listed below for your state, in "State Child Support Enforcement Agencies."

You can register your support order with the state agency whether your spouse is self-employed or works for an employer and whether or not you have arranged for income withholding. If your spouse is self-employed, you can arrange for payments to be made through the agency rather than directly to you. If you're garnishing wages, you can arrange for the payment to go from the employer to the agency and then to you.

When you do get in touch with the agency, be prepared to provide all the information it will need. Your support order (or settlement agreement) should include basic identifying information for you, your spouse, and each of your children, including each person's date of birth, Social Security number, and current contact information. In addition, you'll need to give the agency:

- your court case number and a copy of the order of support
- information about your spouse's employment, including contact information for your spouse's employer, and
- your spouse's driver's license number and the identifying information for any professional license your spouse holds (for example, if your spouse is a doctor, lawyer, architect, or contractor).

Start right away establishing a good relationship with the folks at your child support office by doing your part and providing the information they need to do their jobs. You'll probably be assigned to one worker who will be in charge of your case, but keep track of every contact you have with the agency and who you talked to so that you can always trace the history of your case.

The state has great resources and can be an enormous help to you. At the same time, they're working with a lot of cases, so be patient and don't expect immediate results.

If You're the Recipient: Enforcing Child Support Orders

Getting a child support order from the court isn't that difficult—it's getting your payments regularly that can be hard. You may be worried about getting your support checks because your spouse is self-employed or has a sporadic income stream, or because you simply don't consider your spouse trustworthy. And you're probably not off base in being concerned— millions of dollars in child support goes uncollected every year.

While Your Divorce Is Pending

If your divorce is not yet completed and you haven't been to court yet, you may have an informal agreement with your spouse about support while your divorce is pending. You may even have written it down. However, you can't enforce that agreement until you go to court and get an order from a judge making it official. So if your spouse has stopped paying for necessary expenses, you'll have to go into court right away for a temporary order. See Chapter 5.

If you're in a mediation process, you should immediately report to the mediator—and your consulting lawyer, if you have one—that your spouse isn't making good on your agreement. The mediator may have you and your spouse come in for another session, at which you can find out the reason for the nonpayment and discuss how to protect your children's right to support. Your own lawyer may need to get involved at some point.

Once You Have a Court Order

Once you have a court order, whether your divorce is final or not, you can enforce the support order if your support check doesn't arrive. If you arranged for payment to be made through an income withholding order or through your state child support enforcement agency (or both), you have automatic enforcement help from either the employer or the agency.

If your agreement is for direct payment from your spouse to you, you have more to do.

If you have (or had) a lawyer, immediately tell your lawyer that there's a problem with the support. Most likely, the first thing the lawyer will do is write to your spouse or to your spouse's lawyer. If that doesn't work, establishing an IWO is probably your next best step.

If You're the Paying Spouse

Sometimes it may feel as though you are paying out practically your whole paycheck and going without, while your spouse is living comfortably with the kids in the house that used to be your home too. Try to keep some perspective on the situation. When you lived with your spouse and kids, you probably put most of your money into the household kitty, and a lot of that contribution was about providing a house, clothes, and food for your children. The same is true now.

If you really can't pay what you owe, or your situation changes, you'll need to ask the court to have your support amount modified. (See "If Circumstances Change," below.) Whatever you do, don't just stop paying. Failure to pay court-ordered child support is a crime. That means that under certain circumstances, a warrant could be issued for your arrest and you could be put in jail for up to six months for a first offense, and two years for a repeat arrearage. And there are a lot of possibilities short of that that could make your life pretty miserable. State agencies have the power to dip into your bank account—even if you own it jointly with someone else (like a new spouse). Many states can suspend your professional license and your driver's license if you have serious support arrearages.

State Child Support Enforcement Agencies

State	Agency
Alabama	dhr.alabama.gov/services/Child_Support_Services/Child_Support_Enforcement.aspx
Alaska	www.csed.state.ak.us
Arizona	www.azdes.gov/dcss
Arkansas	www.dfa.arkansas.gov/offices/childsupport/Pages/default.aspx
California	www.childsup.cahwnet.gov
Colorado	www.childsupport.state.co.us
Connecticut	www.ct.gov/dss/site/default.asp (Click "Support for Children")
Delaware	dhss.delaware.gov/dhss/dcse
Dist. of Col.	http://csed.dc.gov
Florida	dor.myflorida.com/dor/childsupport
Georgia	dcss.dhs.georgia.gov
Hawaii	ag.hawaii.gov/csea
Idaho	www.healthandwelfare.idaho.gov/Children/ChildSupport/tabid/76/Default.aspx
Illinois	www.childsupportillinois.com
Indiana	www.in.gov/dcs/support.htm
Iowa	dhs.state.ia.us/Consumers/Child_Support/ChildSupportIndex.html
Kansas	www.srs.ks.gov/services/Pages/CSE.aspx
Kentucky	chfs.ky.gov/dis/cse.htm
Louisiana	www.dss.louisiana.gov (click "Child Support Enforcement")
Maine	www.maine.gov/ag/children_families/child_paternity_support.shtml
Maryland	www.dhr.state.md.us/blog
Massachusetts	www.mass.gov/dor/child-support
Michigan	www.michigan.gov/dhs (click "Child Support" link)
Minnesota	mn.gov/dhs (click "Partners and Providers" for child support link)
Mississippi	www.mdhs.state.ms.us/cse.html
Missouri	www.dss.mo.gov/pr_cs.htm

State Child Support Enforcement Agencies (continued)

State	Agency
Montana	www.dphhs.mt.gov/csed/index.shtml
Nebraska	dhhs.ne.gov/children_family_services/CSE/Pages/CSEhome.aspx
Nevada	http://dwss.nv.gov (click link for "Child Support")
New Hampshire	www.dhhs.nh.gov/dcss/index.htm
New Jersey	www.njchildsupport.org
New Mexico	www.hsd.state.nm.us/csed (click "Looking for Assistance")
New York	https://newyorkchildsupport.com
North Carolina	www.ncdhhs.gov/dss/cse
North Dakota	www.nd.gov/dhs/services/childsupport
Ohio	jfs.ohio.gov/OCS
Oklahoma	okdhs.org/programsandservices/ocss
Oregon	www.oregonchildsupport.gov
Pennsylvania	www.humanservices.state.pa.us/csws
Rhode Island	www.cse.ri.gov
South Carolina	www.state.sc.us/dss/csed
South Dakota	dss.sd.gov/childsupport
Tennessee	www.state.tn.us/humanserv/cs/cs_main.html
Texas	www.texasattorneygeneral.gov/cs
Utah	www.ors.state.ut.us
Vermont	dcf.vermont.gov/ocs
Virginia	www.dss.virginia.gov/family/dcse.html
Washington	dshs.wa.gov/children.shtml
West Virginia	www.wvdhhr.org/bcse/
Wisconsin	dcf.wisconsin.gov/bcs
Wyoming	http://dfsweb.state.wy.us/child-support-enforcement/index.html

Don't Try Playing Dead

One divorced father was arrested and put in jail for failure to pay about $4,000 in child support. He escaped, and a few months later the court got a phone call from a relative saying he'd been killed in a bar fight, so authorities stopped looking for him. Twenty-seven years later, his ex-wife called the sheriff and said the deadbeat dad was alive and living in South Carolina—and she was right. The four grand was now about $30,000 in arrearages. His current (and fourth) wife filed divorce papers immediately. And if that dad thinks he's getting out of the support obligation because he's in jail, he's got another think coming—being incarcerated doesn't automatically end child support, although the amount may be adjusted to take reduced earnings into account.

Most states report nonpayment to the credit bureaus, affecting your credit rating. All report to the federal "new hire database," which means that if you try to change jobs, your prospective new employer can find out that you are behind in your child support. You can have your passport denied and your tax refunds intercepted. Some states list nonpaying parents on public Web pages. Child support obligations don't go away, either—in most states, there's no limit on how many years can pass between the order and collection of the support payments. Even if you file for bankruptcy, you can't wipe out your obligation to support your children.

How Long Support Lasts

Generally, parents' support obligations end when their youngest child becomes an adult in the eyes of the law—usually at 18, but sometimes older depending on the state. However, some states require parents to continue paying child support as long as the child is a full-time student in high school, college, or trade school, up to a certain age. And some pay even longer—see "College Expenses," below.

Certain events end your child support obligation no matter what else is going on in your child's life or yours. You are no longer obligated to pay support if your child:

- becomes emancipated, meaning that before the legal age of adulthood in your state, the child goes to court and is declared an "emancipated minor"—someone with the same rights as a legal adult
- joins the military, or
- gets married.

> **TIP**
>
> **Get insurance.** You have an obligation to support your kids until they are adults, but what if something happens to you in the meantime? You should have a disability insurance policy that replaces your income if you become unable to work (especially if you are self-employed). You should also have life insurance that names your children as the beneficiaries and names someone to manage the policy proceeds for your kids until they are adults. Your former spouse would be the natural choice, but if you don't feel comfortable with that, at least try to choose someone who'll be able to get along with your ex.

Terminating Parental Rights in Order to Terminate Support: Not a Popular Idea

The courts and legislatures take child support responsibilities very seriously. In an Ohio case, a divorced father argued that he shouldn't have to pay past-due child support after he allowed his ex-wife's new husband to adopt his child. Because his rights were terminated by the adoption, the father said, he no longer had any obligation to support the child. The judge agreed that the father no longer had an ongoing support obligation, but wouldn't let him off the hook for past-due payments.

In another case, the divorcing parents agreed that the husband would relinquish parental rights in exchange for not having to pay child support. The divorce court allowed the agreement, but the appeals court said no after the state child support enforcement agency intervened. The court said that the termination of the father's rights was not in the child's best interest, no matter what the parents agreed. As a matter of public policy, courts want kids to have two parents who are responsible for their welfare, if at all possible.

And in a New York case, a mother attempted to facilitate the adoption of her child by her brother, so that she and the child's maternal uncle would be the parents and the child's father would have his rights terminated. The court refused, finding that the father's consent to the adoption was based on a promise that the mother would agree to reduce his child support arrearage. In essence, the parties were trying to terminate parental rights in order to end support, and the court wouldn't do it.

College Expenses

College expenses can be a challenging issue when you're negotiating a divorce settlement. Many parents, believing that a college degree is vital to their child's success, agree to continue paying as long as the child is in school or until the child reaches age 22. When you're negotiating about the duration of child support, however, it's important to consider the impact of your child's college expenses on your own retirement planning. Remember that there are lots of resources out there for college students, including student loans, grants, and school financial aid.

Financial aid rules can also be confusing. The Free Application for Federal Student Aid (FAFSA, available at www.fafsa.ed.gov) is an application for federal college aid that you fill out and use for any schools you're interested in. Eligibility for aid is based on the household income of only the custodial parent—but if the custodial parent has remarried, the stepparent's income will be considered as well.

No Good Deed Goes Unpunished

One cooperative divorced mother agreed to share her son's college expenses with her ex-spouse on an equal basis, even though her ex made more than three times as much as she did. After the son enrolled in college, the father got a job at the same school, which entitled the son to significant tuition discounts. Did the father and son pass those discounts along to Mom? They did not—in fact, they colluded in preparing false tuition statements showing the full amount of tuition, rather than the reduced amount that the son actually owed. When the mother finally got wise, she sued the father and son for fraud and breach of contract—and won on appeal. Needless to say, she was relieved of any further obligation to support her son.

If Circumstances Change

It's a given that as your kids grow, their needs—and the cost of meeting them—will change. Teenagers can be a lot more expensive than toddlers. There will no doubt be unexpected changes, too, and you may find yourself wondering how to pay for tutoring for a child with reading problems or music camp for a child who shows promise.

Your own circumstances can also change. You may lose your job or get a better one, or get hit with a huge hike in the premiums for your kids' insurance. It's also possible that your custody arrangements may change over time, so that the children spend a lot more time with you than when the court order was entered.

Timing is everything ...

"After living with her mom for five years, Amy moved from Houston to New York to live with me when she was 13. I had just started making lots more money than I did at the time the divorce was settled, and my ex-wife had asked for an increase in her child support a few months before, but when Amy started living with me that was the end of that request. Amy never went back to her mom's, and my ex never asked me for another penny."

—**Divorced dad**

The bottom line is that whatever the reason, if there's a change in circumstances, you can always seek a change in the amount of child support that was ordered when your divorce became final. The court has the power to change child support until your kids reach adulthood, so if you can't work something out with your spouse, you can always go to court. And you're not allowed to make an agreement saying that you won't change support for a certain period of time. The court always can make a change. There's more about modifying support in Chapter 15.

![caution icon] **CAUTION**

Don't unilaterally decide that you're changing the amount of support you'll pay. If you're the one paying support and you have a big life change, such as losing your job, don't just start paying less and think everything will be all right. As discussed above, there are severe penalties for failing to pay court-ordered child support—plus it will have a major negative impact on your kids. Talk to your former spouse. If that doesn't get you anywhere, go to court and ask the judge to reduce your support obligation.

Taxes and Your Children

You're probably used to taking your kids into account when you do your taxes each year. With your divorce, there's more to think about, including how you'll share exemptions, credits, and deductions and how you and your former spouse will file.

Tax Basics

If you pay child support, you can't deduct it; if you receive it, it's not income. In other words, child support payments are tax neutral. (The rules for spousal support are different; see Chapter 11.)

Exemptions for Dependents

When you file your personal income tax return, you are allowed one exemption for each person you claim as a dependent. The dependent exemption amount changes periodically; for 2013 it was $3,800. Your child qualifies as a dependent if all three of these conditions are met:

- the child is under 19 at the end of the year, is under 24 and a full-time student, or is disabled
- the child lived with you for more than half the year, and
- the child didn't provide more than half of his or her own support during the tax year.

This means that most children living at home qualify as dependents— and that most children are the dependent of the parent who has physical custody, because the child lives with that parent for more than half the year.

However, you can agree that the noncustodial parent may take the dependent exemptions for your children, or for some of them. If you're the noncustodial parent, you can take the exemption under the following circumstances:

- you and your spouse are legally divorced, are separated under a written separation agreement, or lived apart for the last six months of the tax year

- your child lived with you or your spouse, or both, for at least half the year
- you and your spouse paid more than half of your child's support during the year (the rest can be paid by other relatives or public benefits), and
- your divorce order or separation agreement says that you can take the exemption, or your spouse signs a declaration giving up the exemption.

Your settlement agreement will be incorporated into your final divorce order, so saying what you want to do about the exemptions in the settlement agreement will take care of the last requirement. The custodial parent can give up the exemption for one year, all future years, or specified future years (for example, the next five years, or alternating years until the child is an adult).

Divorcing parents with more than one child sometimes consider splitting exemptions, with each parent taking the exemption for one child. You can certainly do this, but check first to see whether it really means a tax advantage for both parents. If you're not sure what to do about your exemptions, have a tax professional calculate what your taxes would look like if one parent takes all the exemptions and if the exemptions are split. Then do whatever is most advantageous for both of you.

If you and your spouse make a decision about the exemptions, include it in your settlement agreement. If you later agree that you want to change your decision, you can shift the exemptions by using IRS Form 8332. Because of the requirement that your agreement about dependent exemptions be in writing, be sure to use the form—don't just make the change yourselves.

Head of Household Status

If you have physical custody of at least one child, you may be able to file as head of household—it's a filing status, like "married" or "single." Your tax rate usually will be lower than if you file as single or married filing separately, and you will receive a higher standard deduction.

You can file as a head of household if you:

- are unmarried or "considered unmarried" (see below) on the last day of the tax year
- paid more than half the expenses of keeping up your household during the year, and
- had a qualifying person living with you for more than half the year (a dependent child is a qualifying person).

What does it mean to be considered unmarried? You have to meet five requirements:

- You must file separately from your spouse.
- You must have paid more than half the expenses of your household during the tax year.
- Your spouse must not have lived with you for the last six months of the tax year.
- You must have had custody of your child for more than half the time during the tax year.
- You can claim the dependent exemption for your child (you meet this test even if you've voluntarily agreed to allow your spouse to claim the exemption).

Tax Credits

In addition to the dependent exemption, there are a number of potential tax credits available to parents:

- **The child tax credit** provides a credit for a child who's under 17, didn't provide more than half of his or her own support during the tax year, and lived with you for more than half of the tax year—unless you are a noncustodial parent taking the dependent exemption for that child by agreement with your spouse. In that case you can take the child tax credit as well.
- **The child care tax credit** can be taken only by the custodial parent and only if you file jointly; the credit reimburses you for child care expenses up to a certain amount.
- **The education tax credit** applies to either a custodial or non-custodial parent and follows the dependent exemption; it's a tax credit for post-high-school education expenses.

- **The earned income tax credit** applies only to a custodial parent, and is available only to parents with earned income below a certain amount (in 2013, it was $37,870 for one qualifying child, $43,038 for two, and $46,227 for three or more).

RESOURCE

Check out the IRS publications. You can learn everything you wanted to know—and more—about divorce and taxes in IRS Publication 501, *Exemptions, Standard Deduction, and Filing Information*, Publication 504, *Divorced or Separated Individuals*, Publication 972, *Child Tax Credit*, and Publication 503, *Child and Dependent Care Expenses*.

Health Insurance

These days, health insurance can be an important part of child support. Very often, a parent's employer provides medical insurance for the entire family through a group insurance plan. There's no reason the kids can't stay on the same plan they've been on during the marriage if that's what you and your spouse agree to. If the parent whose plan it is must pay for the insurance, the other parent may kick in something toward the cost, or factor the cost into the child support calculations. Make sure that your settlement agreement also addresses the issue of who will pay for uninsured medical expenses—if it doesn't, the parent with primary custody may end up getting stuck with those expenses.

Most parents are glad to maintain kids on their health insurance plans, and there's generally no problem with the employer in doing so—after all, divorce doesn't make any difference in the parent–child relationship between the employee and the kids. But occasionally, an employer will balk at covering kids who aren't living with the employee parent, and, of course, it's always possible your spouse could flake out on paying insurance premiums or providing you with insurance information.

Whenever children are insured by a noncustodial parent, the custodial parent should secure the employer's obligation to continue coverage and the right to get information from the employer and the insurer, with a

Qualified Medical Child Support Order (QMCSO) from the court. And if you decide not to get an order, make sure your settlement agreement says you have the right to do so later if you choose to.

If you have a lawyer, the lawyer will prepare the order. It's also possible that the company itself has a form that you can use. If not, you should be able to prepare it yourself using the summary plan description from your spouse's group health care plan. You can get the summary plan description by writing to the plan administrator, whose contact information should be included in whatever documents you have related to the group health insurance.

The summary plan description should state the requirements for preparing a QMCSO. The order must state at a minimum:

- the name and last known mailing address of the participant (the employee spouse) and the name and mailing address of each child with a right to receive coverage
- a description of the type of coverage to be provided by the plan (for example, "group health and dental insurance")
- the period of time that coverage is to be provided, and
- the name of each plan to which the order applies (the plan administrator or a human resources employee at your spouse's company can give you this information if you don't already have it).

You'll need to prepare the order in time to have it signed along with the rest of the paperwork for your divorce. If you're preparing the order yourself, you can ask the human resources people or the plan administrator at the employer to review it before you submit it to the court, and to give you a letter saying it meets with their approval. That way, you won't have them later saying that it's not a valid order.

RESOURCE

See what it looks like. There's a sample QMCSO in *Divorce & Money: How to Make the Best Financial Decisions During Divorce*, by Violet Woodhouse with Matthew J. Perry (Nolo).

TIP

You can keep your health insurance, too. If you have been covered under your spouse's insurance and you don't have other coverage of your own, you are entitled to continue your coverage for up to three years under a federal law called COBRA. That law is discussed in detail in Chapter 11.

Yours, Mine, and Ours:
Basics of Marital Property

Most of us own a lot of stuff. And from houses to hostess towels, everything that you own—along with all of your obligations—must be accounted for in your divorce. Even property that you had before you were married and that you consider to be yours separately must be identified and included in the process.

This chapter will help you finalize your inventory of assets and obligations and give you the basics of what property will be divided between you and your spouse. The next chapter explains how the property can be divvied up by you and your spouse, or if that fails, by a judge.

Taking Inventory

If you filled out the property inventory forms discussed in Chapter 2, you already have some idea of what there is to divide, on both the credit and debit sides of the ledger. Now it's time to take a closer look. And if you haven't done those worksheets yet, now is the time.

What Do You Own?

Your asset list should include everything that belongs to you or your spouse, whether the property is shared or is one person's alone, and whether the property is tangible (a house, a stereo system, a car) or intangible (mutual funds, retirement accounts). Your list should also note whether you believe that any of the items on it are the separate property of either you or your spouse.

What Do You Owe?

You also need to inventory everything that you owe to any person, business, or other entity. Again, make a note on your list next to any obligation that you believe may be solely your responsibility or solely your spouse's. If you're not sure, and the information below doesn't help you, you may need to ask an attorney to help you figure out whether certain things are joint or separate.

What Property Gets Divided

When you get divorced, everything you own or owe falls into one of two categories: marital property or separate property.

In a few states, both marital and separate property may be subject to division at divorce, depending on the circumstances. These states are sometimes known as "kitchen sink" or "all property" states. Some commentators divide these states further, into "true" kitchen sink states (in which the judge routinely considers and divides both types of property) and "hybrid" kitchen sink states (in which the judge will consider awarding separate property belonging to one spouse to the other spouse only in certain circumstances, such as when the nonowner spouse would otherwise be left with very little after the divorce). Because court interpretations of these laws are evolving, our list includes states of both types.

In most states, however, only marital property is divided at divorce. You get to keep your separate property. For this reason, what is marital and what is separate can become a contentious issue.

Kitchen Sink States		
Alaska	Massachusetts	Oregon
Arkansas	Michigan	South Dakota
Connecticut	Minnesota	Utah
Hawaii	Montana	Vermont
Indiana	New Hampshire	Washington
Iowa	North Dakota	Wisconsin
Kansas	Ohio	Wyoming

Marital Property

Generally, marital property is everything that either of you earned or acquired during your marriage. So, for example, money you earned at work and put in your own checking or savings account is marital property when you get divorced. So is the car you bought and made payments on from that account.

There are some important exceptions to that rule—for example, money that only one of you inherited is not marital property. These exceptions are discussed in "Separate Property," below.

Sometimes separate property is turned into marital property by how you treat it. In some states, the only way property can be changed from separate to marital is if the spouses agree in writing. But in other states, there may be room for argument if one of you:

- placed property that was originally separate into both spouses' names
- placed property that was originally separate into accounts that already included marital property (this is called commingling), or
- devoted significant amounts of time to increasing the value of the property or asset, as opposed to simply allowing it to appreciate as a passive asset. For example, if you own a brokerage account that's your separate property and you spend lots of time buying and selling stocks, your spouse might acquire some interest in the asset because your time itself is basically considered a marital asset. However, your spouse's interest will be only in the appreciation during your marriage—your efforts don't turn the entire asset into marital property. And "routine" attention to investments doesn't count.

In community property states, the terms "marital property" and "community property" are interchangeable.

Separate Property

Separate property belongs only to you or only to your spouse. There are some differences in how separate property is defined in different states, but the same general rules apply most places. The most common forms of separate property are:

- property one spouse owned before the marriage
- gifts received by one spouse before or during the marriage
- property acquired during the marriage in one spouse's name (in a community property state, must be purchased with the spouse's separate funds) and never used for the benefit of the other spouse or the marriage
- inheritances received by one spouse before or during the marriage
- property that the spouses agree in writing is separate
- property acquired by one spouse using separate property assets with the intention of keeping it separate, and
- some personal injury awards (in general, the portion of the award that repays you for lost earnings is marital property, while any award for pain and suffering is separate).

But My Mother Gave Me That!

It's often difficult to divide property that has sentimental value—especially gifts that were given to the couple, or one member of the couple, by friends or family members. In general, gifts to one spouse are considered that spouse's separate property—but spouses often have different memories about who the intended recipients were. And people often feel that a gift given to the couple by one spouse's family should stay with that spouse.

You should be able to hash out issues like this without a lawyer. But if you just can't agree, you may have to get sworn statements from family members or friends about how the gift was intended.

Identifying Community Property

In general, in community property states, partners own equally almost all property either one acquires during marriage, regardless of whose name it is in.

Community Property States		
Alaska*	Louisiana	Texas
Arizona	Nevada	Washington
California	New Mexico	Wisconsin
Idaho		

* In Alaska, you have community property only if you and your spouse signed an agreement creating community property rights.

Each spouse's income is also owned half by the other spouse during the marriage. The major exceptions to community property are gifts given to one spouse, property either spouse owned before the marriage and kept separate during the marriage, and inheritances, all of which are the separate property of the person who receives them. "Separate Property," above, lists some other categories of property that don't fall into the community pot.

Issues arise at divorce if you mixed up your community money or assets with separate money or assets or put lots of money or effort during marriage into a property or business that originally belonged to one spouse. Other issues can be confusing, too. A few examples of how to apply the rules are shown in the table below.

In the third example in this table, if the husband put the money into a joint account but immediately spent $10,000 of it on a piece of sculpture that he owned in his name only, the sculpture could be considered his separate property. As long as he could trace the funds used to buy the sculpture and prove that they were a separate property gift, a judge would be likely to treat the item purchased with those funds as separate property too. But courts are all over the map when it comes to characterizing property as marital or separate, so you'll have to check the rules in your state if you have property that's not clearly one or the other.

What's Community Property?		
Property	**Separate or Community?**	**Reason**
Jewelry wife inherited during marriage	Her separate property	Property inherited by one spouse remains that spouse's separate property
A video camera husband received as a gift from his brother	His separate property	Property given to one spouse alone remains that spouse's separate property
$15,000 given to husband as gift and put into a joint checking account that both spouses used for joint expenses	Community property	The gift money was originally husband's separate property, but placing it in an account that both spouses used made it community property
A boat, owned and registered in the husband's name, bought during the marriage with income he earned	Community property	It was bought with community funds (money earned during the marriage)
A business that the wife started before the marriage, that the couple worked at together during the marriage	Part separate property, part community property	Appreciation of the business's value during the marriage is at least partially community property because both spouses earned it; wife gets to keep part of the value of the business as separate property because she put in the resources to start the business

Getting Financial Information

How do you know you have a complete inventory of assets and debts? You don't, unless you and your spouse share whatever information you have about your joint and separate finances. It's very common for courts to require that you disclose at least the basics of your financial situation to your spouse. If you don't know much about your finances—maybe your spouse always handled those things, while you took care of other matters—the initial disclosure will at least help you know what more to ask for. (For what you'll have to disclose, see Chapter 5.) If your divorce is uncontested, it may be all you need. But if you don't think you've got all the information you need to negotiate, do some more digging. If you're headed for trial, your lawyer will probably make use of formal pretrial "discovery" techniques to get complete information about financial matters from your spouse. (See Chapter 5.)

As part of your negotiation, you may have to hire financial experts to put a monetary value on certain assets. (And you will very likely have to pay for them, unless your lawyer can persuade the judge that your spouse should cover the cost.) For example, retirement plans are an important asset that must be taken into account at divorce. But certain kinds of plans, like pensions, are difficult to value because their value is in the future, when the employee spouse retires. To find out the value of that kind of plan, you'll need to hire an actuary. There's more about that in Chapter 10. You may also want an expert to appraise your family home or other real estate, such as a vacation home.

Is Your Spouse Hiding Assets?

Even with all the procedures in place to help you learn about your spouse's finances, you may suspect that your spouse is not being completely forthcoming with you. Don't ignore your concerns. You can't make the right financial decisions in your divorce without complete information.

Red Flags

People can be very creative when it comes to hiding money. Here are some warning signs to look out for.

The value of your assets looks lower than you remember. It's possible that your spouse anticipated the divorce and has been withdrawing cash or equity from any number of places—from brokerage accounts to the equity in your home.

Your spouse's income looks oddly low. One way to hide income is to take the extremely simple step of asking an employer to increase withholding so that the net amount of a paycheck is lower.

Your spouse is reluctant to share information with you. For obvious reasons, if your spouse resists your efforts to gather information, be alert.

What You Can Do

If you think there's been significant wrongdoing, you probably want a lawyer to help you, to make sure that whatever information you gather will be admissible in court. Here are some tactics to help you get the facts.

Get tax returns directly from the IRS. If you suspect your spouse of misstating financial information—especially income or deductions for a business your spouse owns alone—on disclosure forms, get copies of your spouse's business and personal (if you filed separately) tax returns for the past three years directly from the IRS. Don't rely on returns that your spouse gives you. Use IRS Form 4506—your spouse will have to sign it, but if necessary, you should be able to get a court order requiring this.

If your spouse owns a business, hire an expert. There are a surprising number of ways that money can be hidden when there's a business involved. These include:

- paying "salary" to friends or relatives that is then given back to the business owner
- delaying deals that would profit the business or increase its value
- making deals that temporarily decrease the value of the business so that money is taken off the books
- purchasing artwork, rugs, furniture, or other valuable items in the name of the business to increase expenses and depreciation write-offs
- writing off receivables, which are part of the value of a business, and
- inflating payables, which decrease the value of a business.

You get the picture. And unless you are in the same line of business as your spouse and know everything there is to know about the ins and outs of the specific enterprise, you will be well served by getting yourself some help in this situation. Forensic accountants have special training in reviewing business records to determine what the true value of a business is and whether there's anything inappropriate going on financially.

If the business existed before the marriage, an accountant can also help you figure out what portion of the appreciation in the value of the business occurred before the marriage and what portion occurred during the marriage. This can be a highly technical calculation, and there's little chance you would be able to figure it out yourself.

Use the financial discovery methods. The methods outlined in Chapter 5 and above can help you gather information for as far back as you think might be relevant.

Hire a private investigator. An investigator can search out assets in your spouse's name, even those your spouse has taken a good deal of trouble to hide. Offshore accounts, corporate subsidiaries, and misuse of cash in a retail business are all things an investigator can check for. A thorough asset search might cost you anywhere from about $200 to $1,500.

Be careful to hire someone reputable—if you have a lawyer, it's best to have the lawyer hire and supervise the investigator. If you're doing it yourself, try to get a recommendation from a lawyer. Don't just go to the phone book or the Web.

You can try finding assets yourself through one of the many services available on the Internet. But unless you have a starting place—a type of account you think your spouse might be using, a corporation whose tracks you can follow, or a sophisticated understanding of possible financial shenanigans—you won't have any way of knowing how thorough the search is. In that case, you're probably better off hiring a professional.

RESOURCE

Learn more about assessing your financial situation. Check out *Divorce & Money: How to Make the Best Financial Decisions During Divorce*, by Violet Woodhouse with Matthew J. Perry (Nolo), for tons of information about evaluating your assets and debts and strategizing about dividing your marital property.

Yours, Mine, and Uncle Sam's: Dividing Property

D ividing your property, just like everything else in your divorce, can be done the hard way or the easy way. And again, the easy way—working it out with your spouse instead of duking it out in court—is the recommended course. Try to remember that your stuff is only stuff. Some of it may have sentimental value, but it's a good idea to avoid fighting even over that. Trying to "win" the financial part of your divorce will cost you much more, in the long run, than putting your energy into figuring out what is fair and workable for everyone.

You're in Control

Before looking at the nitty-gritty of how the law views property division, remind yourself that you can divide your property however you want to, if you and your spouse can agree. You are in total control of the property division—all you need is the court's approval once you've made the decisions and written them up properly. And the judge will approve any reasonable division of property the two of you come up with.

You have the same options when it comes to negotiating your property division that you have when it comes to making decisions about your children. You can:
- work with your spouse directly
- work with your spouse through mediation
- use collaborative attorneys to help you negotiate, or
- fight it out using lawyers who represent you in a contested case, and let a judge or an arbitrator decide.

This chapter tells you how a judge might divide your property if you went to trial. You can use it to help you figure out what seems fair in your own divorce. But you and your spouse might well agree on something quite different, because you factor in things that are personal, not legal. For example, maybe your only valuable asset is your home. If you're the primary caretaker of the children and you and your spouse want it to stay that way, your spouse might agree to a buyout figure that's less than half the value of the house so you can stay there with the kids. This would be perfectly acceptable to a judge reviewing your settlement agreement.

Negotiating a property settlement is not easy, but don't sell yourself short just to get it over with. Take the time you need, get as much help and advice as you want, and consider all your alternatives before making decisions.

RESOURCE

If you don't know where to begin negotiating. Especially if you have a wide variety of assets and a long marriage where spousal support is likely to be an issue, an expert called a divorce financial analyst can be a big help. A divorce financial analyst can sit down with you, as well as your spouse or your lawyer, and help you consider all the different possible scenarios for dividing your property, advising you about the pros and cons of each. Chapter 16 has more.

How Judges Divide Property

How a judge would divide your property depends on where you live. For purposes of property division at divorce, there are two kinds of states: community property and noncommunity property states.

TIP

Spousal support is a whole other ballgame. Spousal support is a separate issue from property division, and it's dealt with in Chapter 11. Property division can affect support, however. Property is divided before support is set, and a spouse who gets a large share of the property might not also be awarded spousal support.

Community Property States: Equal Division

Only nine states use community property rules, which provide that most property acquired during a marriage belongs to both spouses unless a couple agrees otherwise.

Community Property States		
Alaska*	Louisiana	Texas
Arizona	Nevada	Washington
California	New Mexico	Wisconsin
Idaho		

* In Alaska, you have community property only if you and your spouse signed an agreement creating community property rights.

The theory of community property is that during the marriage, property is owned equally, and at divorce it must be divided equally unless the parties agree otherwise. However, the practice is somewhat different.

Only California, Louisiana, and New Mexico always divide property equally. In Idaho, Nevada, and Wisconsin, judges start with a presumption that property should be divided equally—but a spouse who wants a different outcome can argue for one and may be able to convince the judge.

In Arizona, New Mexico, Texas, and Washington, courts are required to give each spouse a "fair" share of the community property. In those states, fair usually means equal or something close to it—otherwise, there wouldn't be much meaning to the concept of community property.

Equal division doesn't mean that every single asset has to be split in half—that's just not practical (or desirable, usually). The court just makes sure that when everything is totaled up each spouse ends up with property of equal value.

Just because community property is distributed more or less equally to the spouses, it doesn't mean there won't be any arguments about who gets what. It does mean that the biggest fights are usually about whether certain items are community or separate property, and about the value of certain items of property.

> ### If You Moved From a Noncommunity Property State
>
> What do you do if you got married and acquired a bunch of property in a noncommunity property state, and then moved to a community property state, where you're now getting divorced?
>
> Property that you and your spouse bought in your old state and still own is called "quasi-community property." At divorce, it is treated just like community property. For example, if you purchased a car in a noncommunity property state with joint funds, but put title in only one spouse's name, that spouse would own the car as separate property at divorce in that state. But if you moved to California with the car and then divorced, the car would be considered quasi-community property, and its value would be divided equally at divorce.

Noncommunity Property States: Equitable Division

In noncommunity property states, while you're married you own the income you earn separately. If you have property in your name, you also own it and have the right to manage it during the marriage, even if both of you paid for it or were given it. But at divorce, judges do not simply give property to each spouse based on whose name is on the property's title. To do so could lead to obviously unfair results in some circumstances. For example, say a couple decides that the wife will stay home to raise their children, and the husband deposits his paycheck into a bank account that is in his name only. If he were allowed to keep all that money at divorce, the wife's contribution to the family would be completely ignored.

Equitable distribution is intended to ensure that a spouse whose name isn't on the title still gets a fair share of the couple's property. It rests on the premise that each spouse contributes to the marriage and to the acquisition of property and income, even property and income that has only one spouse's name on it.

The Basic Rule

The judge's job is to divide your property "equitably"—meaning in a fair way, but not necessarily equally. Equitable division may mean that one of you might be awarded property in lieu of support—especially if you were married for a long time. Instead of ordering long-term spousal support, judges sometimes prefer to award property that will serve the same purpose—giving the dependent spouse a standard of living comparable to that of the marriage, but without requiring ongoing ties between the former spouses.

In a few equitable distribution states (listed below), the judge starts with a presumption that assets should be divided equally. Then the judge hears arguments from both spouses about why property shouldn't be divided equally. For example, one spouse might assert a much greater financial need than the other. The custodial parent might ask to keep the house, even though it's worth more than the rest of the assets together, because it's in the children's best interest to stay in the family home.

States That Begin With a Presumption of Equal Division of Assets		
Arkansas	North Carolina	Oregon
Florida	North Dakota	West Virginia
Indiana	Ohio	Wisconsin
New Hampshire		

In states that don't start with a presumption of equal division, state law usually says that the division should be "equitable" and "just." The judge will use the factors described below to reach a result that meets that standard.

Factors a Court Considers in Dividing Property

The judge in your divorce case, if you and your spouse can't divide your property yourself, will consider a number of factors to determine a fair division of property. Each state has its own set of factors but also gives judges the freedom to consider anything that seems relevant to your situation.

If both you and your spouse own roughly equal assets and have roughly equal earning capacity, it's easy. But if one of you would come away from the marriage much less well off than the other if you each simply took your own assets, then the judge tries to even things out. The length of the marriage is a major factor in how equal the judge will want things to be—the longer the marriage, the stronger the argument is for an equal division and for a division that will leave the lower-earning spouse as close to the marital standard of living as possible. By contrast, in a short marriage, if one spouse made a much greater contribution to accumulating marital wealth than the other, the higher-earning spouse will probably get a greater share.

Decisions about dividing property are similar to decisions about spousal support, because they relate to the same issue: how assets should be distributed so that both spouses can live as comfortably as possible after divorce. Both spouses' age and state of health tell the judge something about their needs, as do their job histories, need for retraining, and likely earning capacity.

The judge will also look at whether either spouse has significant separate assets. If you have a family trust that means you'll be set for life, or are expecting a large inheritance or the vesting of significant stock options, the judge will likely consider those holdings.

The judge will consider whether there's been any wrongdoing, such as hiding assets or squandering marital property. If your spouse squanders your joint money on gambling, sells a jointly owned asset for much less than it's worth, or buys expensive items against your wishes, a court could use the final property settlement to even things up. (The legal terms for throwing away money like this are "waste" or "dissipation.") Just making bad decisions or poor investments doesn't usually count as waste; there has to be some wrongdoing involved.

Fairness is always an issue, too. For example, a judge in Virginia refused to approve a settlement that gave the husband all of the property and left the disabled wife indigent, with nothing received except forgiveness of the loan on the house (which the husband received). Even though the wife agreed to the settlement, the judge considered it unconscionable and wouldn't approve it. And in two different divorce cases, spouses sought to "reform" a property division agreement—meaning to change it retroactively—because they had received assets that turned out to be worthless when Bernard Madoff's Ponzi scheme came to light. In one case, the court refused to revise the agreement retroactively, saying that the man could have redeemed the account at the time of the divorce; in the other, the judge said that because the accounts had never really existed, there was nothing to redeem and it wasn't fair for the husband to lose out. And in an extreme case, an appeals court approved the divorce court's award of 90% of the marital property to a husband whose wife was convicted of trying to have him killed.

Other factors the judge could consider include:

- whether there are children, how much time each parent will be spending with them, whether the children have special needs, and whether their ages mean that staying in the family home is important for them
- contributions that either spouse made to the other's training, education, or career advancement
- whether either spouse gave up a career to stay home with the kids
- the potential for marital property to grow in value
- how easy it is to distribute an asset (liquidity), and its present value
- how property is titled (in a few states, the court won't order one party to transfer title to the other, but will require that money or other untitled property be transferred instead)
- potential tax consequences of various distribution scenarios
- separate debts that each spouse is obliged to pay, and
- fault, in some circumstances (see Chapter 5).

Some judges will also consider the sentimental value of certain assets; others only look at ownership and value. When you try to negotiate a settlement with your spouse, review all these factors and consider how they might tip the balance in your situation. It may serve as a reality check if you aren't able to agree. And don't forget how much you could spend in time or lawyers' fees arguing about each issue. Better to compromise some and come away with an agreement that feels fair to you than risk having the judge focus on factors that aren't in your favor.

What to Do With the House

In many—if not most—divorces, the family home is the couple's largest asset. It can also be a very emotional item. Very likely, you and your spouse decided in happier times that it was where you wanted to spend your lives together, and it may be where your children have lived most of their lives. This can make it difficult to let go and to assign a value to it.

Because the house is so valuable and so important, it can be the linchpin of negotiations for a property settlement. Deciding what you're going to do with the house often helps put other property issues into perspective, both financially and emotionally.

There are three common ways to deal with a family home at divorce:

- put it on the market
- agree that one spouse will buy out the other, or
- agree that you'll continue to own the house together.

Here's how each option looks. (If you are facing foreclosure or your property is worth less than the mortgage, see "If You're in Financial Crisis," below.)

Sell

If neither of you wants to—or can afford to—stay in the house, you can put it on the market and try to get the best possible price for it. Keep in mind that before the sales proceeds can be divided, you'll have to pay off the mortgage, any equity line or second mortgage, and the brokers' fees. You'll also have to pay any capital gains tax that might apply to the sale proceeds. (See "Your House and Capital Gains Tax," below.) These expenses are one disadvantage of selling, especially if market conditions aren't good for sellers. Another disadvantage is the need to uproot the kids at a difficult time for them.

But there are advantages, too. Both spouses get money to start over, and it may help you make a clean break—neither of you will have to deal with the memories of better times in the family home.

Once you've decided to sell, you'll be faced with a lengthy and detailed process that involves a number of projects. Each of these projects takes hard work in the best of times, and the emotional upheaval that comes with divorce doesn't make them any easier.

Picking an agent. While in general, it's fine to sell a house without an agent, it's not recommended when you're in the middle of a divorce—the added stress is really not necessary. Try not to spend a lot of time arguing about who your agent will be. If you were satisfied with the agent who worked with you when you bought the house, see whether that person is available. If you're starting from scratch and having trouble agreeing, each of you should pick a friend or relative, and have those two people agree on an agent. Or you can each choose an agent and have those two agents select a third to sell the house—if the first two agents are willing to do it with no listing in the offing. (They probably will if they both work for the same realty company and you agree that they can pick someone in their company.)

Settling on an asking price. Take the agent's advice about your asking price—that's one of the main reasons you're using an expert instead of selling the house yourself. Turning that decision over to the agent will eliminate one potential conflict. If you think the agent's opinion is really off-base, you might need a different agent (or a reality check of your own).

Preparing to show the house. Getting the house ready can be the most difficult part of the sale process. There's often some work that needs to be done—minor repairs, painting, and the like—before the house is ready to be shown, so you need to agree on where the money for that will come from. If both of you have moved out by the time you put the house on the market, you can leave the place to be staged by the agent. If one of you is still living there, you'll need to get things cleaned up, get the clutter out of the way, and probably remove some of the furniture. If this work falls mostly on one person, you might need to figure out a way to compensate that person for the extra effort.

Reviewing offers. You'll have to work together when it comes time to review offers from potential buyers, especially if you live in a place where the real estate market is volatile. Your agent can advise you, of course, but ultimately you'll have to make the decision jointly.

Dividing the cash. Finally, you'll have to figure out how to divide the proceeds. In general, that shouldn't be too complex—the escrow company can distribute the money, after paying off all the obligations on the house and making whatever other payments you've agreed to. (For example, you might pay off marital debts with the proceeds of the house sale, in equal or unequal shares depending on your agreement. See "Dividing Debt," below.) And if one spouse has been making postseparation mortgage payments, that spouse has probably (unless the payments were interest only) been reducing the mortgage amount and increasing the equity. Unless the mortgage payments are in lieu of child or spousal support, the increase in equity may increase the amount to be divided between the spouses after the closing costs and obligations have been paid. The distribution should be adjusted to account for the paying spouse's contribution.

For example, imagine that a year passes between your date of separation and the date your house is sold (not an unusual scenario). During that time, your spouse has made all the mortgage payments, in addition to paying child and spousal support. Each month, $1,700 of the $2,200 payment goes to interest, and $500 goes to principal. That means that over the course of the year, your spouse has reduced the principal on your loan, and thus increased your joint equity in the house, by $6,000— using separate property. Your spouse would be justified in arguing that when the profit from the sale of the house is divided, the division shouldn't be equal. Instead, your spouse should get back the $6,000 in equity that was earned as the result of the payments during the separation before the rest of the sale proceeds are distributed.

Negotiate a Buyout

Another way to deal with the family home is for one spouse to buy out the other's interest. Often, the custodial parent buys out the noncustodial parent so that the children can stay in the house. The advantages are obvious: The house provides continuity and stability for the kids, and you don't have to sell if market conditions aren't good. In any buyout, each party bears a risk. The selling spouse may lose out on future appreciation, and the buying spouse may end up feeling the price was too high if the property depreciates in the future. A buyout can also be a financial stretch for the buying spouse.

Standing on principle isn't always in your interest ...

A woman who owned a large, valuable home with her husband said, "When we split up, we agreed he would buy out my share of the house. But then he said the most he'd pay was $5,000 less than what I should get using even the lowest appraisal we'd gotten. He just sort of stood there and said, 'So sue me.' I was so angry. I called my friend and said I just couldn't accept this final mistreatment—I was going to insist on putting the house on the market.

"My friend gave me some great advice. She said that given the value of the house, $5,000 wasn't that huge an amount—even $10,000 really wasn't, in the scheme of things. She asked me whether I really wanted to have to stay in close communication with my husband right now about getting the house ready for sale and dealing with the agent, the offers, and all that. She said that once the brokers' fees and expenses of sale were thrown in the mix I could end up losing more than the $5,000 I was so mad about.

"Basically, my friend said I should take what he was offering and get on with my life. It was the best advice I ever got. I took the money and we were done. After a while I wasn't even mad anymore—making the decision not to engage in the house-selling project with the person who was the object of my righteous anger also meant I didn't spend more time thinking about the injustice of it all."

A buyout can occur over time, with both spouses keeping an interest in the house for a while—that scenario is discussed below in "Continue to Co-Own the House," and whatever agreement you make about a gradual buyout would be included in your settlement agreement. But often, the buyout is completed as part of the divorce settlement. The buying spouse either pays money to the selling spouse—usually by refinancing the house and taking out a new mortgage loan—or gives up other marital property worth about as much as the selling spouse's share. For example, the wife might keep the house in exchange for giving up her share of investment and retirement accounts.

Because you won't have a real estate agent involved in a buyout, you'll have to use another method to determine the fair market value of the property. If you've recently had the house appraised or if you and your spouse have similar ideas about its value to begin with, you might not have to fuss much about this. If you don't agree easily, or you want a bit more information, you can ask a real estate agent to provide information about recent sale prices in your neighborhood for houses comparable to yours (these are often called "comps"). You can also go online to one of the sites that will estimate your home's value if you type in your address, like zillow.com or eappraisal.com.

But there are a lot of differences between houses, and comps are not always the most accurate way to determine the fair market value of a house, nor is an online estimate. A more accurate method is to hire a real estate appraiser. This will be more expensive—probably $300 to $500—but if you disagree about the house's value, it's a good way to settle the question. If you continue to disagree, you may have to ask a mediator to help you work out an amount you can both live with, or agree to some other method, like averaging multiple appraisals.

Once you've agreed on the fair market value for purposes of the buyout, you may decide to adjust it, for any of a variety of reasons. Here are a few common adjustments:

Broker's fee. Although you won't be hiring a broker, the buying spouse sometimes negotiates to have an amount equivalent to half of the standard broker's fee deducted from the agreed value. This is because the buying spouse may incur broker's fees later when the house is finally sold. Some states don't allow this, though, requiring that the buyer pay all the closing costs, including the entire broker's fee, whenever the property is sold. Your lawyer or mediator should be able to tell you what the rules are in your state. If you're doing your divorce yourselves, this would be a good time to look for a piece of advice from an attorney or a knowledgeable real estate agent. For now, just know that if you foresee selling the property in the near future, you may want to consider continuing to hold it jointly until then, to avoid losing out when the closing costs come due.

Deferred maintenance. If there's work on the house that you put off during the marriage that needs to be done soon, the buying spouse can try to persuade the selling spouse to knock the buyout price down somewhat. Likewise, if the selling spouse owes the buying spouse money to even out the property division, lowering the sale price is one way to take care of that debt.

Spousal support considerations. There's also the possibility that the selling spouse might agree to a lower purchase price to avoid paying spousal support. For example, if the wife is buying out the husband's share of the house so that she can stay there with the kids, she might agree to forgo spousal support if the husband will sell his interest for a much lower-than-market-value price. Be careful with this, however—it may negate the tax advantages that sometimes come with spousal support. (See Chapter 11.)

Refinancing issues. In most cases, a buyout goes hand in hand with a refinancing of the mortgage loan on the house. Usually, the buying spouse applies for a new mortgage loan in that spouse's name alone. The buying spouse takes out a big enough loan to pay off the previous loan and pay the selling spouse what's owed for the buyout.

For example, you and your spouse might have a mortgage loan with a principal balance of $150,000, and an equal amount of equity ($150,000) in your house. If you are buying out your spouse's half of the equity, you would need a loan for at least $225,000. You'd pay $150,000 to pay off the original loan, then pay $75,000 cash (half of the total shared equity) to your spouse, to become the sole owner of the house. The transaction would proceed just like a sale to a third party, with your spouse signing a deed transferring ownership of the property to you, and an escrow company taking care of most of the paperwork and transfers of funds.

Most likely, the transfer of deeds and money will all happen at the same time at a "closing" with the escrow company. If you are the selling spouse, this is the best scenario for you. If there's not going to be a closing, make sure the refinance is completed and you've gotten your money before you sign a deed.

If you're the buying spouse, make sure a title search is done to see that there are no liens (legal claims—for example, for back taxes) or other "clouds" on your title. The title company handling the closing should do this for you. See Chapter 15 for more on making sure all the important paperwork is taken care of.

Releasing One Spouse Without Refinancing

In some cases, it's not necessary to refinance the house when one spouse buys out the other. Instead, the spouse who's keeping the house signs a document releasing the other one from responsibility for the existing mortgage. The mortgage holder must approve this arrangement, and the buying spouse will probably have to fill out the same application form as if applying for a new loan. You might want to do this if:

- interest rates or other loan terms are not as favorable as those under your current loan
- the buying spouse is trading other assets for the house or doesn't need cash to accomplish the buyout, and
- the buying spouse qualifies for the loan independently.

Not all mortgage lenders will agree to this arrangement, called a "release of coborrower." But if you're interested in it, there's no reason not to find out.

Don't forget to also remove the selling spouse from the title, as well.

Continue to Co-Own the House

It's not unusual for spouses to continue owning the family home together, especially where kids are involved. For example, if one of you wants to buy the other out but can't afford to do it all at once, you might agree that payments can be made over time while both of you keep an interest in the house. It's also an option in a weak real estate market if you believe things are going to improve. Or you might delay the sale until a specified event, perhaps your youngest child's graduation from high school. (This is called a "deferred sale.")

There are pluses and minuses to continuing to share ownership. If the custodial parent can't afford to buy the other one out, then the obvious advantage is that the kids get to stay in the house anyway, providing an important sense of security and continuity for them. It can make a buyout possible by spreading payments over time.

Apartments aren't so bad ...

A divorcing couple with an eight-year-old son agreed that they would continue owning the house together until their son was in high school, though the husband moved out. The wife said, "I could have asked for more spousal support, but Greg really took the high road where the house was concerned. He'll be renting until our son is in high school—with this big loan on his record, no way will he be able to buy another house. It was a big sacrifice and it definitely made me more willing to compromise on other issues. We worked everything else out really easily after that was resolved."

The disadvantages of keeping the house jointly can be pretty significant, though. Because you are both responsible for paying the entire mortgage, a credit report for either of you will show the entire amount of your mortgage. Having such a large debt on your record, especially if you are not living in the house, can make it difficult to get credit for other purposes. You also bear the risk that your spouse will make late mortgage payments that will hurt your credit rating.

There's also a fair amount of accounting involved. You must decide how you will share the mortgage and upkeep expenses and who can take the mortgage interest deduction. For example, even if you pay equal amounts toward the monthly mortgage, you can agree that one spouse who would benefit more from it gets to take the entire mortgage interest deduction, in exchange for increased support or some other equalizing payment.

It also means that you must continue to be involved with your spouse. Of course, if you are parents, that's already true, so this may not feel like a big additional burden. But if you anticipate that it will make the emotional disentanglement more difficult, think twice before you agree to this long-term commitment.

You run the additional risk that the spouse not living in the house might have a change of heart later and want (or need) to sell sooner than anticipated. Your settlement agreement should set a specific time that the house can be sold—if it does, the agreement will govern. But anyone who's really determined to get out of an agreement can make your life miserable in the bargain—for example, by claiming that the agreement was entered into under duress and forcing you into a court fight over that issue. So if you think the decision might not stick, don't make it in the first place.

If you own the house together for a significant period of time after your divorce becomes final, you also risk losing the important tax benefit of IRS Section 1041, which is the rule that says transfers between spouses as a result of a divorce are not taxable. Section 1041 applies as long as the transfer takes place within a year of the divorce becoming final, or as long as it's "related to the ending of your marriage," which means it's made under a written agreement or order and occurs within six years of the date your divorce becomes final (after six years, you lose the tax benefit no matter what). So make sure you don't just make a handshake agreement. Make the agreement to keep the house a part of your written settlement agreement, and get the court to approve it so that it becomes a court order. This may also protect the nonresident spouse from losing the capital gains exclusion of $250,000, which applies only to an owner who has lived in the house for two of the five years before the sale—unless there is a written divorce agreement for co-ownership extending beyond that time frame.

Finally, consider two important risks. First, what would happen if one spouse died while you were still co-owners? Each of you has the right to leave your share at death. If you've agreed that one of you will stay in the house until the kids are a certain age, you could also agree that during that period you'll each leave your share of the house to the other, so that the resident spouse can continue to stay as you planned. This requires that you both make wills immediately.

The second risk is that one spouse will be sued by creditors or file for bankruptcy. In either of these cases, that spouse's share could be seized, possibly even resulting in a forced sale. There's really no way to protect against this, so if you believe it's a meaningful risk, don't go the co-ownership route.

> **RESOURCE**
>
> **Can't decide what's best for you?** Figuring out how to deal with this valuable asset—including whether you can actually afford to stay in the house—can be challenging. If you want to do a detailed analysis of your options using financial worksheets, take a look at *Divorce & Money: How to Make the Best Financial Decisions During Divorce*, by Violet Woodhouse with Matthew J. Perry (Nolo). You might also want to consider consulting with a divorce financial analyst. See Chapter 16. If you're over 50, there are some special issues to consider, addressed in *Divorce After 50: The Unique Legal and Financial Challenges*, by Janice Green (Nolo).

If You're in Financial Crisis

If your house is worth less than you owe on it, or if you're behind in your payments, then you'll have a different conversation about how to deal with the property in your divorce. You can still sell the house or stay in it as co-owners, but you may also have to negotiate—as a team—with your mortgage lender or other creditors for some kind of change in the terms of your loan. There are a number of options in this situation—none of them great, but all of them giving you at least the knowledge that you're dealing with your financial problems head on.

RESOURCE

There's a lot to know. This section is just an overview of some of your options, but there are lots of details you'll want to understand if you're dealing with financial problems at divorce. *The Foreclosure Survival Guide*, by Stephen Elias (Nolo), explains foreclosure and options for avoiding it in detail. *Selling Your House in a Tough Market*, by Alayna Schroeder and Ilona Bray (Nolo), could also be helpful if you decide to try to sell. And if the final crisis can't be averted, see *How to File for Chapter 7 Bankruptcy* and *The New Bankruptcy: Will it Work for You?*, both by Stephen Elias (Nolo).

CAUTION

Read your mail carefully. If you've missed payments or have any other problems on your credit record, you've probably been bombarded with mail about ways to avoid foreclosure or get out of debt. A great deal of this mail is from private companies hoping to profit from your misfortune, and you should ignore it. But never ignore mail that comes from your bank or mortgage lender, because it may contain useful information about your loan.

Short sale. In a short sale, you sell your house to a buyer for less than the amount of the mortgage loan, and the bank agrees to release its lien on your home. For example, if your house is worth $250,000 and your loan balance is $300,000, your buyer pays $250,000 and the bank agrees to release its lien even though you are "short" $50,000. You walk away with no house—but you've avoided having a foreclosure on your credit record. A short sale isn't great for your credit, either, but the general thinking is that it's less bad than a foreclosure. What happens if the bank refuses to approve the short sale and release its lien? You won't be able to sell because no reasonable buyer will want your house with the bank's lien still attached, and no title company will issue title insurance to cover the property.

Make sure you won't be responsible to repay the deficiency (the remaining balance of the debt) after the short sale closes. Ask your lender and get its answer in writing, or check your state's laws to see if lenders are prohibited from collecting deficiencies after short sales. Also, be sure you review the sale agreement to make sure it really provides for you to be off the hook for the shortfall—some unscrupulous lenders may agree to a short sale and then try to sneak language into the agreement saying that you're responsible for the whole amount, or for homeowner's association dues or property taxes.

You're more likely to get your short sale approved if you have only one loan on the property. If there's a second mortgage or a home equity line of credit, it's a much more complicated and lengthy process, in part because you'll have to get the approval of yet another lender who stands to suffer a loss on its investment.

It's crucial that you talk to a tax professional before entering into a short sale, because the amount that you are short for the mortgage may be considered taxable income to you in some circumstances. Unless you're considered insolvent at the time of the short sale, meaning that your total debts are greater than your total assets (personal property and equity in real estate), the amount of a second mortgage will be considered taxable to you.

Loan modification. If the lender agrees to modify the terms of your loan, you may be able to keep your house. The lender probably won't reduce the principal in most cases, unless the bank mishandled your loan from the outset or made errors in a prior modification, which might give it an incentive to accommodate you. But you may be able to get a lower interest rate or an adjustment in the length of the loan so that your monthly payments are reduced. The lender may also agree to put any late payments on the back end of your loan, so that you're no longer delinquent.

The lender might allow one spouse to be taken off the loan as part of the modification process, though most lenders prefer a refinance for that purpose. So if you don't have good enough credit for a refinance, you may need to use loan modification as a way to keep the house, even though it stays in both of your names, until the market turns around and you're able to sell it or your financial situation improves and you can refinance and complete a buyout.

The federal government provides subsidies for some loan modifications, to encourage banks to work with homeowners to keep their houses. Many of these programs require that the homeowner be suffering a financial hardship and qualify for assistance on the basis of income. Each bank has its own criteria for loan modification, so you'll need to find out—perhaps with the help of a lawyer or another professional—what your lender's rules are.

Why would a lender be willing to negotiate a loan modification or agree to a short sale? In this economy, banks and other lenders are dealing with significant losses. In many cases, they will lose more if they foreclose on your property or you file for bankruptcy than they will from modifying your loan or absorbing the loss in a short sale. It's a financial decision for them—often it's better in the long run for the mortgage lender to keep you in the house, which gives you some leverage.

SEE AN EXPERT

Get help. Start with the federal Housing and Urban Development (HUD)-sponsored website at www.makinghomeaffordable.gov. This site offers resources and contact information for HUD-certified organizations that provide free help to debtors in all states, as well as basic information about loan modifications, short sales, foreclosures, and the like, and advice about how to avoid predatory foreclosure rescue scams.

You can hire a lawyer or financial professional to negotiate on your behalf if you're considering a short sale or a loan modification. You may get much more attention from your lender if you have someone working on your behalf—banks are often more comfortable speaking with professionals or agencies, believing that homeowners are overly emotional and don't understand the financial ins and outs of the negotiations. Another advantage of having help is that you can be sure that you're not missing anything in the contracts or in terms of the big-picture consequences of the decisions you're making. Don't go with any organization that's not HUD-certified or that promises results that seem too good to be true.

Deed in lieu of foreclosure. If there's no way you can continue making the payments on your house, but you don't want a foreclosure on your record, some lenders will accept a return of the property in exchange for allowing you to walk away from the loan. With a deed in lieu, the lender loses the balance of your loan, but if it can recoup that loss—or at least a significant part of it—by selling the property, it will come out better in the end. (Make sure you get your lender's agreement to forgive the deficiency in writing.) Deeds in lieu of foreclosure are used more often with investment property than residential property, and these days, most lenders won't do them—but it's worth checking if you think it's better for you than a foreclosure.

Foreclosure. Foreclosure rules differ quite a bit from state to state. Some states have what are called antideficiency statutes that prohibit lenders from coming after you for a delinquent loan balance, or for property taxes, after the house goes into foreclosure; others leave you on the hook for the balance owed after the property is resold. If you own a condominium that is foreclosed on, you may remain on the hook for homeowners' association expenses. And if you have a second mortgage or an equity line of credit, it's likely not going to be covered by the antideficiency law.

Foreclosures are either judicial—meaning they are processed in court, you end up with a judgment on your record, and the entire process is public—or nonjudicial, meaning it's a private transaction between you and the bank, although when the bank puts a "foreclosure sale" sign up outside your house, your privacy is lost. Either way, your credit record will show a foreclosure for seven years.

Bankruptcy. Many homeowners try to save their homes by using credit cards to pay expenses and even to make house payments. By the time they realize they can't continue to make house payments, they're in way over their heads with consumer debt and can't make those payments either. Bankruptcy might help you save your house. In Chapter 7 bankruptcy, you can wipe out most or all of your consumer debts, freeing up money for your mortgage. In Chapter 13 bankruptcy, you repay unsecured debtors through a three- to five-year repayment plan, often at a steep discount. With reduced payments on consumer debts, you may be able to afford your mortgage. You can also make up mortgage arrears through your Chapter 13 plan and may be able to strip off (remove) second or third mortgages in certain situations.

Whether you file for bankruptcy jointly or individually depends on your situation and what type of bankruptcy you file. If you want to file a Chapter 7 bankruptcy, it's often best to do so jointly because then both spouses are freed from debts. Most Chapter 7 bankruptcies can be completed within a few months. On the other hand, filing a joint Chapter 13 bankruptcy with a spouse you plan to divorce is rarely a good option. Most divorcing couples do not want to be tightly tied together financially for the duration of the three- to five-year repayment plan.

There are other considerations that arise when deciding whether to file jointly or individually. For example, if your state allows you to double exemptions, you may be able to protect more property if you file jointly. On the other hand, because you must include both of your incomes in a joint bankruptcy, you might not qualify for Chapter 7 bankruptcy if you file together.

It is possible to do both a loan modification and a bankruptcy, and still end up keeping your house. You'll need the help of a lawyer or HUD-approved housing assistance agency.

See Chapter 14 for more about bankruptcy, including what to do if your spouse files for bankruptcy after your divorce is final.

RESOURCE

Know your rights and your options. The federal office of Housing and Urban Development (HUD) provides a great deal of useful information on its website at www.hud.gov. You can find warnings about foreclosure recovery scams, advice about saving your home, and links to free housing counseling and other programs like the Neighborhood Assistance Corporation of America (www.naca.org). You must help yourself by finding your mortgage loan documents and reading them to understand your obligations. And become familiar with your own state's laws. You can find resources for your own state at the HUD website, by clicking on "avoid foreclosure" from the home page and then on the link for state and local resources.

Dividing Your Other Assets

The things you own are valuable to you for lots of reasons—some that make sense, some that might seem crazy. Sometimes giving up the handmade placemats you got for $10 on your vacation in Peru is harder than deciding that you can live without the $2,000 plasma TV. Dividing up your property won't always be easy, but try not to drag it out.

Household Items

Some parts of the process are fairly simple. To start with, agree that each of you keeps your own clothing, jewelry, and personal effects. (In most cases, gifts that one spouse gives the other become the recipient's separate property, so you're probably not going to recover the anniversary Rolex or necklace.) If you're living separately, you've most likely separated those items already. Likewise, you may have divided up some of the furniture and kitchen items. If you want to be sure that each of you is getting furniture and other household items of approximately equal value, you can probably do a quick Internet search to find their current fair market value. This is one place where you really want to save your money by doing it yourselves, even if you have lawyers. Shelling out lawyers' fees to argue about who gets the sectional sofa just doesn't make economic sense.

Instead, make a list, check it twice, and come up with a proposal about who gets what, which you can present to your spouse. If your spouse is the one who moved out, and some of your favorite things went along, put those on your list too—possession isn't nine-tenths of anything where marital property is concerned.

Symbolic value ...

One twice-divorced man compared his two split-ups: "After my first marriage, I just walked away and left her with everything. I thought it would be too painful to sit there dividing the record albums. We didn't have much then anyway. I never had any regrets about giving my ex all of it. The second divorce was much harder, because we'd accumulated a lot more stuff and I cared about it a lot more. For some reason, I was determined that I wanted the really expensive, good standup mixer that was in our kitchen, even though I knew I could buy myself a new one. I did the cooking and it was my favorite toy. I was willing to trade just about anything for it and I laughed at myself later, but it meant something to me at the time."

Try to develop a plan that gives your spouse things that are valuable not just in terms of money. For example, a dining room set that your spouse spent hours refinishing to a perfect shine might be much more valuable to your spouse than something else of the same or even greater monetary value. Your spouse may not accept your initial proposal in its entirety, but it should get you off on the right foot.

If you and your spouse are able to be in the same room without too much drama or anxiety, you can simply take turns picking items. You could also do it by email, first creating a list that you both think is pretty complete, and then sending messages back and forth choosing items. You should come out with a fairly even split this way unless one item is significantly more valuable than everything else. If that's the case, you might want to just leave that item out of the equation and figure it out separately.

However you decide to do it, keeping it simple and keeping the lawyers out of it should be your goal.

Assets With Fluctuating Values

The value of stocks, bonds, mutual funds, and other market-related items is always changing. On any given day, you can know their value, but over time that value can definitely change quite a bit. (It's also true of real estate, but the fluctuations tend to be more gradual.)

Given that your divorce won't be completed for months after your separation, how should you deal with assets that rapidly fluctuate in value? You have a couple of choices:

- Assign each asset a value as of the date of separation and stick with it, even if the actual value is different when you distribute it. Often, you won't be dividing the actual asset, but trading it for something else of equal value. If you do, then each of you takes a risk. The one who kept the volatile asset takes the risk that it will decrease in value; the one who took something else risks having given up an asset that increases in value. Be willing to live with whatever decision you make, or use another method of division.

- Divide the actual asset or account. For a stock trading account, this would mean that each spouse takes a portion of the shares of each stock and moves it into a separately held account. If you were to do this, you would simply take whatever number corresponds to your percentage of the marital property—for example, if you live in an equitable distribution state and you agree to keep or are assigned 60% of the marital assets, you would take 600 out of 1,000 shares of stock.

Before you do the dividing, of course, you need to consider what you want to keep. If you or your spouse invested together in real estate, mutual funds, or art, you may have emotional attachments to some of them just as you do to your house or your personal property. Try to be detached and look at what it really makes sense to keep. Do you want to know you can get your money out of an investment when you need it, or are you willing to wait while long-term bonds mature? Get some advice from a financial planner who can help you consider your long-term goals.

Valuation Dates

When an item of property is valued can also become a point of contention in your divorce case. It happens most often with the family home, the value of which may change between the date the divorce is filed and the date you actually divide your property. The value may even change, as it did in one recent case, between one hearing date and another; given the fact that some family law hearings and trials are held over a period of months, this isn't that unusual. In most cases, the court will order that the property be valued as of the date of the latest hearing or negotiation, not as of the date of divorce.

Assets You Could Easily Overlook

Certain kinds of property seem to exist at the edges of people's consciousness, as minor parts of financial life. But some of those things have significant value and should be divided along with everything else. These include:

- tickets for sporting or cultural events (especially those involving long-term rights to season tickets)
- frequent flyer miles
- club memberships
- stock options
- patents, copyrights, and other intellectual property, and
- bonuses, overtime, and vacation and sick pay (not all states consider these marital property, however).

Some of these items, such as frequent flyer miles, can be divided between you. (Contact the airline to find out its rules about division; generally you'll just have to provide a copy of your agreement and instructions for the division.) Others generally will go to one spouse with the other taking money or assets of equivalent value.

Stock Options

Stock options are a unique type of asset. They are very common in technology companies, and are becoming more common in other industries. A stock option is an option to purchase stock from your employer at a specified point in the future, at a price that's fixed when you get the option. For example, say that when you're hired, your company gives you the option to buy 1,000 shares of stock at $1.25 per share on your third anniversary at the company. On that date, you can buy up to 1,000 shares at that price. If the stock is worth $2 when you exercise your option, you can buy it for $1.25 and immediately sell it for $2 a share, or hold on to it in hopes it will appreciate even more. If you buy and keep shares and their value goes down, you're stuck with that—even if the value goes down lower than what you paid for the shares.

Stock options are vested when you have the right to exercise them. They're difficult to deal with at divorce, because some states treat them as property, and some treat them as income, and because they're often received before marriage but vested during marriage, or received during and vested after, creating ambiguity about whether they are marital property. A spouse might own options that don't vest until years after the divorce, at which time they might be extremely valuable or worth virtually nothing—making valuing them at the time of the divorce difficult. (Some states don't consider them either property or income, because they don't have a clear value and because they can be lost if the owning spouse leaves the company.)

Complicating things further is the fact that many stock options aren't transferable, so the owner spouse can't simply transfer half of the options to the other spouse, leaving both spouses with the same potential risk or benefit. And transfers (if they're allowed) may create tax consequences, especially for the recipient spouse.

Unless you're positive that your stock options are basically worthless and will stay that way, you should consult a lawyer about how to divide them. Some divorcing couples enter into an agreement that requires the employee spouse to hold a certain number of stock options on behalf of the nonemployee spouse and to follow the nonemployee spouse's instructions about when to exercise the options and sell the stock. (At that point, the sale proceeds might be taxable to the person who sells them, so you'd have to account for that consequence in your agreement.)

SEE AN EXPERT

Don't try to figure out stock option division yourself. If either you or your spouse has stock options, you definitely should consult a lawyer about how to divide them. For general information about stock options, see www .mystockoptions.com. Click the link for "Life events" for articles and FAQs— some free and some available for a fee.

Many companies now offer employees restricted stock units (RSUs) instead of stock options. Like stock options, RSUs are granted at one time with a vesting schedule at a later date (or dates). The difference is that once RSUs vest, the employee actually receives shares of stock rather than simply having the option to buy the shares. In most cases, an employee who leaves the job before the RSUs vest will lose any unvested units. As a result, in addition to being a reward for past work, RSUs serve as an incentive to stay in the job. For the nonemployee spouse, accepting unvested RSUs means betting on the employee spouse's staying in the job long enough to receive the units when they vest—and also on the shares' value being worth waiting for.

Deferred Compensation and Paid Time Off

Stock options aren't the only form of compensation that can be difficult to value or distribute in a divorce. Some employees are subject to performance-based deferred compensation, including salespeople who receive commissions a significant time after making sales.

In one case, a financial consultant working at a large investment firm was working toward a $100,000 bonus given at the conclusion of ten years of employment if specific goals were met during those ten years. When he divorced his wife, he was two years away from the goal and was in line for the bonus based on his performance. The divorce court found that the money had been 80% earned at the time of the divorce, and that the near certainty of the husband's receiving it justified including the expected $80,000 in the equitable distribution of the marital property—even though the money was still technically an expectation. Another court might have ordered that the husband compensate the wife for the marital share when the bonus was actually received.

Paid vacation and paid time off can also be a valuable asset, but only if it is actually paid to the employee in the form of cash will it be treated as marital property. Otherwise, it only has value to the employee, and because it's not certain that the employee will ever receive a cash payment in lieu of time off (the employee may use up all the paid time off instead), courts don't generally award any paid time off to the nonemployee spouse. However, a cash reimbursement for unused leave upon an employee's retirement or upon otherwise departing a job may be considered marital property if the payment was made before the divorce was final.

Pets

Anyone who has pets knows that relationships with our furry, feathered, or even scaly friends can mean a lot to us. In a divorce, pets can generate conflict rivaling the toughest child custody battle.

Pets are legally considered property, and courts generally treat them as such at divorce. Most judges don't rule on "custody" but instead make a simple ruling that the animal belongs to one spouse. (Overwhelmingly, that spouse is the wife.) In the absence of such a ruling, at least one court has decided that a pet was part of the "personal effects" of the spouse with whom the dog was living.

Recently, however, some judges have issued orders that provide for shared custody of pets—most often dogs—and that consider the best interests of the pet, not just the desires of the owners. Some have even reviewed "bonding evaluations" done by pet experts who observe both spouses with the dog and report to the court which human has the stronger connection with the dog.

Of course, you won't be surprised to hear that the best way to deal with your pet at divorce is to negotiate an agreement that either allows one of you to keep the pet or provides for sharing on an agreed-upon schedule. If you really can't do that, and if you feel really strongly about this issue, you can push for a shared custody order and take your chances in court.

RESOURCE

Lawyers specialize in pet issues in divorce. Many state bar associations have animal law sections, and their members would be a good bet if you want someone to represent you in a pet custody fight. You could also try an Internet search or check out the website of the National Association for Biomedical Research, Animal Law Section, at www.nabranimallaw.org. The site lists court cases involving pets and divorce, all of which list the lawyers involved.

Genetic Material

More and more couples are using the techniques of assisted reproduction—medical intervention in the conception of children—as they seek to have children. One widely used method is in vitro fertilization, where embryos are created outside a woman's body and then implanted in hopes of establishing a pregnancy. This procedure often results in unused embryos that are stored for possible later use. Ideally, the couple creating the embryos signs an agreement at the time of fertilization that addresses how to dispose of any unused embryos. However, if they don't, and then the couple divorces, a difficult legal issue arises about who owns the embryos and what should be done with them.

Questions of social policy and medical ethics make the legal questions complex. In some states, doctors are prohibited from destroying genetic material and may only return it to the couple who created the embryos (who may destroy it themselves), implant it in the woman whose genetic material it is, or implant it in the womb of another woman with the donors' permission.

A few divorcing couples have gone to court over who gets ownership of stored embryos, and also to litigate the question whether one spouse can use the stored embryos after the divorce to establish a pregnancy and have a child, over the objections of the other spouse. In general, courts have concluded that one divorcing spouse can't use stored embryos to procreate without the other's permission. However, in at least one case in Pennsylvania, a judge awarded frozen embryos to a divorcing wife because she was sterile as a result of cancer treatment, and using the embryos would be her only chance to have a child genetically related to her.

Donor sperm is more likely to be considered marital property subject to division between the spouses, because a partner using donor sperm would not be creating a child using the other spouse's genetic material.

SEE AN EXPERT

If ever there were a situation where a knowledgeable lawyer is required, this is it. If you have stored embryos and don't know what to do with them, look for a lawyer who specializes in assisted reproductive technology by looking on websites related to infertility or surrogacy, or checking the member directory for the American Academy of Assisted Reproduction Technology Attorneys at www.aaarta.org. Or use any of the resources listed in Chapter 16 to find a lawyer.

What to Do With a Family Business

If one of the 23 million small businesses in the United States is among your marital assets, you're in for some special headaches. Trying to run your business during the upheaval of divorce and trying to decide its future while your own future may feel unknowable are big challenges. The business is a little bit like another child—you undoubtedly have an emotional investment in it, you must figure out what's best for it during the separation period, and you must make a long-range plan for it.

Day-to-Day Operations

If you and your spouse have both been running the business on a daily basis, then the first question to ask is whether you can continue to do that during the divorce. For many people, that kind of day-to-day contact is difficult during a divorce, and the many small decisions that must be made every day create too many opportunities for friction in a situation that's already fraught with tension. One way to deal with this is to split your time at the business, alternating days or weeks. Another is to divide decision-making responsibilities into categories of tasks. A third is for one spouse to back off for a while and allow the other one to manage the business.

This last option might be the easiest from an emotional standpoint, but it raises other questions. Will the spouse staying with the business be compensated in any new or different way for taking over the tasks of the spouse who backs away? How much compensation will the spouse bowing out be entitled to? How can the spouse who's out ensure that things continue to function well?

Especially if there's been conflict about how to run the business— not a stretch of the imagination where you've decided to divorce— there have to be some ground rules about what can and can't happen during the separation. (These rules are in addition to the most basic rule that business partners always owe each other standard "fiduciary" duties not to do anything detrimental to the business.) You probably know well what the hot-button issues are—anything from advertising, improvements, and inventory choices to staffing or accounting practices.

It's a good idea to prepare an interim written agreement that sets out those limits. Unless there's a pressing business reason to make big changes, the gist of such an agreement should be that during the separation period no big decisions or changes should be made, to the greatest extent possible.

How Much Is the Business Worth?

Before you can decide on a long-range plan for your business, you have to determine what the business is worth.

Valuing a small business is a tricky thing, and no two people will come up with exactly the same estimate. If one divorcing spouse is keeping the business and the other is selling or exchanging shares in the business for other assets, each one wants the value to come out a certain way.

In some business fields, there are certain rules of thumb or formulas to get a rough estimate of value. For example, you might take the year's profits multiplied by five, or triple the value of the inventory. These are very rough guides, and you should always consult an expert in the specific industry to learn how to refine them with specific information. A lot of other factors can go into figuring out a buyout price, including:

- what comparable businesses have sold for recently
- assets and inventory
- debts and obligations
- potential for income from the business, and
- terms of payment (a buyer who can pay cash can usually get a lower price).

At divorce, an essential part of valuation is determining whether the property is wholly marital, partially marital and partially separate, or wholly separate. (Marital and separate property are explained in Chapter 9.) Most small businesses involve at least some marital share, even if one spouse owned the business before the marriage and the other didn't work there. When one spouse puts a significant amount of energy into maintaining or enhancing the value of an asset during a marriage—and anyone who knows a small business owner knows how much work it is to be the boss—then a marital interest is created. (This is called the rule of "marital effort.") The premise is that in order to give all that attention to the asset, the spouse must be getting support from the other partner and from the existence of the marriage itself.

Obviously, figuring out how much of the business's value is marital property and how much is separate is not always easy. You'll probably want the help of a lawyer, an accountant, or a business appraiser who's familiar with the type of business you own.

And unless the value of your business is relatively low—$250,000 or less—and you and your spouse easily come to an agreement about its value and what to do with it, it's probably worth your while to talk to an expert about a reasonable value. There's more about this below.

Keeping things running ...

"We had just bought the café when things started to get difficult in our marriage. We kept working together to make the business function, and even though we had trouble getting along at home we worked really well together—especially because we made sure there were boundaries. I managed the day shift and David took nights, and we spent an hour overlapping to exchange information and make decisions. Even when we decided to divorce, we kept working together—we still own the café together now and both of us still manage it daily. Our working relationship is much better than our marriage was."

—Divorced business owner

Long-Term Plans

Looking at the big picture, you have three options:

- sell the business to a third party
- have one spouse buy out the other immediately, or
- continue co-owning the business for an indefinite or a specified period, with an eventual sale or buyout.

If you and your spouse decide that one of you will keep the business in exchange for a cash payment, you'll have to consider how you'll structure the buyout. Very few business purchases (which is essentially what this is) are made with cash on the barrelhead; instead, they are made over time.

If you're the spouse whose interest is being purchased, you'll probably be getting an agreement for payment over a period of years. Make sure you also get some kind of security for that agreement, just as you would if you were financing the sale of your business to a stranger. The security can take the form of a lien on real estate, a mortgage, a promissory note, or a cosigner who guarantees payment. Consult a lawyer about the best way to secure the debt in your particular situation.

If your business is incorporated, there will probably be a stock transfer at divorce whether you do an internal buyout or sell to a third party.

Professional Practices

A professional practice, like that of a lawyer or dentist, presents special issues when it comes to valuation. Most of the value of a business like this is in its goodwill—the reputation that the professional has in the community and the resulting income stream from repeat and word-of-mouth business. Valuing a professional practice can be difficult because goodwill is, of course, intangible. One simple and common way is to take annual billings and multiply them by 75% to 150%. For example, if annual billings total $150,000, the value of the business including goodwill would be between $112,500 and $225,000. Some courts use that method, while others consider it as a factor in dividing other assets or setting support, but not in setting the value of the practice.

That's a big range, of course. Where on the spectrum the business's value lies depends on factors such as whether billings are up or down from the previous year, whether large accounts are secure, whether capital expenditures will be necessary in the near future, and whether any of the goodwill of the business rests on factors that will change as a result of the divorce (such as one spouse leaving a position in the office, possibly resulting in a loss of client loyalty).

There's also a lot of variation in how states treat goodwill at divorce. Some don't consider it at all. Others distinguish between "personal" goodwill attributable to the individual professional, and "enterprise" goodwill arising from the reputation of the practice itself. Those states generally divide only the value of the enterprise goodwill.

SEE AN EXPERT

Whether you're doing a buyout or selling to a third party, don't transfer your business without help and more information. This section only touches on the most basic issues. You'll definitely need the advice of a tax professional and probably a business lawyer in order to make the right decisions, and if your business involves stock, you must get advice on the process and consequences of transferring stock.

The Complete Guide to Buying a Business and *The Complete Guide to Selling a Business*, both by Fred Steingold (Nolo), explain valuation in detail and can help you if you're considering a buyout or a third-party sale.

If possible, find someone who has experience in the industry. Accountants, appraisers, actuaries, and lawyers are all good sources of help. The National Association of Certified Valuation Analysts at www.nacva.com, can help you find a professional.

A website at www.valuationresources.com lists different resources that can help you work toward a reasonable valuation of a family business in the context of your divorce.

Dividing Debt

It's a rare married couple that has only assets and no debt. And just as you are required to divide all your assets, you need to deal with your debt—including determining what you're both responsible for and what's separate. The same general rules that govern assets also apply to debt.

What's Marital and What's Separate

If you live in a community property state, you're responsible for debts incurred during your marriage whether or not your name is on them. If you live in an equitable distribution state, debts in your spouse's name should be considered your spouse's alone. However, even in those states you are responsible for debts your spouse took on in your name without your knowledge. The only exceptions are:

- if the credit was used for items that only your spouse would use, and you didn't know about the purchases, or
- if the debt was incurred in anticipation of the divorce and with the intention of making you responsible for it in the period before you and your spouse separated, in which case most courts would not force you to pay any share of the debt. But it can be difficult to prove just what a spouse had in mind.

As an example, if your spouse made a big purchase with a credit card that has your name on it, without your knowledge, you may end up responsible for the debt. The judge will look at all the circumstances of how the debt was incurred, including whether you consented to it at any point, and whether you—or your kids—benefited from what was paid for. This means that if your spouse used a credit card to buy expensive furnishings for your oldest child's first dorm room, you may be held liable for the debt even if you would have purchased the furniture for much less. But if the debt was incurred to buy sporting equipment or expensive clothing that only your spouse would use, you might be able to persuade the court to consider it a separate debt and get your spouse to pay it. (The credit card company, however, will still consider it a joint debt.)

Education loans are a special type of debt. If you got a student loan before you were married, it's yours to keep at divorce. If you were using joint funds to pay it off, consider it a gift from your marriage—but the rest of it is now your sole responsibility again.

If you took out a student loan during your marriage, in most cases, you and your spouse are jointly responsible for it. However, if you used the loan funds only to pay for educational expenses and you divorced before your family got the benefit of your education, some courts will give you full responsibility for the remaining balance on the loan.

Handling Joint Debts

The most common and best way to deal with joint obligations is to pay them off—either with the proceeds of the sale of the family home or with other available assets. This strategy has numerous advantages, including ease, certainty, protection of your credit record, and the opportunity to make a clean break and a fresh start.

Because a house very often changes hands in a divorce, the transaction may give you the chance to take out enough cash to deal with your debts and allow both of you to start with clean slates. Even if one spouse is buying out the other's interest in the house, there will most likely be a new loan, and the buyout price can take the debt into account. (See "What to Do With the House," above.)

For example, say you are buying out your spouse's share of the house. You've agreed that the total equity is $80,000 (the market value is $260,000 and your mortgage loan balance is $180,000). You owe your spouse $40,000. And let's say your joint debts total $12,000.

You're getting a new mortgage loan that will allow you to take out the cash you need to pay off your spouse, so you get a loan for the amount of the original mortgage, plus $46,000. You pay off the mortgage, pay your spouse $34,000, and use the remaining $12,000 to pay off the debts. Result: You each paid an equal share.

Another option is to keep sharing responsibility for debts after your divorce, but this entails certain hazards. For example, if you and your spouse agree that you'll each pay half of the monthly amount due on a joint credit card you used during your marriage, and then your spouse doesn't make the payments, it will affect your credit record (and your credit card balance).

If you do agree to share responsibility for your marital debts, make sure you get an "indemnity agreement" from your spouse, either in your marital settlement agreement or a separate document. The agreement should state that if either of you doesn't live up to agreements about paying debts, the other can go into court to get repaid. Going to court would be a big hassle, but having that option is better than just hoping everything will work out.

Dealing With Debt: Assessing Your Options		
Option	**Pros**	**Cons**
Pay off debt when property is divided	Protects your credit rating Ensures no postdivorce hassles over debts Clean break; make a new start in your postdivorce life	Coming up with the money can be difficult if you have significant debt
Continue sharing	Don't have to come up with money to pay off debts	Risk to your credit rating Risk of conflict later
Divide debts and each take responsibility for some	You have control over the debts you keep Don't have to come up with money to pay off all debts	Risk to your credit rating if spouse defaults Creditor can still come after you for payment of the debts assigned to your spouse

Even if your spouse agrees to take on a debt, if it has your name on it or even if you were married when it was incurred, the creditor can still come after you for payment if your spouse defaults. In short, your settlement agreement isn't binding on Visa. So if your spouse agrees to accept as separate debt $5,000 in credit card charges made during the marriage, and is also receiving a distribution of $30,000 from a brokerage account, arrange for the brokerage firm to issue two checks: one for $5,000 made out to the credit card company, and one for $25,000 made out to your spouse.

Handling Separate Debts

If you get a ruling from a court—or an agreement from your chastened spouse—that your spouse will pay for debts incurred for his or her sole benefit, make sure that these separate debts are paid when assets are distributed to each of you—which is likely to be around the time that you submit your final settlement agreement and judgment papers to the court at the end of your divorce process.

If You Can't Pay Your Debts

Financial problems are often a source of conflict for couples; unfortunately, the problems don't disappear once you decide to end your marriage. If you have serious problems with debt, you and your spouse need to work together to resolve those issues before you can finalize your divorce.

Bankruptcy is one option when your debt situation seems impossible, and it does have the advantage, in most cases, of totally eliminating much or all of your debt with no tax consequences. However, it's a matter of public record and stays on your credit report for ten years. In addition, you may have to disclose the fact of your bankruptcy on applications for a job, a loan, or an insurance policy, and it affects your ability to get credit. (Keep in mind, however, that if you are in financial trouble, your credit is probably already shot.) Chapter 14 discusses what to do if you need to file for bankruptcy (or if your spouse files while your divorce is pending or after it's completed). There are steps you can take to avoid bankruptcy, however, that may work better for you.

Negotiate with creditors. One way to reduce your debt or get payments under control is to negotiate some sort of settlement or deal with the creditor or collection agency. The key to this strategy is communication. It's best to notify creditors as soon as you have trouble paying your bills. But even if you've missed quite a few payments, it's often worthwhile to contact your creditor.

If you can come up with some cash, you can work with a creditor to reduce the total amount you owe, generally by paying a lump sum that is less than the total amount owed. For example, if you owe $10,000 to a credit card company, it might agree to accept $6,000 in full payment of the debt, as long as you pay it within 60 days of agreeing to the settlement. Usually you'll make between one and three payments; the longest most creditors want to wait for a settlement payment is a year, and you'll have to negotiate hard to get that much time.

If the creditor has reported late payments on your credit report, as part of the negotiation, ask that the creditor remove the negative information. If the creditor agrees, make sure you get written confirmation that the debt will be considered "paid in full" and that the creditor will submit a Universal Data Form (a standard form creditors use to report to credit reporting agencies) deleting the "account/trade line" from your credit report.

The most commonly negotiated debts are consumer credit accounts, personal loans with finance companies, debt collection lawsuits, and vendor accounts for small businesses. You'll need cash to make the payment. If your work hours or pay have been reduced because of the economy, you might be a good candidate for debt negotiation because you still have some income. The same is true if you can borrow from friends or family to make the settlement payment.

> **CAUTION**
> **Watch out for the tax consequences.** If you settle a $10,000 debt for $6,000, the creditor could issue an IRS Form 1099 report of miscellaneous income, indicating that you received $4,000 of debt forgiveness, which you would have to report and pay tax on. Not all companies do it, but it's not in your control.

> **CAUTION**
> **Be cautious about debt relief companies.** There are thousands of companies advertising services for "debt settlement," "debt negotiation," "debt consolidation," and the like. Be very careful of these companies—take a look at "Working With a Credit Counselor," below. Stay away from companies that offer guarantees, require significant monthly fees, require that you pay a percentage of your savings, promise that there will be no negative impact on your credit report, or claim that they can improve your credit report by removing negative information. None of these claims are true, and any company that makes these promises is only after your money.

Hardship payment plan. Some creditors will set up a hardship payment plan if you can show that you're unable to make your payments or pay a lump sum to settle the debt. You may be able to negotiate a lower interest rate or lower monthly payments, or both, most often on a temporary basis. The creditor will also usually adjust any past due payments by moving them to the back end of the loan, so that you no longer have to pay late fees. A hardship payment plan is specific to the creditor, the debtor, and the situation—in other words, it's very individualized. You will need to work with the creditor to come up with a plan that will work for you. The creditor may agree to accept hardship payments for six months or a year, and sometimes longer, but not more than a few years.

Hardship payments work for people whose financial problems are likely temporary—for example, they've lost a job but expect to get a new one soon, or they only have a few credit cards and a relatively low total owed so there's every expectation they'll be able to return to their original interest rate or increase the monthly payment within a reasonable, predictable period.

Working With a Credit Counselor

You can try negotiating with creditors on your own, and if you're a good advocate and have the patience, you may get good results. For some people, though, it's helpful to have assistance from a credit counseling agency. If you are looking for help, be very careful in choosing a credit counseling service—especially in a challenging economy, the credit counseling industry is home to some less than scrupulous businesses.

How do you find an ethical credit counseling service? First, make sure the agency is a "nonprofit credit counseling agency." That's not the end of the inquiry—some agencies that are officially nonprofit will still hit you with hidden fees and other unethical practices—but it should be the beginning. Next, take the time to check out a number of different agencies. The Federal Trade Commission suggests finding an agency that offers in-person counseling, and offers the following tips:

- A reputable agency will send you information about its services— for free—without requiring you to provide any personal information.
- Check out any agency you're considering using with your state attorney general (consumer protection division), the local and online Better Business Bureau, and a local consumer protection agency, if you can find one.
- Get a specific price quote, in writing, and a clear written description of the services you're going to receive. Get every agreement in writing—don't rely on any promises made orally.
- Look for an organization with a range of offerings: In addition to debt negotiation, it should provide budget counseling, debt management, and advice on planning and saving. Ask whether it will help you with an ongoing financial management plan that will help you avoid having more problems in the future.
- Find out how employees are paid and trained. If they're paid more for getting you to sign up for certain services, watch out. Try to use an organization whose employees are trained by an outside organization.

Working With a Credit Counselor (cont'd)

- If you're using a debt management plan, contact your creditors to verify that they're truly agreeing to what the company says they are.

RESOURCE
More information. Check out the Federal Trade Commission website at www.ftc.gov for a wealth of information. Also, the National Foundation for Credit Counseling is a 60-year-old nonprofit credit counseling network, providing information and links to credit counseling agencies at www.nfcc.org. For comprehensive information about credit problems, see *Solve Your Money Troubles: Debt, Credit & Bankruptcy*, by Margaret Reiter and Robin Leonard (Nolo).

It's also possible to do a combination of lump sum settlement and hardship arrangements.

The creditor's incentive for reaching a settlement or granting you a hardship deduction is that in many cases, it will end up with more than it would if you filed for bankruptcy (even compared to Chapter 13 bankruptcy, where you pay back some of what you owe).

If you are interested in a debt management plan, be particularly careful in choosing an agency to help you. Consumer advocates warn that many consumers are worse off when they pay high fees to DMP providers because this money could be used to pay creditors. And some shady DMP providers fail to make payments to creditors, leaving the debtor worse off than when the process started.

Debt management plans work pretty much the same as debt nego-tiation, discussed above, and have the same downside—having a lot of negotiated accounts will negatively affect your credit report.

Tax Consequences of How You Divide Property

Many of the transactions that go along with divorce, like transferring property from one spouse to another, are tax-neutral events. In other words, neither of you will owe any tax (or get any tax benefit) as a result. Transfers between spouses generally are exempt from income, gift, and capital gains tax anyway, and transfers related to a divorce are included in that rule. So, for example, if you own a house, but it ends up with your former spouse when you divvy up all your property, your spouse won't have to pay income tax or capital gains tax relating to the transfer, and you won't have to give a thought to gift tax. The tax basis (the value of the property for tax purposes) of the home won't change. Nor will the property taxes increase for the spouse who is keeping the home. (Of course, if you sell your house to someone else, capital gains tax will apply. See "Your House and Capital Gains Tax," below.)

There are, however, some tax issues you need to be aware of when you are negotiating your property division.

> **CAUTION**
>
> **Unmarried same-sex couples need tax assistance.** Although married same-sex couples now enjoy the same tax benefits as opposite-sex couples, most of the federal tax laws that govern marital property don't apply to couples in domestic partnerships and civil unions. How to file taxes and how to deal with property division can be much more complex for same-sex couples, who often must find accountants with specialized knowledge in this area.

Transfers of Deferred Benefits

If you're considering a settlement in which you'll be receiving tax-deferred financial assets of any kind in your divorce, consult a tax expert before agreeing to anything. A transfer of a tax-deferred asset, such as an IRA, is tax free if it's transferred directly into the nonemployee spouse's IRA—in other words, as long as it's rolled over. But if the nonemployee spouse wants to take the money directly, the employee's plan is required to withhold 20% of the amount paid and pay it to the IRS. (The 10% early withdrawal penalty that normally would be due if the nonemployee spouse was younger than 59½ is waived if the transfer is related to a divorce.)

Your House and Capital Gains Tax

Whether and how the capital gains tax affects you during your divorce depends on what you are doing with your house. In general, transfers of property between divorcing spouses are nontaxable. But there are circumstances where the capital gains tax—a tax on profits from sales of property where the gains exceed a certain amount—does apply to transfers that are made as part of your divorce.

The Basics

If you sell your house, you and your spouse can each exclude the first $250,000 of gain from your taxable income. The capital gains exclusion applies only to your "principal residence," which is defined as a home in which you've lived for at least two of the five years prior to the sale. A vacation house doesn't count.

What's "gain"? In the simplest terms, taxable gain is the selling price of your home, minus the selling expenses, minus your adjusted "basis." Basis is the amount you paid for your house or the amount it cost you to build it, with some pluses and minuses for improvements and tax benefits. Of course, being tax related, your basis is not always simple to figure out.

If You Sell Together

If you and your spouse sell your house at the time you're getting divorced, the capital gains tax applies. But you're entitled to exclude a total of $500,000 of gain from tax if you lived there for two of the five years before the sale. (If either spouse is in the military that five-year period can be extended for up to ten years under some circumstances.) And if you bought the house less than two years ago the exclusion may be reduced.

Buyouts

After a buyout, the selling spouse doesn't need to worry about capital gains tax because the sale was part of the divorce. But if you buy out your spouse, stay in the house, and later sell the house to a third party, capital gains tax will apply to that sale. You may exclude the first $250,000 of gain—as long as you've lived there for two years before selling, or meet one of the IRS exceptions to that rule.

Co-Owning the House

For a spouse who continues to own the house but doesn't live in it, there's a risk that the $250,000 exclusion might not apply when the house is sold. To avoid losing the exclusion, it's important to have written documentation of the agreement that called for one spouse to stay in the house and the other to leave but remain a co-owner. If it's clear that the arrangement was pursuant to a divorce settlement or court order, then the nonresident spouse can still take the exclusion on the basis of the resident spouse's occupancy of the house during the required period of time.

RESOURCE

Capital gains can be confusing. If you have questions about your basis, whether your gain is over the exclusion amount, or other aspects of capital gains taxes, try looking for the answer in IRS Publication 523, *Selling Your Home*, or ask your attorney or tax preparer to help you figure it out.

Retirement Benefits

Take a deep breath, because it's time to consider something you may not think about much or understand very well: your retirement benefits. These assets tend to hover in the background and not take much of your attention most of the time, yet they can be an extremely important element of your divorce. Pay careful attention to how you deal with them.

In almost all states, the retirement benefits that you saved up during your marriage are marital property, subject to division between you and your spouse when you divorce. However, benefits that you accrued before the marriage are your separate property.

This section discusses four types of retirement benefits. They're all very different, and you'll use different methods to determine their value and divide them.

Defined Benefit (Pension) Plans

Defined benefit plans, or pensions, used to be common, but nowadays they've mostly disappeared unless you're a highly compensated executive. If your company offers a defined benefit plan, it's an automatic benefit of employment—your participation isn't voluntary, and you don't make any choices about contribution levels or anything else. The benefits accrue while you work for the company, and when you retire you get either a lump sum distribution or a monthly payment. The payment amount is either preset under the terms of the plan or determined by a formula that takes into account your years of service, salary, and other factors.

Withdrawing Money From Retirement Plans

If you want to buy out your spouse's share of your own retirement benefits (or the house, for that matter) by paying cash, your retirement plan might look like a ready source of funds. Generally, you can't take money out of a defined benefit (pension) plan. If you have a defined contribution plan, such as a 401(k), you can borrow or withdraw your own money— the contributions you have made—at any time. But withdrawals have serious penalties. First, if you withdraw money before you are 59½, you will probably have to pay a penalty. Second, if the contributions were tax deductible when you made them (as some traditional IRA contributions are), you'll have to pay tax on what you take out in the year you take it.

You can borrow money from your own (non-IRA) retirement plans, but unless the loan was for the purpose of purchasing a home, you have to repay it within five years. If you don't, the loan will be considered a withdrawal, and you'll owe taxes and penalties.

For everything you ever wanted to know about getting money from your retirement accounts, see *IRAs, 401(k)s & Other Retirement Plans: Taking Your Money Out*, by Twila Slesnick and John C. Suttle (Nolo). To understand the issues in the context of divorce, check out *Divorce After 50: Your Guide to the Unique Legal and Financial Challenges*, by Janice Green (Nolo).

In almost all cases, pension money becomes available only when the employee-spouse retires. When you get divorced, all you can do is to decide what percentage of the payment each of you will eventually get.

Valuing the Plan

Defined benefit plans are difficult to value, because the payout is planned for the future and money has a different value in the present than it will in the future, and because a number of factors go into projecting the future monthly payment, including salary levels and years of service. You'll need an actuary to figure out the present value and then calculate the marital share.

When you have the actuary evaluate the defined benefit plan, the result is going to be a formula that uses three pieces of information:

- The actual amount that the employee spouse will get (usually monthly) upon retirement
- The share of the benefits that is marital property (for example, if the employee spouse worked for 20 years and was married for 15 of those years, 75% of the benefits are marital property and the remaining 25% belongs to the employee spouse alone), and
- The percentage of the marital share that the employee spouse is receiving

You'll know the last two items at the time of your divorce, but you won't usually know the first item until the employee spouse retires.

If you're the nonemployee spouse, your spouse's attorney might try to talk you into estimating the amount and agreeing to a fixed monthly payout starting when your spouse retires. Don't agree to that. Make sure the actuary creates a formula for the court order using the factors listed above, so that you get your full share of the pension benefits, in the form of a percentage rather than a preset amount, when your spouse retires.

Dividing the Defined Benefit Plan

Just as you can arrange for one spouse to buy out the other's interest in the house, you can make a similar buyout arrangement with a defined benefit plan. Or you can agree to have the benefits divided later, when they come due. Each option has pluses and perils, and you need to consider carefully before deciding. Here is how each option works.

Keeping your own pension and giving your spouse equivalent assets. This is a common way of dealing with retirement benefits, because it is clean and simple. But it may not always be the best for the spouse being bought out if that person doesn't have other tax-deferred savings. To accomplish a buyout, you'll ask an actuary to figure out the present value of the benefits and calculate the share that your spouse is entitled to. You'll then give your spouse other marital assets or a lump sum cash payment.

If each spouse has retirement benefits, there will be a certain amount of offset. For example, say that you and your spouse each have defined benefit plans through your jobs. An actuary determines that the present value of the marital share of your pension is $40,000 and the present value of the marital share of your spouse's is $60,000. That means that to equalize things, your spouse needs to pay you $10,000 (half of the difference) or give you other assets worth that much.

If you're buying out your spouse's share of your pension, your spouse must sign a special form with your employer, making clear that the benefits are yours alone after the divorce. The employer will provide the form if you ask for it.

A spouse may sometimes trade a share in retirement benefits for the marital home. If you're considering such a trade, consider the long-term ramifications. If you don't have future retirement income of your own, giving up your share in your spouse's benefits may leave you scrambling to plan for your future.

When trading pension benefits for any marital asset, be very cautious and get the advice of an expert. There are very few circumstances in which you should trade the present value of a pension for an asset of exactly the same fair market value. Retirement plans are extremely valuable because of the value of tax-deferred growth. A retirement account with $10,000 in it today is worth more than $10,000 cash because the pension's tax-deferred status gives it greater growth potential.

Splitting the benefits at retirement. Actually dividing a defined benefit plan is more complicated, because it requires a separate court order.

However, especially because many women don't have retirement benefits of their own, it is sometimes a necessity. It may also make sense where there aren't enough other assets to equalize the division—in other words, if the spouse who earned the retirement benefits can't afford to buy out the interest of the other spouse.

To have retirement benefits distributed in the future, you'll need to ask the court to approve a Qualified Domestic Relations Order or QDRO (pronounced "quadro"). The QDRO directs your retirement plan administrator to distribute the benefits at your retirement according to the percentages that you agreed to or that a judge ordered.

SEE AN EXPERT

Get a lawyer! You'll need a lawyer to draft a QDRO, which is a technical document that needs to be just right. Mistakes can cause benefits to go down the drain instead of to the nonemployee spouse and can trigger undesirable tax consequences. There are lawyers who do nothing but draft QDROs, and if you don't already have a lawyer, the actuary who calculates the value of your benefits can refer you to one. (Don't use an Internet document service for this.) The QDRO will probably cost about $500, but it's worth whatever you pay for it. You need a similar order if one of you is in the military or is a government employee, but the details are different—another reason to hire a lawyer who knows the difference and can draft the document you need.

Defined Contribution Plans

Much more common than pensions are defined contribution plans such as 401(k) plans. These plans are voluntary and require your active participation in getting yourself enrolled and managing your benefits. You often have control over how much you contribute to the plan each month through salary deferrals, and your employer may or may not contribute as well.

The value of a defined contribution plan can be determined as of the date of your divorce, because it's possible to distribute the money right then—it has a present, rather than just a future, value. To find out the value of your defined contribution plan, contact the plan administrator or review your most recent annual statement. Your employer is required by law to provide you each year with a summary of the plan's assets and a statement of your benefits. Many provide them quarterly.

Valuing a defined contribution plan and determining how much of the funds are marital property requires that you figure out how much you contributed before and during your marriage, as well as the rate of gain or loss during those periods.

These calculations aren't really doable by mere mortals—it's well worth your while to hire an expert. An actuary can calculate the value of your retirement savings and figure out what portion should be divided between you and your spouse and what portion is yours alone. An actuary will probably charge between $250 and $1,000 for the job.

For example, if you worked for your company for 15 years, ten of which were during your marriage, then approximately two-thirds of your 401(k) account is marital property (the amount won't be exactly two-thirds, because return on investment has to be taken into account—that's why you need an actuary). You and your spouse agree to split the marital share of your retirement equally, so you ask an attorney to prepare a QDRO instructing your plan administrator to roll over half of the two-thirds into your spouse's tax-deferred individual retirement account.

Dividing Defined Contribution Plans

Defined contribution plans are much simpler to divide than are pensions. Once an actuary calculates what portion of the benefits is separate and what portion is marital property, you can simply roll over the nonemployee spouse's share of the account into another tax-deferred savings vehicle at the time the divorce is final.

Some plans, including 403(b) plans for employees of educational institutions, require a court order (a QDRO, discussed above) before they'll do the rollover; some require only a letter from you, along with a copy of your divorce order. Ask the plan administrator what you'll need.

Vesting and Marital Property Rights

When you have a defined contribution plan, you need to pay attention to the concept of "vesting." Being vested means you actually own the benefits and are entitled to receive them at retirement (or when you leave your job). You always own the portion of your benefits that you contributed yourself; where vesting comes in is in relation to the portion your employer contributes. The vesting schedule should be set out in the plan document and, in most cases, in your employee handbook. Often you'll vest in a certain percentage per year until you become fully vested after you stay at the company for a defined period of time.

Vested benefits are always considered marital property. States treat nonvested benefits differently at divorce. Some states consider them separate property, and you don't have to divide them at divorce. But some states consider nonvested benefits marital property, which means you'll have to account for them—and possibly pay your spouse for a share of benefits that you don't yet own. If you change jobs for any reason, you could lose those benefits and never get what you bought from your spouse. If you have nonvested benefits and you think a job change is in the offing, consider negotiating to have the nonvested portion of the plan benefits divided when they vest, not at divorce.

CAUTION

Roll the money over, not out. Don't have the plan administrator distribute the funds directly to either spouse. The funds could become subject to withholding at the time of the transfer if you do. Instead, make sure you do a "trustee-to-trustee" transfer directly from one spouse's tax-deferred account into the other's.

Military Benefits

There are some quite specific requirements for distributing military retirement benefits. Chapter 12 is about divorce and the military and includes a section on retirement benefits.

Social Security

Social Security isn't considered property subject to division. But the South Dakota Supreme Court has held that one spouse's Social Security benefits could be indirectly considered as an offsetting factor in dividing property. Other states have reached the opposite conclusion. If your marriage lasted less than ten years, you don't need to think about Social Security issues—you're not entitled to receive either survivor or retirement benefits based on your relationship with your spouse.

If the marriage was longer than ten years, you're 62 or older, and your former spouse is entitled to or receiving benefits, you can collect retirement benefits on your former spouse's Social Security record, at least until you remarry. If you get married again, you will lose the right to collect on your former spouse's record unless the second marriage ends, too, in which case you regain your right to collect. If you're close to the ten-year mark when you decide to divorce, think about waiting a bit to get the final divorce judgment, so that the ten-year period will have passed.

Money Now and Later

If you and your spouse start dividing your assets and debts and find that it looks like one spouse will need to pay a sizable chunk of cash to the other, it can cause cash flow problems.

For example, imagine that your spouse wants to keep the house, which has equity worth $70,000. Your spouse also keeps a car worth $10,000 and you keep the more valuable car, worth $20,000. You also keep your entire brokerage account, worth $20,000. You divide all your other assets equally. That means you're getting assets worth $40,000 and your spouse is getting assets worth $80,000. To make everything come out evenly, your spouse will have to pay you $20,000—half of the difference, so that each of you gets $60,000 in assets.

To avoid taking money out of the house, your spouse asks you to accept a payment of $10,000 now and a promissory note for the rest of what you're owed, which will be paid over several years. Do you give your spouse a break by accepting the note?

Start with the fact that money now is worth more than money later. There's the risk that you won't get paid at all, of course, and you also must consider inflation and the time value of money (what you lose by not having the money to invest). If you're inclined to be cooperative— and by all means, do so if you're able to—do a couple of things to take care of yourself. First, make the loan for as short a term as possible. Second, don't hesitate to ask for a reasonable rate of interest, so the money will be worth as much to you over time as it would be now. And of course, get the promise to pay in writing.

RESOURCE

Learn the time value of money. There are standard formulas for determining the time value of money, and you can use free calculators at www.tcalc.com to figure the present value of the proposal your spouse is making. There's also a present value chart in *Divorce & Money: How to Make the Best Financial Decisions During Divorce,* by Violet Woodhouse with Matthew J. Perry (Nolo).

Spousal Support and Health Insurance

Of the many reasons that divorce is so stressful and difficult, making the money that's been supporting one household stretch to support two is high on the list. For women, in particular, concerns about making ends meet can cause a lot of anxiety. Despite the ever-increasing percentage of married women who work, the 2012 census found that women still earn about 77 cents for every dollar men earn. Most women suffer financially in divorce. The prospect of returning to paid work after time spent at home raising kids can also be a source of worry.

Spousal support, also called "alimony" or "maintenance," is designed to help a lower-earning spouse make it through the divorce and the transition into a new single life. (Rules about continuing health insurance coverage after divorce exist for the same reason.) Depending on the length of the marriage and the degree to which one spouse was financially dependent on the other, support can last for many years. However, the nationwide trend is for courts to award spousal support in fewer and fewer situations, and for shorter times when they do award it, because it's so common for both spouses to work or at least be able to return to work. According to one expert, spousal support is awarded in fewer than 15% of divorces nationwide.

In the past few years, there has been a wave of so-called "alimony reform," with a number of states revising their support laws in ways that the proponents consider more in line with the current realities of how couples earn and work. For example, under a 2012 Massachusetts law, alimony ends when the recipient has been living with a new partner for more than three months, and also ends automatically when the recipient reaches retirement age for Social Security purposes. The law also places time limits on alimony for marriages that ended before the 20-year mark was reached. As this book goes to press, alimony reform bills are pending in Florida and New Jersey.

One concern about these new rules is that a few states include provisions for retroactive modification of spousal support. That means that a recipient could be forced to pay back support that was already received. Because support is often negotiated as part of the entire settlement package when the divorce is finalized, opponents argue that it is unfair to allow for retroactive modifications—and it seems likely that judges would decline to implement those provisions in cases where the result would be an adjustment in the overall settlement.

A number of states have established (or are considering) guidelines for spousal support, similar to those already in place in all states for child support. Both payers and recipients may welcome the greater predictability that guideline formulas could bring to the process of negotiating support. Maine, New Jersey, Oklahoma, Pennsylvania, and Texas all have established guidelines. Some counties in California also provide guidelines, but these apply only to temporary support pending the completion of the divorce. Spousal support after the divorce is final is still a question for the judge.

Given all these changes, if you are managing your divorce on your own, you might want to pay particular attention to current law in your state. You may want to consult an attorney to get the lowdown on the rules that apply to your situation.

Basics of Spousal Support

Whether one spouse is entitled to support from the other after the divorce starts with the question of need. Will one spouse require financial help to maintain a standard of living close to what the couple had during the marriage? There's no hard and fast rule, but in general, the longer the marriage, the stronger the presumption that support is appropriate. A marriage of more than ten years is generally considered a marriage "of long duration" and usually carries with it a starting assumption that some support will be awarded. However, even after a long marriage, if you and your spouse both earn about the same amount and have roughly equivalent assets, a judge is unlikely to award support.

In any event, spousal support is still an element of some divorce settlements and judgments, and it's definitely something you should raise if you believe you will need it. Don't be too proud to ask—in most cases, if you aren't able to completely support yourself immediately after your divorce, it's because of sacrifices that you made while you were married.

This goes for both men and women. Men who earn significantly less than their wives and need support are just as entitled to ask for it as women are.

20-20 hindsight ...

" I didn't even explore whether I could have gotten alimony," says one young divorced military spouse. "I thought I wouldn't need it and I didn't want to ask him for anything, and we really rushed through the whole thing, too. Now it turns out I could really use some help and I wish I'd thought about it more then."

In most cases, property is divided first, and then support is set. That's because who gets property is a factor in determining an appropriate level of spousal support. You and your spouse might decide, for example, that one of you gets more of the property instead of getting support. A judge could make the same decision, awarding one spouse the majority of the property and assets to ensure a comfortable future without a need for spousal support.

Of course, if at all possible, it's best not to leave those decisions up to the judge. Spousal support is as unpredictable as the rest of a contested divorce case, and you're both a lot better off working out an agreement yourselves than you are turning it over to a judge.

Where the High Road Leads

What does it mean to take the high road where support is involved? It doesn't mean being noble and giving up your right to ask for support, nor does it mean turning over your whole paycheck to your lower-earning spouse. It simply requires that both of you take an honest look at your needs and abilities and try to come to a fair agreement that's structured in the most advantageous way for both of you. (There's more about how to think about that in "Tax Planning When You Pay or Receive Support," below.)

Types of Spousal Support and How Long They Last

Spousal support falls into two broad categories: short-term support and long-term or permanent support. "Reimbursement" support is a kind of long-term support. A spouse may also get temporary support before the divorce is final.

What type of support is ordered, and how long one ex-spouse must help support the other, are as much in the judge's discretion as is the amount of support. Some judges start with the assumption that support should last half as long as the marriage did, and then work up or down from there by looking at certain factors. (See "How Courts Set the Amount of Support," below.) Most states don't have guidelines for the duration of support, but some do—for example, in Texas and Indiana, payments are limited to three years except in special circumstances. In Utah, support can't last any longer than the marriage did. And in some states, the marriage must have lasted at least ten years for a court to order support at all. The duration of support also depends on the nature of the support. The discussion of each type of support, below, addresses how long each might be expected to last.

It's possible that a former spouse might receive more than one kind of support at the same time. For example, if a spouse is getting rehabilitative and short-term support, then when the spouse is employed again, the rehabilitative support would end. The short-term support would continue until its termination date.

Temporary Support While the Divorce Is Pending

You and your spouse don't need to wait until everything in your divorce is settled to work out spousal support arrangements. In fact, the support issue may be most important immediately after you separate, to support the lower-earning spouse while your divorce is in process. Some states—or certain counties—have guidelines for temporary spousal support, though many don't. If you live someplace where guidelines are available, you can use those to set an amount of support. Otherwise you'll negotiate based on need and ability to pay.

It's always a good idea to make a written agreement about temporary support. (For one thing, payments are tax deductible only if there's a signed agreement. See "Tax Planning When You Pay or Receive Support," below.) If you can't agree on a temporary support amount, then you'll probably spend some time in court arguing over it. If you have a right to support, it starts as soon as you separate, so get yourself to court right away. Temporary support ends when your divorce is finalized and short-term or long-term support begins. In some cases, temporary support is the only spousal support received if the spouses agree on no ongoing support or if the court finds the marriage was too short or there is no need for support beyond the temporary period. Chapters 3 and 5 discuss in more detail agreements and court proceedings for temporary support orders.

Short-Term and Rehabilitative Support

Short-term support is appropriate when the marriage itself was quite short. (This type of support lends itself to the possibility of a lump-sum payment instead of monthly checks. See "Paying Spousal Support in a Lump Sum," below.) Short-term support lasts only a few years, and its precise ending date is set in the court order or settlement agreement.

Rehabilitative support, sometimes also called "bridge the gap" support, is a specific kind of short-term support, designed to help a dependent spouse get retrained and back into the workforce. It generally lasts until the recipient is back to work. Generally, that date isn't set in advance—the agreement is that the support payments will stop when the recipient completes a retraining program and becomes employed in the industry. The recipient is responsible for diligently pursuing the training or course of study and then searching for work. The other spouse is responsible for paying the support until that point—and a payer who suspects the recipient isn't really trying to complete an education or get work can ask the court to reduce the support amount or set a termination date. The person asking for the modification would have to prove that the other ex-spouse was not working hard enough.

Long-Term or Permanent Support

Permanent support may be granted after long marriages (generally, more than ten years), if the judge concludes that the dependent spouse most likely won't go back into the workforce and will need support indefinitely. Some states don't allow permanent support.

Even so-called "permanent" support does eventually end. Of course, it ends when either the recipient or the payor dies. It also may end when the recipient remarries. And in about half the states, it ends if the recipient begins living with another person in a marriage-like relationship where the couple provides mutual support and shares financial responsibilities. (Just having a roommate doesn't count.)

Reimbursement Support

Reimbursement support is the only type of spousal support that's not completely based on financial need. Instead, it's a way to compensate a spouse who sacrificed education, training, or career advancement during the marriage by taking any old job that would support the family while the other spouse trained for a lucrative professional career. Generally, both spouses expected that once the professional spouse was established and earning the anticipated higher salary, the sacrificing spouse would benefit from the higher standard of living and be free to pursue a desirable career. If the marriage ends before that spouse gets any of those expected benefits, reimbursement support rebalances the scales by making the professional spouse return some of what was given during the marriage.

Because it's not tied to need, reimbursement support ends whenever the agreement or court order says it does. Its termination generally isn't tied to an event like the supported spouse getting work or remarrying.

How Courts Set the Amount of Support

Leaving a support decision in the hands of a judge is risky business. This isn't like child support, where the formulas are clear and pretty rigid. In most states, the amount and duration of spousal support payments are entirely up to the judge. Obviously, it's preferable for you and your spouse to keep control of decisions about spousal support. If the two of you can agree to an amount of support and how long it will be paid, then that's what the judge will order. It's the only way to predict what's going to happen.

Only about a dozen states give judges even general guidelines for calculating support. In these states, the judge uses a formula that takes into account the length of the marriage and the spouses' incomes to calculate a starting figure. Then the judge factors in other circumstances to arrive at a final amount and decide how long the payments will last. Here's a look at some of those circumstances.

Need and Ability to Pay

Once the court decides that one spouse is entitled to support, it will try to quantify that need and the other spouse's ability to pay. The judge may take into account:

- how property is being divided in the divorce
- the standard of living during the marriage, and the dependent spouse's ability to maintain that standard in the absence of support
- each spouse's separate income, assets, and obligations (states define "income" differently, with some including unearned income and others limiting the definition more strictly)
- the length of the marriage (more significant in deciding how long support will last than in determining the amount)
- whether the spouses lived together before they were married and whether any part of the cohabitation should be included in the length of the marriage (some states don't consider this factor at all)
- each spouse's age and health
- the needs of the children, and whether child care responsibilities affect the dependent spouse's ability to return to work
- whether the dependent spouse left the workforce to be a homemaker or raise children
- how long the dependent spouse has been out of the workforce, that spouse's marketable skills, and what retraining might be necessary

- contributions that either spouse made to the other's training, education, or career advancement
- the possibility that either spouse may acquire assets in the future (such as the maturing of stock options or a large inheritance), and
- any other factors that the judge thinks should be considered.

Earning Capacity

In addition to looking at actual income, a judge may examine each spouse's ability to earn money. The idea here is that if you could earn significantly more than you are, but voluntarily choose a lower standard of living, your spouse shouldn't have to suffer financially because of it.

If either you or your spouse has skills or education that you are not using—for example, if you are trained as a lawyer but are working as a sculptor—the court can "impute" to you a higher income than what you actually have. You may be ordered to pay support consistent with your earning power, not your actual income. And if you're the recipient spouse, you might get support that's consistent with your ability to earn, rather than what you actually earn—or you may be ordered to fend for yourself.

Shirking doesn't pay ...

" My ex-wife was a nurse. She left me for a guy she met while taking a photography class, then quit her job to try being a photographer. Her income went down to about a quarter of what it had been, and she wanted me to pay her support—even though I had the kids most of the time, too. I said I'd pay support according to what her nursing job paid—which meant I would be paying just about nothing. She fought me at first, but then I think her lawyer told her she was going to lose. She went back to nursing."

—Divorced father of two

Fault

In some states, you can argue that fault should be considered in setting spousal support (you can make this argument whether or not you filed for divorce on the basis of fault). If the higher-earning spouse committed adultery, was abusive, or is for some other reason at fault for the divorce, the support payment may be increased. Of course, as the saying goes, you can't get blood from a turnip. If there's only a certain amount of support that your errant spouse can afford, the court won't order an unrealistically high payment. More commonly, the spouse who receives support has payments reduced because of fault.

A table in Chapter 5 shows the impact of fault on property division and on spousal support—refer to it to see how your state views fault.

Beyond Spousal Support

Spousal support is usually just a temporary measure, designed to keep one spouse from running into financial trouble immediately after a divorce. Even if you're receiving support, you are ultimately responsible for your financial future. Make a one-year, three-year, and five-year plan for where you want to be in your life, and include what kind of work you want to be doing and what you want in terms of salary and benefits. If you received significant property or other assets in the divorce settlement, invest them wisely and with an eye toward the future. Learn to budget, if you haven't yet.

Negotiating Support With Your Spouse

Before you start negotiating with your spouse about support, look carefully at the factors judges consider (discussed above). They may help you in your negotiations—and if you can't agree, at least you'll know what the judge may take into account.

> **SEE AN EXPERT**
>
> **Your mediator or lawyer can help you.** If you're using mediation or collaborative law to resolve your divorce case, you can work with the professionals to figure out how much support is appropriate. If you're in a contested divorce, your lawyer will help you come up with an amount based on all of the factors described above.

Evaluating Your Spouse's Resources

Whether you're the one who'll be receiving or paying support, you need information to negotiate effectively. Otherwise, you can't feel comfortable that the support you agree to is adequate for your needs—or consistent with your ability to pay.

Almost all states require both spouses to make some financial disclosures as part of the divorce proceeding. This is true even if it's clear which spouse will pay support—the recipient spouse's resources are important to determining need, and the paying spouse's to determining ability to pay. If you have been responsible during the marriage for all of the financial ins and outs, you're certain that there's nothing you don't know about your spouse's financial situation, or you trust your spouse's word 100%, you won't need to ask for more. Otherwise, make sure the following things are included in the forms that you're both required to fill out. And if they're not, use the discovery methods described in Chapter 5 to get the additional information you need.

You'll need to know about:

- **Your spouse's separate assets.** If your spouse has separate assets, you're entitled to know their value. (The judge may consider them if called upon to decide a support amount.)
- **Income and expense information.** You definitely want a detailed monthly income and expense report—which should be one of the forms your spouse is required to give you—to show you where your spouse's money is going. If the expense report shows $500 being spent every month on dining out, and all you can afford are microwave dinners while watching "American Idol," you'll surely want to point this out. At the other end of the spectrum, if

your spouse is seeking a large amount of support while you know that separate liquid assets are available for daily expenses, get the information that will prove it.

- **Bonuses, overtime, and benefits.** Don't forget income from things like bonuses and overtime, even though they're not completely predictable. If your spouse has regularly received a bonus or lots of overtime pay, you can average the amount received in the last few years and use that figure. Likewise, pay attention to things like stock options and the value of work-related benefits, such as unused vacation pay and sick pay, company-paid vehicles, and health insurance benefits. All of these items have a measurable value that should be factored into a spousal support negotiation. You may need to ask for your spouse's employee manual or other work-related benefits information to find out what the company's policies are on accruing sick and vacation time, so that you know what's there.

Evaluating Your Needs

Given that you'll be required to prepare a monthly income and expense disclosure anyway, use it to determine how much support you need. Look at the difference between your expenses and your income, and then factor in whatever resources you have and look at the list of factors above. Because there's usually no standard formula, all you can do is decide what you think you need and ask for it. That will get the negotiations started.

TIP

Remember, nothing's getting cheaper. If you're the person getting support, once you've settled on an amount, you may want to include a provision for increasing the amount each year—a cost of living adjustment (often shortened to COLA). You can tie the increases to the national or a local COLA index (available online), or assume an annual increase of a specific percentage.

Paying Spousal Support in a Lump Sum

Spousal support doesn't have to be paid a month at a time. In fact, you and your spouse may prefer one lump sum payment, for emotional reasons as much as anything else. The recipient doesn't have to worry that the support payments won't arrive on time (or won't arrive at all) if the paying spouse suffers a reversal of fortune or simply stops paying. In addition, if the recipient wants to buy a new house or start a business after the divorce, the lump sum payment can be a good way to get started. The paying spouse gets to take care of the obligation in one fell swoop and never bother with monthly payments. Both spouses get to avoid the ongoing entanglement.

Why doesn't everyone do this, then? Lots of people can't afford the big payout, for one thing. And although spousal support payments are tax deductible, a huge deduction in one year might not be as valuable as a number of years of smaller deductible payments. On the other end, the recipient spouse won't be able to count on the regular income from ongoing support, but instead must invest and manage the lump sum. If you're thinking about taking a lump sum payment for spousal support, consider your own financial habits. What are you likely to do if you suddenly have a large sum of money available to you? If you're something of a spendthrift, work out a plan beforehand for investing the money so that it doesn't get frittered away.

Most important, lump sum spousal support raises important and sometimes complicated tax issues. The tax hit can be significant for the recipient spouse, who must include the entire amount on that year's return as taxable income.

You also have to be careful that the IRS doesn't view the payment as a property settlement instead of support and try to challenge the paying spouse's deduction. This problem arises if the amount of support goes down significantly from one year to the next in the first three years. (See "Tax Planning When You Pay or Receive Support," below.) You can do this in your settlement agreement, which should set out the amount of support agreed upon over time and then state that it will be paid as a lump sum. You can also get around the tax issues by stating in your agreement that the support payment is neither deductible nor taxable—as long as it works both ways, you're allowed to choose.

> **SEE AN EXPERT**
>
> **Consult an attorney or accountant.** Before deciding to go ahead with a lump sum payment, talk to a professional about the tax consequences.

Payments to Third Parties

In certain circumstances, the paying spouse can make payments to third parties instead of to the other spouse and have those payments considered spousal support. In order to be tax deductible as spousal support, the payments must be made under an agreement or order in your divorce case. So, it takes some planning if you want to make this kind of arrangement.

Payments to a third party can include payments for medical costs, housing expenses, tuition, or anything else that is provided for under your divorce order or settlement agreement. For example, if you're required by the divorce decree to pay the mortgage, insurance, and property taxes on the family home even though your spouse now owns it, those payments can be considered spousal support.

Why would you use third-party payments? If your spouse is getting extended (COBRA) coverage under your group health insurance plan at work, the employee spouse might want to pay the premiums through payroll deductions. Either spouse might want to have spousal support paid directly to a third party if the spouse receiving support isn't the greatest financial manager. For example, if you know your spouse isn't good about paying the mortgage on time, you might want to make sure your kids' living situation is secure by paying the mortgage yourself. If you're the spouse getting support and are worried about your ability to save up enough of your support to pay your school tuition each quarter, you might ask your spouse to do it for you and deduct the amount from monthly support payments.

Planning for Possible Disability or Death of the Supporting Spouse

If the supporting spouse dies unexpectedly, the recipient will suffer a sudden, and possibly catastrophic, loss of income. To protect against that possibility, it's prudent to purchase a life insurance policy with the recipient spouse as the beneficiary. It's also not unreasonable to buy disability insurance to protect against total disability, which would render the supporting spouse unable to pay as agreed. Some courts will even order the purchase of insurance as a term of settlement.

In either case, if you're the recipient spouse, it'll probably be up to you to ask for the insurance and to try to get your spouse to pay for the policy. If you're negotiating with your spouse, make this part of the negotiation. If you're in court, you can ask the judge to order that insurance be provided and decide who pays for it. If possible, have the policy placed in your name, so that you're sure it can't be terminated without your knowledge. The down side of this is that the premium payments will probably count as support and be taxable income to you. Most life and disability insurance premiums aren't enormously costly—term life insurance is really inexpensive—but you should at least consider the tax factor. And definitely ensure that your settlement agreement or court order provides that you can have direct access to the insurance company for the purpose of confirming that the policy is in force and the beneficiary designation is as agreed. (If you can't do that, try to arrange to be the person notified if there is a lapse in premium payments.)

How do you know how much insurance to purchase? The same actuary who helped you determine the value of the retirement plans (see discussion of using experts in Chapter 10) can perform some calculations that will give you the present value of the support you're expecting in the future. For example, the actuary might tell you that you'll need a $300,000 life insurance policy to replace support you would lose if your spouse died in the next few years.

Changing the Amount of Spousal Support Later

Spousal support is different from child support in many ways, and perhaps the most important is that while a court can change the terms of a child support order until the child is a legal adult, in most states, you can end or limit the court's power over spousal support. In other words, you can build in—or preclude—future modification of the support obligation. All you and your spouse need to do is put a provision in your settlement agreement that states how spousal support can be modified. If a judge decides on spousal support for you, the judge will also decide whether and under what circumstances support can be modified later.

If you're negotiating an agreement about spousal support, you can state that the amount can't change at all, no matter what happens. (One Missouri man might have regretted making such an agreement when the court ordered him to continue paying support to his ex-wife even though she allegedly tried to have him killed.) The paying spouse might agree to this if the likelihood of a downward reduction seems slim (as where employment is secure or assets are high). The recipient spouse might think it would be easier to persuade the other to pay a higher amount if there's a no-change provision, and it also means that support should keep coming even if the paying spouse's employment situation changes.

If you want some future flexibility, you might state that the amount can change only if:

- both ex-spouses agree
- the court orders it
- either spouse's income changes by a specified percentage, or
- one spouse becomes disabled.

If you don't have a modification provision in your settlement agreement, and you can't agree later to a change, then your state's law will control the matter. Most courts allow modification if there is a significant change of circumstances. Some states, however, won't modify spousal support at all—they allow courts to make orders only about child support after the divorce is final. (And in Texas, the support amount can only be modified downward!)

Often, a court will order a temporary modification, just for the period of changed circumstances. For example, if you are paying support and you lose your job, the court might reduce your support obligation for six months or until you find a new job, whichever happens sooner. If at the end of six months, you still haven't found work, you'd have to return to court and ask for additional time.

Tax Planning When You Pay or Receive Support

When you're negotiating with your spouse or arguing in court about the level, type, and duration of spousal support, tax issues should never be far from your mind. This section explains the basic rules and major concerns for each spouse—but it's likely that you'll need some assistance in making decisions about support, as discussed below.

Basic Rules

Spousal support must be reported as taxable income by the recipient and can be deducted by the paying spouse, unless you agree otherwise. (This is the opposite of child support, which is neither taxable nor deductible.) In general, a higher earner will be looking for deductions, and a lower earner will not have to pay much tax on the amount of support received. Any increase in tax for the recipient can often be offset by the significant tax savings for the higher earner, who can make up the difference to the recipient either with an additional payment or in another way. For example, the paying spouse might agree to simply pay the recipient spouse's tax liability.

You can, however, make spousal support payments nontaxable and nondeductible as long as it goes both ways and you both agree (you'll state as much in your marital settlement agreement). You might do this if the spouse receiving support is in a higher tax bracket than the paying spouse (this would be unusual, but might happen if the recipient spouse is receiving reimbursement support and has significant assets), or if the paying spouse doesn't need the tax deduction and the recipient spouse doesn't want to report the income.

> **TIP**
>
> **Just ignore it.** If you do decide to make spousal support nontaxable and nondeductible, the recipient spouse should simply not report the income on that year's tax return.

If You Receive Support

If you receive spousal support, you need to plan for the potential tax impact of the income. Unlike an employer, your former spouse won't withhold any taxes from your support check. If you're staying at home to care for young children and have no other source of income, paying estimated tax each quarter (to both the IRS and your state) may be a good way to avoid taking a tax hit at the end of the year. If you have a paying job, then increasing withholding from your paycheck is another way to offset the potential impact of support payments.

You may need to spend some time looking at different payment scenarios and how they play out tax-wise, by calculating what your tax liability would be if you received a certain amount of support and what benefit your spouse would receive from the tax deduction. You can check your potential tax liability at the IRS website at www.irs.gov, where tax tables are available. Or you can ask a tax professional to help you look at the tax impact of different amounts of support, so that you can figure out the optimal amount—that is, the amount that puts the most money in each person's pocket after taxes are taken into account.

> **RESOURCE**
>
> **Let the tax man help you, for once.** The IRS offers a number of publications that may help you as you negotiate support. IRS Publication 505, *Tax Withholding and Estimated Taxes*, is one, and IRS Publication 504, *Divorced or Separated Individuals*, is another. Both are available at www.irs.gov or by phone request at 800-829-3676.

Payments made to third parties on your behalf (see above) are treated just as though they were paid to you—you have to include them in your taxable income. So, for example, if your former spouse pays the mortgage directly (and this is provided for in your settlement agreement or court order) you must report that amount as income.

If You're Paying Support

You can deduct spousal support payments on your income tax return, but not child support or property distributions. So the IRS scrutinizes support paid in the first three years to make sure that you didn't disguise property distribution or other postdivorce obligations, like attorneys' fees, as deductible support. If the divorce agreement calls for higher payments in the first postdivorce years and lower payments later, and the IRS believes the early payments are in lieu of property division or other nonsupport items, it can go back and "recapture" retroactive taxes. If your agreement calls for a reduction of $15,000 or more in spousal support during year two or year three after your divorce, you may find Uncle Sam knocking at your door to discuss recapture.

When you negotiate your spousal support agreement, it's important to make sure that you don't tie the termination of spousal support to anything related to your kids—for example, the time they leave home or when they finish college. If you do, the IRS might consider the payments child support rather than spousal support—and child support payments aren't tax deductible.

If you're making payments to a third party instead of to your spouse, but you've agreed (in your settlement agreement) that the payments constitute spousal support, for tax purposes those payments are treated as if they were paid to the recipient. In other words, you can deduct them (at least in part) as support payments. Certain payments are not fully deductible, though, including payments related to a jointly owned home. If you and your spouse continue to own the home together and you pay all the expenses, you are allowed to deduct only half of the mortgage payment as spousal support. But you can take half of the mortgage interest deduction as well.

The real estate taxes and homeowners' insurance are even more complicated, and deductibility depends on how you hold title to the property. Check IRS Publication 504, *Divorced or Separated Individuals*, for the lowdown on third-party payments as spousal support.

Keeping Health Insurance in Force

Making sure that health insurance continues after divorce is a major issue for most divorcing people. The vast majority of Americans get their health care through employment, and many people are insured through their spouse's employment benefits. Because of this, there's a federal law, called COBRA, that requires insurers and employers to provide ongoing medical insurance to divorcing spouses for a period of time.

> (!) CAUTION
>
> **Unmarried same-sex couples may not get COBRA benefits.**
> COBRA is a federal law, and the federal government doesn't recognize same-sex domestic partnerships and civil unions. Some employers and insurers may choose to allow former same-sex partners to retain coverage under COBRA, but if they don't, there's not much you can do about it. Married same-sex couples, however, should be eligible for COBRA coverage.

Staying Insured Through Your Former Spouse With COBRA

No, it's not a scary snake. In fact, the Consolidated Omnibus Budget Reconciliation Act (COBRA for short) is the opposite of frightening—it is a critical safety net for employees who lose their jobs and for spouses who are divorcing the person whose employment is their source of medical insurance.

All private employers with 20 or more employees are covered by COBRA. Most states have a similar law for employers with fewer than 20 employees. Employees of public entities are not covered by COBRA, but some states have laws that parallel COBRA and may cover public employees. If you're not eligible for COBRA, check with the human resources department of your spouse's employer to find out whether another type of continuation coverage is available.

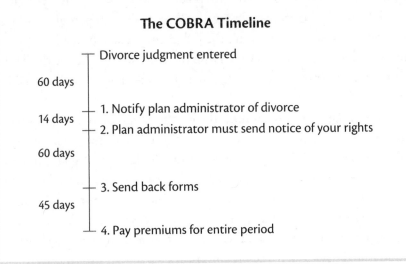

COBRA provides that when an employee insured by a group policy gets divorced, the employee's former spouse can remain covered for up to three years on the group insurance policy. The nonemployee spouse must pay for the benefits, but can be charged only as much as the employer is paying for them plus a 2% administrative fee. After three years, the nonemployee spouse is entitled to convert the group insurance to a private policy with equivalent benefits without the insurance company requiring medical tests or records, but most people don't because it's just too expensive. Generally, only someone who is otherwise uninsurable would take advantage of that provision.

If you're the spouse receiving coverage under COBRA, you need to know when the 36-month period begins. Most insurance plans start the period when the final divorce order is issued by the court. Because many months go by between when you and your spouse separate and when your divorce is final, you may get a significant amount of coverage before the clock even begins ticking on the COBRA limit. Check the terms of the plan to be sure. You are entitled to a copy of the plan upon request. The human resources folks at your spouse's employer can also advise you, but they may not be as familiar with the details of the plan as you might expect. (To get the maximum possible time, if the plan says that the final judgment is the event that starts the 36-month period running, it's a good idea to wait until after the judgment is entered to advise the employer about the divorce. Otherwise the employer might use the date that the notice was received as the starting point—and courts have said that's okay.)

COBRA has strict time limits. The employee spouse must notify the plan administrator of the divorce—generally, through the employer— within 60 days after the court issues the final judgment. If your spouse is the employee, make sure this gets taken care of. To be completely certain it happens, you may want to do it yourself. The plan administrator then has 14 days to send you notice of your right to elect COBRA coverage. You then have 60 days to send back the forms electing coverage, and 45 additional days to pay the premiums. It's a good idea to return the paperwork right away, both to be sure that nothing goes wrong and to avoid having to pay lots of premiums at once.

After you've elected coverage, for the most part you won't need to go through your spouse for any of your COBRA transactions. You'll pay your premiums directly to the insurer and use your coverage just like any other member of the group.

RESOURCE

Learn more about COBRA. If you have general questions about COBRA and divorce, call the plan administrator or the Employee Benefits Security Administration (part of the Department of Labor) toll-free hotline number, 866-444-EBSA (3272). You can also go to the Department of Labor website at www.dol.gov/ebsa and read consumer FAQs on COBRA.

COBRA is a great benefit and one that you certainly want to take advantage of, but it's also time for you to think about what coverage will be available to you once your COBRA coverage ends. If you're pretty certain that you'll eventually get a job with health care benefits—or if you already have a job that provides coverage, but you're opting for COBRA because your spouse's coverage is better—then it's obviously not as important. But if you are retraining, or for some other reason you don't expect to be employed when the 36 months end, you definitely need to explore your options.

Affordable health insurance may be available under the Affordable Care Act (ACA), also known as Obamacare. You can search for coverage on www.healthcare.gov, the federal government's ACA website, or you can go to www.legalconsumer.com/obamacare and search for information about your state's insurance marketplace.

RESOURCE

Special issues if you're older. Health care can be even more complicated if you're over 50, and especially if you're approaching Medicare age. See *Divorce After 50: Your Guide to the Unique Legal & Financial Challenges,* by Janice Green (Nolo).

Special Rules for Military Spouses

If your spouse is in the military, special rules apply when it comes to medical benefits, and COBRA does not apply to you or your kids. The kids can keep their military medical benefits, but you'll have to find another option after a brief transition period. Chapter 12 has the details.

Military Divorce: Special Issues

I f you are one of the nearly 1.1 million active duty American military personnel stationed around the world—or if you're married to someone who is—you'll be dealing with some divorce issues that don't affect civilians. You'll probably need legal counsel (see below). But before you hire an attorney, or while you're working with one, this chapter can help by explaining what the issues are, how they may affect you, and how you can make sure you're doing what you need to do.

Having one's spouse in the military affects:

- where your divorce will be filed
- how support is calculated
- custody and visitation decisions, and
- pension rights and other benefits.

In all these areas, servicemembers have certain rights and obligations that are very different from those of civilians.

> **CAUTION**
>
> **Don't try this at home.** Unless the servicemember in your family has been in the military an extremely short time and you have limited assets, you absolutely shouldn't negotiate your divorce or sign a settlement agreement without at least consulting a lawyer experienced in military divorce. Most likely, you're going to want to hire a lawyer to represent you all through the divorce. (You may be able to get some free legal help through the military; see "Resources," below.) Finally, if you are working with an attorney who does not have experience in this area, you can ask your attorney to use this chapter as a jumping-off point to find additional information about how to protect your interests.

Beginning a Divorce

From the start, a military divorce can involve questions that other couples don't face. Case in point: Where should you file for divorce?

Where Should You File?
Jurisdiction, Domicile, and Residence

Your divorce won't be valid unless the court that grants it has what's called "jurisdiction" over you and your spouse. That's true for every divorce, but in addition, federal law provides that in order to make court orders relating to a military retirement plan enforceable, certain special jurisdictional requirements must be met. (If retirement benefits aren't an issue in your divorce at all, you can refer to Chapter 3 for information about where to file.)

To ensure that the court you choose has jurisdiction over a military retirement plan, you must file for divorce in a state:

- where the military spouse is domiciled
- where the military spouse is a resident, or
- that you and your spouse both agree to.

Remember that wherever you file, the laws of that state will govern your divorce—not those of the state where you married or the state where your spouse lives, if those are different.

Where Is Your Domicile?

If you're a servicemember, domicile is defined as your permanent home, sometimes also called the "state of legal residence." You also have a "home of record," which is the state you lived in when you joined the military. This is an accounting term and doesn't affect domicile.

You can keep a domicile even while not living there, if it has been your home and you intend to return and live there permanently. Being registered to vote and paying state income tax in a state are two strong indications that you intend to return. Some other indications of your domicile include:

- the address you use on your federal tax return
- where you own a home
- where your immediate family (spouse and children) lives
- where you register your car
- where you are registered to vote, and
- the residence you declare in documents such as a will or an insurance policy.

It's possible for spouses to have different domiciles. Be sure that you base your choice of where to file on the servicemember's residence or domicile.

Some states let servicemembers file for divorce if they are stationed there, even if a servicemember doesn't intend to make it a permanent home. But there's a theoretical possibility that another state might refuse to recognize a divorce that's based on a rule like this, sometimes called a "faux residency" law. It's better to file where you are domiciled under the rules discussed above.

Where Are You a Resident for Divorce Purposes?

Most states require you to live in the state for a certain period (commonly, three to 12 months) before you can file for divorce there. (Chapter 3 lists each state's residency requirements.)

Some states require physical presence to establish residency, but most states consider military members who are absent from the state because of military service to remain legal residents during their absence.

The bottom line is, don't fudge on where you file—especially if you're a civilian spouse. Retirement benefits are too important to risk losing because your case was filed in a location where the court doesn't actually have jurisdiction over both spouses.

Consent to Jurisdiction

If you and your spouse agree about where you want to bring your divorce action, you don't need to worry about jurisdiction. If you both participate in the divorce action without challenging jurisdiction, then the final judgment would probably stand up against a legal challenge later.

If You or Your Spouse Is Overseas

If you are stationed overseas or married to someone who is, you can still file in the United States. The proper place to file is the state where you are domiciled or meet the residency requirements, as described above. If you're a servicemember stationed overseas, you'll need an attorney in the United States to help you file at home.

Filing in the States from a distance is preferable to trying to get a foreign divorce, even though the foreign divorce might seem attractive if you're stationed where divorce is easy and inexpensive. The military won't honor a pension division order from a foreign country, and it's hard to know for sure that your divorce judgment itself will be respected when you return to the States.

Serving Divorce Papers on Your Spouse

The process of serving (delivering) papers to a spouse who is in military service can be more complicated than in a nonmilitary case. But service is the way that a court takes jurisdiction over the nonfiling party, and you need to get it done.

Serving Overseas Personnel

It may be difficult to get the paperwork to a spouse who is stationed overseas—especially if you've been separated for a while and you're not sure where your spouse is. If your divorce is uncontested and you just need to get the paperwork to your spouse, you can accomplish service by mail just as if you both were living stateside. Chapter 3 explains how.

If you can't reach your overseas spouse or you find that mail service is likely to be refused, you may be able to seek help from a commanding officer or base commander. But in most cases, you'll need a lawyer's help. Getting someone to serve papers personally on a military base in a foreign country is not a simple process—it's regulated by international treaty and varies from country to country—and you need the help of someone who's done it before.

Locating Your Spouse

It's possible for married people to lose track of each other, especially if they've been separated for a long time without getting around to formalizing their divorce. It's also possible that one spouse might deliberately try to elude the other. In either case, if you want a divorce, the missing spouse needs to be located or you need to get permission to proceed without the other spouse's participation.

If you're trying to find a civilian spouse, see Chapter 3 for information about how to look for your spouse and how to ask a court to excuse you from the personal service requirement if your search doesn't succeed.

If you're looking for a missing servicemember, you may have a challenge ahead of you. If you know your spouse's Social Security number, you're one step ahead of the game. Even without that, a copy of your spouse's military identification card will be very helpful. Without either one, you're really going to have an uphill battle.

If you do have a Social Security number, you can try a number of ways to locate your missing spouse.

Military locators. Each branch of the service has a Worldwide Military Locator Service. Not all of them are online yet. If you write or call, you'll need to explain who you are and why you are searching and provide all the information you have about your missing spouse. An experienced attorney should be able to expedite your search. Another resource is the National Archive at www.archives.gov/veterans/other-resources/find-vets.html. There are also a number of sites that aren't affiliated with any government agency, like www.gisearch.com and www.vetsearch.com.

Base commander. You can try contacting the base commander at the last known military base, to see whether the commanding officer has information about your spouse's new assignment.

Legal Assistance Office. The military has a group of lawyers called "legal assistance attorneys" (LAAs) whose job is to help servicemembers (and their families) with nonmilitary legal issues. An LAA might be able to help you find out your spouse's current whereabouts. You can get help from an LAA who is in a different branch of the military from your spouse. To find a legal assistance office, try the Legal Assistance Locator at http://legalassistance.law.af.mil/content/locator.

Military Locators	
Army:	Army World Wide Locator Commander, U.S. Army Enlisted Records & Evaluation Center 8899 East 56th Street Fort Benjamin Harrison, IN 46249-5301 Telephone: 866-771-6357
Army Reserve or Retired:	U.S. Army Human Resources Command 1 Reserve Way St. Louis, MO 63132-5200 Telephone: 800-318-5298 or 314-592-0000
Navy Active Duty:	Navy World Wide Locator Navy Personnel Command (PERS 312F) 5720 Integrity Drive Millington, TN 38055-3120 Telephone: 901-874-3388, Option 1 or other questions Option 4
Air Force Active Duty:	HQ AFPC/DPDXIDL 5550 C. Street West, Suite 50 Randolph AFB, TX 78150-4752 Telephone: 210-565-2660
Marine Corps:	Headquarters, US Marine Corps Personnel Management Support Branch (MMSB-17) 2008 Elliot Road, Room 201 Quantico, VA 22134-5030 Telephone: 703-784-3942
US Coast Guard:	Commander Personnel Service Center U.S. Coast Guard Stop 7200 4200 Wilson Boulevard, Suite 1100 Arlington, VA 20598-7200 email: ARL-PF-CGPCCGlocator@uscg.mi or try MR_customerservice@uscg.mi

Federal Parent Locator. If child support is involved, you might be able to make use of the Federal Parent Locator Service at www.acf.hhs .gov/programs/cse/newhire. There's more about this tool in Chapter 8, about child support enforcement.

Other Internet sources. The "Globemaster U.S. Military Aviation Database" is a private website that contains links to all branches of the U.S. armed forces, and provides extensive information, including a locator for U.S. military personnel: www.globemaster.de.

Serving Someone on a U.S. Military Base

Because military bases are closed communities with careful scrutiny of anyone going in and out, you might think it's nearly impossible to serve a spouse who lives on a base. This isn't true, however. On a U.S. base, you should be able to serve your spouse following the instructions in Chapter 3.

Each branch of the military has its own rules about service of process, and most have people whose job description includes facilitating service. (In the Marines, for example, that person is called the "civil process officer.") Some branches of the service, including the Army, have a policy of assisting with service on military personnel on U.S. bases, and certainly service won't be hindered by your spouse's superior officers. It's not that common, but depending on where the base is, you may even be able to send a deputy sheriff or process server onto the base to serve the papers.

Having said all this, though, if you're not in a position to serve a cooperative spouse by mail as described in Chapter 3, it's probably best for you to have an attorney help you with service. A local attorney with expertise in military matters will most likely know how things operate at the base, and you'll save time and money by taking advantage of this expertise. In some states, you may also be able to ask your attorney to request permission from a judge to serve an uncooperative spouse by registered mail.

The Servicemembers Civil Relief Act

A federal law called the Servicemembers Civil Relief Act (SCRA) gives servicemembers special treatment in court proceedings at home, so that they're not distracted from their duties. The law is intended to "provide for the temporary suspension of judicial and administrative proceedings and transactions that might adversely affect the civil rights of servicemembers during their military service." (50 U.S.C. Appendix § 502(2)). In other words, a case involving a servicemember can be delayed if the servicemember can show that harm would result if it went forward. (A statement from the servicemember's commanding officer is required to prove the potential harm.)

If you're the military spouse, the SCRA can keep the court from issuing permanent orders that will affect you for a long time to come. If you're the nonmilitary spouse, the SCRA can feel like an endless stalling tactic. In a divorce case, special treatment under the SCRA usually means the servicemember can have extra time to respond to legal papers or arrange to appear at a hearing. As a result, an order for support or for a change in custody that the civilian spouse wants can be delayed. And the entire divorce proceeding can be delayed so that it takes longer to get a final judgment than it would otherwise take. This means the parties stay married, which of course affects a number of issues including tax filing status and the ability of either spouse to remarry.

The SCRA also protects the servicemember from having a default judgment entered for failure to respond to legal papers within a specified time limit. (See Chapter 3 for more about default judgments.)

The SCRA applies to all divorce-related proceedings, including requests for custody, support, or property division.

SEE AN EXPERT

Get help if you're seeking or fighting a stay (order to delay proceedings) under the SCRA. Whether you're a servicemember who wants to invoke the protections of the SCRA or a civilian spouse trying to get some court orders in place, you'll probably need a lawyer's help.

Other Things the SCRA Does

- Protects servicemembers and their families from eviction from rental housing
- Limits interest on credit obligations (such as loans or credit cards) to 6%
- Provides tax protections for servicemembers whose spouses work in states other than the state where the servicemember is stationed.

    For more about how the SCRA can protect your family, see www .military.com/benefits/legal-matters/scra/faq.

Custody and Visitation

Sharing custody of children after a divorce is always challenging. For military personnel, custody and visitation can be complicated by frequent moves and uncertainty about future deployment.

Custody, Visitation, and the SCRA

Although the SCRA lets a servicemember delay judicial proceedings, children need stability and some measure of predictability in their lives. Courts deciding custody disputes involving a military parent generally try to balance the SCRA with the children's needs. Often, those needs trump the SCRA.

Even when a servicemember has been granted a delay under the SCRA, a court may make an order for temporary custody so that the child's living situation isn't put on hold and so that the military parent can't do an end run around the civilian parent's rights. For example, in one case a servicemember left his daughter with his mother, the child's grandmother, and when his ex-wife sought custody, tried to invoke the SCRA to prevent the court from entering an order. The court transferred custody to the child's mother, refusing to apply the SCRA stay where the child's welfare and the parent-child relationship were at stake.

In a similar case, a servicemember left her child with her new spouse despite the fact that she and her ex-husband shared joint custody of the child, and the court refused to apply the SCRA to prevent a change of custody and granted the father primary custody rights.

Often, it may not be clear which state has jurisdiction over the child. The Uniform Child Custody Jurisdiction Enforcement Act (UCCJEA) is a law in every state that determines jurisdiction for all children, including children of military personnel. The rules that apply to where a custody action can be brought are complicated—they often rest on where a child has lived for the six months before the action is brought—and can sometimes work against a servicemember. For example, a mother who lives in California may be deployed overseas and leave her child with her husband. If he decides to file for divorce while she's deployed, and moves to Arizona for longer than the six-month period necessary to establish jurisdiction, the wife may find when she returns that she's subject to a custody action in Arizona even though her permanent home—and the former home of her child—is in California.

RESOURCE

More about custody. There's more about the UCCJEA in Chapter 7 and at www.ncjrs.gov/pdffiles1/ojjdp/189181.pdf.

If you're in the military and you want to avoid a result like this, you can ask your spouse (when you separate or when you are deployed) to sign an agreement about where your child's permanent home is. This will allow you to avoid a fight over jurisdiction if there's a custody dispute when you return from your deployment.

The servicemember's protection against default judgments also applies to child custody proceedings. This is a relatively new rule and there aren't many cases to provide guidance, but it appears to mean that while a servicemember is deployed, a civilian spouse can't persuade a court to enter a permanent child custody order on the basis that the servicemember parent fails to appear and argue against the change.

A number of states have also enacted laws that affect child custody where servicemembers are involved. Some of the state laws go further than the SCRA, stating that no permanent change in custody can be made while the servicemember is deployed. Some provide that a servicemember's absence due to military service can't be counted against the servicemember when a court is considering the factors that affect a custody determination—in other words, the lack of contact with the child can't be used as a factor.

Preparing a Parenting or Family Care Plan

Divorcing parents need a parenting plan, to set out how they plan to care for the kids after divorce. (Chapter 6 discusses parenting plans and how to negotiate and create one; Chapter 13 deals with marital settlement agreements and how to incorporate parenting plans.)

When one or both parents are in the military, you have additional things to think about when you draw up these important agreements. One thing you might consider adding is a discussion of alternate parenting plans for different possible scenarios. In other words, prepare a plan that will be in place if the servicemember parent stays on the military base in the local area, and another plan that you'll follow if the servicemember parent is transferred a significant distance away or deployed overseas. Having these discussions in advance will make things a lot easier if and when the military parent's living situation changes.

Military rules say that any servicemember who becomes a single parent or marries another servicemember must let the military know immediately. Then, within a specified period of time—30 days for active duty members and 60 days for reservists—the servicemember must submit to a commanding officer a Family Care Plan that makes provisions for the children in the event of the servicemember's short or long-term absence. Short-term absence is defined as 30 or fewer days; a long-term absence is 31 days or more.

Usually, the other parent will care for the children in the servicemember's absence, but in some circumstances, the caregiver might be another member of the family, like a grandparent, an aunt or uncle, or a nonrelative.

Having Someone Else Visit Your Kids When You Can't

Judges in Iowa and Illinois have held that a servicemember may delegate visitation rights to a family member while the servicemember is deployed at a distance that makes personal visits impossible. The courts concluded that letting other family members exercise the servicemember's visitation rights would help children feel more connected with their absent parent. The same is not necessarily true for custody, though. A Wisconsin court held that a servicemember's spouse—the child's stepparent—was not entitled to exercise the servicemember's visitation rights.

RELATED TOPIC

Dealing with shared custody at a distance. When one parent is living a great distance away, it's especially important for the custodial parent to support the child's relationship with the distant parent by facilitating whatever form of contact is possible—phone, email, webcam, or sending cookies and pictures by mail. Chapter 6 contains suggestions.

Overseas Visitation

It's not out of the question for an older child to visit or even live with a military parent stationed overseas. For the most part, this isn't any different than when civilian parents living far apart must arrange for visitation and make decisions about where their kids will live. See Chapters 6 and 7 for the basics of child custody and visitation, including who pays for travel expenses—an issue that is often important where one parent is in the military.

Unfortunately, sometimes a servicemember parent takes advantage of the distance and fails to return the child to the United States when the visitation or custodial period ends. In essence, this is parental kidnapping, and the U.S. military rightfully frowns upon it. Regulations require the military to turn over to civilian authorities—the police or State Department—a servicemember who violates a valid child custody order, and to assure the return of the child. (For more about parental kidnapping, see Chapter 14.)

Because of the high stakes, it's especially important to make a clear plan for custody and visitation when one parent is living overseas. Include very specific terms for travel plans, including dates for the child's departure from and return to the United States.

Support for Children and Spouses

Like everyone else, servicemembers are legally required to support their children. Just as is true with custody and visitation orders, the Department of Defense policy is to require servicemembers to comply with support orders. In fact, the military provides for sanctions, including punishment as severe as separation from military service, for failure to pay support. (Possibly for this reason, support compliance rates are significantly higher among military personnel than among civilians.)

RELATED TOPIC

More about child and spousal support. You can learn the basics of child and spousal support in Chapters 8 and 11.

Calculating Pay

One of the challenging things in a military divorce is figuring out the servicemember's actual income for purposes of calculating support. Military personnel receive a base salary, plus a housing allowance that is computed on the basis of the servicemember's location, family commitments, and pay grade. There are also pay differentials for hazardous assignments and other variations in responsibilities.

Although each branch of the military has its own guidelines for family support, these guidelines are intended to be used only when the servicemember and spouse haven't been able to agree on support and there is no court order in place. Before turning to the military guidelines, you should calculate support based on the guidelines of the state where your case is filed. To do this, you'll need to know the servicemember's income as well as any payments the servicemember is making for health insurance or work-related day care for the kids.

If you don't know your servicemember spouse's income, don't use a tax return to try to find it out. Portions of military pay are tax free, and you'll be using an amount that is too low. What you need is something called a Leave and Earnings Statement (LES). The LES will show you basic pay and also allowances such as housing, as well as information about how many dependents the servicemember is claiming and how much accrued leave is available (which may be relevant if the servicemember is invoking the SCRA and seeking to delay a hearing date based on unavailability of leave).

Getting an LES is not always a simple matter—you may have to submit a Freedom of Information Act request to the military if your spouse won't provide the LES. You'll probably find it helpful to have an attorney work with you on this, but you also could seek the help of a child support enforcement agency. (See Chapter 8.)

Another issue to consider is "in-kind" compensation. In some circumstances, it's appropriate to factor in housing, meals, and other in-kind compensation to justify a higher support award because these forms of compensation reduce the servicemember's overall expenses. Many states have rules providing that housing and food allowances should be included for purposes of calculating income even though they are not considered income for federal tax purposes. However, the military no longer provides most meals, instead paying a food allowance in most base locations. (In the field, however, meals are still provided.)

Spousal Support (Alimony)

Like child support, spousal support (also called alimony or spousal maintenance) is mostly controlled by individual states. Each state has its own rules about the circumstances under which one spouse should support the other and how long the support should last. Chapter 11 addresses spousal support.

Enforcement of Support Orders

Mobilization isn't an excuse to stop paying child or spousal support. Even when a servicemember is deployed out of state or overseas, it's quite simple to keep support coming through automatic deductions from the servicemember's pay.

On the other hand, if a servicemember stops paying, enforcing support orders can be challenging. The SCRA can be a factor in child and spousal support cases, allowing the servicemember to delay a hearing where the civilian spouse is asking for support payments.

Chapter 8 deals with child support, lists child support enforcement offices in every state, and advises on how to get an income withholding order.

Special Issues for Reservists: Support Orders

When you're establishing a support order that applies to a reservist, you need to think ahead to what might happen if the reservist is called up. When a reservist is mobilized, pay from a civilian job generally ends—and so does any garnishment of that pay. One way to avoid this result is to obtain a support order that calls for a generic garnishment on any full-time employment, not just on the spouse's current job. This way, the supported spouse can have the garnishment transferred to the military pay when the reservist is mobilized.

Otherwise, especially if the reservist is deployed overseas, filing for a new support order and accomplishing service will be challenging—and the SCRA won't help.

Special Issues for Reservists: Modification of Support

A reserve servicemember's total salary might be reduced by mobilization. Reservists who suffer a loss of pay upon mobilization don't get an automatic reduction in support, because they're likely to regain their previous salary when they return to civilian work. However, depending on the anticipated length of the deployment and the amount of the reduction, the servicemember may want to seek a temporary reduction in the support payment.

The first place to look for the reduction is to the civilian spouse. If the servicemember parent and the civilian spouse have a cooperative relationship, the ex-spouse will probably agree to a temporary reduction while the reservist's civilian pay is reduced. If you make such an agreement, put it in writing. Otherwise, the servicemember must file a motion with the court, asking for a reduction in support. If that's the plan, the servicemember should get an attorney who can help to get the hearing expedited or make arrangements for the servicemember to participate from a distance.

> TIP
> **It's important to modify support right away.** Under federal law, any missed child support payment is immediately "vested," which means the obligation can't be discharged for any reason, even if the parent files for bankruptcy or a court later modifies support. In other words, a court can't make a retroactive modification of support. So if you're a reservist whose upcoming mobilization will reduce your income significantly, and you and your spouse don't agree about the modification, make sure you go to court now and request a change in your support obligation before your deployment.

Medical Benefits

The medical benefits program available to active duty servicemembers, retirees, and family members is called TRICARE. To qualify, each eligible person must have complete and correct information on file with the Defense Enrollment Eligibility Reporting System (DEERS). There are a number of different types of TRICARE plans, but basic TRICARE coverage is free to a servicemember and the servicemember's family, with no copayments or prescription costs.

After a divorce, a servicemember's children continue to qualify for TRICARE. Unfortunately for civilian spouses, unless you meet some pretty stringent requirements, you will no longer qualify once you are divorced. You get to keep your TRICARE coverage only if all of the following things are true:

- You don't qualify for health insurance through your own employment.
- You haven't remarried.
- You meet the requirements of the 20/20/20 rule, meaning that you were married for at least 20 years, your spouse has at least 20 years of military service, and there was at least a 20-year overlap between those two time periods. (Lesser benefits are available to spouses who meet a 20/20/15 rule, meaning the overlap was at least 15 years.)

For example, say you were married in January of 1990 to a spouse who was already in military service. If your spouse is still in the military when you divorce any time after January of 2010, you'll continue to get TRICARE coverage because you were married more than 20 years, your spouse was in the military more than 20 years, and those time periods overlap. In contrast, if you married in 1990, your spouse joined the military in 1994, and you divorced in 2011, you'd have the 20 years of marriage but not the 20 years of military service.

COBRA, the insurance continuation law discussed in Chapter 11, does not apply to spouses in a military divorce. But there is something called the Continued Health Care Benefit Program (CHCBP) that offers transitional insurance benefits designed to help you move from TRICARE to coverage through your civilian employment. CHCBP can also provide coverage for preexisting medical conditions during the period that your new policy excludes them, if any. Rates aren't cheap (currently $1,193 per quarter for individuals and $2,682 per quarter for families, plus an enrollment fee) but they're not the highest, either.

CAUTION

Don't wait to get your insurance ducks in a row. You have only 60 days after you lose your military medical benefits to apply for CHCBP coverage.

RESOURCE

Get the details. Check out www.humana-military.com/chcbp/main .htm for more information about CHCBP.

You can keep the CHCBP coverage for up to 36 months. It's possible that some people may be able to keep the coverage longer if they meet certain criteria—they must have been enrolled in TRICARE at the time of the divorce, must not be covered under any other health insurance, must not remarry before reaching age 55, and must either receive a portion of the servicemember's military retirement or be the beneficiary of the Survivor Benefit Plan, discussed below. If you meet all these criteria, ask an attorney to advocate for your right to maintain your CHCBP insurance coverage.

If you no longer qualify for military medical benefits, it doesn't mean that your former spouse is automatically off the hook for your health insurance or health care expenses. You may want to negotiate to have your health insurance expenses taken care of as part of your support in the overall divorce settlement package.

You should also explore whether you can get comparable coverage at a lower cost under the Affordable Care Act. Check www.healthcare. gov or your own state's marketplace website. You can find state-specific information at www.legalconsumer.com/obamacare.

Dividing Property

Dividing personal property or real estate in a military divorce isn't all that different from dividing it in a civilian divorce. Chapter 10 explains pretty much all of what you need to know about this issue. The most important element of property division is dealing with a military pension, and that's addressed next.

Pensions, Insurance, and Other Benefits

Though it operates under very different rules than the private sector, the military is still an employer. It provides a variety of employment benefits, including medical and pension benefits, life insurance, and various other opportunities. All of these benefits of employment are subject to division in your divorce according to the law of the state in which you are getting divorced.

Military Pensions

The military has some special rules regarding pensions and divorce.

There are three different retirement plans that might apply to servicemembers, depending on when they joined the service: Final Basic Pay, High-3, and CSB/REDUX. The terms of each of these plans are complex, and civilian spouses will need a lawyer's help in identifying which plan the military spouse has and protecting their rights to a share of the benefits. There are a number of ways that a servicemember can make choices that benefit the servicemember at the expense of a civilian spouse, and you need to be sure you have a lawyer who is alert to all of these possibilities.

The 10/10 Rule and the USFSPA

Many people incorrectly believe that a civilian spouse in a military divorce can receive a share of the servicemember's retirement only if the parties meet the 10/10 rule: married for at least ten years with the servicemember having at least ten overlapping years of military service. (The rule is also sometimes referred to as the 20/10/10 rule, with the 20 referring to the number of years of service necessary for the servicemember to reach retirement eligibility.)

This isn't true, though it's easy to see where the misconception came from. For the military to pay a portion of a servicemember's retirement *directly* to a divorced spouse, the 10/10 rule must be met. But even if the marriage doesn't satisfy the 10/10 requirements, a court can still divide the military retirement—it just can't be paid out directly by the military. You'll have to collect it from your spouse when he or she receives it.

It is up to the states to decide who gets what portion of the pension, in the same way they would decide how to divide a pension belonging to a civilian spouse. However, the Defense Finance and Accounting Service (DFAS) will pay only up to 50% of the pension directly to a spouse who meets the requirements. If the court awards more than that, the military spouse must make up the difference by direct payments.

Direct payments from DFAS also require a Military Pension Division Order (MPDO). This is similar to the Qualified Domestic Relations Order (QDRO) described in Chapter 10, and, like the QDRO, it's crucial that you have an experienced attorney draft an MPDO for you to make sure your rights are protected now and in the future. This can't be overemphasized—the DFAS has a high rate of rejecting MPDOs. It's imperative that you find an attorney with experience in drafting these important documents.

The Uniformed Servicemembers' Former Spouses Protection Act (USFSPA)

The USFSPA is a federal law intended to offer some financial protection to certain former spouses of servicemembers. Congress passed the USFSPA to clarify that states are permitted, though not required, to treat military retirement pay as a marital asset subject to division at divorce. (The states' other option is to treat it as the separate property of the servicemember.)

Dividing a Military Pension

Military pensions are "defined benefit plans," which means they are true pensions—participation is mandatory, and payments at retirement are calculated using various factors including length of service. In most cases, the pension won't be paid out until the servicemember actually retires.

If the servicemember is already retired when the divorce begins, then the amount to be divided at divorce is easily determined. If not, if you're doing anything other than dividing the pension equally at retirement, then the marital share of the pension will have to be calculated by an actuary or other expert. That process, and the options for dividing a defined benefit plan, are explained in detail in Chapter 10. In brief, however, the civilian spouse has the option of waiting to receive a share of the benefits when the servicemember retires, or accepting a lump sum buyout either for cash or in trade for other marital assets.

> CAUTION
>
> **Make sure your calculations are specific to the military.** The military has its own mortality tables and other presumptions that affect the retirement calculation. If you hire an actuary to value a military pension, make sure the actuary uses the appropriate assumptions. Your attorney or actuary can also buy software designed to do these calculations.

Some lawyers think that it's usually better for a civilian spouse to take the lump sum at divorce, rather than staying enmeshed in a system that is somewhat unpredictable, as you'll see as you read on. In fact, the very unpredictability of factors like the servicemember's survival until retirement, eligibility for retirement, and rank and pay grade at the time of retirement, lead some courts to refuse to make a decision at the time of the divorce. Instead, they enter a so-called "wait and see" order and retain the right to make a decision about the benefits at the time the servicemember is eligible for retirement or actually retires, whichever comes first. This means ex-spouses can look forward to additional legal fees and engagement with each other at some unknown future date—not a prospect most divorcing spouses relish.

Another situation in which you might want to take a lump sum instead of waiting for your military spouse to retire is where you don't qualify under the 10/10 rule to have the military pay your share of the retirement directly to you. If you wait, you'll be relying on your former spouse to pay you your share, and if many years have passed between your divorce and your spouse's retirement, it may be difficult to enforce the order if your spouse fails to live up to its terms.

What Gets Divided?

Federal law provides that state courts may divide only "disposable retired pay" in a divorce. Disposable retired pay means the servicemember's gross retirement pay, minus any amounts that the government takes back through deductions—for example, prior overpayments, court-martial fines or forfeitures, or premiums for the Survivor Benefit Plan (discussed below). It's crucial that any order dividing retirement benefits use the language "disposable retired pay" so that it's clear what's being divided.

Also excluded from disposable retired pay are disability pay benefits. This means that a servicemember who receives disability benefits as a result of a disability sustained during the marriage may withhold the disability benefit amount from the amount of disposable retired pay that can be divided in the divorce. And a servicemember whose disability begins after the divorce can elect to take a lump sum disability payout that reduces or eliminates pension payments.

In general, there's not much a spouse can do about this. But recently, a Maryland appellate court held that the ex-wife of a servicemember who was discharged because of permanent disability was entitled to receive her share of the lump sum that her husband elected to receive instead of his pension. The court said that the payment didn't violate the rule that disability benefits aren't included in pension payments, because the court ordered the husband to pay the wife out of his assets generally, not specifically out of the disability award.

When Can You Get Your Retirement Share?

As discussed above, it's possible you might agree to take a lump sum buyout of your share in your military spouse's retirement. You'd receive that when you settle your divorce. If you don't, you'll be waiting to get your share later—but what does later mean? Your spouse may continue working for many years after becoming eligible for retirement benefits, while you may want to start receiving your share of those benefits as early as possible. In many states, you'll be able to include a provision in your divorce judgment that says you're entitled to receive your share as soon as your former spouse becomes eligible for retirement. This should be a date you can figure out and include in your judgment.

Bankruptcy and Retirement

An award of a share of military retirement is considered a nondischarge-able debt, just like support obligations. This means that a military spouse who files for bankruptcy still owes the other spouse a share of the pension. (See Chapter 14 for more about bankruptcy.)

Career Status Bonus and Combat-Related Special Compensation

Some servicemembers opt for the retirement plan called REDUX, which gives the servicemember the option of taking a midcareer bonus, called a Career Status Bonus (CSB) of $30,000 when the servicemember reaches 14½ years of service. In exchange, the servicemember takes a reduction in pension benefits.

The DFAS website unequivocally states that as a bonus, the CSB is not divisible in a divorce action, but such a statement isn't binding on state courts. In fact, many courts will require that a servicemember compensate a former spouse for any reduction the servicemember causes in the retirement benefits to which the spouse is entitled.

However, it's possible for a servicemember to opt for the CSB without a spouse's consent and even without the spouse's knowledge—especially if the servicemember's eligibility for the CSB occurs some time after the divorce is final. If you think your spouse has received a CSB, make sure you find out. And make sure that your marital settlement agreement or judgment states that your spouse must inform you—and compensate you—if a CSB comes into play.

Combat-Related Special Compensation (CRSC) is a form of compensation that injured veterans may receive if they meet certain qualifications, including having a combat-related injury. When a veteran opts to receive CRSC, other benefits are affected, and CRSC funds are not divisible by courts in a divorce, because they are neither property nor retirement pay. Talk to a lawyer with expertise in military issues about whether your spouse might qualify for CRSC, and about what provisions you might want to make to protect yourself from losing your share of retirement benefits.

The Survivor Benefit Plan

The Survivor Benefit Plan (SBP) is a form of annuity that allows retired servicemembers to leave a death benefit to specified survivors, including a former spouse. The servicemember pays premiums through a payroll deduction starting after retirement. Unless a court orders otherwise, the servicemember has control over the amount of the benefit and the beneficiary. Upon the servicemember's death, the beneficiary receives a lifetime annuity—for most beneficiaries, currently 55% of the retired pay the servicemember would have been entitled to if he or she retired on the date of death.

The SBP is a way that a former spouse can continue receiving something after the servicemember's death. Whether a divorcing spouse wants to negotiate for SBP coverage depends on all the circumstances of the divorce, but don't ignore this valuable benefit. And pay attention to its time limits and the requirements to finalize the SBP order. You'll need a lawyer's help to be sure you're doing this correctly.

The Thrift Savings Plan

Servicemembers also may participate in a Thrift Savings Plan (TSP), which is similar to a private employer's 401(k) plan. The servicemember contributes a percentage of basic pay (no more than 7%) to the plan, with no matching by the military employer. The TSP is completely separate from the military pension and is treated as a separate asset at divorce. If you're a civilian spouse, you may not even know whether your spouse is participating in the TSP. Be sure to find out so that if it exists, this asset can be included in your negotiations.

Early Separation Payments

It's unlikely that the armed services will be offering early separation incentives to servicemembers in the near future. (In fact, it seems more likely that servicemembers would be offered enlistment and reenlistment bonuses.) But if there is such a payment to divide in your divorce, you should know that states have differed widely in their treatment of early separation payments. Some treat them like retirement benefits and others like income. Be sure to consider such payments an element of your settlement negotiations.

Accrued Leave

Every servicemember accrues 30 days of paid leave each year. The maximum that can be accrued, with a few exceptions, is 60 days. Each month of accrued leave is worth the same as a month's pay. State divorce law applies to accrued leave just as it does to retirement pay, and states differ as to whether accrued leave is property to be divided. Generally, your state's rules about accrued leave will be the same as the rules about unused vacation and sick pay in civilian jobs. (See Chapter 11.)

Civil Service Rollovers

A little-known fact about military retirement is that servicemembers who move from the military into a federal civil service job can roll over their military retirement benefits into that new job's retirement plan. The result is that the military pension disappears, and the funds reappear in the retirement plan for the new job.

If you're counting on payments from an ex-spouse, you don't need to worry. To roll over military pension benefits into civil service retirement, a worker must authorize the Office of Personnel Management to deduct any amounts due to a former spouse under a valid court order. Still, make sure that your settlement or divorce judgment includes language stating that the servicemember won't convert military into civil service retirement benefits without consent from the former spouse and that if a conversion occurs without your consent, you're entitled to receive the equivalent of what you were entitled to from the military pension.

Life Insurance

Life insurance is often a good way to secure ongoing support obligations. If your final divorce judgment says that one spouse must pay child or spousal support, make sure that the paying spouse's life is insured in an amount that will compensate for the loss of support if that spouse dies. (See Chapter 11.)

This rule, of course, applies to military spouses as well, and is especially important for active duty military personnel. But one note of caution: Make sure that you obtain private life insurance, and don't rely on the Servicemembers Group Life Insurance (SGLI). It's important for the recipient spouse to own the insurance policy, so that spouse keeps control over the beneficiary designations (to make sure the kids remain the beneficiaries). The law says that servicemembers always retain control over the beneficiary designations under the SGLI, regardless of court orders or marital settlement agreements that state otherwise.

Tax Issues

The Military Family Tax Relief Act helps servicemember taxpayers by creating less stringent rules for capital gains tax exclusions (see Chapter 10 for basics of capital gains) as well as death benefit payments. Also, if you are a servicemember who owes back taxes, you may get a break in the form of a deferral or relief from interest and penalties if you can prove that your ability to pay was affected by your military service. Any of these issues may come into play in your divorce if you are dividing liability for back taxes or selling a home.

Military servicemembers can qualify for head of household status and can transfer dependency exemptions just like civilian taxpayers. (See Chapter 10 for more about taxes and divorce.)

RESOURCE

The Legal Assistance Office can help. Tax matters are within the scope of the Legal Assistance Offices that are available to help members in every branch of the service. In addition, many military bases operate a tax center every year from January through April.

Domestic Violence and Other Abuse

If you are concerned about domestic violence or child abuse, see Chapter 14 for information and resources that are useful for both civilian and military spouses. But be aware that the military deals with issues of family violence in some different ways than civilian authorities do. The policies, procedures, and rules described below apply mostly when the abuser is a servicemember. If you're a servicemember being abused by a civilian, you're probably going to have to use civilian methods to prosecute the abuser—though sometimes a base commander will bar a civilian abuser from the base to protect a servicemember.

The Department of Defense has two programs in place to deal with abuse within the family: the Family Advocacy Program and the Military Justice system. All military personnel are required to report any suspicion of family violence to the Family Advocacy Program, which will assign an investigator. The investigator reports to a commanding officer, who decides whether the charges are substantiated and then whether the offender should be offered counseling or be subject to discipline under the Military Code of Justice.

> **CAUTION**
>
> **Family Advocacy Program counseling isn't confidential.** Unlike many civilian counseling programs, which protect participants through therapist-patient privilege, counseling under the military's Family Advocacy Program isn't confidential. Information provided to the investigator can be used in later military or civilian prosecution against the offender.

A base commander can also issue a Military Protective Order, requiring the servicemember to stay away from the spouse or child being abused. Civilian authorities won't enforce a Military Protective Order, so it won't help if you want an abuser kept away from your civilian workplace, your kids' off-base schools, or other places off base where you feel unsafe. For that, you'll need a restraining order from a civilian court. (See Chapter 14.)

Penalties for a finding of abuse can be severe for the servicemember, up to and including discharge from the service. Many spouses married to servicemembers are reluctant to report abuse because they fear the military spouse's career will be damaged and that the family will suffer financially as a result. However, federal law protects the civilian spouse if a servicemember is discharged as a result of abuse of a spouse or dependent child—and it's irrelevant whether the discharge followed a court-martial or was imposed administratively by a commanding officer. The civilian spouse is entitled to "transitional compensation" from the military for 12 to 36 months after the military spouse's discharge.

In addition, a civilian spouse can receive the equivalent of retirement payments directly from the military if the servicemember was denied retirement because of the spousal or child abuse. The civilian spouse can obtain an order from a divorce court under the provisions of the Uniformed Services Former Spouse Protection Act for payment of the amount the servicemember would have received if his or her military career had continued. The military will honor the payments. The Family Advocacy Program can help if you're a civilian spouse who wants to take advantage of this rule.

Postdivorce Follow-Up

Chapter 15 explains how to ensure you've taken care of all the small (but important) postdivorce tasks that are easy to forget or put off.

In addition to the items discussed there, there's a lot of paperwork and record keeping involved in military service, and both spouses should be sure to update all records, usually by notifying a commanding officer.

Resources

For more information about divorce and the military, here are some useful sources.

The website www.statesidelegal.org focuses on the unique legal needs of servicemembers, veterans, and military families, especially those with limited financial resources.

Try the Armed Forces Legal Assistance Office website, http://legalassistance.law.af.mil/index.php. Be cautious in relying too much on this source, as not everything is as accurate or complete as you might want it to be. However, there's some good basic information for divorcing servicemembers and their families.

To find the Family Advocacy Program nearest you, go to the Homefront website at www.militaryinstallations.dod.mil.

The American Bar Association's Family Law Section's Military Committee provides information and resources at www.abanet.org/family/home.html. Click the link for "committees" and then "military" to find the committee's home page.

The divorcenet.com site has articles about military issues at www.divorcenet.com/military. Check dates to make sure the information is relatively current.

The website of Marshal Willick, a Nevada attorney, at www.willicklawgroup.com, contains links to many of Willick's publications, including "Division of Military Retirement Benefits in Divorce." Willick is also the author of *Military Retirement Benefits in Divorce: A Lawyer's Guide to Valuation and Distribution*, published by the Family Law Section of the American Bar Association.

The Military Divorce Handbook, by Mark E. Sullivan, is a comprehensive resource. Sullivan has also authored numerous articles, pamphlets, and information sheets on the subject. An Internet search for "military divorce" will turn up many of his shorter, more accessible works.

Chapter 16 provides general legal resources and some instructions about doing your own legal research. ●

Getting It in Writing: Preparing Your Marital Settlement Agreement

U p to this point, the term marital settlement agreement may have seemed abstract. You know you need one, but why is it important? And where will it come from? If you've already worked out some issues with your spouse, or even just begun discussing them, then you're already making progress toward your final agreement. This chapter will answer those questions and outline the issues that you must be sure to address in your agreement. And, to show you what the final product might look like, there's a sample agreement at the end of the chapter.

Even if you think your divorce will end up in a trial, you should still try to come up with an agreement on at least some of the issues, and not leave every decision to the judge. And keep in mind that most contested divorces end up settling out of court—frequently at the last minute. Any work you do negotiating a settlement agreement won't be wasted.

The only times you don't need a settlement agreement are when you're getting a summary divorce, or when your state's forms give you room to include your agreements.

What It Is, What It Does

A marital settlement agreement (sometimes shortened to "MSA") is the document that spells out everything you and your spouse agree to regarding property, custody, and support. It describes:

- how you intend to divide your property and debts
- your agreements about child and spousal support
- how you will share parenting responsibilities, and how you will deal with any issues that come up relating to raising your children, and
- how you will deal with any conflicts that arise later.

Commonly, these agreements contain a lot of detail. For example, yours might set out whether support will be paid by check or by automatic transfer and how you'll choose the real estate agent who will list your house.

Once you've finalized your MSA, you submit it to the judge, who approves it and makes it part of your final divorce order. Because the agreement has the force of a court order, both parties are likely to comply with its terms, which gives everyone some degree of confidence about the future.

Creating the Agreement

To create a marital settlement agreement, you and your spouse must make hard decisions about your property and your children. There are many issues to consider and negotiate. To make sure that your agreement addresses everything it should, refer to the checklist below. You may not need to include every single item in the agreement itself—for example, if neither of you changed your name when you married, you need not include a section about returning to your old name. But you should touch on all of them in the negotiations, if only for the purpose of confirming they don't apply to you.

When you've covered everything, your agreements must be put in a final document. If you use mediation or hire a lawyer, then the mediator or lawyer will likely prepare the settlement agreement for you. Or you may want to start with a free template from the Internet, and use it along with books and other Internet research to create a draft agreement, which you then have reviewed by lawyers. Another option is to pay an Internet business to gather information from you and then prepare an agreement for you, or pay a legal document preparer (if this service is available in your state) to do the same thing. Chapter 16 has details about each of these options.

Most of these issues are included in the sample agreement at the end of the chapter.

Negotiations

Negotiating with your spouse and putting together an agreement will take time, so be patient and put the priority on doing it right, not doing it quickly. This section addresses each issue that you'll need to include in your agreement.

At the end of this chapter, there's a sample MSA for a fictional couple, Cynthia and Howard. Their divorce isn't the very simplest divorce—or the most complex—a couple could possibly have. Their negotiation process is described throughout the chapter, to give you an example of how the issues in a negotiation work together and how the process works.

Cynthia and Howard's Story

Cynthia, a nurse administrator at a nonprofit agency, and Howard, a civil engineer, lived in a house they bought with savings and some help from both sets of parents. Both of them had good jobs with benefits. They had two daughters, Sarah and Maya, ages seven and nine. After each girl was born, Cynthia took six months off and then worked half time, increasing her hours to 30 per week when Maya started kindergarten. Howard worked a fairly predictable 9-to-5 day when he was in town, but his job required frequent travel. His absences were one factor in the growing emotional distance between them, and after almost 11 years of marriage, they separated.

After the initial shock of the decision wore off, Cynthia and Howard were able to agree that they wanted to divorce as amicably as possible for the sake of the children. They also agreed that they'd try to do the divorce themselves instead of hiring lawyers—they figured they would save money and Cynthia was good at doing research and paperwork. She went to the bookstore and purchased a couple of divorce guides, and did some Internet research to get started. Their marriage counselor agreed to act as a mediator and help them to make decisions about their kids and their property.

What Your MSA Should Cover

☐ Child support

☐ Spousal support

☐ Health, life, and disability insurance

☐ The house and other real estate

☐ Cars and other vehicles

☐ Household items (furniture and furnishings)

☐ Personal items, including clothing, jewelry, tools, and athletic equipment

☐ Stocks, bonds, and mutual funds

☐ Bank accounts

☐ Retirement plans and pensions

☐ Family business or professional practice, including accounts payable and receivable

☐ Pets

☐ Art work

☐ Frequent flyer miles, season tickets, and other miscellaneous assets

☐ Stock options

☐ Parenting (separate parenting agreement should accompany MSA)

☐ Name changes (you, your spouse, or the children)

☐ Credit cards and other debts

☐ Tax payments and distribution of refund

☐ Fees for mediation, lawyers, and counselors

☐ Social Security benefits

☐ Modifying the agreement later

☐ How disputes will be resolved

☐ Which state's law will govern in the event of a dispute

Housing

One of the first decisions you'll need to make is where each of you will live and what will happen with the house if you own one. Chapter 10 deals with this question in detail. Whatever you decide, make sure that your MSA is specific about the timing of the various changes. For example, if you're both still living in the house, the agreement should include a date that one of you is going to move out. If you're transferring it, set a date that the paperwork will be signed. If the person staying is getting a loan to buy the other person out, put a time limit on getting the financing in place. The dates need to be realistic—don't leave only two weeks for getting a new mortgage if you haven't even begun looking.

Parents often make agreements about continuing to live in a certain proximity to their children or not to move out of the area or out of state for a specified period of time. If you both have stable work situations and can afford to live in the same area, this is a great way to avoid future conflicts over one parent's desire to move away.

By the time Cynthia and Howard separated, the balance on their 15-year mortgage was $145,000, with a monthly payment of $1,100. They estimated the house was worth about $295,000, and that their equity was approximately $150,000. The house was in a nice neighborhood, an easy commute for Cynthia and a slightly longer one for Howard.

Howard and Cynthia were both very attached to their house. They had worked hard on landscaping the yard, building a deck, and gradually perfecting the interior. Cynthia wanted to stay there with the kids and have Howard move out. He was reluctant, but finally agreed. He found an apartment in a fourplex about half a mile away. It wasn't cheap, but they agreed it was important for him to stay close so that the girls could easily go back and forth.

The more difficult question was what would happen to the house in the long run. At first, Howard was adamant that he didn't want to sell the house—either to a third party or to Cynthia in a buyout. He had put too much work into it and cared about it too much. He also thought it was going to appreciate even more, and he didn't want to miss out on that. He argued that they should continue to co-own the house for another five years and then assess their situation, and he was willing to stay in rental housing during that period if that's what it would take. But he wasn't sure that would be necessary—because the loan on the house wasn't enormous, and he had a good salary without a lot of other debt, he might be able to qualify for a loan on another small place.

Cynthia, who was inclined to make a clean break, wasn't sure about joint ownership. She knew she didn't have a choice about continuing to parent with Howard, but she didn't want to have to continue making decisions with him about financial matters. She also disagreed about the real estate market, believing the house's value wasn't going to increase much. She did want to stay in the house, though, so her position was that Howard should allow her to buy him out of his interest. On the other hand, she was worried that she wouldn't be able to afford a buyout—she'd have to take a larger loan to cover the buyout payment to Howard. She wasn't sure she'd qualify on her salary alone, and also was anxious about the prospect of higher monthly payments. The current mortgage was already stretching her budget since Howard had moved out.

They struggled over the issue until the mediator suggested they table it for a while and look at some of the other issues. He reassured them that sometimes issues that seemed very different were, in fact, intertwined, and suggested that the house question might become clearer as they resolved other things.

Expenses and Support Payments

Your MSA needs to address who will pay what to whom, and how and when. Chapters 8 and 11 explain your options for child and spousal support as well as ways you can enforce support payments. If you're going to use your state's child support enforcement agency, put something in your agreement that says so. Don't forget to include the date or conditions under which spousal support will end.

You and your spouse may have agreed to child support payments that are different from the guideline support that your state would order based on your incomes and your time-share. If that's the case, you may need to include some very specific language in your agreement stating that you are aware that you're deviating from guideline support, why you are doing so, and assuring the court that your children's needs will be met by the support amount. Some states have laws about exactly what you need to say in your settlement agreement if you're deviating from guideline support, so make sure you find out what you need to include. Otherwise you risk having your agreement sent back to you for correction.

You can allow for future changes in your agreement by including a provision for meeting again at a certain point to reconsider the support amounts. If your children are young, or it looks like one of you is going to have a job change that will affect your income, putting in an automatic review date is a great idea. Also include a provision that any changes you make later will have the same force as your original agreement as long as they're made in writing and signed by both of you.

In addressing support, don't forget to include whatever agreements you've made about paying for college and other extra expenses.

> With Cynthia and Howard, short-term needs dominated the initial discussion. Cynthia's $37,500 salary (she worked 30 hours per week but had been considering going back to full-time) was just enough to make the monthly mortgage payment, pay the utility bills, and buy groceries. All of the other expenses, including clothing, activities for the kids, transportation, and larger annual expenses, like homeowners' insurance and property taxes, were going to have to come out of Howard's $95,000 salary—which would also have to pay for his housing and living expenses.
>
> Each of them prepared an expense budget and compared them. Their initial calculations indicated that having Howard pay Cynthia $1,000 per month in child support and $500 per month in spousal support would

mean that they both could make ends meet. The $6,000 annual increase in taxable income (from spousal support) to Cynthia would not affect her tax bracket, and the deduction would help Howard slightly.

They used a child support calculator they found on the Internet to check their state's guidelines, and found they weren't far off from guideline support. (At the time, they also learned that the deductibility of the spousal support relied on having a written agreement about the payments, so they prepared an interim agreement stating what the payments would be and which portion would be considered spousal support.) They also included a savings plan for the girls' college educations.

Parenting

It's a good idea to make your parenting agreement an attachment to your MSA, rather than including all the parenting information in the MSA. Especially if your agreement calls for review dates and anticipates changes, making it a separate document gives you flexibility. If you're anticipating changes, include a provision that changes automatically become enforceable when they are written down and signed by both of you. Otherwise, you'll have to go back to court every time you make a change in your parenting schedule, to try to get it approved by a judge. Also, it makes each document a more manageable length.

Include something in your parenting agreement about how you're going to work it out if you disagree about parenting issues. If you have a marriage counselor or mediator, you might agree to a certain number of sessions with that person to try to work it out. If you make your parenting agreement without any help, take some time to figure out together who could help you if you get stuck—a mediator, custody evaluator, or child development expert are all good choices. Try to pick a specific person if possible. If you can't, pick someone who will help you break a tie if you disagree. The last thing you want is to be stalled out just trying to figure out whom to see when you need help on something to do with your kids.

Chapter 6 defines types of custody and explains different parenting arrangements that people make. Chapter 16 lists resources, including sample parenting plans available on the Internet.

RESOURCE

Building a Parenting Agreement that Works: Child Custody Agreements Step by Step, by Mimi Lyster Zemmelman (Nolo), provides excellent sample clauses for every issue you might want to deal with in a parenting agreement.

Cynthia and Howard easily agreed that Cynthia would continue to be the primary caretaker for Sarah and Maya, just as she had been during the marriage. They were also in sync, at least in principle, that Howard should spend a significant amount of time with the girls. It was when they got down to the brass tacks of what that meant in terms of actual time that things got harder than either of them anticipated.

Howard suggested that the girls spend three nights a week with him when he was in town, and he also wanted to share equally in their vacation time. While supportive of his relationship with the girls—and knowing it was best for them to continue having a meaningful relationship with their dad—Cynthia was concerned because Howard sometimes was paralyzed by depression. At home, he would retreat into his study and not come out all evening, making it clear that no one was to disturb him. The girls found this baffling and a bit frightening, and they felt their dad was unpredictable. Cynthia didn't want to agree to an extensive schedule of visitation if Howard wasn't going to be an effective parent during the time the girls were with him.

These discussions were painful for both parents, but ultimately they came to an agreement that both could live with. Howard's visits started off on a fairly limited basis, and he agreed to monitor his own emotional state and to cancel the visit if he was feeling really down. With the counselor's advice, they came up with a way to talk to the girls about the uncertainty of their visitation schedule. Understanding that his relationship with his daughters was on the line, Howard also agreed to get some counseling of his own and to consider other treatment to help with his depression. They also agreed that if Howard couldn't care for the girls himself during his visitation time (because of travel or other obligations), Cynthia would have the first option to keep the girls with her, and would have approval of any other caregivers Howard proposed. As the primary custodial parent, she didn't feel Howard should have approval over child care choices, and Howard felt perfectly comfortable with her decision making about this.

Over time, Cynthia and Howard worked out all the rest of the agreements they'd need to create a comprehensive parenting plan. The only other sticking point turned out to be the issue of Sarah's learning disability. Cynthia favored a plan to send her to private school, while Howard felt that some extra tutoring should take care of it. They compromised by agreeing on tutoring for the next school year, and then sending her to private school if the tutoring didn't seem to help.

Howard and Cynthia's parenting plan is Exhibit 1 to the sample marital settlement agreement at the end of the chapter.

Personal Belongings

You do have to divvy up personal and household items. (Chapter 10 suggests some ways to approach this.) But to keep things simple, don't list specific items in the body of your MSA. If you have already divided your personal items, you can just say that each of you will keep what you've already got. If you want to make lists of the items you're each taking, make them attachments to the MSA.

It's a good idea to state that you believe you each got things of equal value, or if the value was very different, to say so and then say how you're going to equalize it or why it's not equal.

For the most part, Cynthia and Howard divided their personal belongings without a great deal of fuss. They easily agreed that they each would keep their own clothing and personal effects. They then went through the house together to make an inventory, and sat down at the kitchen table and divided everything—including the kitchen table. Howard had already taken a few things to his new place, and they included those things on the list so that they would have an accurate value for everything they divided. Cynthia agreed that Howard could keep all of the tools, and also agreed to continue storing them at the house and to let Howard come and use the workshop in the basement once a week as long as he gave her 24 hours' notice.

As it turned out, the value of the items that Cynthia kept, because she was staying in the house, far exceeded the value of the property that Howard took with him—in fact there was about a $10,000 difference. Knowing that the issue of the house was still open, and that there were other assets yet to consider, they made note of the difference and moved on.

Cars

It's common with cars for each spouse to keep the car they usually drive, and equalize any disparity in their value by trading other property or paying cash. If you have a joint car loan, though, make sure you don't forget to include it in your division of debt and make provisions for either paying it off or transferring the debt into the sole name of the person who's keeping the car. And don't forget to do the paperwork to transfer ownership and change your insurance.

Cynthia drove a late-model Prius worth about $18,000, which they were still paying for. The car loan had a balance of about $10,000. Howard was driving a slightly older Lexus that was paid off and had a blue book value of about $23,000. Both were happy to keep the cars they were currently driving, but Cynthia worried about her ability to make the continuing payments on the Prius, which were over $300 a month.

Because the values of the two cars were almost equal, the real issue was what would be done with the obligation on the Prius. Neither party was too excited about taking on those payments, so Cynthia suggested that they pay off the car loan when the house was refinanced. This brought them back around to the issue of the house, which Howard continued to insist shouldn't be refinanced at all, as they should continue to own it together. For the time being, they added the cars to the list of issues yet to be decided.

Bank and Other Accounts

By the time you're preparing your MSA, you should have already closed most of your joint accounts and established checking and savings accounts of your own. If you have investment accounts, however, you might have left them in both names while you decided how to divide them. Your MSA sets out what you decide. The agreement should say what's going to happen with your accounts and how—including who will do the paperwork and when. Include realistic deadlines for getting things done.

Cynthia and Howard had joint checking and savings accounts, but when they separated they each set up separate checking accounts and split the money from the joint accounts in half. They closed the joint accounts immediately. They also each had individual retirement accounts with roughly equal balances. They agreed that they each would keep their own IRA.

Cynthia had a separate brokerage account in which she held some stock that she had inherited from her grandfather about six years before. She had never liquidated any of the stock, had never placed Howard's name on the account, and had never deposited any money into that account, so there was no question that it was her separate property. The agreement reflected that and confirmed the account to Cynthia.

Cynthia and Howard also had a joint brokerage account that held stocks and mutual funds that they had invested in over the years. The account had originally belonged to Howard. When they began living together, the assets in it were worth about $12,000. By the time they got married, they had deposited funds together and the holdings had grown to a value of $19,000—and by the time they separated, growth and additional investment had increased the value of the account to nearly $60,000.

This brokerage account generated some spirited discussion in their counseling session. Howard wanted back the money that was in the account at the time he put Cynthia's name on it. Cynthia knew from her research that because Howard had put her name on the account and they placed marital funds into it, the entire account was legally marital property. Howard didn't disagree with her about the law—he just felt that the rule wasn't fair in these circumstances.

The counselor challenged Cynthia to take some time to consider what she felt was fair, apart from what she knew about the legal rules. He didn't give her advice or ask her to come to any particular conclusion, but he did ask her to consider the overall picture of the decisions they were making, and what would work for them both.

Miscellaneous Assets

Chapter 10 identifies some assets that are easy to forget about but that need to be considered in dividing your property and included in your MSA. You might put them in the section on personal belongings, or in a separate paragraph, as in the sample agreement. Identify each item clearly and describe its value and how it's being disposed of.

Howard was a baseball fan and for many years had season tickets for the local minor league team. These were paid for with marital funds and clearly were a marital asset but, just as clearly, Cynthia did not want them. They were worth about $1,600, and Cynthia and Howard agreed that he would pay Cynthia for her share of the tickets. They also discussed the value of Howard's frequent flyer miles, which were significant, given the amount of travel he did. While they were married, they used his frequent flyer miles for most of their family vacations, and he still had a large balance. Neither of them knew how to value the miles in monetary terms, but Cynthia didn't want to just abandon her interest in them. Howard suggested that he would simply give Cynthia miles whenever she wanted them, but she didn't want to have to ask each time.

Nothing Cynthia had read so far had said anything about the miles, so she did some more Internet research. At first she found conflicting information. One article said that frequent flyer miles were impossible to value, and one said that they were impossible to divide because they weren't transferable. Finally Cynthia called the airline and learned that they would split the miles according to the divorce documents—all Howard had to do was submit the final settlement agreement, and the company would make a new account for Cynthia and move half of the miles into it. Howard easily agreed to this.

Debts

Your settlement agreement can call for one person to take over responsibility for certain debts, but it's not binding on the creditors. That's why it's always better to get your debts paid off as part of the divorce, if you can manage it. (Chapter 10 explains more about this.) This element of your MSA should say who's going to take responsibility for what, whether it's keeping the debts or paying them off. Time limits are really important here, especially if there's going to be a payoff. Your best bet is to tie the debt payoff to the division of the assets, and make it happen all at the same time. For example, you might agree to use the proceeds of a refinance to pay off your remaining debts.

Your agreement should say that any debts either of you took on after your date of separation are that person's separate debts, and that you'll pay each other back for anything either person pays on debts that aren't theirs.

Cynthia and Howard didn't have a lot of debt other than their mortgage and the car loan on Cynthia's Prius. However, they did have joint credit cards, two with balances over $5,000. In all, excluding their mortgage they had debt of $23,000, which they agreed they owed equally. Again, Cynthia returned to the idea of paying off the debts with the refinancing of the house, and Howard argued against a sale or buyout. Again, they agreed to table that discussion until they'd reviewed all of the issues.

Retirement Benefits

Retirement benefits are a big issue in most divorces—in some families, they are even more valuable than the family home. If you're going to divide a pension at retirement, you'll need a Qualified Domestic Relations Order (QDRO), which is explained in Chapter 10. Then, your MSA will say how you're dividing the benefits and state that you'll have a QDRO prepared—including who will prepare it for you, how the preparation will be paid for, and when it will be accomplished. You'll need to follow up to make sure all of that happens, as described in Chapter 15.

If you're each keeping your retirement benefits, each nonemployee spouse will need to sign a waiver of rights, which you'll get from your own plan administrator. Your agreement should set out deadlines for accomplishing those tasks, too. Your MSA should state the value of each person's benefits, how the value was arrived at, and what you're doing to equalize assets, if anything. The sample agreement shows how an agreement might look when spouses keep their own retirement plans.

If you are transferring IRAs or 401(k)s, your agreement needs to state that the transfer will be made "trustee-to-trustee," which is another way of saying that you are rolling it over into another account. Otherwise you could end up owing tax and penalties, as described in Chapter 10.

When Howard and Cynthia began discussing retirement benefits, the pieces began to fall into place. Everything they read gave them the same advice: Hire someone to value your pensions! Through his work, Howard knew an actuary firm and he located an actuary who specialized in valuing pension benefits in divorce. Howard and Cynthia both asked their human resources departments for current retirement benefit information and passed it along to the actuary. In about ten days, she gave them a summary of the present value and marital shares of their retirement plans.

The marital share of Cynthia's retirement benefits, which were in a 401(k), turned out to be worth about $70,000 for these purposes. Howard's were much more valuable because he had worked at his job longer and had worked full-time throughout the marriage, at almost double Cynthia's salary. The actuary valued his pension benefits at $220,000. However, some of that had been earned before Howard and Cynthia were married. According to the actuary, the marital share of the pension was about $190,000.

Cynthia and Howard knew that they had two options: keep their own retirement assets and even out the financial disparity using other assets, or continue to own the pension jointly and share it when it came time for distribution. Cynthia felt the same about this as she did about most other things—she preferred a clean break now to a continued relationship. She also preferred the certainty of taking the value out of Howard's pension now. They were both a long way from retirement, and she felt that waiting to receive the benefits later carried some risks for her.

She also saw that the amount she was entitled to, even offset by the likelihood that she would keep her own 401(k), might be enough to help her afford the house, if Howard would agree. His half share of the equity in the house was worth approximately $75,000 (half of the $150,000 equity). The value of her share in his pension was $95,000, and the value of his share of her 401(k) was $35,000, so that he "owed" her $60,000 in retirement money if they agreed to cash out now.

Cynthia asked Howard to reconsider his position on the house buyout. She offered to give up her rights in his pension as partial payment for the buyout, and said she felt they could shuffle the other assets and debts to make it work. He said he would think about it, and after a difficult but helpful discussion with his best friend, he decided to let go of his interest in the house. By the time they returned to mediation the next week, Howard was prepared to agree to the buyout, but he wanted to be compensated for giving up the future appreciation that he was certain the house would bring.

Cynthia still disagreed with him about the certainty of the appreciation, but she was willing to agree to some compensation as long as there was no risk to her. The current market value of the house was about $295,000. She suggested that if she sold the house in the future for more than $350,000, she would give Howard $5,000 to compensate him for the appreciation. If it sold for more than $400,000, she would give him $15,000. Howard quickly agreed to this, and they added the term to their draft agreement.

They also returned to the issue of the brokerage account. Cynthia had considered Howard's position and decided that his point was valid and that he should get credit for at least some of what had been in the account before they moved in together. She proposed that they treat only $50,000 of the account as marital property, and the other $10,000 as Howard's separate property. Howard accepted this proposal as well.

Taxes

What legal document would be complete without a section on taxes? Your MSA should include your decisions on the following tax-related questions:

- whether you'll file income tax returns separately or jointly for the previous and current tax years, or how you'll decide
- who will take the dependent exemptions for your children, or how you'll decide

- how you'll share any refund you get for the last year you file jointly, and
- how you'll pay any tax you owe for the last year you file jointly.

You may have other tax issues. Make sure you include them and clearly state who is responsible for what taxes. And remember that if you are divorced any time up to December 31, you are considered single for tax purposes for that entire tax year. If you want that, make sure your judgment is entered by the end of the year. If there are tax advantages to staying married, make sure it's not.

Howard and Cynthia prepared their marital settlement agreement in August, and while they knew something about the tax consequences of their decisions, they did not yet know what their tax liability for that year would be. They agreed that they would share jointly in the cost of having their taxes prepared by a professional (in the past, they had prepared their own tax returns), would file in the way (jointly or separately) that would be most advantageous to both of them, and would share any tax liability (or refund) in proportion to their incomes that year—in other words, Howard would pay or receive approximately twice as much as Cynthia. They also agreed to use the professional tax preparer in the future to help them figure out the best way to share the dependent exemption for the girls.

Life and Disability Insurance

If support is changing hands, getting life and disability insurance for the paying spouse is a good way to ensure that support would continue even if unforeseen events make that spouse unable to work and earn. Chapters 8, 11, and 15 all deal with this topic.

The agreement should state time limits for buying the insurance or, if the spouse already has it, contacting the insurance company and redoing the beneficiary designations. (Chapter 15 explains why this is necessary.)

> Both Howard and Cynthia wanted to be sure that the girls would be taken care of if anything happened to either of them, so they agreed that they would maintain each other as the beneficiaries of their life insurance through work. Cynthia was also concerned about Howard's becoming unable to work as a result of his depression. While Howard thought this was unrealistic, he knew that accidents are always a possibility and agreed to purchase disability insurance.

Health Insurance

Your MSA should clearly state how each member of the family is going to be insured for medical coverage, which parent is keeping the children insured, and whether one spouse is going to remain insured on the other's group plan under COBRA (the federal law that lets a divorced spouse keep group coverage through the former spouse's employment). The COBRA time limits are particularly important here—Chapter 11 explains what they are, and your agreement should ensure that you both know what your responsibilities are to get the COBRA coverage in place. You also need to say who's going to pay for the insurance and any uninsured medical expenses.

> For Howard and Cynthia, health insurance was another fairly simple issue. Although Cynthia's employer offered group insurance, Howard's coverage was better and they agreed that Cynthia would stay on that coverage, paying the premiums herself, until the COBRA time limit ran out. He would keep the girls on his coverage indefinitely. The agreement reflects this and contains Howard's promise to notify the plan administrator when the divorce is finalized.

Name Changes

If you're going to return to a previous name after your divorce, say so in your MSA. It's likely that the divorce order will have a place to enter the name change, too. If you don't do it at the time of your divorce, you'll have to go through another court process to get your name changed later.

Cynthia decided she wanted to return to using her birth name after the divorce, so she and Howard included a provision in the agreement to that effect. Howard asked that it be made clear that the girls would keep his last name, even if Cynthia remarried, and Cynthia agreed to including that.

Dispute Resolution

You've probably worked hard to get to the point where you're preparing a settlement agreement, and you don't want to end up in court fighting about it later. Disputes could arise about just about anything, including one parent wanting a change in the visitation schedule or support. Include a simple agreement that if you have a problem with the terms later, you'll mediate. Try to agree on a mediator in advance, or to a person who'll break a tie between you if you can't agree.

By the time they were finishing up their agreement, Cynthia and Howard were very satisfied with their out-of-court process, and they wanted to be sure they made every effort to continue to avoid court. To that end, they included a provision in their agreement promising to use mediation before going to court, if they ever had a dispute about any of the terms of their settlement agreement or parenting plan. They agreed to ask their current counselor to continue to serve as the mediator, and agreed to attend at least four sessions of mediation before either of them could file a court action.

"Boilerplate" Provisions

There are a few important provisions that should be in every legal agreement to help avoid confusion later. (Lawyers call this standard language "boilerplate.") For example, it's important to agree that you've both made full disclosure of all the required information about your finances. You should confirm that the written agreement you've made is the only one you have, that there aren't any side agreements that contradict what you've written, and that you intend the agreement to be incorporated into your final divorce order (this last provision is critically important).

You should also say what state law you'll use if you end up in court over your agreement. If one person moves away later and you don't have this provision, you could end up fighting about where you're going to fight.

Making sure you have all the required standard language is one of the reasons that it's a good idea to have a lawyer review your agreement.

Doing the Math

After you've negotiated the terms of your agreement and drafted your MSA, sit down with a pencil, paper, and calculator and do a ledger that shows the value of what each person is keeping. Make sure the division is what you want, whether it's an equal or an unequal division. Double-check the agreement to make sure it says what you want it to say and that the math works out.

After their long series of discussions and decisions, it became clear who was going to get what. Cynthia proposed to buy out Howard's $75,000 share in the house by giving up her share of Howard's pension and paying all of the joint debt. Between that and what Howard owed her for the baseball tickets, the end result of Cynthia's proposal was that she came out with $9,000 more in assets than Howard had. She proposed paying him the difference by taking less from the brokerage account and giving him more, and Howard agreed to the proposal.

Cynthia and Howard drew up a ledger sheet and listed all of their marital assets and debts, and how each item was to be divided. This is what it looked like when they were finished.

Assets	Value	Cynthia	Howard
House (equity)	$150,000	$150,000	
Prius	$18,000	$18,000	
Lexus	$23,000		$23,000
Brokerage acct.	$49,600	$19,600	$30,000
Howard's pension	$190,000		$190,000
Cynthia's 401(k)	$70,000	$70,000	
Baseball tickets	$1,600		$1,600
Household furnishings	$30,000	$20,000	$10,000
Debts			
Loan on Prius	($10,000)	($10,000)	
Credit card debt	($13,000)	($13,000)	
Total	$509,200	$254,600	$254,600

Consulting a Lawyer

When you've done everything you can do to prepare a draft MSA, it's time to take it to a lawyer for review. You don't absolutely have to do this—if you do your paperwork correctly, a judge will approve your divorce without checking to see whether a lawyer's been involved. But it's highly recommended, because your MSA controls everything involved in your divorce and can have an enormous impact on your future. It's time and money well spent.

Chapter 16 has advice on finding a lawyer to review your agreement. (It's a different process than finding a lawyer to represent you in a trial.)

After two months and six visits to the mediator, Cynthia and Howard had a draft marital settlement agreement. It hadn't been an easy process, but they both felt the agreement was fair and workable, and they were glad to have done it themselves. Still, their counselor urged them to have lawyers review the agreement to make sure that it would stand up later and was in compliance with all of their state's laws.

Cynthia was a little afraid the lawyer would try to talk her out of giving up her share of Howard's pension or would want to rewrite the agreement in legalese. Howard was more enthusiastic about the idea, so he got some recommendations from coworkers who had been through divorces and he began calling attorneys. The first lawyer said that she wasn't willing to review the document without doing a full interview and going over all of the financial information related to the marriage, for which she would charge a minimum of $2,500.

After a few more calls, Howard found an attorney who would review the agreement merely for clarity and legality, for an hourly fee of $225. She estimated it would take two to three hours to complete her review and give Howard her opinion. Howard emailed the lawyer the draft settlement agreement, and about a week later had a telephone conference with her. She suggested a few wording changes, but her biggest concern was that Cynthia be advised of her rights with regard to her share of Howard's pension. In her role as Howard's advocate, the attorney cautioned him that if Cynthia gave up her rights without getting advice from a lawyer, the agreement might not hold up if Cynthia later said that she hadn't understood her rights or that she was coerced into signing the agreement. Howard didn't think it likely that Cynthia would challenge the agreement they'd spent so much time working out, but he told her what his attorney had said and urged her to find someone to talk to as well. Cynthia, encouraged by the fact that Howard's lawyer hadn't dismantled all their hard work, got some referrals. Her first phone call put her in touch with a lawyer she liked and felt comfortable with right away.

Cynthia sent the draft, with the changes suggested by Howard's attorney, to her own lawyer and then went in for a face-to-face meeting. The lawyer questioned Cynthia carefully about her decisions. She reviewed the actuary's report on the present value of Howard's pension, and she quizzed Cynthia about her own retirement benefits and her future plans. She made sure that Cynthia understood her right to keep half of the marital portion of Howard's pension, and made sure that she understood to her own satisfaction why Cynthia was choosing to give up this important right. Ultimately, she was persuaded that the value of the house to Cynthia was worth it.

Like Howard's lawyer, Cynthia's attorney wanted to tweak the language of the agreement a little bit. She also suggested that Cynthia add a provision saying that the court would keep jurisdiction over spousal support—meaning that the court could modify the support provisions later if either party's circumstances changed. Howard agreed to this.

Howard paid his attorney about $600 for her two and a half hours of work, and Cynthia paid her attorney $750 for three hours. Added to the $500 they paid for the actuarial review of their pension rights, the $400 in filing fees they paid to the court, and $720 in fees to the counselor for six hour-and-a-half mediation sessions at $80 per hour, the total cost of their uncontested divorce was $2,970.

Marital Settlement Agreement

This marital settlement agreement is made by Cynthia Bean and Howard Bean. It will become effective when both of us have signed it and the court has issued the final order of divorce incorporating this agreement. This document is intended to set out our agreements about the division of our marital assets and obligations and the coparenting of our children, in connection with our pending divorce action and in light of the following facts.

We were married on August 1, 2003, and separated on March 22, 2014. We have two children: Sarah Bean, born March 23, 2005, and Maya Bean, born September 14, 2007.

Irreconcilable differences have arisen between us so that we agree that our marriage is irretrievably broken. It is our intention to live apart permanently and to end our legal marriage.

Cynthia filed for divorce in the Kelsey County Superior Court on May 30, 2014. Howard filed his response on June 14, 2014.

In exchange for the mutual promises made in this agreement, we agree to live separately, divide our assets and obligations, and parent our children according to the following terms:

1. **Housing.** Cynthia will continue to live in and will own our family home at 1970 Canyon Drive ("the house"). We agree that Howard's interest in the equity in the house has a value of $75,000. Howard will take other assets of equivalent value in exchange for his share of the equity, as described in this agreement.

    Howard has rented an apartment at 2111 Bronson Avenue. Howard agrees that until Maya enters high school, he will try to live within five miles of Cynthia and the girls.

    Within 60 days after this agreement becomes effective, Cynthia will complete a refinancing of the loan on the house. She will obtain a loan in an amount adequate to pay off the loan on the Prius automobile as described in Paragraph 5, and to pay the $13,000 in credit card obligations that we owe jointly. Howard will sign a quitclaim deed transferring his interest in the house to Cynthia immediately upon Cynthia providing Howard with documentation of the refinancing being complete and the loan being in her name alone.

    We also agree that if the house appreciates significantly in the future and Cynthia sells it, Howard will receive a portion of the profit. Specifically, if the house

Marital Settlement Agreement, page 2

sells for more than $350,000, Cynthia will pay Howard $5,000 promptly after closing. If the sales price is more than $400,000, Cynthia will pay Howard $15,000 promptly after closing. Cynthia will be solely responsible for any capital gains tax related to the future sale of the house.

2. **Support.** Howard will pay Cynthia $500 per month per child as child support, for a total of $1,000 per month, and $300 per month as spousal support. Payments of half the total monthly support amount will be made by check on the first and the fifteenth day of every month. Cynthia understands that she must report the spousal support to the IRS as taxable income. If Howard is more than one month late with any child or spousal support payment, Cynthia may establish an earnings withholding order through his employer, or arrange to have support paid directly through the appropriate state agency.

   Spousal support will end on the earliest of the following dates: December 31, 2019; the date that Cynthia remarries; or the date that either Cynthia or Howard dies. Until then, the court retains jurisdiction over spousal support.

   Child support will end for each child when that child turns 18. We have made other agreements about supporting our children through college, which are described in the parenting agreement attached as Exhibit 1 to this agreement.

3. **Parenting.** We will share joint legal custody of our children, Sarah and Maya. Cynthia will have physical custody, and Howard will have liberal visitation. The details of the time-sharing schedule, and all the other details of our agreements regarding our children, are described in the parenting plan attached as Exhibit 1 to this agreement.

4. **Personal Belongings.** We have divided our personal belongings and all of the furniture and furnishings in our home. Each of us will keep the personal items currently in our possession, except that the tools in the workshop at 1970 Canyon Drive belong to Howard. We agree that the value of the personal belongings and household furnishings that Cynthia is keeping is $20,000 and the value of the items that Howard is keeping is $10,000, and our overall property division is intended to equalize this disparity.

5. **Automobiles.** Cynthia will keep the 2011 Toyota Prius, and Howard will keep the 2008 Lexus LS. Cynthia will pay the balance due on the Prius loan within 30 days after refinancing of the house is completed and will provide Howard with

Marital Settlement Agreement, page 3

proof that the loan has been paid. Each of us will sign the required paperwork to relinquish our interest in the other's car, as soon as the paperwork is presented by the other person.

6. **Bank and Other Accounts.** We have already closed our joint bank accounts. We have left one joint brokerage account at Charles Schwab that has a balance of approximately $59,600. We agree that $10,000 of that amount is Howard's separate property. To equalize the division of assets, we agree to distribute the remaining $49,600 as follows: $30,000 to Howard, and $19,600 to Cynthia. Each of us will keep the IRA that's in our own name, which we agree have equal values. We agree that each of us will make our daughters the beneficiaries of our IRAs.

   In addition, Cynthia owns a brokerage account at TD Ameritrade that consists of her separate property inheritance from her grandfather; Howard agrees that account is Cynthia's separate property and confirms it to her. Howard agrees to do the paperwork to divide the Schwab account within 14 days of the date of the final divorce order, and Cynthia agrees to sign any documents needed to accomplish the division within 48 hours of presentation to her.

7. **Miscellaneous Assets.** Howard will keep the season tickets for the Norfolk Tides baseball team, which we agree are worth $1,600. We agree that Cynthia is entitled to half of Howard's frequent flyer miles, which will be divided on the date we sign this agreement. Howard agrees to write to the airline immediately after we sign this agreement, instructing it to establish a new frequent flyer account in Cynthia's name and to transfer half of his miles into that account.

8. **Debts.** Cynthia agrees to pay off all of our outstanding debts, as part of the equalizing of the division of assets. Our debts include the balance on the Prius loan, the Chase VISA card, and the MBNA MasterCard. Cynthia will provide Howard with documentation that she has paid off these debts and closed all of these accounts within 60 days of signing this agreement. If she does not provide that documentation, Howard has the right to pay off the debts and seek reimbursement from Cynthia. We have closed all the rest of our joint credit accounts.

   We agree that any debts either of us took on after our date of separation are the separate property of the person who took on the debt. We each agree to indemnify the other from any responsibility for those debts.

Marital Settlement Agreement, page 4

9.   **Retirement Benefits.** Each of us agrees to give up our rights to the other person's retirement benefits. Cynthia gives up any and all interest in all of Howard's pension through his employment at AT Consulting Engineers. Erica Moore, an actuary, evaluated and valued the marital share of Howard's pension at $190,000. Cynthia understands that she is giving up an interest worth $95,000.

Howard gives up any and all interest in all of Cynthia's retirement benefits through her employment at Community Healthcare. These retirement benefits were evaluated by Erica Moore, who valued the marital share at $70,000. Howard understands he is giving up an interest worth $35,000.

We each agree to sign any documents necessary to accomplish the waiver of rights in the other person's retirement plans, as soon as the documents are presented to us by the other person.

We each understand that giving up our rights in each other's retirement benefits means that we will never be able to claim any share of the retirement benefits that were earned by the other person during our marriage. We understand that if we did not waive these rights, we would each have the right to receive half of the marital share of the other person's retirement benefits upon the other person's retirement. We understand that that amount might be greater than the present value of the retirement benefits, and we still agree to waive our rights.

10. **Tax Issues.** We agree that we will hire Sharon Kornbluth, CPA, to prepare our taxes for tax year 2014. She can advise us whether it is more advantageous for us to file jointly or separately. We will take her advice about filing and about which of us should take the dependent exemptions for the children. If either of us has a tax liability for 2014, we will share the tax liability in approximate proportion to our income: Howard agrees to pay 66% of the tax liability, and Cynthia agrees to pay 34%. If there is a tax refund due to us, it will be divided in the same proportion.

For tax years after 2014, we will continue to have Sharon Kornbluth (or another tax preparer we agree upon) prepare our separate tax returns and advise us on the best way to deal with the dependent exemptions for the girls. If one person gets more tax advantage than the other, we'll equalize the difference through a one-time payment or in another way that we agree on.

11. **Life and Disability Insurance.** Howard agrees to maintain Cynthia, Sarah, and Maya as the beneficiaries of his life insurance policy through his employment.

Marital Settlement Agreement, page 5

He will resubmit beneficiary paperwork to the insurance company within 30 days of the divorce becoming final. If Howard leaves AT Consulting and doesn't move directly into a position with equivalent life insurance coverage, he agrees to purchase a life insurance policy with equivalent coverage and to keep it in force until he gets a new job that provides life insurance benefits. In addition, Howard agrees that within 60 days of the divorce becoming final he will purchase private disability insurance that pays a benefit equal to at least 60% of his current salary in the event of his disability. The purpose of this insurance is to ensure that if Howard becomes disabled he will still be able pay child and spousal support. Howard agrees to provide Cynthia with annual confirmation that the policies described in this paragraph are in full force, and to provide confirmation more frequently upon Cynthia's request.

12. **Health Insurance.** Howard agrees that within 14 days of the divorce becoming final, he will notify the human resources department at his work and request COBRA election paperwork for Cynthia. He will give Cynthia documentation that he has notified his employer. Howard agrees to maintain Sarah and Maya on his health insurance for as long as they are eligible, or until he and Cynthia agree otherwise. Howard will pay for Sarah and Maya's insurance coverage. Cynthia will be responsible for paying her own COBRA premiums. We will share all uninsured medical, dental, and vision expenses for the girls in approximate proportion to our current incomes: Howard will pay 66% and Cynthia will pay 34%. If the income ratio changes by more than 10%, the payment ratio will also change. Any changes less than 10% will not affect the income ratio.

13. **Legal Names.** Cynthia has asked the court to restore her previous name, Cynthia Robertson, upon entry of the final order of divorce. Sarah and Maya will keep the last name "Bean," even if Cynthia later changes her last name again, unless Howard agrees otherwise.

14. **Dispute Resolution.** If we have any disputes about the matters covered in this agreement, we will return to see Jeff Gold, MFT, who helped us negotiate this agreement. We agree to attend at least four sessions with Jeff before either of us files any kind of court action. We will share the cost of the sessions equally. Also, we agree that either of us can request a session with Jeff to discuss any of the matters covered in the agreement, even if we aren't having an active dispute, and that upon such request the other will attend at least one session with Jeff.

Marital Settlement Agreement, page 6

15. **Other Agreements.** There are no other agreements between us, written or unwritten, about any matter related to our divorce.

16. **Governing Law.** This agreement will be governed by the laws of the Commonwealth of Virginia.

17. **Disclosures and Obligations.** Each of us has submitted financial disclosures to the other, and we each declare that we have made a full and complete disclosure of all of our assets and obligations, whether joint or separate. Each of us agrees that the other has provided us with full and fair disclosure that has allowed us to make informed decisions about the matters covered in this agreement.

18. **Incorporation Into Judgment.** It's our intention that this agreement will be attached to and made a part of our final order and judgment of divorce and will be enforceable by a court.

    Each of us agrees that other than the obligations disclosed previously and disposed of in this agreement, we have not to date entered, and will not in the future enter, into any financial obligation that would bind the other person.

19. **Attorney Review.** Each of us has consulted a lawyer of our own choosing. We prepared this agreement together, and it has been reviewed by our lawyers.

20. **Waiver of Inheritance Rights.** Each of us gives up the right to inherit from the other unless we inherit under a will or other instrument signed after the date that our divorce was final.

21. **Modification.** This agreement can be modified only by another written agreement between us that supersedes this one.

22. **Clauses Severable.** If any paragraph or term of this agreement is deemed invalid by a court of law, all the rest of the agreement will remain valid and in full force.

23. **Judgment of Divorce; Effective Date.** We agree to submit this agreement to the court along with our request for a judgment of divorce, and to have the terms of this agreement merged into the court's final divorce order.

Howard Bean
_____
Signature

Cynthia Bean
_____
Signature

August 1, 2014
_____
Date

August 1, 2014
_____
Date

Exhibit 1
Parenting Agreement

Howard Bean and Cynthia Bean agree to the following parenting plan regarding our children, Sarah, born March 23, 2005, and Maya, born September 14, 2007.

1. **Custody.** We agree to share joint legal custody and to jointly make decisions on all significant matters relating to our children's welfare. Cynthia will have physical custody, and Howard will have visitation rights as described below.

2. **Visitation.** The girls will live primarily with Cynthia in the family home at 1970 Canyon Drive. They will visit Howard on the following schedule to start with:

    Tuesday and Thursday evenings from 5 to 8 p.m.

    Saturdays from 9 a.m. to 4 p.m.

    Howard will pick the girls up at the house and bring them back to the house. We agree that we would both like Howard to spend more time with the girls. After three months, we will meet to assess how the visitation is going, and if we agree it is going well, we will add one overnight visit with Howard per week. When he is with the girls, Howard agrees to care for them himself, and not to place them in anyone else's care. If he's unable to care for them, he will ask Cynthia to keep them. If she can't, Howard may find another caregiver who Cynthia has agreed is an appropriate caregiver for the girls. If Cynthia needs child care, she'll try to ask Howard first, and Howard's parents next, but she's not restricted from asking someone else.

    Howard is free to call or email the girls any time and agrees to try to call them each night before bedtime when they are not with him.

    Cynthia agrees that Howard's parents can have time with the girls in addition to Howard's time with them; the grandparents can make arrangements directly with Cynthia as they have done in the past. Cynthia will be as cooperative as possible with these visits within the restrictions of the girls' schedules.

3. **Holidays and Vacations.** We will share holidays and vacations according to the following schedule through the end of the 2014-2015 school year. We will reassess and make a new agreement about the summer holiday and the rest of 2015. If we can't agree by April 15, 2015, on how the girls will spend the summer, we will arrange for counseling sessions with Jeff Gold.

Exhibit 1–Parenting Agreement, page 2

2014 Holiday/Vacation Schedule:

Thanksgiving Weekend: The girls will go with Cynthia to her parents' house for Thanksgiving dinner. Howard is welcome to come for dinner if he wishes, and to take the girls to his house on Thursday evening for an overnight visit whether or not he comes for dinner. The girls will stay with him through Saturday at noon, when they will be returned to Cynthia for the rest of the weekend.

Christmas Holiday: The girls will spend Christmas Eve from 4 p.m. with Howard and will stay overnight. Howard will return them to Cynthia's house at 11 a.m. on Christmas day. Cynthia will have them for the rest of Christmas day and night, and on the 26th. We'll share the rest of the winter school break equally or as close to equally as everyone's schedules allow.

New Year's: The girls will be with Cynthia on New Years' Eve, and Howard will pick them up on January 1 at 10 a.m. and bring them home by 8 p.m.

Spring Vacation: The girls will spend the first half of the spring school vacation (Friday afternoon to Wednesday morning) with Howard, and the second half (Wednesday afternoon to Sunday evening) with Cynthia.

Passover: Howard may take the girls to his parents' house for the Passover seder.

4. **Birthdays.** We agree to try to spend time together with the girls on each of their birthdays. Cynthia will arrange birthday parties, and Howard will attend. We'll try to make sure that each of us has time with the girls on our own birthdays.

5. **Schooling.** Cynthia agrees to keep Howard apprised of school events and activities with enough notice that he can attend if he's in town. We agree that Sarah needs tutoring in reading and math. Beginning with the 2014-2015 school year, we will enroll her in twice-weekly tutoring through the Score program. Howard will pay for the tutoring. If, after three months, Sarah's academic performance hasn't improved (in the opinion of both of us and her teachers), we will apply for her admission to Julia Morgan Middle School for the 2015–2016 school year. If we do enroll her at Julia Morgan, Howard will pay 66% and Cynthia will pay 34% of her tuition. (If our income ratio changes by more than 10%, the payment ratio will also change. Any changes less than 10% will not affect the income ratio.) We will split all other school expenses, such as uniforms and supplies, equally. If Sarah's application for Julia Morgan isn't approved, we will explore other options for academic support for her.

Exhibit 1–Parenting Agreement, page 3

6. **Support.** Howard will pay child support as described in our marital settlement agreement. In addition, we agree that each of us will deposit no less than $100 per month (Cynthia) and $200 per month (Howard) into the education savings account that we've established at the Bank of America. When special expenses come up, like music camp or major school trips, we'll discuss how they will be paid for. Our starting assumption is that we'll pay for special expenses in unequal shares, with Howard paying 66% and Cynthia 34%. If the kids need child care during summer vacation, we'll pay for that in the same unequal shares.

7. **Screen Time.** We agree that the girls shouldn't watch or use more than one hour of television or other devices every day, excluding movies that we watch with them. On school nights, the girls must finish their homework before watching television or using an electronic device.

8. **Medical Care.** We each agree to notify the other about any medical or dental care that either girl receives, even if it is routine.

9. **Dating.** We both agree that we won't introduce anyone we are dating to the girls until we have been seeing the person for at least three months. We also agree to tell each other before introducing a new partner to the girls. We agree that we won't have any new partner spend the night when the girls are at our home until we have been seeing the person for at least six months, and until we feel sure the girls are comfortable with the new partner.

10. **Dispute Resolution.** It's our intention to be as cooperative as possible in raising our children and to act in their best interests at all times. We agree to try not to argue in front of the girls and not to discuss difficult parenting issues when they are around. If either of us wants to schedule a session with Jeff Gold to discuss a child-rearing concern, the other will attend at least one session, and we will share the cost equally, regardless of who asked for the session.

11. **Revisions and Updates.** We agree to meet every three months for the first year to talk about how the visitation schedule is going and to make any necessary revisions to the visitation schedule. If either of us thinks it's necessary, we'll ask Jeff Gold to help us with those discussions. We understand that the court will include this parenting agreement as part of the final divorce order in our dissolution action, and we understand that the court will retain the power to make decisions about custody and visitation if we can't agree. If we do make changes in this

Exhibit 1–Parenting Agreement, page 4

parenting agreement, as we anticipate, the changes will be in writing and signed by both of us. As long as we make the changes in writing, the revised parenting agreement will have the same force and effect as the original agreement, and will be enforceable by a court.

Howard Bean
Signature

August 1, 2014

Cynthia Bean
Signature

August 1, 2014

Completing the Paperwork

After your MSA is completed, you're almost done—but you still have to file the final paperwork to complete your divorce. Chapter 3 describes the process of an uncontested divorce, including getting a final judgment.

After finalizing the agreement, the only thing left for Cynthia and Howard to do was the paperwork to finalize their divorce. Cynthia already had the forms that they needed; they completed the forms together and submitted them to the judge along with the final settlement agreement. The forms included a declaration signed by both of them stating that they wanted an uncontested divorce and had come to agreement about division of their property and coparenting their children, and a final order for the judge to sign.

Cynthia and Howard weren't required to go to court to finalize their divorce. It took about four weeks, but eventually they received back the signed order and file-stamped copies of their other forms. Their settlement agreement had been approved by the judge and now had the force of a court order, so that if either of them didn't comply with its terms, the other could ask a judge to intervene. Cynthia's former name was legally restored as part of the judgment.

Critical Care:
When Things Really Go Wrong

sn't every divorce a crisis of sorts, requiring a trip to the emotional emergency room? It surely feels that way when you are dealing with one hazard after another during the process. But this chapter deals with the bigger crises—being in an abusive or threatening situation, having a spouse you can't trust with your kids, or running out of money—and what you can do about them.

In any of these situations, get yourself a good lawyer; you'll need all the help you can get. If you can't afford a lawyer, your local court may provide support for do-it-yourself restraining orders and other emergency orders, and you probably will get some help from shelter workers if you've been battered by your spouse. Low-cost legal services can be difficult to find, but your local bar association should be able to direct you to services in your area.

Chapter 16 offers resources for finding counseling services and suggestions on how to take care of yourself; Chapter 6 deals with children's experience of divorce and how you can help them. Whatever you do, be kind to yourself and know that things will get easier.

Emergency Divorce: When You Can't Afford to Wait

A few states allow abbreviated waiting periods in case of emergency. (Kansas actually has a procedure for an "emergency divorce.") If you can persuade a judge that there is an emergency, such as domestic abuse or a pressing need to leave the state immediately, you may be able to avoid the usual waiting period before your divorce is final.

Domestic Violence

If you are in a violent relationship, your first priority is very simple: Get yourself and your kids to safety. Statistics show that the most dangerous time for women living with batterers is the point at which they leave the relationship. (The vast majority of battered spouses are women, but if you are a battered husband, all of this advice applies to you as well.) This means that you will need to find housing somewhere that your spouse can't find you—a battered women's shelter, a hotel, or the home of a friend your spouse doesn't know. Don't go to your parents' or somewhere else that he's likely to look for you.

If you have time to plan, start putting aside cash—again, preferably somewhere other than your house. Leave some clothes and important items with a friend in case you have to leave your house quickly. And start documenting every incident of physical or emotional abuse in your household, whether it involves you or your kids. Make a note of the date and time the incident occurred, and exactly what happened.

Advice From the Experts

The National Coalition Against Domestic Violence advises that you:

- make a list of safe people to contact
- memorize phone numbers of people or places you could call for help
- keep change (for a pay phone, as you may find yourself without a cell phone) with you at all times, as well as cash for living expenses, and
- establish a code word with family, friends, and coworkers so that you can tell them to call for help without alerting your spouse.

If you have to leave your home quickly with your kids to get away from an abusive spouse, go to court immediately for an emergency order giving you custody as well as a restraining order that requires your spouse to stay away from you. Otherwise, you may be accused of kidnapping.

If you have the resources, hire a lawyer to help you. If you go to a shelter, the staff should be able to help you find legal assistance quickly to file the necessary papers. Many courts have domestic violence resources, including restraining order packets with instructions, clinics with clerks who can help you with the paperwork, or judges who are available to sign restraining orders and custody orders on very short notice—in some places, you have access to the court 24 hours a day. In general, you also will be able to quickly find help with delivering legal documents to your spouse—the local sheriff's office is usually charged with this task. You have to get the papers delivered (served) before they take effect.

Restraining Orders and Pets

A growing number of states now protect family pets in domestic violence situation. Domestic violence pet protection laws generally provide that pets may be included in restraining orders so that the abuser is prohibited from having any contact with pets belonging to the other spouse or a minor child. At least 22 states currently have laws that include provisions for pets in domestic violence restraining orders.

You have the right to keep your address and telephone number confidential if you fear violence from your spouse. So, even if you share custody with your spouse, you can make arrangements for neutral pickup sites or for others to pick up and drop off your kids, and you can have your contact information kept out of the court file. Even if your spouse has been violent with you, if the violence hasn't been directed at your kids, the judge is still likely to order some type of visitation. But you can ask that conditions be put on the visitation, such as supervision or a requirement that your spouse can't drink or use drugs when with the kids, or that certain friends, relatives, or associates of your spouse can't be around the kids.

If restraining orders are in effect, or if you don't think it's safe to be in the same place as your spouse, you can choose a public place to meet for visitation exchanges. Your local police station is a good choice, or you can use a restaurant or another very public setting. In extreme cases, you can ask the court to appoint a visitation supervision monitor and arrange for the dropoff and pickup to be staggered in time, with the monitor watching the kids in between. If you have other creative ideas, propose them to the judge. Most judges will consider any plan that will keep everyone safe and facilitate visitation at the same time.

> **RESOURCE**
>
> **You are not alone.** Look online or check your phone book under "domestic violence" for local agencies, or contact one of these national resources for advice and help locating services in your area:
>
> - The National Domestic Violence Hotline, 800-799-SAFE (7233), provides advice and assistance.
> - The National Coalition Against Domestic Violence, www.ncadv.org, 303-839-1852, has a list of state coalitions that can help you find local services.
>
> Most divorce websites have information about dealing with domestic violence.

If your spouse stalks you after you have separated, get a restraining order. Stalking is a crime just like domestic violence, and you can get the police and the courts involved. Much of the same advice applies to stalking as to domestic violence: Make sure you have the support of people around you and have a safety plan. Check out the website of the National Center for Victims of Crime: Stalking Center at www.ncvc .org/SRC.

Child Abuse

If you discover that your spouse is abusing your children either physically or sexually, take them to a doctor right away, both for treatment and to document what's been going on. You also need to find a good lawyer and an experienced child therapist.

Make sure you stay within the law yourself. Don't just take your children and hide them. If you need to get your kids out of an unsafe situation immediately, then just as immediately you need to get yourself to the courthouse and get an emergency order for custody. You may, however, face some resistance to your efforts to protect your children, in the form of dubious social workers or judges. This is especially true if there's been no previous evidence of abuse during your marriage— in other words, the allegations are coming up for the first time in connection with the divorce. There appears to be a commonly held belief that allegations of child abuse made in the context of divorce are suspect, made to gain an advantage in the legal proceedings. And sometimes, parents are accused unjustly. If you make such a serious claim, you need evidence to back it up.

By no means should this lead you to the conclusion that you shouldn't take every possible step to protect your children. Indeed, for many people the discovery or the escalation of abuse is what leads them to make the decision to divorce. Protect your children, get evidence, and take action.

> CAUTION
> **Never coach your children about what to say to a doctor, therapist, social worker, or court mediator.** Simply reassure them that they are safe and will be taken care of, and let them know that they just need to tell the truth and let the adults figure out what to do.

Kidnapping

One parent absconds with the children far more often than most of us would like to believe. According to the Department of Justice, in 2010 more than 200,000 children were kidnapped by a family member. If your spouse has threatened to take the kids or has significant ties to another country, be wary. (The vast majority of abducted children are recovered, by the way.)

If your children are abducted by your spouse, contact local law enforcement immediately, along with the National Center for Missing and Exploited Children, (www.ncmec.org), 800-843-5678. If you think it's imminent that your spouse may try to leave the country with the kids, contact the federal Office of Children's Issues at 888-407-4747, and inform local law enforcement officials. You should also contact your lawyer right away, so that the lawyer's kept informed and can provide information about your custody rights if need be.

Preventing Abduction

There are some practical steps you can take to prevent abduction and be prepared in case your child's other parent does try to take the child:

- Keep a list of the contact information for your spouse's relatives, friends, and business associates both here and abroad.
- Keep a record of important information about your spouse, including physical description (get a current photograph), passport number (get a copy of the passport if you can), Social Security number, bank information, driver's license number, vehicle description, and plate number.
- Prepare a written description of your kids, including hair and eye color, height, weight, and any special physical characteristics. Update it regularly as they grow and change.
- Take full-face color photographs or videos of your children every six months.
- Have your kids fingerprinted at the local police department.
- Make sure your children know how to use the telephone, including how to make collect calls, and that they know your phone number. Tell them to call you immediately if anything unusual happens.
- In especially worrisome circumstances, you can hire a private investigator to supervise your spouse's visitation secretly. This is an extreme step, and could backfire on you if the investigator interferes with visitation when there's no actual threat to your kids. However, if you believe the risk is high, there are investigators who specialize in this type of surveillance. Make sure you find someone who has experience in dealing with potential (and actual) parental abductions.

Special Concerns About International Abductions

If your children are dual citizens of the United States and another country, be even more watchful. Even if you have their U.S. passports, your spouse may be able to get them passports from their other country of citizenship. You can't force another country not to issue a passport for your child—but you can ask. Send the embassy or consulate a written request, along with certified copies of any court orders you have that address custody and that prohibit your spouse from taking your children out of the country. (Also state in your letter that you are sending a copy of the request to the U.S. Department of State, and then follow up.)

If your child is only a United States citizen, you can request that no visa for the other country be issued. Again, there's no law that requires other countries to comply with such requests, but some countries may comply voluntarily.

To have a U.S. passport issued for a child under 16, the child and both parents must appear in person to apply for the passport. If one parent can't be present in person, the parent who is there must bring a notarized form called DS-3053, "Statement of Consent," from the parent who isn't there. This law applies whether the application is made in the United States or at a U.S. consular office abroad.

If you register with the Department of State's Children's Passport Issuance Alert Program, you'll be notified if the other parent applies for new passports for your kids—or for renewal of an existing passport—any time until they turn 18. You can register with CPIAP by submitting an application and proof of your identity and your parent-child relationship to the Office of Children's Issues (part of Passport Services). Go to www.travel.state.gov and click the link for "Parents' Corner," which in turn will lead you to a link for CPIAP and the details on how to participate in this program.

Once a passport is issued, though, the Department of State doesn't provide any tracking of its use, and there are no exit controls for American citizens leaving the United States. Other countries may have controls at entry points—for example, Mexico requires that a parent traveling alone with a child produce the child's birth certificate and written proof that the other parent has given permission for the travel. But not all countries do this.

Bankruptcy

If your former spouse files for bankruptcy, rest assured that it has no effect on your right to child or spousal support. Debts for past due child or spousal support are not wiped out by bankruptcy. All the same, if your spouse does file for bankruptcy, you should contact a lawyer for some advice about how to proceed. In most cases, you're better off cooperating with the bankruptcy than you would be fighting it—the court will take your interests into account.

There are two types of bankruptcy for individuals:

- **Chapter 7 bankruptcy:** Also called "liquidation" bankruptcy. In a Chapter 7 case, the debtor (the person who filed for bankruptcy) gets to keep a small amount of property; everything else is sold and used to pay creditors. Debts that aren't paid in full are wiped out (discharged). You can't use Chapter 7 bankruptcy to discharge student loans, money owed to the government (like back taxes), or child or spousal support, as discussed below.

- **Chapter 13 bankruptcy:** Also called "repayment" bankruptcy. The debtor comes up with a plan for paying back some or most of the debt over three to five years. Repayment plans can provide for anywhere from zero to 100% payment of debts, depending on how much income the debtor has left over after paying basic expenses. If the debtor completes the plan (many don't), the remaining debt is wiped out (discharged). Often, people use Chapter 13 bankruptcy because their income or assets are too high to qualify for Chapter 7. An advantage to Chapter 13 is that if you are behind in your house payments, you may be able to repay the deficiency over a number of years instead of all at once. The disadvantage is that if you lose your job or for some other reason become unable to make the plan payments, you become responsible for your debts again (as well as the interest that accrued while you were in the bankruptcy process).

When a debtor files for bankruptcy, something called an "automatic stay" comes into play—it means that all creditors are prohibited from coming after the debtor for money owed to them. And when the bankruptcy is completed the debtor's obligations are discharged, meaning they no longer exist. The bankruptcy law says that "domestic support obligations" are not dischargeable in bankruptcy, so they survive the bankruptcy proceeding and continue to exist after it's over.

It's very clear that spousal and child support are domestic support obligations, but property settlements are not always included in the exception and can be discharged in bankruptcy in many cases. The law isn't entirely clear, because the language of the bankruptcy law was changed fairly recently and what is considered a domestic support obligation is somewhat in flux—some states consider a divorced spouse's promise to pay off debts to be a support obligation and thus nondischargeable, and some include attorneys' fees payments as well. Other states reach the opposite conclusion. Also, your state's laws may affect how those debts are treated. If you see that bankruptcy is on the horizon, though, you'd be well advised to accept more alimony and a smaller property settlement, so that your future payments aren't in jeopardy. If your ex-spouse files for bankruptcy, see an attorney to make sure your rights are protected.

Child and Spousal Support

If your spouse files for Chapter 7 bankruptcy—the most common kind—you can continue trying to get past due child or spousal support by garnishing your ex-spouse's wages. And you will be first in line (of all your spouse's creditors) for any property that your former spouse is not, by law, allowed to keep after filing for bankruptcy. So, if your former spouse owns any such property, the bankruptcy trustee (the person appointed by the court to handle your spouse's property during the bankruptcy) will pay your claim before any others. The bankruptcy trustee has a legal obligation to notify you if your spouse files for bankruptcy.

If your spouse files for Chapter 13 bankruptcy, things are handled differently. (In this kind of bankruptcy, your spouse will submit a three- to five-year repayment plan to the court.) You cannot garnish your former spouse's wages. The repayment plan must list back child and spousal support as top priority debts, after administrative costs, which means you will be paid first before any other type of debt. And the plan must provide for 100% payment of the back support. The bankruptcy trustee must keep you advised of the status of the case and the current address of your ex-spouse when the case winds up. The Chapter 13 case will be thrown out of court if your spouse gets behind on support obligations.

Property You're Entitled To

Usually, spouses divide all their property when the divorce becomes final. But if your former spouse files for Chapter 7 bankruptcy and still owes you money under your marital settlement agreement, the debt won't be wiped out by the bankruptcy.

If your spouse files for Chapter 13 bankruptcy, debts owed to you from a property settlement can be wiped out. This means that whatever portion of the debt your former spouse doesn't pay you under the Chapter 13 repayment plan is cancelled. If, however, before the bankruptcy you put a lien (legal claim) on real estate your former spouse owns, you may be in luck. Such debts are "secured" debts and must be paid in full as part of a Chapter 13 plan.

If your spouse agreed to take over joint debts and those are included in a bankruptcy filing, the creditors are likely to come after you, at least in a Chapter 7 bankruptcy (in a Chapter 13, creditors can't come after codebtors—that's why you should pay off your debts wherever possible). You can try to talk them out of it by showing them the divorce order that says your spouse is responsible for the debts, but they're not bound by that in most cases. You're left with the choice of paying the debts or taking a hit on your credit rating. If you do pay the debts, you can sue your spouse for reimbursement—but if your spouse has filed for bankruptcy, you're unlikely to collect anything. ●

After the Divorce

What does it mean to get a final divorce order (also called a "judgment" or "decree")? For starters, it means you have a piece of paper that says you are no longer legally married. Next, it means there are a bunch of details to attend to right away to make sure that your new marital status is reflected in all of your important paperwork and that you've done everything that's required by your final order. Finally, it means you need to know what to do if something goes wrong with the arrangements for custody, support, and property that you carefully hammered out during the divorce process. This chapter deals with all of those issues and a few more, too.

You're Not Done Yet: Ten Postdivorce Tasks You Can't Ignore

Remember how you had to list and divide all of your assets and debts in the course of your divorce? Well, splitting those assets and debts involves paperwork, and this is the time to make absolutely sure that all of that paperwork is in order, all transfers have been accomplished, and all of your ownership documents have been changed to reflect that you are no longer married (and to reflect your new name if you've changed it). There are some other things you should take care of, too, including updating your will, insurance coverages, and beneficiary designations.

1. Read the Court Order and Fix Any Mistakes

When the dust settles and you have a copy of your divorce order and your settlement agreement, take some time and review the entire court order to make sure that it says what you expected and that you understand all of it. Then go through it again, along with this chapter, to make sure you've taken care of everything and can go confidently into your new single life.

What should you do if you find a mistake in the order? If the problem is merely a typographical error that doesn't change the meaning of any of the terms, it's probably best to just leave it alone, no matter how much of a stickler you are for accuracy. But if a provision was left out, something was included that you didn't agree to, or an agreement you did make is stated incorrectly, you need to take immediate action. If someone else prepared the order (like a lawyer or mediator), contact that person first. If your divorce was uncontested, contact your former spouse and see whether you're in agreement about the error. If so, you can ask the court together to remedy the mistake, by submitting an amended order along with a letter signed by both of you asking for the change. If you had a lawyer in the divorce, your lawyer can do this. If your ex-spouse doesn't agree that there's a mistake, consult an attorney about your next step. Amending a final order against the wishes of another party is a tricky business, and you'll need help.

Assuming your review of the final documents doesn't raise any red flags, it's time to take care of business.

2. Get Certified Copies of Your Divorce Order

When you finalize your divorce, you'll end up with a copy of the order that the judge signed saying that you are no longer married and ordering you and your spouse to comply with the terms of your marital settlement agreement. The order will be stamped with the date that it was filed in the court. Most likely, you'll get this date-stamped order in the mail.

You'll need a couple of "certified" copies of your divorce order—they'll probably be required when you ask an insurance plan administrator, a banker, or a real estate agent to do something that's required by the order. Certification is the official seal of approval from the clerk that shows the document is an accurate, official copy of what the judge signed. If you have a lawyer, the lawyer will take care of getting certified copies for you. If you're on your own, take your stamped copies to the court clerk and ask for certified copies. You'll know the difference because the certified copies will have a special seal on them with the court clerk's signature, which may even be embossed (raised). You'll have to pay a fee for the certification.

3. Make New Deeds for Real Estate

If one of you stayed in the family home and bought out the other, you may have already done the paperwork to transfer the house to the one who's keeping it—possibly as part of the refinancing process. But if you haven't transferred the property formally yet, now is the time to do it. (Remember, there are no tax consequences to a real estate transfer if it's related to a divorce, so it's important that you make the transfer soon after the divorce. See Chapter 10.)

If you had a divorce lawyer, the lawyer may have taken care of any required deeds, but double-check to be sure. You need to know where the deed is, anyway, so put your hands on it and make sure the property is in one spouse's name alone. If it's not, you can either ask your lawyer to prepare a deed or do it yourself. Either way, you first need to find out—from your lawyer or through one of the resources listed below—what type of deed you need. Most likely it will be a "quitclaim deed" or a "grant deed." You can get a deed form online, from an office supply store, or from a title company. (Wherever you get it, make sure it meets the requirements of your state—every state has its own rules on what deeds must contain and how they must be executed.) On the form, enter your property's legal description and the appropriate names, sign the form in front of a notary, and record (file) it at the land records office in the county where the property is located.

RESOURCE

Learn more about deeds. Most of the divorce websites listed in Chapter 16 have some basic information on deeds for transferring real estate after divorce. In addition, the following resources can help you with preparing real estate transfer documents

The websites www.udeed.com and www.usdeeds.com offer deed preparation and other assistance with property transfers for a (not insignificant) fee.

For the answers to basic questions, check out Nolo's website at www.nolo.com for FAQs on deeds.

If you live in California, you'll learn everything about deeds and find deed forms in *Deeds for California Real Estate*, by Mary Randolph (Nolo).

4. Transfer Your Personal Items and Cars

Make sure that all of the vehicles you owned together are transferred into the name of the right person. You can usually do this by getting forms from your state department of motor vehicles. Forms are often available online for downloading. The person giving up ownership will need to sign. Then either send or take them in to be processed at the DMV. If you have a car loan, you'll also have to make sure that the spouse who's giving up the car is no longer responsible for that loan. The best way to do that is for the person keeping the car to get a new loan.

If there's stuff in your basement that your spouse is supposed to take, send a gentle reminder that you'd like it gone. Even though it might seem like there's no harm in storing some of your spouse's things, it's a good idea to complete all the terms of the divorce order soon after it's entered. It avoids confusion about what belongs to whom, and it can help you get a sense of closure.

5. Update Insurance Coverage and Beneficiaries

Insurance policies are easy to neglect, but it's important that you review all of your insurance and get it in order. If one insurance agent helps you with all your coverage, schedule a meeting to go over everything. Try to gather as much information as you can, and avoid buying new products right away, except the life and disability insurance that you should have if you'll be paying support. Insurance agents are salespeople first, so maintain a "buyer beware" attitude.

Health insurance. Chapter 11 describes in detail how to use the federal law called COBRA if you're staying on your former spouse's health insurance plan. There are very strict time limits for signing up for continued coverage, so if you've been putting this off, find your paperwork and get it taken care of right away. Verify that the plan administrator has been notified of COBRA election by a nonemployee spouse. Check into your options under the Affordable Care Act as well.

Life or disability insurance. If you own life insurance, you may want to change the beneficiary from your former spouse to someone else. Even if you don't want to make this change, you still have to fill out new forms. That's because in many states, the original designation is automatically revoked by the divorce. So if you want your ex-spouse to get the benefits because he or she would be raising the kids alone in the event of your death, you'll need to fill out a new beneficiary designation form after the divorce is final to make it clear that you still want your ex to be the beneficiary.

If your spouse agreed, as part of your divorce negotiation, to buy or keep life or disability insurance with you or your kids as the beneficiaries, follow up. Your marital settlement agreement should say that you are entitled to get information about the policy. Your postdivorce task, then, is to follow up with a letter to the insurance company letting it know that you have this right, and asking to be notified if there's any change in the policy or any problem with premium payments. Send a certified copy of your divorce order with the provision about your access to information highlighted, and say you'll be checking in regularly to confirm the order's being complied with. Send a copy of the letter to your ex, too.

If you didn't get an order like this from the court, or if your spouse bought the insurance later, then ask your former spouse to voluntarily provide you with documentation that the insurance is in place.

Auto insurance. Contact your insurance company and make sure the vehicle you're driving is properly insured and that you're the only owner of the insurance policy. It's likely that after the car was transferred into your name alone a new policy was issued with you (and possibly your driving-age kids) as the only insured. Get a copy of the declaration page, the sheet that says what coverage you have and who is covered.

6. Update Other Beneficiary Designations and Your W-4

Make sure you've considered all the possible places you might have named your spouse as a beneficiary, and change any of those you want to change. Think about:

- pension plans
- retirement accounts

- payable-on-death bank accounts, and
- securities accounts for which you named a transfer-on-death beneficiary.

Ask your human resources department or the account custodian (the brokerage house where you have an IRA, for instance) to help you be sure you've filled out all the right forms. Under some plans your ex-spouse may have to sign something acknowledging that you're changing beneficiaries.

While you're visiting the human resources folks, check on whether you need to update your W-4. If you've been claiming a withholding exemption for your spouse, you must give your employer a new W-4 within ten days of your divorce becoming final, showing a corrected number of exemptions.

7. Protect Your Retirement Rights

If you and your spouse divided retirement plans, you need to make sure that all the dividing actually happened. If the retirement plan was a defined benefit plan, you undoubtedly asked the court to enter a QDRO, or Qualified Domestic Relations Order, requiring the plan administrator to split pension payments between you and your ex-spouse when the payments eventually become due.

If a QDRO was part of your divorce settlement or judgment, make sure the order actually gets written, signed by the judge, and made a part of your court file. The QDRO is separate from the order that says you're divorced. This is a detail that's easy to overlook, especially if the divorce order doesn't say who's responsible for preparing the QDRO. Generally, the spouse who will be getting benefits from the other's retirement takes charge, but not always. And even if the divorce order says your spouse is supposed to do it, if you're the nonemployee spouse, it's in your interest to make sure the order gets entered so there's no confusion or hassle later—and you don't face the possibility of losing your pension rights.

If you have a lawyer, the lawyer should take care of this. If you don't, then hire an actuary or attorney who specializes in QDRO preparation to help you get the order written and entered.

After the QDRO is signed, get a couple of certified copies from the court. Keep one in a very safe place, along with information about the pension plan so that you know who to contact if you have questions. Send the other to the employer or plan administrator. There's nothing more you need to do until it's time for the pension to be paid out.

RESOURCE

Questions? You can get more information from the Department of Labor's website at www.dol.gov/ebsa (the page for the Employee Benefits Security Administration, which deals with benefits questions). Click the link for FAQs and you'll find information about QDROs.

If the retirement benefits you split were in the form of IRAs or other assets that don't require a QDRO for distribution, you still need to make sure that the division happens. You can't just change the title on an IRA account, or have a check written to you which you then cash or endorse to pay your ex-spouse. You'll be taxed on the money, and penalized for withdrawing it early if you're not yet 59½. Ask the trustee how to properly roll over the money into another IRA in one spouse's name. See Chapter 10 for more about this.

In addition to buying life and disability insurance that would cover spousal and child support in the event of the paying spouse's death, if you are expecting retirement benefits in the future, make sure the life insurance benefit also covers the value of the retirement benefits. Otherwise, if your former spouse dies before retirement, you might lose out.

8. Update Your Will, Trust, and Power of Attorney

If you haven't yet made a new will, do it immediately. Any will that you made during your marriage says that you are married and, most likely, leaves your property to your ex-spouse. In some states, divorce voids provisions in your will that leave property to your ex—but not all states have this rule, so don't count on it. Even if you still want to leave something to your former spouse, you need to change your will to state that you are a single person and restate your intentions.

CAUTION

Make sure you wait until the divorce is final. If you do want to provide for your now ex-spouse in your will, don't make the new will until your final judgment has been entered, officially ending your marriage. If you make the new will before that official date, it may be automatically revoked in short order when the judgment is entered.

If you hold any separate property in trust, you may have already taken the property out of the trust during the divorce. In any case, review the trust document and amend it if necessary. You may want to check with the lawyer who prepared the trust.

If you signed a power of attorney for finances, giving your ex-spouse the right to make financial decisions for you if you're unable to take care of your own affairs, make sure you destroy it. The same goes for a health care directive that names your ex.

Don't procrastinate. The law books are full of cases resulting from arguments between current and former spouses about a person's intent to leave money or property to one or the other. Do your family a favor and be clear about your wishes after your divorce.

RESOURCE

There are lots of resources to help you with estate planning. Whether you want a book, software, or an online will preparation service, there are plenty out there. Many can help you figure out whether you need a lawyer or can prepare your simple will on your own, and some can help you work with a lawyer, too. Here are some of the best:

Quicken WillMaker Plus (Nolo) is interactive software that takes you through a series of questions and then produces a valid will tailored to your state. The program also contains powers of attorney.

You can also make a will or living trust online at www.nolo.com.

Nolo's Quick & Legal Will Book, by Denis Clifford (Nolo), lets you make a simple will.

8 Ways to Avoid Probate, by Mary Randolph (Nolo), explains how you can take advantage of important—and often overlooked—probate avoidance strategies.

Make Your Own Living Trust, by Denis Clifford (Nolo), explains how to create a living trust, transfer property to the trust, and amend or revoke the trust.

9. Confirm That All Bank and Credit Accounts Are Separated

You have probably already closed all your joint bank and credit card accounts, but if there are any left over, take care of them. All you need to do to divide a bank or brokerage account is contact the bank, credit union, or brokerage company—in writing—and instruct them on the terms of your divorce order. (Contact the institution by phone or email to find out where your letter should be mailed.) Send along a copy of the final divorce order and give clear instructions, and send a copy of the letter to your ex-spouse. A sample letter is shown below.

Stock certificates require special treatment. If you have actual certificates (rather than just holding your stock in a brokerage account), you need to send the certificates back to the transfer agent with endorsements by both you and your ex-spouse on the back. Include a copy of your divorce order calling for division, and a letter directing the transfer agent to issue new stock certificates in the amounts stated in the order.

If your settlement agreement makes your spouse responsible for some of your debts, take steps to have those debts transferred into your spouse's name. Notify the creditors of the divorce settlement, and send them a copy of the divorce order that requires your spouse to pay. Legally, creditors can still look to you for payment of the debt (that's why Chapter 10 advises against making this kind of arrangement). But you can at least make a record that your spouse is responsible.

Sample Letter Asking Financial Institution to Split Account

April 2, 20xx

Charles Schwab
Main Office
P.O. Box 765
San Francisco, California

Re: Account Number 1234567

Dear Charles Schwab:

This is to let you know that my former wife, Marla Jackson, and I are now divorced. Our divorce order calls for the equal division of our jointly owned mutual fund account. (I'm enclosing a certified copy of the order.) The account number is above. My Social Security number is 111-222-3333 and my ex-wife's is 444-555-6666.

Please open a new account in my name and transfer 50% of the holdings for each company held in Account Number 1234567 into the new account. Please take my name off the old account, and leave the original account in my former wife's name. If there is a fee for the transfer, please split the fee equally between the two accounts.

Please contact me if you have any questions. Thank you.

Very truly yours,

Bart Jackson

Bart Jackson
444 Rose Street
Berkeley, CA 94710
bjack@yahoo.com
510-555-1222

10. Follow Up on Any Name Change

If you changed your name as part of the divorce order, you'll need to follow up by making sure that all of your official documents reflect your new name. Notify all relevant agencies and companies.

Name Changes: Whom to Notify	
Driver's license and vehicle registration	State department of motor vehicles
Social Security card	Social Security Adminstration (www.ssa.gov)
Credit cards	Issuing companies
Employment records	Your employer
State tax records	State tax authority
Voter records	Registrar of voters for your county
Passport	Passport services office (www.travel.state.gov/passport)
Retirement account	Employer or plan administrator
Deeds and mortgages on real estate	Lender and title company
Insurance policies	Insurance companies
Mail	Local post office
Utilities and telephone service	Individual service providers

Of course, you'll also need to notify your friends and relatives that you'll be using a different name. Some people even send out an announcement of the divorce, adding new contact information if appropriate. You probably won't find a template at your local stationery store, but making up an announcement might be a good way to symbolically put an end to the divorce process and begin your new life.

The Kid Connection

If you have kids, you are undoubtedly well aware that, divorced or not, you haven't seen the last of your former spouse. Your kids will connect you for a long time to come, probably for the rest of your lives. The courts understand this, too. Until your kids reach adulthood the court has the power to make decisions about child custody, visitation, and support.

Child Custody and Visitation

If nothing else, you'll continue to have contact with your ex as you shuttle the kids back and forth. The best thing you can do at the beginning is to comply with the court order exactly, without asking for exceptions or changes, and pay particular attention to being on time with pickups and drop-offs. As time goes by and you all settle into a routine, the changeover days should get easier and involve less stress for everyone (at least until new partners start to get involved—see "Dating and New Relationships," below).

When things get more comfortable, it will become easier to ask for flexibility in the routine when you need it, and easier to provide it when your ex needs it, as well. It's very possible that your parenting plan may need some tweaking as time passes and your kids' interests, activities, and schedules change.

Stay in communication with your ex about everything involving the kids. If you see a change coming that might require an alteration in some part of your parenting plan, such as a change in the days the school band practices or the loss of your regular child care person, start the discussion well in advance. Don't assume that whatever makes the most sense for you will immediately be acceptable to your ex. After all, you are no longer privy to all of the factors that your former spouse must consider. These are great opportunities to practice taking the high road by being as cooperative as you possibly can about whatever adjustments are needed.

If there are significant changes in the way you or your ex wants to handle custody, you may need to go back to court to request a legal change. For example, you might want to ask that physical custody change from joint to sole custody with visitation rights. Or if you compromised during the divorce by giving your spouse physical custody because your job took you out of town a great deal of the time and now you don't travel as much, you might want to ask for a change in the schedule as well as a change to joint physical custody. Again, start by trying to have the discussion with your ex directly, or with the assistance of a therapist or mediator. Just as in your original divorce proceeding, these matters are best kept out of court.

Moving Away

Probably the most disruptive change that's likely to collide with any parenting plan is a custodial parent's desire to move somewhere that will make visits with the other parent significantly more difficult or expensive. There are lots of reasons that such a move might make sense—to the parent who wants to go. But noncustodial parents who spend a significant amount of time with their kids usually resist the idea of a move that leaves them with a lot less time with their kids. And because moving is an all-or-nothing proposition, it's hard for parents to see how compromise could happen.

You may have agreed to a divorce order that says neither of you can move farther than a certain distance away. In that case, if you want to move, you'll have to try to talk your former spouse into modifying the agreement. If there are no restrictions in your divorce order, you'll still be better off starting with a conversation with your ex.

In most states, a custodial parent is free to move unless the other parent can convince the court that the move is for the purpose of frustrating visitation or will harm the child for some other reasons. In some states, however, if the noncustodial parent objects, the parent who wants to move must show why the move will benefit the kids and how the kids will continue to have contact with their other parent.

If you've had a parenting arrangement that's been working well for the kids and you're considering a move, start by inviting your ex-spouse to a session with a therapist or mediator, and raise the possibility. Listen carefully to what your ex has to say about the move, and present your reasons for wanting to go without acting like it's the only possible outcome that could work for you or the kids. Be patient with your ex's reaction.

If you're the parent who fears losing your kids, try to keep your mind open too. There may be ways to keep in close contact with your children even if they move away. It may be that the move would have benefits for them that they can't get where they are living now.

It's possible that all of this open-mindedness won't help you work your way to an agreement about the move, and you may be in for a court fight. There is so much at stake in a battle like this that you almost certainly want a lawyer representing you, whether or not you hired one during your divorce.

The Judge Isn't Always Right

In a Louisiana case, when a mom who had primary custody moved out of state, her ex-husband went to court, asking that their eight-year-old daughter stay in Louisiana with him. A judge ordered that the child live with each parent for a year at a time, alternating back and forth between states, with the other parent having visitation on all holidays and school breaks. When the mother appealed, the appeals court overturned this ridiculous ruling, saying that it would be disruptive to the child's education and socialization, as well as her sense of stability, and thus was not in her best interests. Custody remained with the mom.

Do you need any more reminders of why you shouldn't trust family decisions to a judge?

If You're Not Getting Support Checks

If you're entitled to receive child support and the money isn't coming, you're not alone. Failure to pay child support is an enormous problem in this country. (As of 2008, according to the U.S. Census Bureau, just over 46% of custodial parents received all the child support they were owed while an additional 30% received some, but not all of the support due.) Chapter 8 explains what to do during your divorce that should make it easier to enforce support orders, if it comes to that. If you're not satisfied with what wage garnishment or your state's child support enforcement (CSE) programs are doing for you, you can also hire a private collection agency to go after your ex for child support payments. Be careful with this, though, because the percentage that the agency takes might be higher than it's worth to you, and not all agencies are scrupulous.

If your former spouse moves out of state, enforcing support can be even more difficult. In general, the less parents see their children the less likely they are to make their support payments. If the checks stop coming, you'll need to register your support entitlement in the new state by sending the appropriate forms (which you can get from your CSE agency) to the other state's collection agency. The new state will then make the same collection efforts that your state would. If your ex moved because of work but stayed with the same company, you can also send the forms directly to the employer if that state has its own provisions for wage garnishment.

If you're getting support and then your ex stops paying after a move, it might be worth your while to hire a lawyer to help you get your order registered in the new state. After that, you should be able to take care of follow-up yourself.

Modifying Child Support

Circumstances change, and after you divorce you may find you need a change in the child support arrangement. If you're the paying parent, you might want to lower your support obligation because you're temporarily out of work or you find yourself facing an ongoing extra expense like a chronic illness or caring for a parent. If you're receiving support, an increase in your ex-spouse's income or in your expenses might justify an increase in support.

Either way, try to resolve it with your ex-spouse without resorting to the courts. Don't just stop paying and hope everything will work out—you'll just get further behind, and a debt related to child support is a debt you have forever (even if you file for bankruptcy; see Chapter 14).

If talking it out yourselves doesn't work, go back to your mediator, collaborative lawyer, or counselor, if you had any of those kinds of help during your divorce. If you didn't, find a mediator—Chapter 4 explains how. If you do come to a meeting of the minds, write down whatever you agree to. If you're the payer and your ex tells you over the phone that it's okay to miss a few payments, don't rely on that. If your ex has a change of heart, you could be looking at a court order to make the missed payments later. Get it in writing.

If you can't work something out with your ex, you can go to court and ask for a modification. You're required to show a change of circumstances; simply taking on new voluntary expenses, like a luxury car, doesn't count. Nor does leaving your job voluntarily, even if it's to take a job that is more meaningful to you but pays less. You need to show that something beyond your control is interfering with your ability to support your children at the same level you have been providing.

Moving in with a new partner can affect the amount of child support you receive. Child support is based in part on your income, and if you begin living with someone who is contributing to household expenses that include taking care of your kids, a court might reduce your support accordingly.

Helping Your Kids Deal With Divorce After the Fact

As time passes, the very best way that you can help your kids is by working out a cooperative, minimally conflicted relationship with your ex. Of course, it's important to tell your kids repeatedly that you love them, that the divorce was not their fault, and that they will always have two parents—but the proof is in the pudding, and you need to be a model of maturity in how you deal with the divorce.

This doesn't mean never letting them know that you are stressed or that the divorce brings up some difficult feelings for you. It's fine to talk about those things in general ways, without burdening the kids with the details. But don't express bitterness toward your ex, and don't in any way imply that your ex isn't a good parent or that your kids are wrong to want a relationship with their other parent. Instead, continue to support that relationship in every way you can, so that the kids can be free of guilt and ambivalence.

Even a year or two (or more) after the divorce, make sure you are available to listen to them whenever they want to talk. As they grow and develop, they may need new information or need to process their feelings in a different way. Depending on their ages and personalities, you may need to encourage them to continue to talk about their feelings about the divorce.

You know that divorce is a very stressful event for kids. Even if your child has generally had a positive spin on things and bounced back from adversity pretty easily, keep an eye out for the rough patches that are bound to occur. There's more in Chapter 6 about helping your kids cope with the divorce, and there are parenting resources in Chapter 16.

Modifying Spousal Support

Courts are generally reluctant to change spousal support arrangements, but if you can prove that you gave up your right to spousal support under duress (you were forced or threatened), or that something about the agreement really wasn't fair, a court might change the order. If you are paying spousal support, the court might consider a big change in your ex-spouse's circumstances enough to justify a change. For example, if your ex landed a great job and is doing fine financially, you might be let off the hook for support. And if you lose your own job, you might get a downward adjustment in support, at least temporarily. Chapter 11 describes the different kinds of spousal support and how long they're each likely to last.

Your Right to Social Security

There are lots of rules about just who's entitled to Social Security after divorce. Here are the basics.

If you were married ten years or longer, you can receive Social Security benefits as a widow or widower if your ex-spouse dies—even years after your divorce, and even if your ex-spouse has remarried. Benefits paid to a surviving divorced spouse who is 60 or older will not affect the benefit rates for other survivors receiving benefits, meaning your children's benefits won't be affected if you're over 60, but they may if you are younger. And if you remarry before you turn 60, you lose the entitlement to survivors' benefits from your former spouse, unless your later marriage ends before the death of your former spouse. If you remarry after age 60 (50, if you are disabled), you can still collect benefits on your former spouse's record. When you reach age 62, you can substitute your new spouse's retirement benefits instead of keeping your former spouse's survivor benefits, if the new benefits are higher. Your remarriage would have no effect on the benefits being paid to your children.

RESOURCE

Learn more. Your local Social Security office would be a good source of more information, as is the Social Security website at www.ssa.gov. *Social Security, Medicare & Government Pensions,* by Joseph Matthews with Dorothy Matthews Berman (Nolo), has a detailed explanation of Social Security benefits, including the effect of divorce and remarriage on benefit entitlement. *Divorce & Money: How to Make the Best Financial Decisions During Divorce,* by Violet Woodhouse with Matthew J. Perry (Nolo), also discusses Social Security benefits.

Dating and New Relationships

If you have kids, you'll be dealing with some special challenges as you return to the dating world. You may be ready for dating long before your children are prepared for you to do it, so be extremely cautious in bringing a new love interest home to meet the family. It's natural for the kids to continue wishing that you and your ex will reconcile—possibly even long after you've been with a new partner. There's very little chance that you'll talk them out of it, so just be patient and honest about what's going on. And be cautious. Your kids have been through a big loss, and you don't want to keep repeating it as you search for the right relationship. Especially if you share custody with your former spouse, you have a ready-made schedule for dating: For a while, do it when the kids are with your ex.

Don't be surprised if your ex-spouse also has a difficult time with the knowledge that you are dating. It's probably wise to exercise the same caution with your ex that you do with your kids, and not introduce a new partner until you're sure it's serious—but it's also a good idea to make sure your ex hears it from you, not your kids or a well-meaning friend. And be prepared for your own feelings to surprise you when you learn that your former spouse is dating. Even when you have no ambivalence at all about the divorce—and how common is that?—it can be hard to see your partner of many years in a relationship with someone else.

What can you do? Nothing but take the high road. Acknowledge your feelings to yourself, and talk about them with your friends if you need to. But never give your spouse a hard time about the new partner, and never bad-mouth either of them to your kids. If a big problem arises (for example, it turns out the new mate has a drinking problem or is abusive), of course you'll need to deal with it. But if you just don't take to the new friend, keep it to yourself. You may find that those feelings fade as you get to know each other.

And get to know each other you will. When your spouse gets serious with someone else, you will eventually find that you must integrate the new partner into your daily routine. After all, they may be picking up your kids from school and showing up at their soccer games and piano recitals. Again, give the benefit of the doubt and be patient. There's nothing like the passage of time to soothe difficult feelings.

When you decide to start integrating your own new love interest into your daily life—and especially if your new partner moves in—you'll find even more adjustments to be made. Now, instead of having to negotiate scheduling (and parenting issues) with just your ex-spouse, you'll have to work with your new partner, too. And your kids will have to adjust to the household's new adult, who comes with new ideas about discipline, appropriate behavior, and what kind of snacks should be in the fridge.

Hope Springs Eternal: Remarriage

So you're considering taking the plunge again. Let experience give you wisdom, and consider all the legal ramifications of your decisions.

Spousal Support

Spousal support often ends if you remarry, though living together doesn't generally affect it. It's very likely that your divorce order says that support will terminate if the recipient marries, and even if it doesn't, termination is automatic in some states.

Prenuptial Agreements

If you're thinking about remarrying, you should also be thinking about preparing a prenuptial agreement. The sad truth is that even more second marriages than first ones end in divorce—more than 65%, in fact. And it's likely that you want to protect your children's inheritance rights as well as your own hard-won financial independence.

A prenuptial agreement is a document that lets you and your spouse-to-be make your own decisions about which of your state's marital property and support laws will apply to you and which won't. For example, you could give up your right to spousal support, or agree to keep your property separate so that if you divorce, your spouse isn't entitled to ask for any of your assets.

All states have laws designed to make sure that prenuptial agreements are entered into without duress or fraud. These laws seek to protect the person who's giving up rights, by making sure that person understood everything that the agreement said and wasn't forced into making the agreement. One common requirement is that both spouses have lawyers, to ensure that the spouse who's giving up a right like spousal support has advice about the legal consequences of the decision.

A prenuptial agreement might seem unromantic, but if you've been through a divorce you know just how really unromantic the ending of a marriage can be. The prenuptial agreement means that if your new marriage does end in divorce, you'll already have a plan for the distribution of your assets, and the divorce process should be much easier.

> **RESOURCE**
>
> **See for yourself.** There's much more about prenuptial agreements, with examples and sample clauses, in *Prenuptial Agreements: How to Write a Fair & Lasting Contract*, by Katherine E. Stoner and Shae Irving (Nolo). You can also find help with prenups at www.legalzoom.com and www.uslegalforms.com. You'll need a lawyer to help you with the final agreement, but you can do a lot of the preparatory work yourselves.

Your New Spouse and Your Kids

Remarriage does not affect your ex-spouse's relationship with your children. Your new spouse will be your kids' stepparent, not their parent, and won't have a legal relationship with your kids. That means that if you split up, your new spouse won't have an obligation to pay child support and, in most cases, won't be entitled to ask for visitation. The only way your new partner can become a parent to your kids is by completing a stepparent adoption, which would require the other parent's consent and termination of the other parent's rights.

Getting Help and Helping Yourself

Just because your divorce is over, it doesn't mean that you are done having feelings about your ex, your marriage, or your future on your own. There are lots of things you can do to ease your transition.

Be Prepared for the Final Split

Whether your divorce was quick or drawn out, the day that you receive the final divorce order and know that your marriage is legally over can be harder than you anticipate.

If you have to go to court to have the judgment entered—for example, if your state requires you to appear in front of a judge to confirm that your paperwork is accurate and that you want the divorce—you'll know when that day is coming, and you can get yourself ready. Bring a friend with you if you think it will help. Think about what you might want to say to your spouse, if you think you'll talk (if you both have lawyers and your divorce has been acrimonious, this is unlikely). And think about what you might want to do afterwards: a nice lunch, a strenuous hike, or whatever works for you. Some people will want to take their minds off the event, and others might want someone to sit with them and list all the reasons why the divorce was the right thing to do. It's a good idea to do something, though—even the smallest of rituals to mark the change in your life that is (legally) completed.

If you submitted paperwork for an uncontested divorce, you'll probably just find the divorce order in your mailbox one day. If you would prefer to pick up the papers, then when you submit your papers, ask the clerk whether you can pick them up after they're signed, and find out the procedures for doing that. Then you can choose your day and make whatever plans you want to. At least find out when the papers might be coming and prepare yourself for it.

Get the Help You Need (or Want)

Divorce is a lonely process, and it can often seem that no one around you understands what you are going through. But in fact there are a lot of resources available to you—some, like your friends and family, can help you feel better, and others will provide more practical, professional help.

Friends and family. Don't forget to ask for help—or just for company—from people you are close to. It's easy to isolate yourself after your divorce. Resist that temptation, and spend time with people you enjoy and who make you feel good about yourself. (If every time you see your mother she tells you how disappointed she is about the divorce, choose someone else to visit.) Try to be a person who says "yes" when you're invited to parties, outings, and events. If need be, make a list of invitations you receive and make sure you accept at least half of them.

If you're in a real crisis mode, delegate tasks to your friends and family. If you are reluctant to impose, think about what you would do for the people you love, and how good it makes you feel when you know you are helping them. Then decide you're going to do your loved ones the favor of letting them take care of you. Ask someone to do your grocery shopping or your laundry or watch your kids for an afternoon so that you can rest or go out.

Financial planner. This would be a good time to meet with a financial planner, if you haven't already. You may have received a cash settlement or an order that you'll receive part of your ex's pension later. You need to understand the value of these items (whether there's anything you need to do to maintain them) and what they mean to your financial future. Chapter 16 has advice about how to choose a planner to work with. This is also a good time to get a new credit report and to correct anything that still shows joint ownership with your ex-spouse. Turn back to Chapter 2 for information about how to get a credit report and how to make corrections if they're needed.

Career counselor. If you're returning to work after a hiatus, you might want to invest in some career counseling. If you're considering a career change to go along with your life change, but aren't sure what direction you want to go in, www.careerplanner.com has lots of resources as well as links to other good sites. And the classic book on career counseling is *What Color Is Your Parachute?*, by Richard Bolles (Ten Speed Press). There are tons of other books, too, so head out to your local bookstore and take a look.

Support groups. If you're having a hard time emotionally (and that probably includes just about everyone), consider group counseling. A group of people who have also gone through divorce recently, or a group like Parents Without Partners (www.parentswithoutpartners. org), might be a great place to meet others and get support. Check with your physician or HMO, a local mental health agency, and other local resource centers (like a community center or public library) for support groups for divorcing folks. Some people find the immediacy of Internet chat rooms on divorce can be helpful. If you're involved in a religious or spiritual community, find others who have been through a divorce or a recent loss and make contact.

Individual counseling. A psychologist, psychiatrist, or marriage and family therapist can help you talk through your feelings in individual sessions. Some counselors also use other types of treatment, such as hypnosis, to help free you from patterns of behavior that haven't served you well. Find a licensed therapist by asking people you know (always the best source of referrals) or checking with your local county mental health agency.

Life coaching. A life coach works with you to assess your current situation, establish goals, and work toward achieving them. Life coaching is not therapy. It's directed at developing and achieving measurable goals. To learn more about coaching, check out the website of the International Coaching Federation at www.coachfederation.org.

Learn to Take Care of Yourself

Taking care of yourself can mean a lot of different things. For starters, you need to take care of your physical health. Don't get into bad habits because you feel sorry for yourself—and if you already have bad habits that are making you feel bad about yourself, this is a great time to make a change. Eat right, get plenty of rest, and exercise—you'll be amazed at how much difference these simple things can make in your life. And get a checkup. Even if you feel fine, it's a way of symbolizing that you're moving into a new phase and doing it in good health.

You also need to make sure that you are functioning effectively in your daily life. That means not just getting yourself to work and your kids to school every day—although that can feel like quite an accomplishment in itself—but also making sure that your house and your car are in working order and that everyone's properly fed and clothed.

If your spouse always took care of "handy" tasks around the house, you may need to do some quick self-education. There's a great page at www.divorceinfo.com/guystuff.htm that provides basic information about things like changing the furnace filter and dealing with circuit breakers. And there are some good books on the topic, too. *Yes, You Can:*

Home Repairs Made Easy, by Amy Wynn Pastor (Meredith Books), and *Dare to Repair: A Do-It-Herself Guide to Fixing (Almost) Anything in the Home*, by Julie Sussman and Stephanie Glakas-Tenet (Harper Collins), are both accessible guides to basic home maintenance.

And if you never learned to cook because your spouse took care of all that, it's time to get it together and learn your way around a kitchen. Try *Betty Crocker's Good & Easy Cook Book*, by Betty Crocker (Simon & Schuster), for simple, straightforward recipes. There's also *The Absolute Beginner's Cookbook, or How Long Do I Cook a 3-Minute Egg?*, by Jack Eddy and Eleanor Clark (Gramercy).

And finally, it's important that you take care of your mental and spiritual health. Take the time to nurture yourself in whatever ways work for you—whether it's through volunteer work in your community, involvement in your local church, synagogue, or temple, a yoga or meditation practice, music lessons, a book group, or joining a softball team. There are no rules except that you need to do things that are just for you and that help you move forward and put the past behind you.

RESOURCE
Below are some resources that might help.

Spiritual Divorce: Divorce as a Catalyst for an Extraordinary Life, by Debbie Ford (Harper San Francisco), aims to help you use the lessons of your divorce to create a happier and more fulfilling life for yourself.

Learning From Divorce: How to Take Responsibility, Stop the Blame, and Move On, by Robert LaCrosse and Christine Coates (Jossey-Bass), encourages you to let go of the past and embrace the future by seeing your divorce as a turning point and an opportunity, not a failure.

The Beginner's Guide to Forgiveness: How to Free Your Heart and Awaken Compassion, by Jack Kornfield (audio CDs, Sounds True). A simple spiritual guide by a well-respected meditation teacher.

Forgive for Good: A Proven Prescription for Health and Happiness, by Dr. Frederic Luskin (HarperCollins), the founder of the Stanford University Forgiveness Project, posits the theory that forgiveness is good for you and provides techniques for learning to forgive.

How to Be an Adult in Relationships, by David Richo (Shambala), is for when you think you're ready to return to the world of committed relationships—it's a guide to understanding relationships, learning appropriate boundaries, and attracting a similarly minded partner.

Finally, a well-known book on meditation is called *Wherever You Go, There You Are*, by Jon Kabat-Zinn (Hyperion). Whether or not you have the slightest interest in meditation, try to accept and acknowledge the words of the title. No matter what has happened in the past, and no matter how unknowable and frightening the future may seem, your present is what it is. Some days you'll just be treading water in that present, and other days you might feel all the potential of a future that is yours to create. Make the most of it! ●

Getting Help, Finding Information, and Looking Stuff Up

When you're getting divorced, it's important to remind yourself that you're not alone—lots of others have been there before you, and there's an enormous amount of information and help available to you. We've sorted through some of it for you, and this chapter points you to some of the best information and suggests ways to use the help that's available, including books, the Internet, and professional help of all kinds to help you get oriented to the laws of your state and the general universe of divorce law.

More Great Books

You can get great help from books that deal with divorce, whether you're looking for information and advice on the emotional and psychological aspects of divorce, child custody, money, or grief and loss. Here are some that are particularly useful.

Mediation and Collaborative Divorce

Divorce Without Court: A Guide to Mediation & Collaborative Divorce, by Katherine E. Stoner (Nolo), explains in detail how mediation and collaborative divorce work, provides worksheets to help you find a mediator or collaborative lawyer to work with, and offers examples of how the process might look in individual cases.

A Guide to Divorce Mediation, by Gary J. Friedman (Workman), describes the divorce mediation process and includes 12 in-depth case studies to give you a clear sense of how mediation works.

Collaborative Divorce: The Revolutionary New Way to Restructure Your Family, Resolve Legal Issues, and Move On With Your Life, by Pauline Tesler and Peggy Thompson (HarperCollins), describes the collaborative process.

The Collaborative Way to Divorce, by Stuart Webb and Ron Ousky (Hudson Street Press), is another source for understanding collaborative divorce.

Parenting

Building a Parenting Agreement That Works: Child Custody Agreements Step by Step, by Mimi Lyster (Nolo), walks you through the process of negotiating and preparing a parenting agreement with your spouse, and provides sample clauses for building your own agreement.

Being a Great Divorced Father: Real-Life Advice From a Dad Who's Been There, by Paul Mandelstein (Nolo), offers practical advice for dads trying to deal with the new world order after a separation.

Mom's House, Dad's House: Making Two Homes for Your Child, Revised Edition, by Isolina Ricci, Ph.D. (Simon & Schuster), is the classic text on dealing with shared custody.

Putting Children First, Revised Edition, by JoAnne Pedro-Carroll, Ph.D. (Penguin), is a guide to emotionally intelligent parenting designed to lessen the potential negative impacts of divorce on children.

Helping Kids Cope With Divorce the Sandcastles Way, by M. Gary Neuman, L.M.H.C., with Patricia Romanowski (Random House), helps parents understand what their kids are experiencing during divorce and offers practical advice for communicating with children and helping them to express their feelings. Includes sections for every age group.

The Good Divorce, by Constance Ahrons (Harper), offers hope for a postdivorce family structure that works and encourages parents to work hard on their own relationship as coparents after divorce, for the benefit of their children.

How to Parent with Your Ex, by Brette McWhorter Sember (Sphinx), has an interesting two-books-in-one format, with one side addressing parenting issues from a custodial parent's perspective and the flip side dealing with noncustodial parenting.

"Split: A Film for Kids of Divorce (and their Parents)" is a film made for kids and parents, featuring children's perspectives on divorce. No adults or experts show up in this powerful video. Find it at www.splitfilm.org.

Communication

Difficult Conversations: How to Discuss What Matters Most, by Douglas Stone, Bruce Patton, and Sheila Heen (Penguin), has practical advice about how to prepare for difficult talks and communicate successfully about hard topics.

Crucial Conversations: Tips for Talking When the Stakes Are High, by Kerry Patterson, Joseph Grenny, Ron McMillan, Al Switzler, and Steven Covey (McGraw-Hill) offers useful tools for planning and dealing with the difficult conversations that are inevitable.\ This book appears to focus on business relationships, but its definition of a crucial conversation fits right in with what you'll be dealing with during your divorce: one where "… (1) stakes are high, (2) opinions differ, and (3) emotions run high."

Taking the War Out of Our Words: The Art of Powerful Non-Defensive Communication, by Sharon Ellison (Bay Tree Publishing) suggests using a three-pronged approach of questions, statements, and predictions, so you can learn to communicate nondefensively no matter what your spouse is doing. The related website at www.pndc.com has tips and resources.

Emotional and Psychological Issues

Crazy Time: Surviving Divorce and Building a New Life, Revised Edition, by Abigail Trafford (Random House), focuses on the emotional difficulties of ending your marriage and the divorce process, and how you can come out of it and move forward.

Life After Divorce: Create a New Beginning, by Sharon Wegscheider-Cruse (HCI), offers an optimistic view of postdivorce life and promises to turn an event generally perceived as traumatic into a life-enhancing change.

Chapter 15 lists some additional titles that can help with emotional issues.

Estate Planning

Quicken WillMaker Plus is interactive software that lets you create a valid, state-specific will and health care directive.

Nolo's Quick & Legal Will Book, by Denis Clifford (Nolo), provides step-by-step instructions and forms to create a simple will.

Living Trust Maker, a software program, and *Make Your Own Living Trust*, by Denis Clifford (both from Nolo), will help you create a simple living trust. At www.nolo.com you can make a will or living trust online.

Finances

Divorce & Money: How to Make the Best Financial Decisions During Divorce, by Violet Woodhouse with Matthew J. Perry (Nolo), is a detailed, comprehensive guide to the financial issues involved in divorce. Includes lots of worksheets that can help you make the important decisions about money and property.

The Complete Guide to Protecting Your Financial Security When Getting a Divorce, by Alan Feigenbaum and Heather Linton (McGraw-Hill), is written by divorce financial planners and details how to make sure that what looks like a good settlement now will really benefit you in the long run.

Solve Your Money Troubles: Debt, Credit & Bankruptcy, by Margaret Reiter and Robin Leonard (Nolo), provides practical strategies for getting out of debt and making a fresh financial start.

Credit Repair, by Robin Leonard and Margaret Reiter (Nolo), offers legal information and practical tips on credit reports, budgeting, negotiating with credit bureaus, and building a solid credit history.

Getting Divorce Information and Forms

If you're doing all or part of your divorce yourself, you'll need to find forms and information about the process. Here's how.

When it comes to a court's fill-in-the-blanks forms, you can get most of what you need at your local court. Just walk in and ask the clerk how to get your hands on them. The clerk may send you to the nearby county law library for the forms, but more likely you'll have them handed across the counter to you. They'll probably include some instructions or information about how to get started on your divorce.

There is a mind-boggling amount of information about divorce available on the Internet—you could literally spend days exploring websites that give away or sell information, forms, and services to divorcing spouses. From government-sponsored sites on down to commercial sites trying to make a quick buck, there's a broad spectrum of quality and usefulness. Here is some help sorting through it all to find useful information about your divorce, whether you are looking for your local court's website or want to use an interactive program to fill out your divorce forms.

Court and Court-Related Websites

Many court websites have extensive, free general information about state divorce laws, along with local court rules and forms. Check the list below for the best site in your state for finding information and forms. If the court website doesn't offer much, you'll find Web addresses for the state bar or a local law school—the most likely candidates for offering information and forms.

If you simply want to find information about where your local court is, which branch you should use, filing fees, or clerk's hours, you can usually find a direct link to the court website at www.statelocalgov.net or www.ncsconline.org.

And although it doesn't fit neatly into one of the state boxes, don't forget www.irs.gov, where the IRS offers free information about all the tax issues related to divorce (specific publications are identified throughout this book).

TIP

State websites will help you calculate child support. Most states also have sites dedicated specifically to helping you calculate child support. There's a list of those sites in Chapter 8.

Best Court and Court-Related Websites		
State	Websites	What you'll find
Alabama	http://judicial.alabama.gov/civil.cfm	Link to child support information and child support forms (click on "Frequently Asked Questions" link); general forms not available
Alaska	www.courts.alaska.gov/shcforms.htm	Family law self-help center; extensive family law forms and instructions
Arizona	www.azcourts.gov/familylaw/Home.aspx	Links to forms and other resources
Arkansas	http://courts.arkansas.gov/aoc/forms.cfm	Selected domestic relations forms
	www.arlegalservices.org	Arkansas Legal Aid's website with family law forms and instructions
California	www.courtinfo.ca.gov/selfhelp/	Extensive family law resources; all forms
Colorado	www.courts.state.co.us/Forms/Index.cfm	Extensive family law resources; all forms
Connecticut	www.jud.ct.gov/webforms	All family law forms and do-it-yourself divorce guide available for download
	www.jud.ct.gov/lawlib/law/divorce.htm	Divorce guides and resources
Delaware	http://courts.delaware.gov/Family/index.stm	Information about family law and divorce law; link to forms online
District of Columbia	www.dccourts.gov/internet/public/aud_divorce/main.jsf	Information about family courts; link to forms and instructions online
Florida	www.flcourts.org/gen_public/family/self_help/map.shtml	Information about local self-help centers; divorce forms and other resources
	www.clerk-17th-flcourts.org/Clerkwebsite/BCCOC2/SelfService.aspx	Broward County's pilot program for interactive divorce forms online
Georgia	www.legalaid-ga.org/GA/index.cfm	State legal aid site with links to divorce information and forms by county
Hawaii	www.courts.state.hi.us	Link for "court forms" leads to information and resources, including forms

Best Court and Court-Related Websites (cont'd)		
State	Websites	What you'll find
Idaho	www.courtselfhelp.idaho.gov	Court assistance office's home page lists local offices that can assist you with self-help or low-cost legal services; links to forms and instructions for family law cases online
Illinois	www.law.siu.edu/selfhelp/info/divorce/packets.html	Southern Illinois University School of Law provides instructions and forms for filing for divorce
	www.state.il.us/court/links/circuit.asp	Locations of your local court; some local sites provide forms
Indiana	www.in.gov/judiciary/selfservice/	Links to self-help legal center, child support calculators; general information about self-representation
Iowa	www.iowacourts.gov/For_the_Public/Representing_Yourself_in_Court/DivorceFamily_Law/Forms/index.asp	Information about divorce and forms
Kansas	www.kansasjudicialcouncil.org/DivorceForms.shtml	Family law information and forms
Kentucky	http://courts.ky.gov/courtprograms/divorceeducation/Pages/default.aspx	Divorce information and court locations and rules; not much in the way of forms
Louisiana	http://files.lsba.org/documents/PublicResources/LSBADivorceBrochure.pdf	Louisiana state bar association's pamphlet with general information on Louisiana divorce
	http://louisianalawhelp.org/issues/family-children/divorce	Online resources, including forms for some parishes
Maine	www.helpmelaw.org	State-sponsored site: search "divorce" for pamphlets, resources, and court forms
Maryland	www.mdcourts.gov/family/formsindex.html	Court forms and links to self-help information
Massachusetts	www.mass.gov/courts/selfhelp/index.html	General court information and family law self-help center, including forms

Best Court and Court-Related Websites (cont'd)

State	Websites	What you'll find
Michigan	http://courts.mi.gov/Self-help/center/casetype/Pages/Divorce.aspx	General court and family law information; no forms
	www.michiganlegalhelp.org/self-help-tools/family	Automated forms for each county
Minnesota	www.mncourts.gov/selfhelp/?page=1625	Browse through "Court Forms Categories" section to find relevant forms
Mississippi	www.mslegalservices.org/issues/family-and-juvenile	Extensive information; no forms
Missouri	www.courts.mo.gov/page.jsp?id=10580	Information and link to family court forms
Montana	www.courts.mt.gov/library/topic/end_marriage.mcpx	Extensive information and all court forms
Nebraska	http://supremecourt.ne.gov/self-help/#families	Forms and instructions for simple divorce
Nevada	www.nevadajudiciary.us/index.php/viewdocumentsandforms/SelfHelpProSe	Standardized divorce forms and resources for self-representation
New Hampshire	www.courts.state.nh.us/fdpp/forms/allforms.htm#divorce	All divorce forms and information; general information about self-representation
New Jersey	www.judiciary.state.nj.us/family	Information about family court; some forms; links to general information about divorce law
New Mexico	www.nmcourts.com/cgi/prose_lib	Forms for uncontested divorce and domestic violence filings only
	www.nmstatelibrary.org/subject-guide-to-nm-resources	State law library resources (scroll down to "Divorce" section)
New York	www.nycourts.gov/divorce/index.shtml	Extensive court forms, divorce information, and information about self-representation

Best Court and Court-Related Websites (cont'd)

State	Websites	What you'll find
North Carolina	www.nccourts.org/Citizens/GoToCourt/Default.asp	Information about self-representation; click links under "civil" heading for family law forms and information
North Dakota	www.ndcourts.gov/court/forms/divorce/forms.htm	Forms for simple, uncontested divorce; links to rules of court and policy on self-represented parties
Ohio	www.ohiobar.org/Pages/LawFactsPamphlets.aspx	Pamphlets on child support, divorce, and divorce mediation
	www.sconet.state.oh.us/web_sites/courts	Links to specific court websites, which have local family law forms for county courts
Oklahoma	www.oscn.net/applications/oscn/start.asp	State court network, with links to a few forms and minimal divorce information
	www.okbar.org/public/Brochures/divorce.aspx	Oklahoma Bar Association brochure on divorce
Oregon	http://courts.oregon.gov/OJD/OSCA/cpsd/courtimprovement/familylaw/pages/index.aspx	Extensive collection of informational material and all family law forms
	http://courts.oregon.gov/OJD/OSCA/cpsd/courtimprovement/familylaw/pages/addresources.aspx	
Pennsylvania	www.pacourts.us/courts/courts-of-common-pleas/	Scroll down to find link to your county's website; counties differ as to the extent of information and forms
Rhode Island	www.courts.ri.gov/courts/familycourt/default.aspx	Family court information about divorce; some forms
South Carolina	www.sccourts.org/forms/index.cfm	Use drop-down menu to find family court forms
South Dakota	http://ujs.sd.gov	Home page of UJS has links to self-help center and forms

Best Court and Court-Related Websites (cont'd)		
State	Websites	What you'll find
Tennessee	www.tsc.state.tn.us/help-center/court-approved-divorce-forms	Court-approved divorce forms
	www.tsc.state.tn.us/programs/parenting-plan	Forms and instructions specific to parenting plans
Texas	www.tyla.org/tyla/index.cfm/resources/general-public/family-law/	Lengthy handbook about representing yourself in uncontested family law cases, with sample forms, from Texas Young Lawyers' Association
Utah	www.utcourts.gov/resources/forms	Divorce information and forms; link to online interactive program that helps you fill out divorce forms
Vermont	www.vermontjudiciary.org/gtc/family/marriagerelated.aspx	Extensive forms and family law pamphlets
Virginia	www.courts.state.va.us/forms/district/jdr.html	Family court forms
	www.vsb.org/site/publications/divorce-in-virginia	Information on divorce in Virginia
	www.fairfaxcounty.gov/courts/circuit/pdf/fba-h-53.pdf	A pro se divorce package for Fairfax County
Washington	www.courts.wa.gov/forms	Extensive forms and information on all aspects of divorce law
West Virginia	www.courtswv.gov/lower-courts/family-forms/index-family-forms.html	Extensive forms and informational material on all aspects of divorce law
Wisconsin	www.wicourts.gov/forms1/circuit/index.htm	Family law self-help site offers instructions, forms, and interactive program for completing forms. Click on the "Family" link.
Wyoming	www.courts.state.wy.us/DandCS.aspx	Basic legal information and all divorce; forms and instructions

Other Websites

There are many, many commercial (and some nonprofit) websites that contain legal information about divorce. Some have a specific bent, like www.divorceasfriends.com, which encourages people to work toward an amicable divorce whenever possible and www.womansdivorce.com, which directs advice and information at divorcing women.

Lots of individual lawyers and law firms maintain websites and, increasingly, blogs, with free information about their states' laws. Some include forms—even when a state fails to make the forms available online. Try entering your state's name and the word "divorce" into a search engine like Google or Yahoo!, and look at some lawyers' websites. You can find a great deal of state-specific information that way. You might even find a lawyer you want to work with. You can't always rely on these sites to be current, though, so be careful.

The following chart lists some websites and blogs that offer useful information, links, and resources.

You can buy divorce "kits" online that purport to include all the paperwork you'll need for under $50, but you'll get what you pay for— the marital settlement agreement forms won't be state specific, and the other court forms may not be current. Your forms may be rejected by the court, putting you back at square one. You'll be far better off paying more for truly state-specific materials (and you'll still be paying a lot less than you would pay a lawyer). The services listed below in "Web-Based Services" offer state-specific filing forms.

Good Noncourt Divorce Websites

Website	What You'll Find
www.divorcenet.com	General and state-specific articles; directory of lawyers, mediators, and financial professionals
www.distanceparent.org	Resources for parents who live too far away from their kids for frequent in-person contact
www.divorcesupport.com	State-specific information and links to divorce-related products and divorce professionals
www.divorceinfo.com	One of our favorite divorce information websites. Articles, FAQs, and specific information for every state, organized in an accessible way
www.divorcetoday.com	General and some state-specific divorce information; links to professionals and document preparation services
www.divorcecentral.com	Legal, personal, parenting, and financial resources; links to support groups, professional directories, and assistance with divorce paperwork
www.divorcemagazine.com	Features on divorce and relationships; links to state-specific materials and divorce-related products; directory of divorce professionals
www.totaldivorce.com	From a consortium of divorce lawyers; referrals and state-specific information, including links to divorce laws for each state
www.divorceonline.com	Information, resources, and links to document preparation and divorce-related professionals
www.divorcelawinfo.com	Information, resources, links to divorce-related professionals, and document kits without online assistance
www.divorcehelpline.com	Extensive information and links to resources; help for California residents in completing uncontested divorces
www.bonusfamilies.com	Information and resources for divorced coparents and stepfamilies
www.aaml.org (American Academy of Matrimonial Lawyers)	Model parenting plan and general divorce guide at low or no cost (click "publications" link)
www.womenslaw.org	Information and resources about domestic violence and other legal issues
www.parentingplan.net	Parenting plans for downloading, including standard plans, plans where one parent is in the military, and plans for supervised visitation
www.sharekids.com	Online coparenting system for managing shared custody

Good Noncourt Divorce Websites (continued)	
Website	**What You'll Find**
www.nolo.com	Articles about property, custody, and representing yourself; related books on divorce; lawyer directory
www.justia.com	Lots of free information, including case law and statutes
www.alllaw.com	Lots of free information, including child support calculators

Help With Negotiations

If you and your spouse need help negotiating the terms of your divorce settlement, but aren't beyond the point of being able to communicate or compromise with one another, you might want to try divorce mediation. You'll have the help of a neutral third party, called a mediator, who will sit down with both of you to try to help you resolve all of the issues in your divorce. The mediator doesn't make any decisions; that's up to you and your spouse. But a mediator can be a huge help in communicating with each other and coming to an agreement. Mediation is increasingly popular throughout the legal system, and especially so in family law cases. It's affordable, it's civilized, and it works. Chapter 4 deals with divorce mediation in depth. You can also ask a lawyer to coach you in your negotiations. See "Legal Advice," below.

Financial Advice

There are quite a few types of financial professionals who can get involved in a divorce. You won't need to hire them all, but paying for some expert financial help during divorce is sometimes a very wise investment.

Accountants

Even though a lawyer may be the first kind of professional you think of when it comes to a divorce, you may find just as much occasion to seek help from an accountant. An accountant can help you figure out the tax consequences of:

- spousal support (whether you pay or receive it)
- property division
- filing status on your income tax return, and
- dependent exemptions.

An accountant can also help you prepare your tax returns and keep your finances in order by working with you on budgeting and organization. And a specialized forensic accountant is trained to find hidden assets and financial wrongdoing.

Personal referrals are a great way to locate an accountant you can work with. If you have a lawyer helping you with your divorce, the lawyer will surely know trusted accountants. If neither of these avenues gets you there, you could try a website like www.cpadirectory .com, which lists accountants by area and verifies that their licenses are current.

Actuaries

Actuaries are financial professionals whose job is to evaluate risk—in other words, to try to predict the future to the greatest extent possible. In a divorce, the most common job for an actuary is to value retirement benefits by predicting the future return on the marital portion of a spouse's pension. How they do that is pretty technical; that's why you hire them.

The best way to find an actuary to help value your retirement plan is through a lawyer. If you don't have one yet but you're planning on hiring a lawyer to review your settlement agreement or do some other limited task, consider getting a jump on that and asking the lawyer for a referral to an actuary. You can also find referrals on some divorce websites (see "Other Websites," above).

You might want to try to find an actuary who's a member of the American Academy of Actuaries and the American Society of Pension Professionals and Actuaries (ASPPA), so that you'll know the actuary's focus is on retirement benefits.

Credit Counselors

If you have lots of debt and are having difficulty managing it, a credit counselor may be able to help you get back on track. Some nonprofit agencies offer credit counseling services, both locally and through national agencies such as the National Foundation for Credit Counseling. (See www.nfcc.org or call 800-388-2227.) You may also find credit counseling at local universities, military bases, or credit unions. There's much more on credit counseling in "Dividing Debt" in Chapter 10.

Financial Planners

A financial planner can help you both during and after your divorce by reviewing your current financial situation, advising you on settlement proposals and their financial and tax consequences, and working on budgeting and financial management so that you feel secure about your finances as you enter your new life as a single person.

Ask your lawyer or accountant for a referral—and if you have friends who are happy with financial planning help they've received, get names from them as well. You can also check the website of the Financial Planning Association at www.fpanet.org. Financial planners are certified by the Certified Financial Planner Board of Standards, Inc., at www.cfp. net. You can find referrals there, too. Free financial planning services are often available through banks and investment firms.

Divorce Financial Planners

A special kind of financial planner, called a divorce financial planner (DFP) or divorce financial analyst, can work with you and your lawyer or your spouse to evaluate various settlement scenarios. The DFP will try to help you find a win-win division of property, taking into account each spouse's needs, goals, and tax situation.

A DFP can also help you plan investments, advise you about withdrawing money from your retirement plan to fund current needs, and help you with retirement plan rollovers. You can work with a DFP on your own to get advice on settlement proposals and options, or together with your spouse to brainstorm solutions to your property division dilemmas.

The Institute for Divorce Financial Analysts offers certification to planners. It can help you find one through its website at www .institutedfa.com, which also answers FAQs and provides information. Another organization, the Association of Divorce Financial Planners, offers referrals and also has links to useful publications and divorce information on its website at www.divorceandfinance.com.

Document Preparation Services

If you don't want to handle everything in your divorce yourself, but don't think you need to hire a mediator or lawyer either, consider a middle path: hiring a nonlawyer to help you just with the paperwork. You won't be getting help with the negotiation, as you would in mediation, or legal advice, as you would if you used a lawyer. But you will get welcome, experienced help with preparing the court paperwork. Some document preparation services also take care of filing papers with the court or give you instructions on court filing procedures.

You can use these services only when you and your spouse have completed your negotiations and know exactly how you want to settle your divorce. You'll have to know how much support will be paid and what you're going to do with your property and debts. If you haven't yet worked out these questions, you aren't ready for the document preparation phase of your divorce.

Some document preparation services operate small offices; others work entirely online.

Legal Document Preparers

In some places, there are businesses that prepare the paperwork for uncontested divorces. These folks used to be called paralegals but are now most commonly referred to as legal document preparers, or LDPs.

Legal document preparers aren't allowed to give you individualized legal advice. (Only licensed lawyers can do that.) All they do is prepare forms, using the information you supply, and file them with the court. So when you visit a document preparation business, you'll get a questionnaire that asks you for the information the preparer needs to fill out court forms for your county. The LDP will transfer the information onto the forms, and then either you or the LDP can file them with the court.

The fee for doing the paperwork for an uncontested divorce varies from about $175 to $700, depending on where you live, whether you have children, and whether you need a separate settlement agreement (which depends on how your state's forms are structured).

To find a legal document preparer, first ask your divorced friends and acquaintances whether they used one, and what the experience was like. If that gets you nowhere, look online or in the yellow pages under "legal document assistant," "paralegal," or "typing services." You can also search the Internet using those terms and your state's name, to learn more about how LDPs operate in your state (some states limit their activities) and get referrals.

Web-Based Services

Some document preparation services interact with customers only through the Internet, which may be a boon to you if no walk-in service is available close to where you live. You'll answer questions on the website, and the forms will emerge from your computer or be mailed to you a few days later. You'll need to file the forms with the court and do the rest of the legwork yourself.

The main differences among the sites are how quickly your paperwork is available to you and price. Most online preparation services charge from about $139 to $300.

Online Document Preparation Services	
Site	**How long it takes to get your documents**
www.legalzoom.com	5–7 days by mail
www.ourdivorceagreement.com	Immediate, online
www.completecase.com	Immediate, online
www.divorcetoday.com	2–3 days
www.onlinedivorce.com	A few hours, online
www.divorcesource.com	Various options online or by mail

CAUTION

Do your homework. We're not recommending any of these online services, just listing them for your convenience. Before you plunk down any money for document preparation services, check out the company. Some sites display a seal for the Better Business Bureau online, which means you can check on a report for that company at www.bbbonline.com. Not having the seal doesn't mean that the product isn't good, but use your judgment and spend some time looking around for what will work best for you. And while getting your documents immediately may seem appealing, check to be sure they're being reviewed before you get them.

Legal Advice

Sometimes you want some personalized guidance on legal matters, from someone who's handled lots of divorces and knows the pros and cons of the options you face. That's when you call a divorce lawyer.

Ways to Work With a Lawyer

The traditional way to work with a lawyer during divorce is to hire the lawyer, pay the fee, and then turn everything over to the expert. That's still the model many divorce lawyers follow (and expect you to follow), but it isn't the only way to go. A lawyer can work for you as a coach, a mediator, a collaborative representative, or an advocate out to get you the best possible deal. You can also hire a lawyer to handle only specific parts of your divorce.

One way to ensure that your case doesn't get away from you is for you and your spouse to use collaborative lawyers. Collaborative lawyers try hard to work with you and your spouse to settle divorce cases out of court—and if you or your spouse later insist on a trial, you'll have to hire new lawyers and start over. (See "Collaborative Divorce," in Chapter 1.)

Another way to use a lawyer is as a consultant when you are working with a mediator. In fact, some mediators require that both spouses have attorneys of their own, called consulting attorneys, throughout the process. Even if they don't require it, many mediators will make sure that you at least have a lawyer look over the settlement agreement before you sign it. (See Chapter 4 for more about mediation and consulting lawyers.)

A consulting lawyer can explain your rights and the legal procedures you're dealing with, provide referrals to other professionals like actuaries or appraisers, help you decide whether a settlement offer meets your needs, or give you advice about any aspect of your divorce.

You can ask a lawyer to serve as your coach, answering questions and helping you negotiate as you do your own divorce.

Finally, you can ask a lawyer to help you only with specific tasks. This can make expert help much more affordable. Lawyers in many states are experimenting with something called "unbundled" legal services, meaning that you can hire a lawyer to represent you for just a specific part of your case.

So, for example, you could file your own divorce case, schedule a hearing (and file papers yourself) about how much child support should be paid while the divorce is proceeding, and then hire a lawyer just to come to the hearing and represent you in front of the judge. Or you could hire a lawyer to look over the marital settlement agreement that you and your spouse prepared yourselves after working with a mediator.

What a Lawyer Can Do for You

- Help you with paperwork and deal with the court so you don't have to
- Advocate for you in negotiations and try to settle the case
- Help you inventory and assess your assets and debts, especially if you have significant assets or complicated financial arrangements
- Advise you during mediation
- Help you evaluate who owns what, especially in situations where you merged property you owned before the marriage with property you acquired during it
- Help to protect you and your kids if your spouse is physically abusive or abuses drugs or alcohol
- Keep the process moving forward if your spouse is unresponsive or impossible to talk to
- Keep the playing field level if your spouse has an aggressive lawyer who you think will try to take advantage of you
- Help track down assets your spouse is hiding

How to Find and Choose a Lawyer

Chapter 5 explains how to find a lawyer if you're embroiled in a contested divorce. Much of the advice there will also help you if you're looking for a lawyer for uncontested cases, so be sure to check it out. Here's some more advice for other circumstances in which you might be hunting for a lawyer.

If you're looking for a lawyer to consult with you during mediation. Chapter 4 explains how to find a mediator, and you can look for a consulting attorney the same way:

- If you have a business lawyer or accountant, ask for referrals.
- Ask your friends and family who are divorced whether they used mediation and have a consulting attorney they would

recommend. If they had an attorney for a contested divorce, see whether they're willing to ask that attorney for referrals.

- Search www.mediate.com or www.acrnet.org for divorce mediators, many of whom also provide consulting attorney services.
- Use links on divorce websites.
- Look in the phone book under "mediation" or "dispute resolution" for attorney-mediators who will serve as consulting attorneys.

If you're looking for a collaborative lawyer. Collaborative divorce is a very specialized way of practicing divorce law, so you'll need to find a lawyer who's been trained in the process. It may be harder to find personal referrals because collaborative law is relatively new, but ask around. Perhaps you'll find that someone you know recently settled a divorce using collaborative law and can recommend an attorney. Otherwise, ask family law attorneys, who should be aware of who's practicing collaborative law in the community.

It's also likely, if you live in a metropolitan area, that there are local collaborative law organizations. Try an Internet search for your area along with the terms "collaborative law," "collaborative divorce," and "collaborative attorney." You should get sites for local organizations as well as for local attorneys who practice collaborative law. You can also contact the International Academy of Collaborative Professionals at www.collaborativepractice.com. The website has links to collaborative professionals all over the country.

If you're looking for a lawyer to review documents or make a single appearance in court. If you want a lawyer for a single task, such as appearing in court or reviewing a document, try the tips in Chapter 5 for finding a lawyer. But your first question should always be whether the lawyer is open to working on only part of your case. Some lawyers won't do it, believing that without knowing every single thing about your case they can't provide good services. So before you waste time on questions about experience or billing practices, find out whether you're barking up the wrong tree.

For this kind of search, the lawyer directory at www.nolo.com may be a good resource for you. Each lawyer with a profile in the directory answers a series of questions, including whether the lawyer is willing to review documents and coach clients who are representing themselves.

Other Ways to Look Things Up

It's possible that you might want to look up specific laws, rules, or forms for your own state. For example, you might want to find out the waiting period for your state or get a sample form for asking to be excused from having to serve papers on your spouse. This kind of research can seem intimidating, and it is very specialized in some ways. But it's not hard to learn once you know a few basic methods and get the lay of the land. There are a few different ways you can find legal information.

Library Research

Nearly every county has a public law library. Ask the court clerk where you would find the nearest law library that's open to the public—often it will be in the courthouse, a state-funded law school, or a state capitol building. Some local public libraries also have law books.

Law librarians are trained to work with novice legal researchers. They can't give legal advice or explain the information that you find in the law books, but they will nearly always be very helpful about pointing you to the right area of the library or finding specific books.

Because divorce law differs so much from state to state, it's hard to say exactly what resources you might find in your local law library. But you will definitely find all of the following:

- the text of your state's laws on divorce and family issues (statutes and regulations)
- published court decisions (cases) that interpret the state law, and
- legal articles, books, and sets on specific topics that explain the law in depth.

Here's a quick look at each of these resources.

Statutes and Regulations

The basic law of your state can be found in the state's statutes (also called laws or codes), which are the laws made by your state's legislature. Ask the law librarian to show you where the "annotated" codes are—these contain the statutes plus supplemental material like descriptions of cases that interpret the laws and cross-references to articles about the topic.

Most state laws are divided into sections, sometimes called "codes"— for example, you're likely to find that the "Family Code" or "Domestic Relations" chapters contain the divorce laws for your state. If there's no separate family code, the laws are probably in the Civil Code. Look in the index under "divorce" to find the code you're looking for and narrow down the sections. The codes are numbered, and once you find the general area you should be able to find the law you need using the table of contents in the code book itself. Ask the law librarian for help if you're not finding what you need.

Finding the law won't always help you immediately, as statutes can be difficult to read and understand. After you've reviewed them, you can look through the "annotations," which are brief descriptions of cases that mention the code section you're interested in, to see whether there are any cases that might help you understand what the law actually says. Also, be sure to look in the back of the book to see whether there's a paperback addition ("pocket part") that shows changes in the law since the book was printed.

Court Decisions

In addition to the laws made by the legislature, judges' rulings in individual cases are collected and published. These are usually appeals cases, not ordinary trials. If you see a case in the statutory annotations or in another source that you want to look at, you'll need to decipher the case's "citation," which tells you what volume the case is published in—a fairly simple task once you know the trick.

Let's use the case of *In re Marriage of Brown v. Yana* as an example. It's a California case related to custody and moving away. There are two different citations for the case: 37 Cal.4th 947 and 127 P.3d 28. In each citation, the first number refers to the volume of the set, the second letter/number combination refers to the set of books the volume is in, and the third number refers to the page where the case begins.

"Cal.4th" means the *California Reports*, 4th Series. Once you've found the series, find Volume 37 and turn to page 947. The second citation is to the *Pacific Reporter*, 3rd Series. (This set of books includes decisions from courts in several West Coast states, not just California.) Once you've found the series, find Volume 127 and turn to page 28.

Not all law libraries have the state reporters—some only have the regional ones. But both of these volumes contain exactly the same cases.

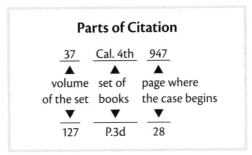

Parts of Citation

37	Cal. 4th	947
▲	▲	▲
volume of the set	set of books	page where the case begins
▼	▼	▼
127	P.3d	28

Background Resources

You may also want to look up information in a legal encyclopedia—the two major national ones are called the *ALR* and *Am.Jur*. You can search the index by subject—for example, custody or visitation—and then review brief summaries of cases on that subject. If you find cases from your state, you can look them up as explained above.

It's very likely that your state has practice manuals and form books related to family law. Ask the law librarian to show you where they are and give you a crash course in how to use them.

Online Legal Research

Most of the websites listed in "Getting Divorce Information and Forms," above, have links to legal research websites, and the list includes general legal research websites like www.nolo.com, www.alllaw.com, and www.justia.com. To get your state's laws, you can also go to www.totaldivorce.com, where the divorce laws are separated out from other state laws and presented in an easy-to-review format. You can often find the full text of laws and cases online just by putting the citation into a search engine.

RESOURCE

If you want to learn more. *Legal Research: How to Find & Understand the Law,* by Stephen Elias and the editors of Nolo (Nolo), explains in detail how to find legal information and resources and can help you find your way around the law library and the Internet.

All of these resources, along with everything else you've learned here, should help you take charge of your divorce and prepare for your future. Good luck. ●

Appendix

You can use the forms in the appendix by making copies to fill out. You can also download any of the forms and worksheets at:

www.nolo.com/back-of-book/NODV.html

When there are important changes to the information in this book, we'll post updates on this same dedicated page. You'll find other useful information, such as author blogs and podcasts, as well.

Financial Inventory (as of _____)

ASSETS	Date of Purchase	Owned Separately	Account Number (if relevant)	Current Market Value ($)
Cash and Cash Equivalents				
Cash	_____	☐ Yes ☐ No	_____	_____
Checking accounts	_____	☐ Yes ☐ No	_____	_____
Savings accounts	_____	☐ Yes ☐ No	_____	_____
Money market accts.	_____	☐ Yes ☐ No	_____	_____
Tax refunds anticipated	_____	☐ Yes ☐ No	_____	_____
Other	_____	☐ Yes ☐ No	_____	_____
			Subtotal	_____
Real Estate				
House/condo/coop	_____	☐ Yes ☐ No	_____	_____
Vacation home	_____	☐ Yes ☐ No	_____	_____
Income properties	_____	☐ Yes ☐ No	_____	_____
Unimproved lot	_____	☐ Yes ☐ No	_____	_____
Other lot	_____	☐ Yes ☐ No	_____	_____
			Subtotal	_____
Personal Property				
Motor vehicles	_____	☐ Yes ☐ No	_____	_____
Furniture	_____	☐ Yes ☐ No	_____	_____
Home furnishings	_____	☐ Yes ☐ No	_____	_____
Electronic equipment	_____	☐ Yes ☐ No	_____	_____
Computer system	_____	☐ Yes ☐ No	_____	_____
Jewelry	_____	☐ Yes ☐ No	_____	_____
Clothing	_____	☐ Yes ☐ No	_____	_____
Collections (coin, stamp)	_____	☐ Yes ☐ No	_____	_____
Animals	_____	☐ Yes ☐ No	_____	_____
Artwork	_____	☐ Yes ☐ No	_____	_____
Other	_____	☐ Yes ☐ No	_____	_____
			Subtotal	_____

Financial Inventory (continued)

ASSETS	Date of Purchase	Owned Separately	Account Number (if relevant)	Current Market Value ($)
Investments				
Life ins. (term)	_____	☐ Yes ☐ No	_____	_____
Life ins. (whole life policies)	_____	☐ Yes ☐ No	_____	_____
Stocks	_____	☐ Yes ☐ No	_____	_____
Bonds	_____	☐ Yes ☐ No	_____	_____
Mutual funds	_____	☐ Yes ☐ No	_____	_____
Annuities	_____	☐ Yes ☐ No	_____	_____
IRAs	_____	☐ Yes ☐ No	_____	_____
SEP-IRA	_____	☐ Yes ☐ No	_____	_____
401(k) plans	_____	☐ Yes ☐ No	_____	_____
Other retirement plans	_____	☐ Yes ☐ No	_____	_____
Partnerships	_____	☐ Yes ☐ No	_____	_____
Accounts receivable	_____	☐ Yes ☐ No	_____	_____
Other	_____	☐ Yes ☐ No	_____	_____
			Subtotal	_____

LIABILITIES	Date Incurred	Account Number		Total Balance Due ($)
Secured	_____	_____		_____
Mortgage	_____	_____		_____
Mortgage	_____	_____		_____
Deeds of trust	_____	_____		_____
Home equity loans	_____	_____		_____
Liens	_____	_____		_____
Motor vehicle loans	_____	_____		_____
Bank loans	_____	_____		_____
Personal loans	_____	_____		_____
Other	_____	_____		_____
			Subtotal	_____

Financial Inventory (continued)

LIABILITIES (cont'd)	Date Incurred	Account Number	Total Balance Due ($)
Unsecured			
Student loans			
Bank loans			
Personal loans			
Credit card balances			
Judgments			
Taxes			
Support arrears			
Other			
		Subtotal	

Net Worth Summary

Assets

Cash subtotal $ _____

Real Estate subtotal   _____

Personal Property subtotal   _____

Investments subtotal   _____

Total Assets $ _____

Liabilities

Secured subtotal $ _____

Unsecured subtotal   _____

Total Liabilities $ _____

Net Worth (assets minus liabilities) $ _____

Monthly Income

Wages or Salary	Spouse #1	Spouse #2
Job 1: _____		
Gross pay, including overtime:	_____	_____
Subtract:		
Federal taxes	_____	_____
State taxes	_____	_____
Social Security	_____	_____
Medicare	_____	_____
Union dues	_____	_____
Insurance payments	_____	_____
Child support withholding (from previous marriage)	_____	_____
Other deductions (specify): _____	_____	_____
Job 2: _____		
Gross pay, including overtime:		
Subtract:	_____	_____
Federal taxes	_____	_____
State taxes	_____	_____
Social Security	_____	_____
Medicare	_____	_____
Union dues	_____	_____
Insurance payments	_____	_____
Child support withholding (from previous marriage)	_____	_____
Other deductions (specify): _____	_____	_____
Job 3: _____		
Gross pay, including overtime:	_____	_____
Subtract:		
Federal taxes	_____	_____
State taxes	_____	_____
Social Security	_____	_____
Medicare	_____	_____
Union dues	_____	_____
Insurance payments	_____	_____
Child support withholding (from previous marriage)	_____	_____
Other deductions (specify): _____	_____	_____

Monthly Income (continued)

	Spouse #1	Spouse #2
Job 4: _____		
Gross pay, including overtime:	_____	_____
Subtract:		
Federal taxes	_____	_____
State taxes	_____	_____
Social Security	_____	_____
Medicare	_____	_____
Union dues	_____	_____
Insurance payments	_____	_____
Child support withholding (from previous marriage)	_____	_____
Other deductions (specify): _____	_____	_____
Total Employment Income	$_____	$_____
Investment Income		
Dividends	_____	_____
Interest	_____	_____
Leases	_____	_____
Licenses	_____	_____
Rent	_____	_____
Royalties	_____	_____
Other deductions (specify): _____	_____	_____
Total Investment Income	$_____	$_____
Other Income		
Bonuses	_____	_____
Trust income	_____	_____
Loans payable income	_____	_____
Alimony or child support (from previous marriage)	_____	_____
Pension/retirement income	_____	_____
Disability income	_____	_____
Social Security	_____	_____
Public assistance	_____	_____
Other deductions (specify): _____	_____	_____
Total Other Income	$_____	$_____
Grand Total Monthly Income	$_____	$_____

Daily Expenses

Week beginning _____

Expense	Mon.	Tues.	Wed.	Thurs.	Fri.	Sat.	Sun.

Monthly Expenses

	Proj.	Jan.	Feb.	Mar.	April
Home					
Rent/mortgage					
Property taxes					
Renter's insurance					
Homeowner's insurance					
Homeowners' association dues					
Landline telephone					
Cell phone					
Gas, electric					
Water, sewer					
Cable TV					
Internet access					
Garbage					
Household supplies					
Housewares					
Furniture, appliances					
Cleaning					
Yard or pool care					
Maintenance, repairs					
Credit and Loans					
Credit card payments					
Personal loan payments					
Other loan payments					
Food					
Groceries					
Take-out food					
Eating out					
Coffee/tea/snacks					

May	June	July	Aug.	Sept.	Oct.	Nov.	Dec.

Monthly Expenses (continued)

	Proj.	Jan.	Feb.	Mar.	April
Wearing Apparel					
Clothing, accessories					
Laundry, dry cleaning, mending					
Self-Care					
Toiletries, cosmetics					
Haircuts					
Fitness (massage, yoga, health club)					
Health Care					
Insurance					
Medications, vitamins					
Doctors					
Dentist					
Eye care					
Therapy					
Transportation					
Car payment					
Registration					
Insurance					
Road service club					
Gasoline					
Maintenance, repairs					
Car wash					
Parking, tolls					
Public transit, cabs					
Parking tickets					

May	June	July	Aug.	Sept.	Oct.	Nov.	Dec.

Monthly Expenses (continued)

	Proj.	Jan.	Feb.	Mar.	April
Entertainment					
Music					
Movies, video					
Concerts, theater, museums					
Sporting events					
Hobbies, lessons					
Club dues or membership					
Books, magazines, newspapers					
Computers, software, apps					
Dependent Care					
Child or elder care					
Clothing					
Allowance					
School expenses					
Toys, games, entertainment					
Lessons, activities					
Pet Care					
Grooming, boarding					
Vet					
Food, toys, supplies					
Education					
Tuition or loan payments					
Books, supplies					
Travel					
Life Insurance					

May	June	July	Aug.	Sept.	Oct.	Nov.	Dec.

Monthly Expenses (continued)

	Proj.	Jan.	Feb.	Mar.	April
Gifts & Donations					
Holidays					
Birthdays, anniversaries					
Donations					
Personal Business					
Supplies					
Photocopying, postage					
Bank & credit card fees					
Lawyer, accountant, or other professional fees					
Taxes					
Savings and Investments					
Deposit to savings					
Deposit to retirement account					
Deposit to college fund					
Purchase of stock, bonds, or mutual funds					
Other					
Total Expenses					
Total Income					
Total Expenses					
Difference					

May	June	July	Aug.	Sept.	Oct.	Nov.	Dec.

Index